GENEALOGIES OF SPECULATION

Also available from Bloomsbury:

PRESENT TENSE – A POETICS
Armen Avanessian and Anke Hennig

THE NEW PHENOMENOLOGY
J. Aaron Simmons

SPECULATIVE REALISM
Peter Gratton

SUBJECTIVITY AND IDENTITY
Peter V. Zima

STUFF THEORY
Maurizia Boscagli

GENEALOGIES OF SPECULATION

MATERIALISM AND SUBJECTIVITY SINCE STRUCTURALISM

Edited by
Armen Avanessian and Suhail Malik

Bloomsbury Academic
An imprint of Bloomsbury Publishing Plc

B L O O M S B U R Y
LONDON • OXFORD • NEW YORK • NEW DELHI • SYDNEY

Bloomsbury Academic
An imprint of Bloomsbury Publishing Plc

50 Bedford Square	1385 Broadway
London	New York
WC1B 3DP	NY 10018
UK	USA

www.bloomsbury.com

BLOOMSBURY and the Diana logo are trademarks of Bloomsbury Publishing Plc

First published 2016

© Armen Avanessian, Suhail Malik and contributors, 2016

Armen Avanessian and Suhail Malik have asserted their right under the Copyright, Designs and Patents Act, 1988, to be identified as Authors of this work.

All rights reserved. No part of this publication may be reproduced or transmitted in any form or by any means, electronic or mechanical, including photocopying, recording, or any information storage or retrieval system, without prior permission in writing from the publishers.

No responsibility for loss caused to any individual or organization acting on or refraining from action as a result of the material in this publication can be accepted by Bloomsbury or the author.

British Library Cataloguing-in-Publication Data
A catalogue record for this book is available from the British Library.

ISBN: HB: 9781472591678
PB: 9781474271295
ePDF: 9781472591692
ePub: 9781472591685

Library of Congress Cataloging-in-Publication Data
Genealogies of speculation : materialism and subjectivity since structuralism / edited by Armen Avanessian and Suhail Malik.
pages cm
Includes bibliographical references and index.
ISBN 978-1-4725-9167-8 – ISBN 978-1-4742-7129-5
– ISBN 978-1-4725-9168-5   1. Realism. I. Avanessian,
Armen, editor.
B835.G43 2016
149'.2–dc23
2015028981

Typeset by Fakenham Prepress Solutions, Fakenham, Norfolk NR21 8NN

To Robin Mackay – in admiration of his construction of a twenty-first century philosophy.

CONTENTS

Acknowledgements ix
Contributors x

Introduction: Speculative Genealogies – *Armen Avanessian and Suhail Malik* 1

Part 1: Genealogy 27

1. Foreign Territory: The Promises and Perils of Speculative Realism – *Steven Shaviro* 29

2. Reflections of a Rotten Nature: Hegel, Lacan and Material Negativity – *Adrian Johnston* 41

3. For a Realist Systems Theory: Luhmann, the Correlationist Controversy and Materiality – *Levi R. Bryant* 70

4. Deleuze: Speculative and Practical Philosophy – *Sjoerd van Tuinen* 93

Part 2: Languages of Speculation 115

5. Iteration, Reiteration, Repetition: A Speculative Analysis of the Sign Devoid of Meaning – *Quentin Meillassoux* 117

6. Language Ontology – *Armen Avanessian* 199

7. The Realist Novel and 'the Great Outdoors': Towards a Literary-Speculative Realism – *Arne De Boever* 217

8. Materialist Reason and its Languages. Part One: Absolute Reason, Absolute Deconstruction – *Suhail Malik* 238

Contents

Part 3: Science   269

9 Underlabouring for Science: Althusser, Brassier, Bhaskar –
Nathan Coombs   271

10 Formalism, Materialism and Consciousness –
Dorothea Olkowski   300

11 Subtending Relations: Bacteria, Geology and the Possible –
Myra J. Hird and Kathryn Yusoff   319

Index   343

ACKNOWLEDGEMENTS

Armen Avanessian and Suhail Malik thank Christoph Cox and Diann Bauer for their helpful comments on early versions of the Introduction, and to Robin Mackay and Mortiz Gansen for their attentive and generous commitment to translating Quentin Meillassoux's chapter.

With Nathan Coombs, we thank Edinburgh University Press and Bloomsbury for agreeing to simultaneously publish parts of chapter four of *History and Event: from Marxism to Contemporary French Theory* as parts of chapter ten of this volume.

Together with Myra J. Hird and Kathleen Yusoff, we'd also like to extend our gratitude to Scott Loughheed for his assistance with the references to chapter twelve. Myra J. Hird gratefully acknowledges the Social Sciences and Humanities Council of Canada for funding her research.

CONTRIBUTORS

Armen Avanessian's books include, among others, *Irony and the Logic of Modermity* (2015), *Present Tense. A Poetics* with Anke Hennig (2015), *Überschrift. Ethik des Wissens – Poetik der Existenz* (2015), *Speculative Drawing* with Andreas Töpfer (2014) and *Metanoia: Ontologie der Sprache* with Anke Hennig (2014). Avanessian has been a Visiting Fellow at both Columbia University and Yale University, and taught extensively in art academies in Europe and the US. He is editor in chief at Merve Verlag Berlin and founded the bilingual research platform Speculative Poetics (www.spekulative-poetik.de).

Arne De Boever teaches American Studies in the School of Critical Studies at the California Institute of the Arts, where he also directs the MA Aesthetics and Politics programme. He is the author of *Narrative Care* (2013), *States of Exception in the Contemporary Novel* (2012), and coeditor of *The Psychopathologies of Cognitive Capitalism: Vol. 1* (2013) and *Gilbert Simondon: Being and Technology* (2012). De Boever edits *Parrhesia: A Journal of Critical Philosophy* and the critical theory/philosophy section of the *Los Angeles Review of Books*. He is also an Advisory Editor for *boundary 2*.

Levi R. Bryant is a Professor of Philosophy at Collin College, Texas. He has written widely on poststructuralist thought, systems theory, psychoanalysis, and speculative realism. He is the author of *Onto-Cartography: An Ontology of Machines and Media* (2014), *The Democracy of Objects* (2011) and *Difference and Givenness: Deleuze's Transcendental Empiricism and the Ontology of Immanence* (2008).

Nathan Coombs is a Leverhulme Early Career Research Fellow in the Department of Sociology, University of Edinburgh, and author of *History and Event: from Marxism to Contemporary French Theory* (2015). He has published in *Journal of Political Ideologies*, *Theory & Event*, and *The European Legacy*, among others.

Contributors

Myra J. Hird is Professor and Queen's National Scholar in the School of Environmental Studies, Queen's University, Canada (www.myrahird.com), and is a recently elected Fellow of the Royal Society of Canada. Hird is Director of the *genera Research Group* (gRG), an interdisciplinary research network of collaborating natural, social and humanities scholars, and Director of *Waste Flow* (www.wasteflow.ca), an interdisciplinary research project focused on waste as a global scientific-technical and socioethical issue. Hird has published eight books and over sixty articles and book chapters on a diversity of topics relating to materiality.

Adrian Johnston is Professor in the Department of Philosophy at the University of New Mexico at Albuquerque and a faculty member at the Emory Psychoanalytic Institute in Atlanta. Recent publications include *Adventures in Transcendental Materialism: Dialogues with Contemporary Thinkers* (2014), *Prolegomena to Any Future Materialism, Volume One: The Outcome of Contemporary French Philosophy* (2013) and *Badiou, Žižek, and Political Transformations: The Cadence of Change* (2009). He is the coauthor, with Catherine Malabou, of *Self and Emotional Life: Philosophy, Psychoanalysis, and Neuroscience* (2013). With Todd McGowan and Slavoj Žižek, Johnston is a coeditor of the book series *Diaeresis* at Northwestern University Press.

Suhail Malik is Reader in Critical Studies at Goldsmiths, London, and was 2012–15 Visiting Faculty at the Center for Curatorial Studies, Bard College, New York. Publications include *On the Necessity of Art's Exit From Contemporary Art* (2016) and 'The Ontology of Finance' in *Collapse VIII* (2014). With Christoph Cox and Jenny Jaskey, Malik is coeditor of *Realism Materialism Art* (2015) and, with Thomas Keenan and Tirdad Zolghadr, of *The Flood of Rights* (forthcoming, 2016).

Quentin Meillassoux is Professor of Philosophy at Université de Paris 1, Panthéon Sorbonne. He is author of *Science Fiction and Extro-Science Fiction* (2015), *The Number and the Siren* (2012) and *After Finitude: An Essay on the Necessity of Contingency* (2008). Meillassoux is a frequent contributor to the journal *Collapse*.

Dorothea Olkowski is Professor and Chair of Philosophy at the University of Colorado, Colorado Springs, Director of the Cognitive Studies Program, and former Director of Women's Studies. She is the author/editor of ten

Contributors

books including *Postmodern Philosophy and the Scientific Turn* (2012), *The Universal (In the Realm of the Sensible)* (2007) and *Gilles Deleuze and the Ruin of Representation* (1999), and of over 100 articles including essays, book reviews, encyclopedia articles, translations of her work, and collaborations with artists.

Steven Shaviro is the DeRoy Professor of English at Wayne State University. He writes about science fiction, music videos, and process philosophy and speculative realism. He blogs at The Pinocchio Theory (www.shaviro.com/Blog).

Sjoerd van Tuinen teaches Philosophy at Erasmus University, Rotterdam and coordinates the Centre for Art and Philosophy (www.caponline.org). Publications include *Speculative Art Histories* (forthcoming), *De nieuwe Franse filosofie* (2011) and *Sloterdijk. Binnenstebuiten denken* (2004), and editorship of *Deleuze and The Fold: A Critical Reader* (2010) among others. His forthcoming book is *Matter, Manner, Idea: Deleuze and Mannerism*.

Kathryn Yusoff is a Senior Lecturer in the School of Geography at Queen Mary University of London. Her work focuses on political aesthetics, geophilosophy and environmental change (including climate change, extinction and the Anthropocene). She is currently working on *Geologic Life*, a book examining the genealogies, geoontologies and geographies of the Anthropocene.

INTRODUCTION: SPECULATIVE GENEALOGIES
Armen Avanessian and Suhail Malik

The early drama surrounding the philosophical movement called Speculative Realism, inaugurated in 2007 at the eponymous conference at Goldsmiths, London, revolved around its leading claim to overthrow the very basis for both poststructuralism, whose various strands had by then become the prevailing critical and theoretical doctrines in the arts and humanities, and also analytic philosophy's self-imposed modesty in limiting itself to problems circumscribed by language and empiricism. For all of their mutual and historical antagonism, each of these established paradigms limit philosophical and theoretical claims to the finitude of language, history, thought and subjectivity – with significant anthropocentric assumptions guiding their respective research programmes (multifarious though these may otherwise be). These paradigms propose that the social and cognitive conditions of thought restrict and shape what can be thought and repudiate the claim that there can be knowledge of the real as such other than in terms of its cognition and discourses.[1] In this, they propose social, cultural, psychosymbolic or pragmatic variants of what in physics is called the anthropic principle and, in philosophy, of Immanuel Kant's argument that the world as humans know it is mediated by their intrinsic conditions of knowledge, with the consequence that what is outside of human knowledge can not be known 'in itself'.[2] By contrast, speculative realism (SR) reconstructed a broadly metaphysical set of claims, emphasizing among other things (though not always consistently among all the stances captured under the term) that knowledge of the real as such could be attained without anthropological bias, that the Enlightenment project is sustainable despite the rigorous and often devastating criticism it has received, that philosophy offers a route out of the anthropocentric construction of how objects interrelate between themselves or, in apparent contradiction, that rational thought itself is but a byproduct of larger processes in which the human merely takes its part but not as their primary condition. In short, that philosophy could apprehend the real as such in its independence from the conditions of its being thought.

While this is a necessarily over-simplistic picture of the complexities and divergences within any of the designated movements, it nonetheless captures the basic demands and provocation of SR: the repudiation if not condemnation of now-dominant poststructuralist and analytic-philosophical stances and constraints. The institutional and theoretical realignments and abreactions to these realist provocations against poststructuralist conventions constituted the drama already mentioned, the terms of which are worth quickly rehearsing here in order to give a broad outline of the debates and contentions addressed by this volume as a whole and the individual chapters. Those sympathetic to SR's claims have seen in it a route to break out of the deadlocks, incapacities and dead ends of the fatal self-regard that poststructuralism had become. On the one hand, it proposed a way of revalidating the truth claims and objectivity of science, technology, calculation and instrumentality, all of which continue to be challenged if not repudiated by poststructuralist doctrines as part and parcel of its insistence on the social construction and unfixity of all meaning, knowledge and practice. This latter repudiation of instrumental rationality was itself a theoretically organized countermanding of the remorseless, industrially organized horrors of mid-twentieth-century totalitarian regimes, the exploitative and subjugating regime of industrial capitalism in the nineteenth century, and the conformism of the bureaucratic state capitalism of the post-Second World War period. On the other hand, though not wholly distinct to the concerns just mentioned, some strands of SR propose a political counterclaim to the by-then evident incapacities and debilitating contradictions of poststructuralism as an intellectual and anarcholeftist political project that has, despite its claims and stances, become a conventional academic doctrine in the arts, humanities and some social sciences.

This doctrinal incapacity and historical self-nonrecognition of poststructuralism has particularly telling ramifications for its often-rehearsed claims to have political traction. Despite the vigour and constant invention of this broad school of academic and cultural theory, by the mid- to late 1990s poststructuralism seemed to present a less and less effective practical or political challenge to the consolidation of neoliberal activism and reorganization over that same period (and since). This ineffectivity and institutional *dis*-traction, if it can be put this way, is not just at the level of the admittedly broad and ill-defined field of 'politics' or 'society' but reaches to the very specific domain of the higher education sector and cultural institutions in which poststructuralism is primarily transmitted in Western Europe and particularly the United States. These institutions are now integral to the economic and social organization of those regions in which poststructuralism has been fully established and central to the institutional formation of the arts and humanities by the early 2000s. Yet, despite its impressive analyses and criticisms of neoliberal social, political and technoscientific reconstruction over the period, it has been almost wholly powerless in countermanding these transformations of its own sociopolitical conditions – if, that is, it has not rather been actively incompetent by indirectly abetting those transformations.[3] (Analytic philosophy finds itself quite far away from direct engagement with these concerns in its content – though of course not as an institutional-sociological discipline – so the paradoxes and limitations identified here are less pressing for it.) That domestication of poststructuralism is attributable to some degree to its continued and indefatigable fetishization of the movements of 1968, which has left those who advocate for it somewhat unable to contend substantially with the social conditions and politics in place half a century later. And while this immobility in part explains poststructuralism's current limitation as a continually transformative political programme, its failure is also attributable – and perhaps more so – to the drawing down of political ambitions it has warranted and cultivated. Cultural leftism's embrace in the 1990s of postmodernism, identity politics, and the turn to ethics (via the human rights settlements) as its primary organizing determinants of a social justice agenda that militated against standardization not only ruled out any appeal to the 'grand narratives' of modernity as the basis for leftism but, more actively, sought to delegitimize any such universalizing criteria.[4] The incapacitation of overarching narratives of emancipation or justice coupled with the sensitivity to singular, irreproducible and even untransmittable political claims and social demands so carefully identified by poststructuralist doctrine has resulted in social, cultural and political demands being formulated primarily in terms of subjectively organized claims that caution against extending beyond themselves for fear of imposing a microimperialism. Concomitant to this reduction of political horizon is the requirement that all political ambitions do not amount to more than their ad hominem or socially constructed formation and limitation, and that praxes that continue to propose that knowledge is not ethnoculturally specific but universal and objective – such as science in both its theoretical and practical branches – are to be treated as a suspicious modernist anachronism. In an uncomfortable but also revealing twist of political logics, this latter relativization of science and its truth claims as being culturally if not even subjectively specific have more recently been adopted by religious and populist right-wing political forces (especially in the United States) to countermand rationally constituted and evidence-based policy demands.[5]

Given these benighted conditions, and in direct contrast to poststructuralist conventions, SR vindicated the reconstruction of a 'grand narrative' politics. This big-picture project of a rationally organized long-term project – a vindicated Enlightenment of sorts, captured under the term 'Left Accelerationism' – has sought to advantageously mobilize the knowledge and operational developments made by technosciences alongside other complex and complexifying social and material factors.[6] This politically directed offshoot of SR takes these complex social factors as objective forces that allow the attainment of emancipation by their construction of social bonds and semantics that, contrasted to poststructuralist premises, do not presume or suppose unfixity *against* reason. Other fronts of SR, gathered in their distinct 'object-oriented' and neomaterialist variants, put emphasis on how a noncognitive semantics and social relationality is constituted equally between things of all kinds rather than premised on the centrality of the human actor or, more particularly, recognized forms of conceptual and cognitive apprehension.[7] Here, human modalities of apprehension and relationality are only one among others that, for all of their particularly and dominance for us, have no particular privilege among other modalities. This proposal is highly attractive in the face of the increasing pressure of material, technical and natural processes at the microlevel of personal and even subindividual engagement, the mesolevel of networked social processes, and the macrolevel of the globality of climate change, each of which leads to the weakening of traditional-modern anthropic determinations of these processes, if not the outright subordination or even elimination of the human as a factor or determinant of how things are with one another, and also of what they mean to one another.

Despite their common critique of anthropocentric conditions of knowledge or relationality, these variants of SR are somewhat inchoate with one another and its fragile unity fell apart not long after the launch conference. Yet, with regard to the pivotal role of conceptual apprehension as a condition for their respective claims to realism, it remains the case that these reworkings of the task of 'critical' thinking continue to look to move past and transform the limitations of poststructuralism, if not to countermand and repudiate its primary determinations. However, the prevailing sense of 'critique' after Kant is the mitigation of cognitive and rational overreach into speculative claims; and, with poststructuralism and postwar Frankfurt School critical theory, it is generalized to mean forms

Introduction: Speculative Genealogies

of thought antagonistic to and disidentified from dominant ideology and power. It's not at all obvious to then suppose that the terms 'critique' or 'critical' are then the right ones for the task set by speculative realism. For object-oriented approaches in particular, it's moreover not apparent that the move they advance takes place in the dimension of thought at all insofar as such conceptual cognition remains, to date, anthropically specific. This affirmation of nonanthropic relationality is itself in marked contrast to the advocacy of a postcritical – that is speculative – conceptual thought as the condition for apprehending the real typical of the neorationalist strand of SR exemplified by Brassier and Meillassoux. Nonetheless, these various strands of SR are united not only by their common historical adversary. As identified by many of the individual chapters of this volume, the one positive, cogent organizing feature that continues to permit the legitimate use of SR as a coherent term is their subscription to Quentin Meillassoux's diagnosis of what he has influentially called correlationism. For Meillassoux, correlation is:

> any philosophy that maintains the impossibility of acceding, through thought, to a being independent of thought ... [Consequently,] we never have access to any intended thing ... that is not always-already correlated to an 'act of thinking' ... Correlationism posits that thought can never escape from itself so as to accede to a world not yet affected by our subjective modes of apprehension.[8]

In holding that the real is an effect of the conditions of its apprehension and social-semantic construction, poststructuralism is but an instance of correlationism and it is this *general* theoretical-conceptual condition and its ensuing limitations that (despite serious disagreements among them) current and future variants of SR look to surpass to gain access to the real beyond thought.

The trenchant attacks on poststructuralism by SR are and will continue to be met by countercriticisms of SR itself. While some of this could be straightforward reactive hostility and suspicion between obviously adversarial stances, more salient criticisms of SR can focus on how the demotion of anthropic determinations by object-oriented approaches leads to the abjuring of judgement and semantically organized social practice – including politics – as necessary premises for the purposive transformation of the conditions of which it speaks.[9] Equality of objects and the concomitant subordination or elimination of subjecthood as a condition of praxis risks undermining the very possibility of constructing an active, directed and transformative demand, and might even mitigate against it for fear of reinstating an anthropocentric overreach (a kind of macroimperialism over objects). Worse yet, the theoretical equivalence of social and natural objects quickly leads to the naturalization of social and technical organization thereby contributing to the reinstatement of political-ideological forces as simply neutral systemic elements of objecthood out of reach of semantic and volitional determination. On the other hand, variants of SR vindicating Enlightenment precepts, albeit highly revised ones, stand accused of resuscitating the very blindness to the violent ethnocentric power hierarchies and sociologies that claimed reason and its universalism as their legitimating term.[10] The primary referents here are the putatively 'civilizing' missions of Western European colonialism since the early nineteenth century, and also the subordination of all subject- and social-identifiers that were deemed not to have rational capacities in part or as a whole. Specifically, poststructuralist criticism – especially in its postcolonial, feminist and queer theory formations – has done important, trenchant work in undoing the fixed, ethnocentric standard of reason as a term – if not *the* term – of legitimacy. Coupled to the advocacy of postmodern multifarious self-legitimating 'small narratives' against the 'grand narratives' of Western modernity, these antifoundationalist advances have importantly undermined the standardizing modern (and, for that matter, ancient) conventions of reason and universalism as criteria for political and theoretical praxes. Such criticism has correctly learnt from and contributed to the shattering of sociohistorical power away from the white European men, and in terms other than those overtly and subtly set by that constituency, who not only wielded and maintained their state and civil power by appeal to reason but also formulated its modern doctrines.[11]

These criticisms are reinforced by the insights of mid-twentieth-century Frankfurt School critical theory on the cogent deployment of rationalism by European powers since the eighteenth century to legitimize colonialism as a 'civilizing mission' and also, later, by totalitarian states to formulate and prosecute their genocidal persecutions within Europe.[12] In addition, along a similar axis, this critical stance contends that the rationalism of capitalist liberal democracies reinforces standardized forms of subjectivity and indoctrination through their emphasis on consumption and, more recently, social individualism.[13] In broad terms, the Frankfurt School distinguishes between an 'instrumental reason' (a model of ends-directed rationality) conducive to these and other pernicious and oppressive effects and another mode of reason without ends that leads to cognitive and social emancipation (formulated by

Kant as the work of reflective and aesthetic judgements, both of which are then distinct to the ends-directed judgements of the understanding). In no less stylized terms, for poststructuralism reason as such is ineliminably a social and power effect which cannot be distinguished from the violent and oppressive historicopolitical forms of domination that have legitimized themselves precisely through claims to their own rationally constituted universalism (although for Michel Foucault, following Nietzsche in this regard, power is also a positive term of transformation).[14] Poststructuralism's theoretical and ideological work has effectively contributed and protected – if it has not in fact transformed – the very terms by which sociocultural recognition takes place in favour of its multiplicity. And on the basis of these countervailing recognitions of historically and newly subordinated sociopolitical constituencies and forms, vindicating a rationalist project can be at best regarded as a regression from the theoretical and political advances made in the past forty years, if not just an obdurate naivety.

The apparently antagonistic if not directly incompatible theoretical, social and historical premises and identifications of poststructuralism and SR (on both of its main fronts) pivot primarily on the terms and constraints of the construction of meaning, action and systemic traction. These antagonisms are, as noted, not only those of their respective political demands, but extend to the basis of their respective constitutions and how they are to be attained. Yet, given that most sides of this dispute broadly espouse leftist emancipatory claims, some pragmatic political reconciliation or alliances between poststructuralist developments and those in SR could be envisaged. For example, as certain strands of neomaterialism have already proposed, poststructuralism's emphasis on the unfixity and sociosubjective malleability of meaning and the experience of the Other as (de)structuring condition for all of these primary terms can be expanded to all material as well as ideological systems in which the human subject is not the defining condition.[15] Or, some recuperation of the rational determination of social organization that does not return to instrumental rationality, or which multiplies and localizes rationalities such that sociohistorically specific universalisms are incapacitated, could reconcile the interests of neorationalism to those of postcolonialism and the affirmation of singularities.[16] Similarly, Foucault's affirmation of power as a means of resubjectivization countering socially repressive power – a stance vigorously attacked by Marxists and anarcholeftists at the time – may be a model for the revived interest in 'alienation' as a positive condition for emancipation via social complexification asserted by Left Accelerationism.[17]

If anything, however, the incompatibilities are much starker and more contentious with regard to the respective *theoretical* formulations and commitments of SR and poststructuralism than are their respective political ambitions. While the just-proposed schematic research programmes may be attractive in the name of broad politically organized alliances, the theoretical and conceptual bases remain mostly at odds: if the subject or 'sentience' is, in however complex a sense the term to be elaborated, the referent and locus for the construction of meaning and the operations of the social, then the more expansive notion of the sociality of objects between themselves – and at wildly divergent scales – remains constitutively unavailable. Equally, however capacious the grand narrative of a rationally constituted universalism may be, it must assign legitimacy-granting authority to itself alone and thereby denounce whatever legitimacy the small narratives that sociohistorical particulars (such as cultures or religions) determine for themselves if they do not accord with that universalism. Such a requirement appears at once authoritarian, sovereign, and clearly unable to accommodate a radical alterity – all of which are severely condemned in poststructuralism and surpassed by it.

The standoff between poststructuralism and SR seems, in short, intractable. It is this impasse that *Genealogies of Speculation* looks to overcome by unlocking their historically simplifying and theoretically stultifying opposition. The proposition of this volume is not only that substantial claims and effective traction on current social and cognitive horizons can be better realized by resetting the terms of debate between poststructuralism and SR. It is also that such a resetting enables the realization of more expansive and more trenchant political and theoretical ambitions on both sides of the current dispute. For example, the ostensibly desubjectified realism and engagement with complex sociotechnical systems of cognition claimed by SR makes a demand on poststructuralism: that social counternormative theory recover its diagnostic capacities and gain leverage on sociocultural conditions that in fact now domesticate and welcome poststructuralism's standard claims to undermine and disrupt conventions and authority with singular eventualities and exteriorities. Equally, and on the other hand, the sophisticated accounts of the complexity and interdependence of sociopolitical multiplicities obtained by poststructuralism demand greater nuance and social precision from SR in its conceptualizations of sociotechnical and cognitive constitution, attention to which would take it beyond its own internecine quarrels and avant-gardist postures, both of which have to date waylaid its expansive development and gaining of sociohistorical traction.

Introduction: Speculative Genealogies

But these demands are again mainly politically organized prescriptions for reconciliation; and, as remarked above, the pressing requirement if these expanded ambitions are to be realized is, rather, for the respective theoretical premises to be recast. To that end, *Genealogies of Speculation* provides two main supports: first, to provide the more nuanced and responsible debate required to move past the often-reductive arguments on current speculative thought advanced *by both sides* that have led ineluctably to the impasses and oppositions elaborated above. While the vigour of these provocations, debates and stances has served to rapidly draw attention to the important claims and divergences involved (especially in the unmoderated and affectively dense space of social media and the blogosphere where, it must be acknowledged, much of the dispute outlined here has been most emphatically formulated), this dramatic eruption of a substantial theoretical dispute has, however, also stalled if it has not prevented the thorough and rigorous examination of the proximities, continuities and channels available between poststructuralism and SR. This is the work that *Genealogies of Speculation* looks to present in a synoptic and inaugural manner. The contributing chapters each in their own way venture that substantial cross-contaminations and redeterminations across the stated theoretical divide can be established. That said, while common and convergent concerns thereby appear on both sides of what could be called the correlationist divide, the discussions presented here mostly establish that the incompatibilities across them *do* present substantial problems that importantly prohibit the construction of direct reconciliation or integration across it. These clarifications and elaborations therefore serve to specify the programmes that need to be constructed, as well as their constraints.

To be more exact, and as the second main support for the theoretical recasting called for here, *Genealogies of Speculation* acts as reminder that the various programmes gathered under the headings of poststructuralism themselves advance variants of materialism that proponents of SR broadly deny it. As each of the individual contributions to this volume make clear, materialism is hardly a minor or neglected concern in antifoundationalist thought but is rather one of its primary thematic and methodological interests. The specific and various determinations of materialism presented in the individual chapters are outlined below but, in general terms, the broad issue that emerges from this volume as a whole is not so much *whether* it is SR or poststructuralism that can claim to be materialist theories as such but rather *what* materialism is, how it is to be constructed, and the varying ramifications of these diverse theorizations. It is on this point that – to highlight the full title of this volume – the fundamental question around which all of the above discussion revolves is made explicit: does materialism incorporate or repudiate the subject as a structuring condition of its theorization? And: what are the terms of articulation or presentation of such materialisms? And even: what is the matter of materialism? Though the individual chapters may not each formulate the questions this directly, they nonetheless each provide a response to it.

Notable in this regard is Meillassoux's contribution to this volume, which is the first publication to advance his philosophy beyond the terms of *After Finitude* in 2006 (published in English two years later). As already remarked, it is Meillassoux's term correlationism that more or less unifies the otherwise discrepant philosophies gathered under the term SR by identifying the condition upon which the thereby common adversary operates. Meillassoux's chapter in this volume disambiguates his own formulation of speculative materialism from that of his erstwhile colleagues in SR, remarking that even as each stance in the original SR conference (among others) establishes the conditions for a realism that does not presume human subjectivity or thought as its basis, some such theories – notably the object-oriented variants associated with Graham Harman and the naturalized reason associated with Iain Hamilton Grant – nonetheless posit subject-like attributes outside of any form of organic consciousness as the condition for their noncorrelationism, a general condition that Meillassoux here designates as 'subjectalism'.[18] While Meillassoux grants that these philosophies may be speculative and even realisms, they are for him not at all materialisms – the latter term being reserved for the knowledge of what is outside of all subjectivity *and its proxies*.

Following this schema, the SR theory Meillassoux criticizes has more in common with antifoundationalist poststructuralism than it does with his own speculative materialism. Like Meillassoux, Ray Brassier too argues that philosophical materialism must converge with scientific and mathematical knowledge of the real. Unlike Brassier, however, Meillassoux's Cartesian commitments mean that for him scientific descriptions only have validity if they are mathematically formulated. Nonetheless, for both, the elimination of the biases inherent in subjective and sociohistorical knowledge requires that any such scientific materialism is premised entirely upon conceptual-cognitive determinations of the real. Brassier therefore *stipulates* rather than eradicates conceptual and therefore anthropic cognition as the basis for the materialism that is the noncorrelational knowledge of the real.[19] For object-oriented variants of SR – whose premise is that realism proscribes the human (never mind rational thought or maybe even 'sentience') as a prerequisite for what the relation to the real can be – conceptual thought cannot make any claim to realism, as the nonsubjective relation of objects to one another, precisely because it is a thinking.[20] Moreover, that *rational* thought is the basis for materialism is, in the view of object-oriented SR, the very much worse error of mistaking an idealism for realism, allowing an equivalence to be drawn up between such neorationalist arguments and poststructuralism.[21] Moreover, the neorationalisms that propound a nonfoundational account of reason itself, in the wake of the account of post-Kantian philosophy proposed by Robert Brandom and Richard Rorty before him, only confirm that the conceptually constituted determinations of the real share more with the antifoundationalism of poststructuralism than they might be prepared to admit.

Genealogies of Speculation proposes a change in methodological perspective to the terms of these disputes. What the accusations and counteraccusations between the various allegiances to realism, materialism and antifoundationalism indicate is that these terms, among others, are in fact shifting with regard to what they indicate, and are now at best ambivalent or contingent upon the theoretical schema in which they are deployed. Their mutating semantic and theoretical determinations override their lexical stability. And this schematic instability is wholly to the advantage of the ambitions of this book, for it proposes that the adversarial stances based upon standard theoretical determinations can be surpassed in favour of new theoretical configurations advocated for here. One such reconfiguration is apparent in Meillassoux's chapter itself, which marks a significant step forward in his philosophy since his paradigmatic definition of correlationism in *After Finitude*: contrary to demands that realism requires the dispensing of linguistically organized knowledge claims because these are both primarily anthropically constituted and also, qua language, specific to a culture or discipline, Meillassoux proposes instead that what is real of an extant being can only be known *because* of the unique properties of mathematical sign systems. While Meillassoux's essay overall seeks to establish the conditions and requirements of what he affirms by the term materialism, its second part is directly preoccupied with an extended discussion of written signs: a topic extensively studied in the structuralism that provided the basis for poststructuralism's antifoundationalism. While having language as the primary referent in a discussion of materialism may surprise readers expecting that materialism should refer to that which is removed from what is characteristically anthropic, symbolic and subjectively constituted,

Genealogies of Speculation

Meillassoux's argument makes it clear that what he calls speculative materialism cannot be occasioned without the specifics of mathematical scripts. Similarly, several other contributions to this volume investigate how materialist and realist claims are established not only as a referent of language that is outside of language itself, but also within and as language itself – which is, typically, a focus not only of structuralist and poststructuralist theory but also of analytic philosophy – leading in each case to qualified departures from Meillassoux's argument.

The reorganization of the theoretical space in which realism, materialism and antifoundationalism are established weighs no less on each of the substantive terms in the title *Genealogies of Speculation* and the latent dilemma it presents. If speculative thought or speculation more generally is directed to that which is not (yet) determined by or within that which speculates – in this context, (cognitive) apprehension that is turned towards that which is outside of it, most formidably in the future – attention to the genealogies that give the account of how and why the current conditions, structures and claims have come to be what they are would seem to mitigate against speculatively organized transformation. But as the preceding comments should make apparent, the overall claim of this volume is that as much as the recent 'speculative turn' does not make quite as severe a break from its immediate precursor as is typically portrayed – that is, while speculation is itself somewhat genealogically constituted – the conceptual and lexical rearrangement that speculative thought imposes in order to make the claim *outside* of the cognitive basis for speculation also reorganizes the conditions and schema by which such speculative endeavours are undertaken. It is the outside or the future that recursively rearranges the past, retrieving it otherwise than how it has shaped the present in order to open up another future than the one that has been given by the past.

In the immediate case of this book, the speculative turn itself requires poststructuralism's antifoundationalist to be apprehended as being not only materialist – exactly how is the contention of the contributing chapters – but also as incipiently speculative, thus presenting a *speculative past* for SR that is different from the one that, on the basis of its genealogical determinations, sets up the schematic discrepancies and adversarial stances highlighted above. The first section of this volume is therefore dedicated to the resetting of a speculative past for SR by demonstrating the (perhaps subordinate or obscured) commitments to materialism within poststructuralism. And further before that too: the first chapter by Steven Shaviro, which instructively lays out the leading theses of the four protagonists at the Goldsmiths conference, proposes that the early/mid-twentieth-century philosopher Alfred North Whitehead also proleptically established a distinct speculative realism that tests the current iterations. This test is at the core of Whitehead's later philosophy: whether the bifurcation of nature is overcome. That bifurcation is, Whitehead proposes, the division between the nature *apprehended* in awareness and the nature that is the *cause* of awareness, a division that is more about the generic qualities of both human and nonhuman entities than about the correlational circle. On this basis Shaviro suggests that SR's core contention – whether things in themselves can be apprehended as such without their compliance to the conditions of their apprehension – be displaced and expanded from an epistemological and mainly anthropically organized discussion to one of ontology and nature.

How SR transforms not only what nature is *understood* to be but, more directly, what nature *is* returns as a theme throughout the book. Adrian Johnston's chapter addresses precisely this issue in relation to the constitution of the human subject itself, directly introducing materialism and subjectivity as the two optics through which this volume examines – or tests – SR. Johnston's attentive reading of Jacques Lacan's writings on the helplessness of the human neonate demonstrates that Lacan supposes not only the familiar symbolic and linguistic-structuralist account of psycho-symbolic genesis but also an overlooked material-biological basis for it. The psychogenesis of the subject thereby intertwines the symbolic register with biology. Lacan thus emerges on Johnston's account as a realist and materialist, and even a speculative materialist, in his insistence on the continued disruption of organicity to the symbolic construction of the psychoanalytical subject. Johnston's materialist basis for psychoanalysis enables that praxis to directly engage evolutionary theory on its own terms. Specifically, Johnston shows that the supposed antinaturalism or anorganicity of the psychoanalytical subject is a key feature of natural processes such as evolution and the organic organization of the human brain. The materialism core to psychoanalytic subjectivity yet often disavowed in its theorization is, Johnston contends, incorporated into nonsubjective processes of material organization. With that, Johnston sets the terms for a transformative incorporation of the psychoanalytical subject within SR, challenging its prevailing emphasis on desubjectified processes and relations.

Such a precursion and test of extant SR substantiates the demands of Shaviro's essay. And they converge with Levi R. Bryant's demonstration that the staunch antirealism of Niklas Luhmann's systems theory paradoxically provides crucial tools for SR. The paradox is that, as Bryant demonstrates, Luhmann's rigorous construction of a self-referential systematicity is on the one hand cogent enough to act as an encompassing paradigm for several otherwise incoherent antirealisms, implying that it should be inert as any kind of precursor or contributor to SR. Yet, on the other hand, Luhmann's entire antirealism is based on a simple realist assumption: that there are identifiable systems, meaning that the real is sectioned off from itself. Just as Johnston shows how Lacanian efforts to construct a systemic and immanent symbolic account of psychogenesis flounder in Lacan's own endorsement of an asystemic material base that is transcendent to that psychosymbolic construction, so Bryant shows that Luhmann's necessary distinction between systems and their environments in fact commits him to incorporate externalities and material conditions for the construction of systems to which the systemic account should be inured. Bryant therefore proposes that the highly self-enclosed antirealism of systems theory cannot exempt itself from an astructural realism. This mode of speculation defies the precepts of systems theory, recursively proposing that it is a productive resource for SR rather than inert to it – presenting a test for how the relations between interiority and exteriority (and between interiority and interiority for that matter) are to be cogently constructed.

Gilles Deleuze's 'transcendental empiricism' provides the basis for Sjoerd van Tuinen's examination of the systematicity and asystematicity of thought, of how the externalities of systemic thought direct and shape it, bringing these concerns into direct relation to Meillassoux's philosophy. Van Tuinen argues that Deleuze presents a model for speculative materialism that does not rely wholly on rationalist imperatives as it does for Meillassoux. Rather, Deleuze takes up the tradition of empiricism that is able to attend to and render comprehensible the actuality of becomings, leading to a radical overhaul of the Principle of Sufficient Reason, which posits that everything has an intelligible reason or cause. Van Tuinen shows that counter to Meillassoux's philosophy of speculative materialism, which abandons this principle, Deleuze's theorization of the real as the duality of a virtual-actual couplet upholds it. The result is that the latter philosophy is itself a speculative materialism that not only upholds philosophical responsibilities of providing rational explanations, in a way that Meillassoux's does not, but is also directly immersed and constructive for practice rather than constrained to the theoreticism that Meillasoux also lapses into, according to van Tuinen.

Van Tuinen's chapter in some ways sets up an explicit test for Meillassoux's speculative philosophy. And while Meillassoux's own chapter in this volume directly addresses how he positions Deleuze's philosophy as a whole, what is striking is that this characterization is made on the basis of one of several new developments in his thinking since *After Finitude*. Just as the definition of 'correlationism' in the earlier book has proven to be paradigmatic for philosophical and theoretical debates in the early years after its publication, so the wide-ranging elaborations and innovations of Meillassoux's expanded conceptual system in this major contribution should again change the terms of discussion on the conceptualization and stakes of realism, materialism and speculation. Specifically, Meillassoux establishes that his own speculative materialism has to be sharply demarcated and distanced from what he here calls subjectalism, which is the 'absolutiz[ation of] the correlation of thought and the world through the choice of various traits, all of which are present in human subjectivity'.[22] While subjectalism in part characterizes the philosophies of several of his erstwhile colleagues in SR broadly speaking, what is more broadly significant in this development is that subjectalism is not limited to the cognitive-conceptual dimension as correlationism is. *Any* subjective element 'not only of the subject in a limited sense, as consciousness, reason, freedom', as Meillassoux puts it, 'but of the subject in all its modalities – will, sensation, preconscious life' and so on can provide the basis of subjectalism, whether or not cognitive capacities are invoked.[23] Meillassoux establishes that subjectalism characterizes many systems of thought that may claim to depart from conceptual cognition and the human as their condition for apprehending the real as such but which do so by metaphorizing subjective traits to the absolute-real that is, rather, alien to any subjectalism. Thus escalating the demands on speculative materialism, Meillassoux in this chapter advances the programme of speculative materialism set out in *After Finitude* by establishing the mathematical sign as the condition for a speculative materialism. This real is then rationally known, Meillassoux contends, not only in the dimension of the absolute condition of what can be, which is the ontology established in the earlier book, but now also of what is qua fact. Here, the sign undergoes a radical recasting, as precise and inventive as the deduction of absolute contingency in *After Finitude*. Specifically, Meillassoux proposes that the mathematical sign devoid of meaning, the pure sign, is itself absolutely contingent and rescinds subjectalism, an empirical and semiotic manifestation of the general ontological truth of what can be but one that is rationally and formally manipulated in mathematics. With that, the somewhat Cartesian task of speculative materialism to mathematically apprehend the absolute-real as what it is (in addition to the philosophy of *how* it can be, which is the ontological task accomplished in *After Finitude*) can be met.

What is striking and apparently paradoxical in Meillassoux's argument is that speculative materialism is inaugurated not by removing or renouncing human capacities of conceptual-cognition but instead, and to the contrary, by rational thought *alone* via philosophy (the account of what can be) and mathematics (the account of what is). Furthermore, it is not just thought that permits the apprehension of the absolute-real qua fact but the semiotics of a pure sign that in its absolute contingency is wholly removed from any historical, semantic, or subjective interest, expression or motivation. Meillassoux's speculative materialism is then close to the also nonsubjective determination of language and signs proffered by structuralism (to return to an undercurrent of both Johnston's and Bryant's chapters). It is moreover confirmed as a rationalism, but one that not only offers no reasons (van Tuinen) but also *proceeds* by way of the sign without reason, the sign deprived of meaning; a language of speculation.

Meillassoux's extended essay acts then as a pivotal point in this volume. As well as extending his own formulation of speculative materialism (now categorically and doctrinally distinct from speculative realism), the chapter also draws attention to the sign-system of language and mathematical scientific formalization as prerequisites for that task. Here, the claims of the preceding chapters gain extra traction: does Meillassoux entrench the 'bifurcation of nature', which Shaviro proposes as the leading test for speculative thought? Or is the apprehension of nature by nature itself an instance of subjectalism? Equally, does Meillassoux's even more emphatic repudiation of any trace of subjecthood in his criticism of subjectalism vindicate Johnston's demand for a comprehensive materialist theory of the subject and its formation? Does the pure sign unshackled from structural semantic mobilization, which Meillassoux contends is the condition for mathematics as the privileged discourse of speculative materialism, accord with the asystemic real that Bryant uncovers in Luhmann's otherwise highly correlationist systems theory? Is it an externality to systemic meaning-making yet also the condition for knowledge of the real? And does the knowledge of facts in their absolute contingency, provided by mathematical discourse according to Meillassoux, not contend with the empiricism and praxis that is for van Tuinen the advantage of Deleuze's formulation of speculative materialism? The contention leading this volume is that while these and other questions certainly need further elaboration in the future, the disputes that are thereby occasioned and conclusions arrived at will

Introduction: Speculative Genealogies

in each case require a revisiting and further complexification of the now obviously tenuous division of schools of thought according to the correlationist divide.

The subsequent essays take up aspects of these questions via language and science respectively, while also maintaining the focus on speculative, realist and materialist contentions in poststructuralist thinking. In particular, the chapters in the 'Languages of Speculation' section directly respond to Meillassoux's contribution. Imbricated with Meillassoux's ontological claims on language via the pure sign of mathematics but distinct to them, Armen Avanessian's chapter draws particular focus on the ontological and praxical-transformative dimension of language itself. Language, Avanessian argues, does not only tell of ontologies outside of the linguistic subject. As poststructuralism and some analytic philosophy recognized, language is itself a medium and generator of relationality and therefore ontologically generative, speculative and determined otherwise than by the expressive and intentional capacities of the speaking subject. Somewhat counterintuitively – though also confirming core insights of German Romanticism, structuralist linguistics after Ferdinand de Saussure and C. S. Peirce's semiotics – language is both real and realist with regard to relationality. This last proposition recalls Bryant's proposal on Luhmannian systems as realist despite their ostensible antirealism. What it also does is argue against an object-oriented approach that seeks to establish a general ontological relationality aside from or before language (as a distinctively human capacity). And it furthermore proposes that ordinary language's recursivity – language addresses, refers to and modifies language itself – therefore shapes and transfigures not only language itself but also the ontology of what is. Avanessian thereby challenges Meillassoux's specification of the ontologically committed sign to mathematics and to the sign devoid of meaning alone, arguing instead that *all* language and meaning is certainly realist and maybe itself materialist, but is any case a fabricating *poiesis*.

Arne De Boever's chapter takes up the counterintuitive proposition that language is itself a realism: not only is language the thinking of thought beyond itself but also *how* thought does this. However, for De Boever, it is not just language per se that presents the real in itself in and as language but specifically literature. Contrasting what he identifies as a recent genre of literary-speculative realism against the more traditional genre of representationalist, biopolitical and humanist realism, which is dedicated to truthful accounts of the world and life outside of literature, De Boever advocates for the former as a 'deathly, linguistic approach to literature'.

This does not commit De Boever's analysis to the knowledge of the realm of death that Meillassoux proposes mathematics allows.[24] Rather, reading the dissolute conclusion of Michel Houllebecq's *The Map and the Territory* as a referentless demonstration of the real of language itself liberated from subjective expression – a demonstration of a materialist literature – De Boever argues that Meillassoux's own claims on how literature might present materialism as he, Meillassoux, conceives it remain too beholden to conventional genres of realism. That is – and to return from a very different angle to the contentions made by Avanessian – De Boever proposes that Meillassoux underestimates the capacities and instantiation of a speculative realism, if not a speculative materialism, in ordinary (albeit literary) language.

The distinction between ordinary and formal languages is the organizing axis of Suhail Malik's chapter. Beginning with what he calls the predicament of the languages of reason – according to which the intrinsic though distinct contingencies of ordinary language and formal languages render them inadequate to the universalities and invariances that rational deductions draw up – Malik initially contends that the rationalism underpinning Meillassoux's speculative materialism is, according to Meillassoux's own categories, itself a realism rather than a materialism. But while van Tuinen argues that Meillassoux's commitment to rationalism undermines the latter's claims to a fully fledged materialism, Malik diverges from this conclusion in proposing that it is the prerequisite of Meillassoux's *realism* that leads to an only-formal determination of the absolute-real as necessarily contingent. Furthermore, it leads to a determination of reason itself as an unreason. Both results prevent establishing rational speculative thought as the comprehensively explanatory materialism that Meillassoux endorses as an adequate and sufficient philosophical basis for modern science. Returning to the genealogical identifications of the first section of this volume, Malik proposes that a precursor for such realism, despite its common repudiation by SR, is Jacques Derrida's deconstruction of structuralism, and in particular structuralism's endeavour to establish its own scientificity. However, because deconstruction never rescinds the finitude of thought and language, Malik maintains that the divergence between it and speculative materialism must be upheld. Yet a comparative analysis of the nonmetaphysical sign that each theorization respectively proposes leads Malik to contend that the 'obverse contiguity' of deconstruction and speculative materialism resolves the predicament of the languages of

Introduction: Speculative Genealogies

reason and, no less, provides the basis for establishing the scientificity of a comprehensive speculative materialism.

Highlighting what the realism and materialism of the sign and language have to be as constitutive conditions of modern science and rationalism, Malik's essay acts as a bridge to the final section of the book, 'Science', whose principal concern is how SR can contribute to science as the praxis that has had a leading claim to materialism, that is, to rationally apprehend the real outside of thought. As already noted, this claim is of course highly contested, not least by poststructuralism and some strands of SR, but Nathan Coombs's chapter helpfully addresses Ray Brassier's endorsement of scientific naturalism as the leading paradigm of comprehensive explanatory realism in modernity. Drawing attention to a fundamental theoretical schism in SR between Brassier's epistemological rationalism and Harman's quasiphenomenological networked ontology, Coombs exposes a similar disparity in the trajectory of Louis Althusser's theoretical stances and commitments. Althusser's early allegiances to the mid-twentieth-century French school of rationalist epistemology and history of science led to an antisubjectivist 'scientistic' theory of Marxism and its revolutionary praxis. However, while the insights from rationalist epistemological theory on how discontinuities in structures of thought are occasioned (quite distinctively from the 'paradigm shifts' proposed by Thomas Kuhn) have evident appeal to a Marxism looking to find theorization of revolutionary transformation, Althusser's consequent 'theoreticism' and repudiation of empirical analysis of the actuality of social conditions ends up disabling the very politics it looks to ground. But, as Coombs goes on to show, Althusser's later self-criticism of what he called his 'speculative-rationalist' deviation has important lessons for how today's SR conceives its relation to science. Specifically, with regard to Brassier's project, following Wilfrid Sellars, to endorse science as the paragon of a naturalist-rationalist epistemological endeavour that exceeds conventionalized knowledge of the real is, Coombs contends, liable to perpetuate the same antiempiricism that the early Althusser later recanted. More exactly, it risks formulating a general theoretical account of science that pays little heed to its practice and the distinctions between the various sciences. Coombs proposes that a richer account of scientific ingress into the real-object is to be had in the critical realism propounded by Roy Bhaskar, which bridges Althusser's and Sellars's approaches but also builds its epistemological claims on the basis of scientific practice and plurality without, however, resorting to empiricism. Coombs's genealogy is not then only the story of a likely historical lineage resulting in Brassier's version of speculative realism; like several other of the genealogies proposed in this volume, it also makes specific demands and puts specific pressures on what has preceded the extant formulations of SR in order to reconfigure its future.

Like Coombs, Dorothea Olkowski identifies the influence of mid-twentieth-century French rationalism – Jean Cavaillès in particular – in Meillassoux's speculative realism, resulting in abstractions and formalisms in his account of the real that have little to do with the realities of scientific practice and discovery. While in some ways reiterating Coombs's criticism of Brassier's reliance on Sellarsian rationalism for his account of scientific epistemology, Olkowski's contentions stem from what she characterizes as a broader linguistic turn in philosophy to models derived from languages of logic and formal computation models in the philosophies of language and mind, and of mathematical or logical formalism in particular. The neo-Cartesianism of Meillassoux's 'pure sign' of mathematics would bear out this characterization, suggesting a concomitance with the otherwise distinct criticisms of Meillassoux with regard to his rationalist repudiation of empiricism (van Tuinen), to the formalism of his ontological determination (Malik), to his linguistic idealism (Avanessian) and, mutatis mutandis, with Bryant's argument regarding Luhmann's systematicity and Johnston's on psychosymbolically constitituted Lacanianism (even though the latter are, paradoxically, paradigmatically correlationist). Olkowski proposes that in order to break out of the formalist account of science it is necessary to configure science not according to (neo)Cartesian assumptions – which, she contends, science has anyway discarded in its practice – but by inserting the consciousness of the observer into the account of the scientific system. Olkowski cites Fotini Markopolou's criticism that the standard configuration of observation, in which observation takes place outside of the physical system under investigation, thereby segmenting the unity of the universe, cannot apply when that system is the universe itself, as is the case of cosmology. The scientist describes the system with a view from the inside and, in this, it is Maurice Merleau-Ponty's phenomenology of the flesh that provides for Olkowski the corresponding philosophical account of how science constructs knowledge. Merleau-Ponty's challenge to both empiricist and rationalist determinations of scientific knowledge is made with regard to quantum mechanics, which proscribes any neutral frame of reference and implicitly if not explicitly formulates its theses (as relativity theory also does) on the basis of partial but overlapping views of the included observer. The incarnated 'I think' of the scientist is then ineliminable in the scientific account, entailing the inclusion of her or his consciousness within the account of the scientific result. While this might seem to epitomize the correlationist claim, Merleau-Ponty's materialist because antiformalist (meaning antinominalist) account of physics conceptualizes reality otherwise than by a dichotomy between the in-itself and representation, and so proposes a phenomenological materialism beyond the terms of the correlation.

If Olkowski endorses the inclusion of the noncorrelational subject in the account of science – reiterating from a quite different angle Johnston's demand with regard to the knower as well as the known subject – Myra J. Hird and Kathlees Yusoff present a fourth, and final, paradigm for apprehending the scientific endeavour than those put forward by Malik, Coombs and Olkowski. Hird and Yusoff propose that the scientific endeavour has to be apprehended not just as a descriptive-epistemological task but also as constructive and transformative. Technoscience as it is presented in this chapter is determined by an empirically organized object-oriented analysis of the anthropogenetic transformation of objects and their ontology. Specifically, as the waste and material surplus of contemporary consumption, the objects Hird and Yusoff attend to are more or less ubiquitous with timescales far exceeding those of individual human subjects via their biographies, and thereby inaugurate local, global and geological risks with radically unknown outcomes. The environmental and futural demands made by these objects are themselves to be understood only by their scientific determination. Though sociotechnically produced, the empirical and sociohistorical perdurance of such active – because polluting – objects requires a revision of relationality in which they can no longer be subordinate to intraanthropic consideration: the ethical other no longer has a human face and – to recover a theme from object-oriented strands of SR – relationality may bypass the human actor altogether. Furthermore, Hird and Yusoff propose that it is poststructuralist feminist theory, which stresses the importance of co-constituted material-discursive practices (as several of the contributors to this volume also endorse), that will enable the reconstitution of our epistemologies and ethics according to the already transformed ontologies. This theoretical-geneaological necessity is then imperative for constructing not only the future of the theories adequate to what materialism is and, because of practical exigencies, now needs to be; it is also an imperative to construct the future of the material conditions themselves.

Hird and Yusoff's fundamental displacement of anthropic subjecthood from the centre of the socioscientific framework of waste environments returns the thematics of this volume back to the concerns of the inaugural chapters: how is the bifuraction of nature to which Shaviro draws attention constituted in the conditions of deeptime waste? What are the determining constraints of the here literalized-materialized environment on the construction of semantic-constituting systems as their real that Bryant exposes in Luhmann's theory? And, following Johnston, what does the resultant anorganicity of the environment itself mean for the future of organic life? These questions, fabricated across the span of *Genealogies of Speculation*, could readily be multiplied. But doing so is, precisely, not to close a circle for either this volume or for SR. Attending to the still-viable prospects and lessons of poststructuralism, all chapters *take leave* from a doctrinal consolidation of SR – even Meillassoux's own text formulates important revisions of his earlier formulations to establish clearly stated disagreements with the broad category of SR and, more particularly, several of his copresenters at the 2007 conference. For us, this is not a sign that SR is to be discarded, but rather that it inaugurates a multidirectional wealth of research, even and especially for the theoretical and historical doctrines that correctly see in it an adversary to their established commitments.

Notes

1. For a summary of these positions and their sources, see Steven Shaviro, 'Foreign Territory: The Promises and Perils of Speculative Realism', in this volume; see also Christoph Cox, Jenny Jaskey and Suhail Malik, 'Editors' Introduction', in Christoph Cox, Jenny Jaskey and Suhail Malik (eds), *Realism Materialism Art* (Center for Curatorial Studies, Bard/Sternberg: Annandale-on-Hudson/Berlin, 2015), pp. 16–25.

2. Immanuel Kant, *Critique of Pure Reason*, trans. Werner S. Pluhar (Indianapolis: Hackett, 1996 [original German publication: 1781/87]). On the anthropic principle see John D. Barrow and Frank J. Tipler, *The Anthropological Cosmological Principle* (Oxford: Oxford University Press, 1988).

3. For the logic of the apparently accidental – but in fact fortuitous – role of critique in abetting the transformation of capitalism by providing it with the resources to justify itself newly, especially since the 1990s, see Luc Boltanski and Ève Chiapello, *The New Spirit of Capitalism*, trans. Gregory Elliot (London: Verso, 2007). On the political incompetence of the humanities through the neoliberal restructuring of universities, see Armen Avanessian, *Ethics of Knowledge – Poetics of Existence*, trans. Nils F. Schott (Berlin: Sternberg, 2016).

4. The highly influential account of postmodernity as the delegitimization of grand narratives by small narratives is presented by Jean-François Lyotard, *The Postmodern Condition: A Report on Knowledge*, trans. Geoffrey Bennington and Brian Massumi (Minneapolis: University of Minnesota Press, 1984)

5. For a striking diagnosis and criticism of the philosophical and theoretical legitimacy provided by poststructuralism (among other doctrines) for faith-based claims and repudiations of rational-scientific determinations of the real, see Quentin Meillassoux, *After Finitude: An Essay on the Necessity of Contingency*, trans. Ray Brassier (London: Continuum, 2008), chapter two.

6. See Robin Mackay and Armen Avanessian (eds), *#accelerate: The Accelerationist Reader* (Falmouth: Urbanomic, 2014). In particular: Alex Williams and Nick Srnicek, '#Accelerate: Manifesto for an Accelerationist Politics', ibid., pp. 347–62; and Ray Brassier, 'On Prometheanism and its Critics', ibid., pp. 467–88.

7. See Graham Harman, *The Quadruple Object* (Alresford: Zero Books, 2011) for a synoptic account of Harman's philosophical system; for a broader account of his object-oriented claims, see Harman, *Bells and Whistles* (Alresford: Zero Books, 2013). See also Levi R. Bryant, *The Democracy of Objects* (Ann Arbor: Open Humanities Press, 2011); Ian Bogost, *Alien Phenomenology, Or, What It's Like to be a Thing* (Minneapolis: University of Minnesota Press, 2012), and Timothy Morton, *Hyperobjects: Philosophy and Ecology After the End of the World* (Minneapolis: University of Minnesota Press, 2013). For neomaterialist claims to deprioritize anthropic conditions for knowledge or relationality broadly sympathetic to overtly object-oriented philosophies but distinct to them, see among others: Bruno Latour, *Reassembling the Social: An Introduction to Actor-Network-Theory* (Oxford: Oxford University Press, 2007); Jane Bennett, *Vibrant Matter: A Political Ecology of Things* (Durham, NC: Duke University Press, 2010); Manuel de Landa, *Deleuze: History and Science* (New York and Dresden: Atropos Press, 2010); and Diana Coole and Samantha Frost (eds), *New Materialisms: Ontology, Agency, and Politics* (Durham: Duke University Press, 2010).

8. Quentin Meillassoux, 'Iteration, Reiteration, Repetition: A Speculative Analysis of the Sign Devoid of Meaning', trans. Robin Mackay and Moritz Gansen, this volume, p. 117–97.

9. For this and the next claim, see Ray Brassier and Suhail Malik, 'Reason is Inconsolable and Non-Conciliatory: Ray Brassier in Conversation with Suhail Malik', in Cox et al. (eds), *Realism Materialism Art*, pp. 219–20. See also Peter Wolfendale, *Object Oriented Philosophy: The Noumenon's New Clothes* (Falmouth: Urbanomic, 2014), chapter six.

10. This is a contention of strands of anticolonial and postcolonial theory. For a particularly striking historical example, see Ngugi Wa Thiong'O, *Decolonising the Mind: The Politics of Language in African Literature* (Portsmouth, NH: Heinemann, 1986). The claim has also been prevalent in French poststructuralist feminism countering the bourgeoise patriarchy sociologically

associated with the normative stipulations of rational discourse in European modernity; see for example Catherine Clément and Hélène Cixous, *Newly Born Woman*, trans. Betsy Wing (Minneapolis: University of Minnesota Press, 1986) and Luce Irigaray, *This Sex Which Is Not One*, trans. Catherine Porter (Ithaca: Cornell University Press, 1985).

11. See for example Gayatri Chakravorty Spivak, *A Critique of Postcolonial Reason* (Cambridge, MA: Harvard University Press, 1999); Dipesh Chakrabarty, *Provincializing Europe – New Edition* (Princeton: Princeton University Press, 2007); Aihwa Ong, *Neoliberalism as Exception* (Durham, NC: Duke University Press, 2006). Jonathan Israel contends that sociohistorical emancipatory claims have been formulated and warranted by those previously denied them through the extension or seizing of the Enlightenment's own distinctively philosophical project of materialist and universalist rationalism. See *Democratic Enlightenment: Philosophy, Revolution, and Human Rights, 1750–1790* (Oxford: Oxford University Press, 2013). A related argument, proposing that the democratic precept of the Haitian slave revolt of 1791–1804 informed the modern rationalism of Hegel's philosophy, is proposed by Susan Buck Morss, *Hegel, Haiti, and Universal History* (Pittsburgh: University of Pittsburgh Press, 2009). On the deployment of 'universalism' as a strategic anticolonialist term in the policy coding of post-Second World War human rights regimes, see Lydia H. Liu, 'Shadows of Universalism: The Untold Story of Human Rights around 1948', *Critical Inquiry* 40(4) (Summer 2014): 385–417.

12. Max Horkheimer and Theodor Adorno, *Dialectic of Enlightenment*, trans. Edmund Jephcott (Stanford: Stanford University Press, 2007 [original German publication: 1947]).

13. Herbert Marcuse, *One-Dimensional Man: Studies in the Ideology of Advanced Industrial Society* (Boston: Beacon, 1991 [original publication: 1964]). For a more recent diagnosis along these lines, see Axel Honneth, *Pathologies of Reason*, trans. James D. Ingram et al. (New York: Columbia University Press, 2009).

14. See Michel Foucault, *The History of Sexuality: An Introduction*, trans. Robert Hurley (London, Penguin, 1998), p. 101: 'discourse transmits and produces power; it reinforces it, but also undermines and exposes it, renders it fragile and makes it possible to thwart it'.

15. See Donna Haraway, *When Species Meet* (Minneapolis: University of Minnesota Press, 2007); Karen Barad, *Meeting the Universe Halfway: Quantum Physics and the Entanglement of Matter and Meaning* (Durham, NC: Duke University Press, 2007); and Karen Barad, 'Posthuman Performativity: Toward an Understanding of How Matter Comes to Matter', *Signs: Journal of Women in Culture and Society* 28(3), Spring 2003, pp. 801–31.

16. See Reza Negarestani, 'Where is the Concept? (Localization, Ramification, Navigation)', in Robin Mackay (ed.), *When Site Lost the Plot* (Falmouth: Urbanomic, 2015), pp. 225–51; Fernando Zalamea, 'Peirce and Latin American "razonabilidad": Forerunners of Transmodernity', *European Journal of*

Pragmatism and American Philosophy 1(1), 2009, p. 2. Available from http://lnx.journalofpragmatism.eu/wp-content/uploads/2009/11/09-zalamea.pdf [accessed 12 March 2015].

17. See Mackay and Avanessian (eds), *#accelerate*, in particular: Williams and Srnicek, 'Manifesto', p. 362, and Reza Negarestani, 'The Labor of the Inhuman', ibid., pp. 425–66.
18. Meillassoux, 'Iteration', pp. 121ff.
19. Brassier and Malik, 'Reason', pp. 221–4.
20. In Timothy Morton's pithy formulation, 'sentience is out of phase with objects, at least if you have a nervous system'. See 'Here Comes Everything: The Promise of Object-Oriented Ontology', *Qui Parle* 19(2) (Spring/Summer 2011): 176.
21. Graham Harman, 'I am also of the opinion that materialism must be destroyed', *Environment and Planning D: Society and Space* 28(5) (2010): 772–90.
22. 'Iteration', p. 122.
23. Ibid., p. 132.
24. Ibid., pp. 157–8.

PART I
GENEALOGY

CHAPTER 1
FOREIGN TERRITORY: THE PROMISES AND PERILS OF SPECULATIVE REALISM
Steven Shaviro

The great promise of speculative realism is that it proposes to break open the prison gates of our own all-too-human assumptions, and to bring us into contact with what Quentin Meillassoux calls *the great outdoors* (*le Grand Dehors*):

> the absolute outside of precritical thinkers: that outside which was not relative to us, and which was given as indifferent to its own givenness to be what it is, existing in itself regardless of whether we are thinking of it or not; that outside which thought could explore with the legitimate feeling of being on foreign territory – of being entirely elsewhere.[1]

Speculative realism endeavours to move beyond the framework of the merely human. It seeks an outdoors, an outside, an elsewhere. Such a search is not as easy as it sounds, however. For we usually bring our own habits, assumptions and viewpoints along with us, no matter where we go. Tourists never truly encounter foreign territory: for them, everything is always either just like home, or else interestingly 'exotic' because of its differences from home. But home remains the unvarying point of reference.

In order to avoid being just intellectual tourists and actually to reach the great outdoors we need to escape the habit of always referring things back to ourselves. Going somewhere else is only the first step. We must also remove our own presuppositions about whatever it is that we encounter elsewhere. As Eugene Thacker puts it, it is not enough just to consider the *world-in-itself*, in contradistinction to the *world-for-us*.[2] That just reproduces the old binaries of subject and object, and of mind and matter. Rather, Thacker says, we must actively seek to approach the *world-without-us*: the world insofar as it is not 'given' to us, and that subsists following 'the subtraction of the human from the world'.[3] This means that we must bring our own thought to the point where it is *beside itself*, or *outside itself*. Speculative realism asks us to displace ourselves, so that we may encounter things that absolutely resist being cast in terms of our own habits, assumptions and categories of thought.

All four of the original speculative realist thinkers – Quentin Meillassoux, Iain Hamilton Grant, Graham Harman and Ray Brassier – address the basic situation of the world-without-us: a world that is not made in our image, or to our measure. For Iain Hamilton Grant, even our most abstract theoretical thinking is still an expressive power of Nature itself, on the same order as stellar fusion and planetary convulsions.[4] This means that thought, no less than these other eruptions, is propelled by primordial forces that it cannot grasp or recuperate on its own account. For his part, Graham Harman envisions a world of mysterious objects, none of which can be entirely plumbed by any other.[5] Things continually beckon to one another from their depths, shining with an aesthetic *allure* that cannot be cashed out in the form of knowledge or comprehension.

Meillassoux, meanwhile, insists on what he calls the *ancestral*: the traces of 'events anterior to the advent of life as well as consciousness'.[6] These traces take no account of us; they cannot be regarded as 'given' to us, or as existing 'for us', in any way, shape or form. The discovery of the ancestral marks an 'aporia' for correlationism. And finally, Ray Brassier reminds us that human thought, no matter how grandiose or transcendental it conceives itself to be, is nonetheless bound to physical embodiment, and hence to mortality. It will someday come to an end:

> Sooner or later both life and mind will have to reckon with the disintegration of the ultimate horizon, when, roughly one trillion, trillion, trillion (10^{1728}) years from now, the accelerating expansion of the universe will have disintegrated the fabric of matter itself ... Every star in the universe will have burnt out, plunging the cosmos into a state of absolute darkness and leaving behind nothing but spent husks of collapsed matter. All free matter, whether on planetary surfaces or in interstellar space, will have decayed, eradicating any remnants of life based in protons and chemistry, and erasing every vestige of sentience – irrespective of its physical basis.[7]

The speculative realists thus all write of forces, things, and stretches of time that exceed our grasp – not just empirically, but necessarily and intrinsically. I can imagine the world continuing beyond my own death; but can I imagine there no longer being a 'world' as the correlate of my imaginings?

I can understand that things may exceed the limits of my own understanding; but can I understand the existence of things that are not 'given' in the first place, and hence not understandable even in principle? Questions like these challenge the very limits of pragmatic, human-centred, correlational thought.

The traditional correlationist response to such challenges has been to recuperate them self-reflexively. For I can think even my own inability to think. In this way, every failure or aporia becomes yet more evidence for the power of the mind, and the necessity of the correlation. Kant himself is the master of this strategy. In *The Critique of Judgment*, he describes the experience of the Sublime. We are overwhelmed when we encounter forces that are capable of destroying us:

> Bold, overhanging, as it were threatening cliffs, thunder clouds towering up into the heavens, bringing with them flashes of lightning and crashes of thunder, volcanoes with their all-destroying violence, hurricanes with the devastation they leave behind, the boundless ocean set into a rage, a lofty waterfall on a mighty river, etc., make our capacity to resist into an insignificant trifle in comparison with their power.[8]

And yet, Kant says, we are ultimately confirmed in our own self-consciousness by confrontations of this sort. Sublime spectacles 'elevate the strength of our soul above its usual level', Kant says, 'and allow us to discover within ourselves a capacity for resistance of quite another kind, which gives us the courage to measure ourselves against the apparent all-powerfulness of nature'.[9] Even – or especially – when I face up to the prospect of my own imminent destruction, I triumph. For I thereby affirm the transcendent power of the human mind: its power precisely to imagine such a fate. The power of nature is overmatched by my own power to envision its power. The very fact that I can conceive a limit demonstrates my superiority to this limit.

Kant's recuperative move is repeated again and again in the subsequent history of Western philosophy. Indeed, Hegel turns this Kantian argument against Kant himself, through a kind of philosophical jiu-jitsu. For Hegel argues that the exteriority of 'things in themselves', their resistance to being grasped by the understanding, is a limit posited by the understanding itself.[10] It is we alone who attribute to things the status of escaping their correlation with us. Exceeding the correlation is, for Hegel, itself a correlational category imposed by our own minds. In this way, we are trapped more firmly than ever within what Meillassoux calls the 'correlationist circle'. Kant's claim about the Sublime applies only to our *feelings*; it describes an affective recognition, not a cognitive one. But Hegel turns Kant's demonstration into an epistemological principle that applies to cognition or the understanding. In this way, nothing is allowed to escape the correlation. Hegel eliminates the very possibility of a world-without-us, or of an Outside that is neither positively nor negatively 'relative to us'.

From a strictly logical point of view, the key correlationist assertion – that I cannot think or speak of something without thereby turning it into a correlate of my thought – is undoubtably a sophism. As Brassier puts it,

> To say that I can think of something existing independently of my thought need not be flagrantly contradictory once I distinguish the claim that my thoughts cannot exist independently of my mind, which is trivially true, from the claim that what my thoughts are about cannot exist independently of my mind, which simply does not follow from such a trivial truth.[11]

Nonetheless, it is nearly impossible to put this logical distinction into actual practice. Whenever I think and speak of things insofar as they exist entirely apart from my thinking of them, I risk falling into a *performative contradiction*. For do I not produce a relation between myself and a thing simply by the act of pointing to it? Whenever I approach a thing in this way, I appropriate it as my 'intentional object' (as the phenomenologists would say). The problem is only compounded when we consider that most thoughts and speech acts go well beyond simple designation. To think of something means to understand it in a certain way, to place it within the complex order of what Kant called the categories of the understanding. To speak of something means to enmesh it within the relational web of language.

In other words, once I have accepted the phenomenological principle that 'all consciousness is consciousness of something', I am no longer able to separate things from my perception of them.[12] I may well concede in principle that things transcend my own conceptions of them; but I cannot *detach* them altogether from my own conceptions. Even though 'what my thoughts are about' is logically independent of the thoughts themselves, I am unable to make this separation in practice. I remain trapped, performatively if not conceptually, within the correlationist circle.

The speculative realist thinkers all take this performative dilemma seriously. But they differ greatly in their strategies for getting around it. Brassier remains on the terrain of epistemology. He places his bets on the disjunction between commonsense beliefs and the discoveries of physical science. Brassier claims that 'scientific representation', in contrast to all other modes of understanding, adopts 'a stance in which something in the object itself determines the discrepancy between its material reality – the fact *that* it is, its existence – and its being, construed as quiddity, or *what* it is'. Our concepts of objects never coincide with the objects themselves. But Brassier claims that the scientific method – with its rational procedures and its openness to continual empirical revision – is uniquely able to evade the threat of performative contradiction. It can step outside of the corrrelationist circle, because it is bound to the 'game of giving and asking for reasons' envisaged by Wilfrid Sellars and Robert Brandom. Bound in this way, scientific discourse is forced to acknowledge, and continually correct for, the unavoidable discrepancy at the heart of its own formulations.

Meillassoux invokes physical science in a radically different way than Brassier does. For Meillassoux puts his faith in 'the *absolutory capacity of modern science* – that is to say, *Galilean science*, which proceeds via the mathematization of nature'.[13] In other words, Meillassoux seeks to reestablish 'a Cartesian rather than a Kantian conception of experimental science'.[14] Brassier's notion of science is still (via Wilfrid Sellars) a Kantian one. It doesn't claim to access the nonhuman real directly, but rather values science because its verification procedures can be rationally grounded. Science is an inherently '*self-correcting* enterprise', allowing or forcing us to exercise 'normative commitments that underwrite our ability to change our minds about things, to revise our beliefs in the face of new evidence and correct our understanding when confronted with a superior argument'.[15] In other words, science is still finally a *human* enterprise – albeit one that relies upon 'man qua rational agent, not anthropological object'. It is from within the human, rational realm that science is able to approach a nonhuman and nonconceptual reality.

Meillassoux, to the contrary, values science only on the grounds of its recourse to mathematical formalization. He is not concerned with the way that the self-correcting scientific method would allow us to asymptotically approach a nondiscursive reality. Rather, Meillassoux privileges mathematics as a form of absolute knowledge, which unequivocally provides information about things in themselves, as they exist entirely apart from us:

All those aspects of the object that can give rise to a mathematical thought (to a formula or to digitalization) rather than to a perception or sensation can be meaningfully turned into properties of the thing not only as it is with me, but also as it is without me.[16]

Meillassoux's effort to justify attributing this power to mathematics is still a work in progress. Basically, he argues, rather astonishingly, that mathematics is able 'to grant us access to the Kingdom of the dead … to tell us what death looks like *in our world*'.[17] It is bound up with the 'dead matter' that is all there is to the world, according to Meillassoux, outside of the correlation with human subjectivity. Mathematics has this power because it is '*founded upon signs devoid of signification*' that can be iterated endlessly: 'the singular ontological import of mathematics proceeds precisely from the fact that, unlike ordinary meaning, it makes systematic use of signs that are effectively devoid of all signification'.[18] Mathematical formalism thus supposedly stands apart from any sort of subjective or intrinsic meaning whatsoever. It follows, according to Meillassoux, that mathematical measurement and description uniquely picks out 'what belongs to the world alone', independently of the meanings that we impose upon it. Mathematics is therefore the royal road to the great outdoors.

Grant and Harman approach the performative dilemma in an altogether different manner, without calling upon the authority of mathematics or science. Grant agrees with Brassier that our conceptions of things are always different from, and inadequate to, the things thereby conceived.[19] But Grant rejects Brassier's claim that scientific representation can work to take account of, and diminish, this difference. Instead, Grant breaks down the very dichotomy between my limited, correlational conceptions of things and the things themselves. For the former, no less than the latter, are finite products of Nature's own boundless productivity. Conceptions, like objects, are never adequate to the forces that impel them; for this reason, all correlations between them fail. But conceptions and objects alike are nonetheless products of these impelling forces. My very cognitive performance, or conceptual production, is itself derived from the excess that it is unable to contain or represent. Following Schelling, Grant inverts Kant's account of a Sublime encounter with the overwhelming power of Nature. Instead of discovering a supposed counterpower[20] of my own mind that would overmatch Nature's power, I come to realize that my own mental power cannot be opposed to that of Nature, for it *expresses* Nature's unbounded power already. Any correlation between thoughts and things is dissolved, because they must both be referred back, in the same way, to the processes that continually generate them.

Harman makes no attempt to find a noncorrelational form of knowledge, because he maintains that any such knowledge is impossible. For 'the real is something that cannot be known, only loved'.[21] The sole 'access' that we have to objects – or for that matter that objects have to one another – is allusive and *'indirect'*. The world is filled with 'ghostly objects withdrawing from all human and inhuman access, accessible only by allusion and seducing us by means of *allure'*.[22] Harman here comes close to Alfred North Whitehead's notion of the prospects that entities raise for us (or for other entities) as 'lures for feeling' – though as far as I know he never cites this particular aspect of Whitehead's thought. For Harman, aesthetics precedes epistemology. Causation – or, more generally, any form of influence – is indistinguishable from seduction.

It is at this point that I would like to introduce the philosophy of Alfred North Whitehead (1861–1947), as offering another approach to the dilemma of the world-without-us. There is at least a certain sense in which Whitehead is already a speculative realist *avant la lettre* – though one of a different sort than any of the current group. As Harman has often noted, Whitehead unquestionably breaks with anthropocentrism since he refuses to privilege any sort of human or rational subject.[23] Unlike the Kantians and the phenomenologists, Whitehead does not give any special treatment to the way that the world exists *for us*. What's more, he describes his own metaphysical system as 'a recurrence to that phase of philosophic thought which began with Descartes and ended with Hume': in other words, he self-consciously reverts to what Meillassoux calls 'the absolute outside of precritical thinkers'.[24]

I will not go into the details of Whitehead's 'speculative scheme' here: they are less important than his overall project. Like the great pre-Kantian philosophers, he begins with issues of sensation, perception and thought. But he does not see these as especially human categories, nor as rational ones. Rather, he formulates his principles in such ways that they refer equally to all entities in the cosmos: to the 'most trivial puff of existence in far-off empty space' as much as to human beings, or to God.[25] Whitehead elaborates a mode of explanation with sufficient generality that it can be applied alike to commonsensical human self-understanding, and to the paradoxical discoveries of relativity and quantum mechanics. Rather than asking the epistemological question of how things themselves differ from human projections upon them, he asks ontological questions about the generic qualities of both human and nonhuman entities. By formulating his approach in this way, Whitehead seeks to overcome what he calls *the bifurcation of nature*.[26] This is his term for the division between the nature apprehended *in* awareness and the nature that is the *cause* of awareness. The 'nature which is the fact apprehended in awareness' holds within it the greenness of the trees, the song of the birds, the warmth of the sun, the hardness of the chairs, and the feel of the velvet. The 'nature which is the cause of awareness' is the conjectured system of molecules and electrons which so affects the mind as to produce the awareness of apparent nature.

The poet and the phenomenologist recognize only the nature which is the fact apprehended in awareness; the scientist, on the other hand, sees this as mere illusion, and instead recognizes only the nature which is the cause of awareness. For Whitehead, both of these separate positions are needlessly limited; we need a single account that accommodates both. 'We may not pick and choose. For us the red glow of the sunset should be as much part of nature as are the molecules and electric waves by which men of science would explain the phenomenon'.[27] We get nowhere when, like the phenomenologists and other correlationists, we dismiss the molecules and electric waves and concentrate only on the red glow of the sunset. But we also get nowhere when, like the scientific reductionists, we dismiss the poetic feelings of the sunset altogether, and treat the molecules and electric waves as the only relevant actualities.

One good way to understand philosophical distinctions is to use them as *tests*: trials to which we can submit our own hypotheses. Speculative realism offers us one such test: it asks whether we remain trapped within the correlationist circle, or whether we have found a way to go beyond it and enter foreign territory. Whitehead offers us a somewhat different test: he asks whether we continue to accept the bifurcation of nature, or whether we have found a way to avoid abusively picking and choosing. These tests are not mutually exclusive. In posing his test about the bifurcation nature, Whitehead also steps outside of the correlationist circle. Any philosophy that (in the wake of Kant) divides the world into two, privileging the human subject on the one hand, and opposing it to a world of nonhuman objects on the other, thereby perpetuates the bifurcation of nature – no matter which side of the dichotomy it picks. But the inverse of this is not necessarily true: it is possible to reject correlationism, without for all that overcoming the bifurcation of nature.

By way of conclusion, let us see how the four major speculative realist thinkers differ in the ways that they implicitly respond to Whitehead's test.

Harman easily passes Whitehead's test. Though Harman does not explicitly mention the bifurcation of nature, he discusses a similar distinction posed by the British physicist Arthur Stanley Eddington, who was a student of Whitehead's and an associate of Einstein. Eddington draws a famous contrast between a table as it is viewed by common sense, and the same table as it is understood by modern physics. Eddington's first table is 'a commonplace object of that environment which I call the world … It has extension, it is comparatively permanent, it is coloured; above all it is *substantial*'.[28] Eddington's second table, in contrast, 'is mostly emptiness. Sparsely scattered in that emptiness are numerous electric charges rushing about with great speed', i.e. electrons circling atomic nuclei. Harman proposes a *third table* in contrast to either of these. He insists that neither of Eddington's bifurcated formulations is able to 'exhaust the table's reality … The real table is a genuine reality deeper than any theoretical or practical encounter with it.'[29] Harman and Whitehead thus agree that both the phenomenological and the scientific descriptions of an entity are partial and limited. But where Harman concludes that both descriptions are therefore false, Whitehead concludes that both are therefore true – each in its own particular way. Harman's mysterious 'real objects' are quite different from both what Whitehead calls 'actual entities' and from what he calls 'societies' or 'enduring objects'.[30] Nonetheless, like Whitehead, Harman constructs a vision of the world that rejects the bifurcation of nature.

Grant also resists the bifurcation of nature. There are clear affinities between Grant's conception of nature's productivity and Whitehead's designation of Creativity as 'the universal of universals characterizing ultimate matter of fact'.[31] Through his rereading of Schelling, Grant seeks to forge a *Naturphilosophie* according to which 'nature is considered the condition under which alone anything that can exist does so'.[32] The result is not so much to erase the bifurcation of nature *per se*, as to suggest that both of its sides – the red glow of the sunset, and the molecules and waves – are produced by the same processes, and in analogous ways. The forces of nature are always already at work prior to any division. Both sides of the bifurcation – subjective phenomenology and objective physical qualities – are natural products in the same way. They are both are produced out of, and alike ultimately dissolved back into, nature's groundless productivity.

Meillassoux, on the other hand, knowingly fails the Whiteheadian test. He opens *After Finitude* precisely by reviving the old Cartesian division – regarded by Whitehead as the initial source of the bifurcation of nature – between mathematically formalizable 'primary qualities' that characterize the thing in itself, and 'secondary qualities' that only exist in relation to us. Meillassoux also consistently describes the world-without-us as not having 'any subjective – thinking, psychological, egoic, sensible, or vital – traits'.[33] In this way, Meillassoux reasserts the classical opposition between rational, active mind and, on the other hand, matter conceived as mechanistic, passive and inert. Of course, Meillassoux gives this opposition a strange new content. On the one hand, the brute materiality of lifeless nature is subject to the rule of Hyperchaos, which can make anything whatsoever happen for no reason at all.[34] On the other hand, human thought alone is able to attain an 'intellectual intuition of the absolute'.[35] But both of these terms require the bifurcation of nature as their underlying condition.

Brassier is the most ambiguous of the speculative realist thinkers when it comes to Whitehead's test. As a scientific rationalist, Brassier explicitly rejects what he calls 'the kind of philosophical aestheticism which seems to want to hold up "aesthetic experience" as a new sort of cognitive paradigm wherein the Modern (post-Cartesian) "rift" between knowing and feeling would be overcome'.[36] This seems like a refusal to grant any validation whatsoever to the phenomenological, experiential side of the bifurcation of nature. For Brassier, it would seem, we can only overcome the bifurcation by categorically rejecting one side of it. But the situation is actually more complicated than this. For Brassier also argues that what Wilfrid Sellars calls the 'manifest image' of man cannot simply be *replaced* by the more accurate 'scientific image'. Rather, Brassier agrees with Sellars that the two images need to coexist. For 'the manifest image is indispensable insofar as it provides the structure within which we exercise our capacity for rational thought'.[37] Without the manifest image, Brassier says, quoting Sellars, 'man himself would not survive', and the normativity that grounds scientific discovery would become impossible.[38] Brassier seeks to purge scientific rationality of its 'anthropological' attributes, including its ties to any experiential or affective basis. But he also insists that 'normativity is not found but *made*', and therefore that it has ties to what, for the moment, remain human practices.

In short, Harman and Grant both pass Whitehead's test. Meillassoux unequivocally fails it. Brassier's is the most fascinatingly ambiguous case. Brassier is clearly opposed to the *spirit* of Whitehead's proposition, as he unequivocally supports the scientific demystification of all phenomenological and narratively meaningful claims.[39] This puts him firmly on one side of the bifurcation of nature. But in pragmatic terms, Brassier cannot altogether dismiss the phenomenological side of the bifurcation, since he needs it precisely in order to reach the point where he is able to abandon it. Whitehead would surely have rejected both Brassier's bleak nihilism and his excessive rationalism vis-à-vis science; but the tension between these two sides of the bifurcation of nature is precisely what makes Brassier's thought so rich and compelling.

Notes

1. Quentin Meillassoux, *After Finitude: An Essay on the Necessity of Contingency*, trans. Ray Brassier (London: Continuum, 2008), p. 7.
2. Eugene Thacker, *In the Dust of This Planet* (Winchester: Zero Books, 2011), pp. 2–4.
3. Thacker, *Dust*, p. 5.
4. Iain Hamilton Grant, *Philosophies of Nature After Schelling* (London: Continuum, 2006).
5. Graham Harman, *Guerrilla Metaphysics: Phenomenology and the Carpentry of Things* (Chicago: Open Court, 2005).
6. Meillassoux, *After Finitude*, p. 9.
7. Ray Brassier, *Nihil Unbound: Enlightenment and Extinction* (Basingstoke: Palgrave Macmillan, 2007), p. 228.
8. Immanuel Kant, *Critique of Judgment*, trans. Paul Guyer and Eric Matthews (Cambridge: Cambridge University Press, 2000), p. 144.
9. Kant, *Judgment*, pp. 144–5.
10. G. W. F. Hegel, *The Encyclopaedia Logic: Part I of the Encyclopaedia of the Philosophical Sciences*, trans. T. F. Geraets, W. A. Suchting and H. S. Harris (Indianapolis: Hackett, 1991), pp. 80–108.
11. Ray Brassier, 'Concepts and Objects', in Levi Bryant, Nick Srnicek and Graham Harman (eds), *The Speculative Turn: Continental Materialism and Realism* (Melbourne: re.press, 2010), p. 63.
12. Gilles Deleuze, *Cinema 1: The Movement Image*, trans. Hugh Tomlinson and Barbara Habberjam (Minneapolis: University of Minnesota Press, 1986), p. 56.
13. Quentin Meillassoux, 'Iteration, Reiteration, Repetition: A Speculative Analysis of the Sign Devoid of Meaning', this volume, p. 151.
14. Ibid., p. 155.
15. Ray Brassier, 'The View from Nowhere', *Journal for Politics, Gender and Culture* 8(2) (Summer 2011): 9.
16. Meillassoux, *After Finitude*, p. 3.
17. Meillassoux, 'Iteration', p. 157.

18. Meillassoux, *After Finitude*, pp. 163 and 183 (emphasis added).
19. Iain Hamilton Grant, 'How Nature Comes to be Thought: Schelling's Paradox and the Problem of Location', *Journal of the British Society for Phenomenology* 44(1) (January 2013): 24–43.
20. Ibid., pp. 24–5.
21. Graham Harman, *The Third Table* (Ostfildern: Hatje Cantz, 2012), p. 12.
22. Ibid., p. 12.
23. Alfred North Whitehead, *Modes of Thought* (New York: Free Press, 1938).
24. For Whitehead, see his *Process and Reality* (New York: Free Press, 1978), p. ix; for Meillassoux, see *After Finitude*, p. 7.
25. Whitehead, *Process*, p. 18.
26. Alfred North Whitehead, *The Concept of Nature* (Amherst, NY: Prometheus Books, 2004), pp. 26–48.
27. Whitehead, *Nature*, p. 29.
28. A. S. Eddington, *The Nature of the Physical World* (Cambridge: Cambridge University Press, 1958), pp. xi–xii.
29. Harman, *Table*, pp. 9–10.
30. For Whitehead's distinction between actual entities, which he considers the ultimate elements of reality, and societies, or the objects we encounter in the world, and which are composites of many actual entities, see *Process*, pp. 31–6.
31. Ibid., p. 21.
32. Leon Niemoczynski and Iain Hamilton Grant, 'Physics of the Idea: An Interview with Iain Hamilton Grant', *Cosmos and History* 9(2) (2013): 35.
33. Meillassoux, 'Iteration', p. 120.
34. Ibid., p. 150.
35. Meillassoux, *After Finitude*, p. 82.
36. Ray Brassier, 'Against an Aesthetics of Noise'. Available from http://www.ny-web.be/transitzone/against-aesthetics-noise.html [accessed 23 March 2015].
37. Brassier, 'View from Nowhere', p. 8.
38. Ibid.
39. Ray Brassier, 'I Am a Nihilist Because I Still Believe in Truth', 2011. Available from http://www.kronos.org.pl/index.php?23151,896 [accessed 23 March 2015].

CHAPTER 2
REFLECTIONS OF A ROTTEN NATURE: HEGEL, LACAN AND MATERIAL NEGATIVITY

Adrian Johnston

From the myth of the nongiven to the anorganic – negativities theistic and atheistic

Despite my solidarity with numerous facets of Jacques Lacan's thinking, I consider his central accounts of the emergences of ego and subject to suffer from a major shortcoming: their exclusively ontogenetic status. As I illustrate and criticize elsewhere, Lacan, wavering between epistemological and ontological justifications, strictly prohibits phylogenetic hypotheses and investigations as illegitimate and out of bounds, at least within the limits of psychoanalysis proper as he conceives it.[1] In my critique of Lacan's forbidding of inquiries into phylogenesis, I point out how this highly contentious circumscription of the scope of analytic thought leads Lacan into having direct recourse to biblical and Christian references (despite identifying himself as an atheist and, following Freud, considering psychoanalytic theory and practice to be atheistic in a number of ways).[2] More specifically, in line with his ban on raising queries regarding the historical origins of language and connected social structures, Lacan permits himself an affirmation of the statement 'In the beginning was the Word';[3] concomitantly, he overtly portrays the advent of the symbolic order, a creative genesis obfuscated and mystified by the Lacanian law against all things phylogenetic, as the descent of the 'Holy Spirit' down into the world.[4] For any atheist materialist, Lacan included, this should be deeply troubling.

Dovetailing with this side of the Lacanianism with which I take issue, Jacques-Alain Miller proclaims that 'nothingness enters reality through language'.[5] As I will show below, such a thesis does not actually fit Lacan himself overall, especially considering the latter's realist and materialist depictions of negativities manifest in core concepts of his like the body-in-pieces (*corps morcelé*). However, this stated, Miller's proclamation indeed is able to prop itself up against select sides of Lacan's teachings. What Miller and the version of Lacan he relies on represent is, I contend, a dogma particularly widespread in Continental European philosophy and theory, infected as these intellectual traditions have been and still remain with various idealist, romanticist and negative theological tendencies both avowed and disavowed. Modifying a turn of phrase from American Analytic philosopher Wilfrid Sellars's seminal 1956 essay 'Empiricism and the Philosophy of Mind', I consider the most suitable label for this dogma 'the myth of the nongiven'.

This myth lurks at the basis of each and every appeal to an unexplained factical givenness of the nongiven qua absence, lack, negativity, and so on. Apropos a theory of subjectivity (which is my focus in this context), its supporting background presence is borne witness to by dogmatic invocations of an irreducible, unanalysable Nothingness as the primordial privative cause of the subject (or even as the subject itself). No matter how seemingly sophisticated and intricate the jargonistic gesticulating, these invocations boil down, when all is said and done, to vulgar foot stamping and fist banging.

As regards the myth of the nongiven in relation to certain theories of subjectivity, a bond of complicity is established between them at the dawn of Renaissance humanism with its founding document, Giovanni Pico della Mirandola's 1486 oration 'On the Dignity of Man'. Therein, Pico della Mirandola describes human beings, as distinct from all other creatures and creations, as specially endowed by God with a strange, peculiar natureless nature, an inner absence of form unlike that to be found anywhere else in the abundant, overflowing fullness of the rest of the formed world. Through top-down divine fiat alone, an abyssal groundlessness of pure negativity becomes the metaphysical spark of humans in their crown-of-creation dignity; a rock-bottom emptiness of otherworldly provenance is the privative *Ur*-cause of humanity's distinctiveness.[6]

Jumping ahead to the past century, ostensibly irreligious minds continue to propagate, without critical modifications, permutations of Pico della Mirandola's mythical, theological story of uniquely human voidedness. In the Continental Europe of the last one hundred years generally, and in France particularly, atheists and nonatheists, humanists and antihumanists, and partisans of a range of other apparently incommensurable or incompatible theoretical orientations faithfully reproduce this narrative with varying degrees of self-awareness. Even when decoupled from the Christian framework of 'On the Dignity of Man', assertions of an *ex nihilo*, always-already-there absence, lack, nothingness, void, etc. at and as the heart of subjectivity perpetuate the religious vices of dogmatism, mystification and obscurantism. Through dependence on the myth of the nongiven, those putting forward these assertions either rest on positings of a priori metaphysical 'unexplained explainers' or capriciously baulk at thinking their way through to the underlying foundations of their positions.

Insofar as they staunchly refuse to contemplate the lengthier stretches of human and natural histories (as in phylogenesis and evolution) that anyone with sound scientific sensibilities presumes gave rise to contemporary humanity, Lacan and Lacanians evince belief in a mythical givenness of negativity as nongiven. Apart from the idealist and antinaturalist variants of Lacanianism against which I argue, and even on the most sympathetic materialist, quasinaturalist reading of Lacan (which I try to offer later here), he continues to be guilty of investment in this myth. Within his purely ontogenetic picture, the infant's *corps morcelé* is referred to as if it were the ultimate givenness of a ground-zero origin incapable of further explanation (save for ahistorical, idealist talk about big Others as eternally preexisting and phylogenetically inexplicable symbolic orders into which conception and birth throws children). Severed from its natural connections with phylogenetic and evolutionary histories, the prematurationally helpless body-in-pieces of ontogenesis darkens into being an opaque bedrock of false, fictional absoluteness. The myth of the nongiven hides itself poorly in the cracks and gaps of this barred corpoReal. If these spectres of negativities are not to be exorcized completely after being flushed out of these nooks and crannies within bodies, what is to be done with them? How are they to be rightly situated? To be crystal clear, I do not intend to overturn Lacan's rich dissections of embodiment. Instead, I merely aim to demonstrate that his reflections on these matters are indefensibly incomplete and in need of substantial supplementary supports of sorts with which he likely would not be comfortable (about which I will say more subsequently).

Other figures culpable of providing philosophical refuge and cover for a mysticism of negativity are not hard to identify. Apart from Lacan, his existentialist contemporaries Martin Heidegger, with his unfathomable sendings and ecstatic clearings of Being, and Jean-Paul Sartre, with his unnaturally essenceless existences, are obvious examples (for reasons I go into at length on other occasions, I do not consider G. W. F. Hegel and Karl Marx, despite possible appearances to the contrary, culpable of repeating or resting upon appeals to mystical negativities in the manners I am objecting to in this setting).[7] Flashing forward to today, Alain Badiou and Giorgio

Agamben are two living philosophers influenced by these predecessors and, under such influences, embellishing upon the myth of the nongiven (Slavoj Žižek too sometimes flirts with the danger of continued fidelity to the idol of this mysterious Nothingness).[8] Agamben's human being is a 'man without content', a deessentialized openness (as first glimpsed by Pico della Mirandola, to whom Agamben waves) whose always-second 'nature' is continually subjected to ongoing constructions and reconstructions putting to work its unworkable, inexhaustible potentialities.[9] Similarly, Badiou's human being is a 'voided animal' to be thought by a new 'inhumanism' combining Sartre's humanism and the antihumanism of Lacan, Louis Althusser and Michel Foucault. Badiou equally praises these four French forerunners of his for their unflinching opposition to 'a bad Darwin', although he has yet to indicate whether, for him, there is such a thing as a 'good Darwin' and, if so, what he would look like and what relevance, if any, he would have for Badiouian philosophy. In short, unlike all other animals, Badiou's voided animal cannot be addressed by naturalism, purportedly calling instead for antinaturalist (one might be tempted to say 'supernaturalist') engagements.[10]

The surfacing of Charles Darwin's name at this juncture is fortuitous and fitting. Apart from Kant and Hegel as its twin fountainheads, the vast bulk of what has come to be known as 'Continental philosophy' springs from the (un)holy trinity of Marx, Friedrich Nietzsche and Sigmund Freud (à la Paul Ricoeur's three great 'hermeneuts of suspicion').[11] In my estimation, the almost blanket neglect of Darwin by these philosophical orientations leveraged to the authority of this triumvirate of his approximate contemporaries is symptomatic of a swarm of intellectual and ideological problems plaguing various strains of Continental philosophy and its offshoots. Ironically, Marx, Nietzsche and Freud, unlike so many of their self-proclaimed successors, do not downplay or ignore Darwin's immense significance.

Whereas the majority of Continental philosophers of the past century underestimate the far-reaching radicality of the Darwinian revolution, a sizeable number of Analytic philosophers tend to the opposite extreme of overestimating it (along with Hegel, the figure of Darwin marks a fork of fundamental divergence between the Continental and Analytic traditions). Although I have reservations about hyperbole in Daniel Dennett's trumpeting of Darwinian evolutionary theory as a 'universal acid', I readily acknowledge the incredible potency and magnitude of the Darwin-event (to employ Badiou's language in a fashion he himself probably would not).[12] My wager

Reflections of a Rotten Nature

is that dispelling the myth of the nongiven while nonetheless preserving its insistence on an intimate rapport between subjectivity and negativity – my antipathy toward mystical varieties of lack(s) by no means entails my sympathy toward lack-denying positivisms, presentisms, organicisms, or anything else in these scientific veins – demands evolutionary-phylogenetic explanations of the natural emergences of the denaturalized/more-than-natural negativities inherent to existent subjects qua subjectivity proper (i.e. as irreducible to garden-variety, pseudoscientific naturalisms). For any philosophical or psychoanalytic system reconciled with the natural sciences and allied with (historical/dialectical) materialism, a rapprochement with Darwin's ideas is requisite.

With respect to Lacan's theories of the geneses of ego (*moi*) and subject (*sujet*) in this context, a nonmystical, thoroughly materialist account (one that refrains from conjuring up anything along the lines of the Holy Spirit) of the historical genesis of the ontogenetic ground-zero of the biomaterial body-in-pieces needs the help of Darwin and his evolutionary-theoretic heirs. Without accepting such assistance, Lacanianism leaves itself divided from within by an unsustainable self-contradiction in which it is split between ontogenetic atheism and phylogenetic theism. On this matter, a choice formally configured as a Badiouian 'point' (i.e. a decision between two irreconcilable alternatives with no third way available) thrusts itself forward: In the terms of heavy-handed American popular culture wars bumper sticker sloganeering, this is a choice between the Jesus fish and the Darwin amphibian.[13]

However, Lacan, despite his reputation as an avid antinaturalist, has no qualms whatsoever about leaning upon certain ideas of nature as components of his theoretical apparatus (hence, my critiques of his mystical, theosophical lapses are unexpectedly immanent ones).[14] Although adamantly opposed to the introduction of a crudely reductive biologism as a grounding paradigm for psychoanalysis, he is not, for all that, categorically dismissive of the life sciences. Once in a while, he even permits himself, like Freud, to voice hopes of eventual biological confirmations of analytic theories.[15] To take just one illustration of this known to anyone familiar with Lacanianism, Lacan's concept of 'need (*besoin*)', as per the need-demand-desire triad, is bound up with the biological facticity of protracted infantile helplessness (*Hilflosigkeit*), an anatomical and physiological 'fact' of immense import for psychical ontogenesis in the eyes of both Freud and Lacan.[16] Arising immediately from the very start of the human organism's existence as a bodily being, need is the contingent yet a priori base of the Lacanian libidinal economy, a crucial impetus necessary for propelling the neonate into the combined arms of Imaginary Others (i.e. experientially familiar conspecifics as intersubjective alter egos, caretakers and nurturers as 'like me') and Symbolic Others (such as shared languages, laws, norms, rules, traditions, etc. forming a transsubjective mediating matrix for intersubjective relations, with the latter relations instantiating for and imposing upon the neonate this mediating matrix). Only thereby, thanks to helpless neediness as a natural condition of possibility, is the transition to the complex dialectical mediations of demand and desire prompted. Even though Imaginary-Symbolic imprinting and overwriting via the images and words of others and Others (partially) denaturalizes need – Lacan's talk of 'denaturalization' automatically implies the prior existence of certain natural things as origins or sources[17] – the resulting denaturalized subjectivity ($) remains, to phrase this in a Lacanian style, 'not without (*pas sans*)' a rapport with nature in the guise of its biomaterial body. Or, in alternate phrasing, the never fully denaturalized subject is stuck perpetually struggling with stubbornly indigestible bits and fragments of an incompletely and unevenly domesticated corpoReal.

In a companion piece to the present essay, I highlight the numerous instances in which Lacan, with however many caveats and qualifications, utilizes the notion of the organic in its biological sense.[18] I argue there that his references to this notion, clustering around his recurrent embellishments on the mirror stage, suggest the concept of a nonorganicity that would be different from the merely inorganic as dealt with by the physics and chemistry of the nonliving. On the basis of this reading of Lacan, I hence distinguish between the inorganic and the 'anorganic', with the latter being a Hegelian-type negation of the organic as itself, according to Hegel's *Philosophy of Nature*, a 'negation' als *Aufhebung* of the inorganic; that is, a dialectical-speculative negation of negation disobeying the rule of double negation in classical, bivalent logic as non-dialectical/speculative. In other words, if, as per Hegel, the organic is itself a sublation of the inorganic, then the anorganic sublates the organic (specifically as an internal, self-generated malfunctioning of the latter) without thereby resulting in a simple return to the previous level of the inorganic. After passing through a delineation of the organic and the anorganic *à la* Lacan as exhibited within his accounts of the mirror stage, I will circumnavigate back to the claims in this paragraph by showing how anorganicity, as a more-than-organic transcendence nonetheless immanent to the organic, simultaneously conjoins and disjoins the natural kingdoms of animal organisms and the spiritual/minded regions of human subjects. One of the implications of my extracting this conception of the anorganic from the Lacanian mirror stage is that Lacan himself already suggests a sophisticated neither-reductive-nor-eliminative materialism embracing the sciences without, for all that, allowing itself to be captured by and absorbed into them.

Bodies and brains in pieces – The real nature of the Lacanian mirror stage

Lacan's 1949 *écrit* on the mirror stage is perhaps the single best-known and most widely read piece of his extensive *oeuvre*. Closer to the time of the regrettably lost text on which this *écrit* is based, 1938's lengthy entry in the *Encyclopédie française* on 'The Family Complexes in the Formation of the Individual' already aims to get back behind the reflective surfaces of the moment of identification with the *Gestalt* of the *imago*. (Incidentally, this 1938 essay provides the best available indications of the contents of Lacan's original presentation of the mirror stage at the International Psychoanalytic Association conference in Marienbad in 1936.) Lacan refers in this article to 'libidinal conditions' underlying the onset of the mirror stage properly speaking.[19] A few pages later, he points to 'the vital insufficiency of man at his origins' (specifically, the human being's ontogenetic origins, his/her default 'natural' condition as thrown into the world by conception and birth).[20] The canonical 1949 framing of this stage explicitly connects these two points in 'The Family Complexes' by describing a 'libidinal dynamism (*dynamisme libidinal*)' having to do with the infant's 'motor impotence and nursling dependence' (in other words, prematurational helplessness catalyses the motivationally efficacious movements of certain drives and desires).[21]

In 1948's 'Aggressiveness in Psychoanalysis', another key text as regards the mirror stage, Lacan offers formulations pertaining to biology and the organic consistent with both 'The Family Complexes' and 'The Mirror Stage'. As he explains:

> What I have called the 'mirror stage' is of interest because it manifests the affective dynamism (*dynamisme affectif*) by which the subject primordially identifies with the visual gestalt of his own body. In comparison with the still very profound lack of coordination of his own motor functioning, that gestalt is an ideal unity, a salutary imago.

Its value is heightened by all the early distress resulting from the child's intraorganic and relational discordance (*la discordance intra-organique et relationnelle*) during the first six months of life, when he bears the neurological and humoral signs of a physiological prematurity at birth (*les signes, neurologiques et humoraux, d'une prématuration natale physiologique*).[22]

Between this *écrit* and that on the mirror stage, the adjectives 'affective' and 'libidinal' alternately modify, in 1948 and 1949 respectively, the 'dynamism' serving as a precondition for the advent of this founding event of ego-level identification, with all its denaturalizing consequences for the future vicissitudes of the human creature (as 'a gestalt' with 'formative effects on an organism').[23] Almost certainly, Lacan, apropos this topic at least, considers these adjectives to be roughly equivalent insofar as the dynamizing push of the young subject-to-be into the seductive pull of the mirror's virtual reality is a force generated by the combined powers of the libidinal (that is, motivations) and the affective (that is, emotions). As the above quotation proceeds to stipulate, certain emotions (specifically the 'distress' of negative ones such as fear, anger, anxiety, envy, jealousy, hatred, rage, and the like) motivate the child to invest itself in the 'gestalt' of 'an ideal unity, a salutary imago'. Furthermore, Lacan undeniably situates this dual catalytic configuration of the affective/emotional and the libidinal/motivational as an effect or outgrowth of ontogenetically primordial biological factors, namely, as the preceding quoted passage has it, 'the child's intraorganic and relational discordance during the first six months of life, when he bears the neurological and humoral signs of a physiological prematurity at birth'.

Subsequent moments within 'Aggressiveness in Psychoanalysis' underscore the ground-zero status of such biomaterial conditions. A few pages after the immediately prior block quotation, another paragraph adds:

A specific satisfaction, based on the integration of an original organic chaos (*un désarroi organique originel*), corresponds to the *Urbild* of this formation, alienating as it may be due to its function of rendering foreign. This satisfaction must be conceived of in the dimension of a vital dehiscence (*une déhiscence vitale*) constitutive of man and makes unthinkable the idea of an environment that is preformed for him; it is a 'negative' libido that enables the Heraclitean notion of Discord – which the Ephesian held to be prior to harmony – to shine once more.[24]

Reflections of a Rotten Nature

This is reiterated in the mirror stage *écrit*:

> In man ... this relationship to nature is altered by a certain dehiscence at the very heart of the organism, a primordial Discord (*une certaine déhiscence de l'organisme en son sein ... une Discorde primordiale*) betrayed by the signs of malaise and motor uncoordination of the neonatal months. The objective (*objective*) notions of the anatomical incompleteness (*inachèvement*) of the pyramidal tracts and of certain humoral residues of the maternal organism in the newborn confirm my view that we find in man a veritable *specific prematurity of birth*.[25]

Taking these two extremely similar passages from the same period in the late 1940s together, Lacan posits an 'objective incompleteness' (i.e. an actual absence in biological reality of completeness qua harmony, synthesis, etc.) as a primary negative *Urgrund* of ontogenetic subject formation. This 'original', 'primordial' foundation of biomaterial facticity (including its objective incompleteness) is, as Lacan puts it in 1949, 'prior to ... social determination', 'prior to ... social dialectic' as 'an organic inadequacy of his [man's] natural reality' (*une insuffisance organique de sa réalité naturelle*).[26] In terms of anatomy, physiology and neurology (that is, the three life-scientific dimensions mentioned explicitly by Lacan), the biology of the newborn human 'organism' entails prematurational helplessness, among other conditions; the neonate's discombobulated dependence is precisely a lack of anatomical, physiological and neurological maturation sufficient for it to survive without the sustained, substantial assistance of significantly older conspecifics (who bring with them enveloping Imaginary-Symbolic realities into which they hurl this fragile, vulnerable little being). In 'On a Question Prior to Any Possible Treatment of Psychosis', the *écrit* encapsulating the essentials of Lacan's third seminar on *The Psychoses* (1955–6), the 'specific prematurity of birth in man' is directly equated with the baby's 'fragmented body (*corps morcelé*)', a natural reality throwing the young child into the mirror stage and its 'counternatural features (*contre-nature*)'.[27] Additionally, one should note here the self-subverting dialectical character of a nature that aids and abets its own effacement by 'counternature', namely, a natural autodenaturalization peculiar to the (species-)being (*Gattungswesen*) of humanity. Much later, in his twenty-fourth seminar, Lacan again utilizes the phrase '*contre-nature*'.[28] Likewise, in his 1958 *écrit* 'The Direction of the Treatment and the Principles of Its Power', he speaks of '*antiphusis*'.[29]

As I observed earlier, the hybrid constellations of affective emotions and libidinal motivations making the immature subject-to-be interested in and receptive to the mediations of external identifications are provoked by the state of *Hilflosigkeit*, itself a brute (and brutal) biological fact. This initial bodily state is anorganic in my precise sense, in that Lacan qualifies it as an 'intraorganic discordance', 'an original organic chaos' situated 'at the very heart of the organism' (in Lacan's first foray into the English language, the 1951 paper 'Some Reflections on the Ego' presenting the mirror stage to the members of the British Psycho-Analytical Society, he similarly underlines an 'organic disturbance and discord').[30] In other words, what is at stake here is an immanent negation of the organic that nevertheless is not simply a reversion to the inorganic; this negation is a disruption of organicity arising from within its own (dis)organization (with the words 'organ', 'organic' and 'organism' being etymologically tied to the idea of 'organization'). The human organism's preliminary default lack of organic organization (coordination, integration, wholeness, and the like) is a privative/negative cause, one with ontological standing as both real and material, necessary for helping to set in motion the trajectory running from natural substance to more-than-natural subjectivity. (I will clarify and defend my use of this sort of [quasi-]naturalist and Hegelian language in due course.) At one point in 1955's 'The Freudian Thing', Lacan's realist materialism and carefully qualified naturalism surface when he describes the distinguishing anorganicity of the human organism as 'the congenital gap presented by man's real being in his natural relations (*la béance congénitale que présente l'être réel de l'homme dans ses relations naturelles*)'.[31] Consistent with my concept of the anorganic,[32] Lacan, at the same moment in this *écrit* when he affirms a materialist quasinaturalism, simultaneously breaks with the scientific *Weltanschauung* of organicism generally holding sway in biology and its branches by deriding 'the organism's pseudototality (*la pseudo-totalité de l'organisme*)'[33] – hence his repeated warnings against picturing humans, their bodies included, as sums or wholes (akin to Aristotelian souls).[34]

In the first sentence of the last paragraph of 'Aggressiveness in Psychoanalysis', Lacan speaks of a 'formidable crack (*formidable lézarde*)' in the human being that 'goes right to the very depths of his being (*jusqu'au fond de l'être*)'.[35] Just a few years later in a glossing of the mirror stage in '*Le mythe individuel du névrosé, ou Poésie et vérité dans la névrose*' (1952), he again talks about 'the original chaos of all the motor and affective functions of the first six months after birth (*le désarroi originel de toutes les fonctions motrices et affectives qui est celui des six premiers mois après la naissance*)', 'a profound insufficiency (*une profonde insuffisance*)', and 'a crack, an original tearing, a dereliction (*une fêlure ... un déchirement original ... une déréliction*)'.³⁶ And, in a 1955 session of his second seminar on *The Ego in Freud's Theory and in the Technique of Psychoanalysis*, the mirror stage is grounded in humans' biological inclination towards a transcendence of their biology by virtue of a 'biological gap (*béance biologique*)' internal and inherent to their very being.³⁷ Near the close of this session, Lacan unfurls a thread of continuity between Freud's radical revision of analytic drive theory in *Beyond the Pleasure Principle* (1920), in which ferocious clashes originating within the id between *Eros* and the *Todestrieb* split human beings right down to their bare bones and raw flesh, and the riven biomaterial roots of human subjectivity.³⁸

As is common knowledge among Lacan's readers, the phrase 'body-in-pieces (*corps morcelé*)' is how, from the mid-1930s through the mid-1950s, he tends to designate much of what is summarized in the preceding outline.³⁹ However, what is not so well appreciated is that Lacan does not restrict this phrase's significance to that of a label for an exclusively phenomenological description of the neonate's experience of his or her lived embodiment. Although, as conceded earlier, a phenomenology of embodied emotions and motivations is indeed part of what Lacan's ontogenetic narratives associate with the anatomical, physiological and neurological prematuration of newborns, his metapsychological theories of the interlinked emergences of ego and subject ultimately rest, when all is said and done, on the objective grounds of biomaterial – i.e. nonphenomenological – bases (and these grounds would have to be Real for Lacan to the extent that, as seen, they precede the Symbolic of sociolinguistic mediation as well as the Imaginary of experiential phenomena). A quite striking indication of this is to be found in black and white within the pages of the renowned 1949 mirror stage *écrit* itself. Virtually unseen beneath the noses of this text's countless readers complacently assuming Lacan to be a certain sort of uncompromising antinaturalist thoroughly hostile toward the life sciences, he directly and explicitly connects the body-in-pieces to 'the cerebral cortex' of 'the central nervous system', depicting this brain region as what 'psychosurgical operations will lead us to regard as the intraorganic mirror' (in effect, predicting the eventual discovery, almost fifty years later, of the serendipitously christened 'mirror neurons').⁴⁰, ⁴¹ In other words, Lacan does not limit himself to an analytic phenomenology divorced from, or even opposed to, biology and its branches (such as anatomy, physiology and neurology). Instead, he ambitiously contests the spontaneous organicist picture thinking of the life sciences on their own scientific terrain, with his *corps morcelé* incarnating, among other things, an intrascientific critique of pseudoscientific imaginings of fictitious syntheses and totalities.

The themes I am subsuming under the heading of the anorganic persist into Lacan's work of the late 1950s and 1960s. Two essays in the *Écrits*, 'Remarks on Daniel Lagache's Presentation: "Psychoanalysis and Personality Structure"' (1960) and 'On My Antecedents' (1966), contain contents relevant to the present discussion. In his response to Lagache, Lacan walks a fine line between the natural and the nonnatural:

> It is ... worth recalling that, from the outset, Freud did not attribute *the slightest reality* as a differentiated apparatus in the organism to any of the systems in either of his topographies. For people forget to draw therefrom the corollary that, by the same token, he forbade us to force any of these systems back into the fantasized reality of any sort of 'totality' of the organism (*la realité fantasmée d'une quelconque "totalité" de l'organisme*). In short, the structure of which I am speaking has nothing to do with the idea of the 'structure of the organism', as supported by the most soundly based facts in *Gestalt* theory. Not that structure, in the strict sense of the term, does not take advantage of gaps in the organic *Gestalt* to submit it to itself (*Non que la structure au sens propre ne profite des béances de la* Gestalt *organique pour se l'asservir*). But on the basis of their conjunctions, whether they prove to be based on fission or fissures, a heterogeneity between two orders appears, which we will be less tempted to mask if we grasp its principle.[42]

Lacan's familiar antinaturalist refrains obviously are audible at the start of this quotation in his interpretative insistence on the independence of Freud's topographies (whether the first or the second) *vis-à-vis* the anatomy and physiology of the human body as a piece of nature falling under the explanatory jurisdiction of the natural sciences. Consistent with his self-appointed role as the lone orthodox Freudian of his time, Lacan portrays his own notion of 'structure' (materialized by symbolic orders as the 'objective spirit' of external sociolinguistic arrangements) as testifying to an all-too-rare fidelity to this Freud in particular.

However, in the preceding quotation, Lacan's position is much more subtle and nuanced than that of a straightforward, unqualified antinaturalism. This delicately maintained stance pivots around the matter of how to conceive of the theme of the organic in relation to real human organisms. The second sentence of this passage from the *écrit* on Lagache prohibits interfacing components of analytic metapsychology specifically with 'the fantasized reality of any sort of "totality" of the organism'. That is to say, Lacan here worries more about scientism (the imagined One-Alls of organicism as protoconceptual picture thinking) than science (the actual biology of flesh-and-blood human animals) in terms of potential perils posed to the theory and practice of analysis. In the immediately following sentence, he vehemently underscores that 'the structure of which I am speaking has nothing to do with the idea of the "structure of the organism"'. Here, the etymology of the word 'organism' should be recalled. Insofar as its etymological origins signify 'organization', the phrase 'structure of the organism' arguably is a pleonasm synonymous with '"totality" of the organism'. Hence, Lacan's denial of metapsychological ties to the natural body target precisely this *corps* as *non-morcelé* qua totalized or structured in the sense of organically organized, namely, as envisioned under the influence of organicism, with its lopsided emphases on motifs of balance, harmony, wholeness, and the like. Organicists would count among those whom Lacan, in his contemporaneous *écrit* 'Guiding Remarks for a Convention on Female Sexuality', curtly dismisses in their implicit claims for themselves of 'a messianic access to decisive chemisms (*un accès messianique à des chimismes décisifs*)', with 'decisive chemisms' partly alluding to the eighteenth-century motif of 'elective affinities' and Goethe's thus-entitled novel of 1809.[43] His later 1970s-era reflections on the nonexistent *rapport sexuel* (as an elective affinity between the sexes) similarly are extrapolated into an indictment of envisionings of Nature-with-a-capital-N as a Yin-Yang-style cosmic dance of complementary pairs mirroring (often unconscious) fantasies about masculinity and femininity.[44]

The subsequent fourth sentence of this excerpt from Lacan's response to Lagache – 'Not that structure, in the strict sense of the term, does not take advantage of gaps in the organic *Gestalt* to submit it to itself' – promptly reinforces this anorganic thrust in that it appeals to the fractured and fragmented body-in-pieces as a biological condition of possibility for denaturalizing/more-than-natural structure getting a grip on the anorganic 'first nature' of the human organism (i.e. for the signifiers of the big Other overwriting the real bodily being of the *parlêtre*-to-be). In his contemporaneous eighth seminar on *Transference* (1960–1), Lacan echoes the claim made by this sentence, indicating that the combined material and phenomenal features of the *corps morcelé* establish necessary conditions for ego and subject formation. In resonance with intuitions long ago articulated by F. W. J. Schelling and Hegel,[45] he stipulates:

> In effect, if one starts from the notion of original narcissism, perfect as regards libidinal investment, if one conceives of the primordial object as primordially included by the subject in the narcissistic sphere, as a primitive monad of enjoyment (*jouissance*), with which is identified ... the infant nursling (*nourrisson*), one has difficulty seeing what would be able to lead to a subjective way out (*une sortie subjective*).[46]

Put differently, without the absences and lacks built into the biomaterial foundations of human nature in the form of the neonate's helpless anorganic *corps*, nothing would motivate an exit ('a subjective way out') from what would be an initial (i.e. 'primordial') state of blissful, self-enclosed idiocy, an infantile paradise of perfectly and completely satisfying oceanic oneness (i.e. 'the narcissistic sphere', 'a primitive monad of enjoyment'). The newborn's body is inclined to open up to the impressions and intrusions of mediations imposed by others and Others – the immature child is prodded down the path of both acquiring an ego as well as becoming a subject – thanks to natural deficits Lacan connects to the *corps morcelé*.

The fifth and final sentence of the above block quotation from the Lagache *écrit* – 'But on the basis of their conjunctions, whether they prove to be based on fission or fissures, a heterogeneity between two orders appears, which we will be less tempted to mask if we grasp its principle' – deploys a dialectical-speculative conjunction of continuity (i.e. 'conjunctions') and discontinuity (i.e. 'heterogeneity'). The 'two orders' to which Lacan refers are those of the endogenous body, as natural but anorganic, and exogenous structure, as nonnatural but relying upon exploitable anorganic spots of receptive weakness in the child's living flesh. The dual dimensions of *phusis* and *antiphusis* collide at loci of paradoxical connection-in-disconnection which Lacan, in his later teachings, sometimes struggles to illustrate through recourse to select figures drawn from topology and knot theory.[47] They are enabled to meet up by and in the clearing of incomplete (human) nature, namely, through the anorganic cracks of negativities (whether the materials of a deficiently functional organism or the phenomena of negative affects) pervading the barred corpoReal of the *corps morcelé*.

Turning to 'On My Antecedents', written by Lacan specifically for the publication of the *Écrits*, he therein revisits much of the analytic landscape surveyed here. His remarks in these veins are worth quoting in full.

Addressing the mirror stage (i.e. 'this phase') as irreducible to 'Gestalt theory and phenomenology', he elaborates:

> Must this phase be reduced to a biological crisis (*une crise biologique*)? The dynamic of this phase, as I outline it, is based on diachronic effects: the delayed coordination of the nervous system (*retard de la coordination nerveuse*) related to man's prematurity at birth, and the formal anticipation of its resolution. But to presume the existence of a harmony that is contradicted by many facts of ethology (*une harmonie que contredisant bien des faits de l'éthologie animale*) is tantamount to dupery.
>
> It masks the crux of a function of lack (*manque*) with the question of the place that this function can assume in a causal chain. Now, far from imagining eliminating it from it, I currently consider such a function to be the very origin of causalist noesis, which goes so far as to mistake it for its crossing into reality (*passage au réel*). But to consider it effective due to its imaginary discordance is to still leave too much room for the presumption of birth. This function involves a more critical lack, its cover being the secret to the subject's jubilation (*la jubilation du sujet*).[48]

At this juncture, there should be little doubt that, although Lacan wishes to avoid reducing the analytic account of psychical ontogenesis to its material underpinnings at the level of biology and its branches, his antireductivism is far from pushing him to the opposite extreme pole of an idealist or dualist denial of the relevance of these fields for analytic theories of emergent egos and subjects. The first two sentences quoted above make this abundantly clear. Furthermore, the ethology Lacan has in mind in the third sentence of this passage is that of the human animal in particular. Given 'the delayed coordination of the nervous system related to man's prematurity at birth, and the formal anticipation of its resolution' – i.e. the *Hilflosigkeit* of the *corps morcelé* as a factical biological real(ity) – the life sciences themselves problematize and invalidate the assumptions and suppositions of organicism as a nonscientific constellation of images and ideas frequently accompanying these same sciences ('But to presume the existence of a harmony that is contradicted by many facts of ethology is tantamount to dupery'). Lacan's critique of organicist picture thinking in biology is immanent and intrascientific, rather than external and antiscientific.

Taking the third paragraph of this quotation from 'On My Antecedents', Lacan here seems to be confronting science insofar as it does not (yet) include psychoanalysis (to refer to a question Lacan raises during the same period of his teaching in the mid-1960s: 'What would a science be that included psychoanalysis?').[49] Lacan's main complaint in this confrontation appears to be the metaphysical bias of the modern sciences against the actual material efficacy of absences and lacks, a bias enshrined in what he refers to above as their 'causalist noesis' (i.e. how they think the fundamental, science-grounding concept of causality); he diagnoses their constitutive blindness to fissures, gaps, negativities, and so on. At best, these empirical, experimental disciplines manage to register the tangible effects present in the material real – as Lacan put it, 'to mistake [the crux of a function of lack] for its crossing into reality' – of what he recognizes as causally efficacious nonpresences (i.e. absences relative to here-and-now physical bodies and their presently observable interactions). Post-Baconian/Galilean scientificity, with its questionable a priori positivist presentism, tends to demand 'eliminating' the 'function of lack'. Opposing this, Lacan tears aside the veils of a pseudoscientific organicism tacitly leaning on nonempirical presentist presumptions 'contradicted by many facts of ethology'. He does so through assigning a precise biological materialization of *manque-comme-cause* – namely, the absence of sufficient harmony and maturation intrinsic to the anorganic bodily being of the newborn human organism – a crucial load-bearing position in the analytic architecture of his theoretical apparatus. As realist, materialist and quasinaturalist, this *manque-comme-cause* is also *manque-comme-être* (modifying here Lacan's *manque-à-être*, a phrase typically employed by Lacan and Lacanians in connection with those lacks animating and perturbing the restless desiring subject).

The last two sentences of the preceding quoted passage further reinforce my reading of Lacan as spelled out in this intervention. The sixth sentence – 'But to consider it effective due to its imaginary discordance is to still leave too much room for the presumption of birth' – undeniably warns against reducing the model of the body-in-pieces from the mirror stage to being merely a phenomenological description of neonatal experiences of negative affects and the intentions they motivate. Twentieth-century phenomenology proceeds from Husserlian resistance to the sweeping expansions of the rapidly advancing natural sciences and continues with Heideggerian rubbishing and bemoaning of their relevance. Lacan's refusal of biologistic reductivism by no means drives him into the company of such phenomenological and/or existentialist neoromantics. In fact, here, he insists that limiting the *corps morcelé* to being a nonbiological experience of embodiment separate and distinct from the biological body implicitly concedes to the latter a wholeness and unity that the very biology of the human organism indicates it does not enjoy. That is to say, for Lacan, finding disharmony solely within the sphere of the subjective states described by phenomenology strongly hints at a presupposition to the effect that the objective material real in and of itself is harmonious (i.e. 'the presumption of birth' as an assumption that the neonate's biological body, by ostensible contrast with its fragmented embodied experience, is at least an organic-qua-organized organism). In this context, Lacan's observations insinuate that, as regards modern science, phenomenology and its offshoots are simultaneously too radical in their antinaturalist turnings away from the sciences *and* not radical enough in these turnings away, conceding 'too much' to the fields thus abandoned. Psychoanalysis, on the other hand, promises the initiation of the pursuit of an immanent critique of modern science through which this amazingly powerful edifice can be transformed significantly instead of being indefensibly neglected or untenably dismissed.

In the seventh and final sentence of the prior quotation from 'On My Antecedents' – 'This function involves a more critical lack, its cover being the secret to the subject's jubilation' – the 'more critical lack' to which Lacan refers is that of the biomaterial real(ity) of the *corps morcelé* independent of any and every phenomenal experience of emotions or motivations. Admittedly, not all of the affects included in Lacan's narrations of the mirror stage are negative. The primary positive feeling manifest in this stage is the 'jubilation' – the 1949 *écrit* speaks of a 'jubilant assumption (*assomption jubilatoire*)' – expressed by the joyful, playful quality of the infant's '*Aha-Erlebnis*' moment of recognizing its reflection.[50] In 1966, Lacan emphasizes that this upsurge of enthusiasm is symptomatic of the eclipsing and obfuscation (i.e. 'its cover') of the body-in-pieces qua barred corpoReal by the 'mirages' and 'phantoms' of the register of the Imaginary. Preferences for the fictions of organic harmony bear indirect witness to aversions to the facts of anorganic disharmony.

Thus far, I have illuminated a consistent red thread of interrelated thoughts running uninterrupted through Lacan's intellectual itinerary from the 1930s to the 1970s. I can begin bringing my anorganicist interpretation of Lacan to a close with a final reference to the *écrit* on the mirror stage. Therein, he states:

> These reflections lead me to recognize in the spatial capture manifested by the mirror stage, the effect in man, even prior to this social dialectic,

of an organic inadequacy of his natural reality – assuming we can give some meaning to the word 'nature'.⁵¹

My hunch is that Lacan's hesitations apropos talking about 'nature' have to do with his awareness of just how overloaded this word is with fantasmatic and propagandistic baggage. The Imaginary projections of a conflict-averse organicism place every appeal to anything 'natural' under the threat of immediate (mis)appropriation by those dreaming of unreal onenesses, namely, those having faith in nonexistent big Others that would not be barred. Very much in line with this early concern of his, the Lacan of the 1970s characterizes nature as 'not one (*pas une*)'.⁵² In terms of the human organism, this not-oneness amounts to an affirmation of its anorganicity. During the same period, he similarly urges reconceptualizing the very notion of 'nature' as strangely unnatural insofar as this reconception markedly deviates from long-standing imaginings regarding nature.⁵³ In jarring dissonance with the pleasant, soothing associations with which (w)holistic fantasizings dress up all things said to be natural, the late Lacan, in a 1977 session of his twenty-fourth seminar, *L'insu que sait de l'une-bévue s'aile à mourre*, depicts nature as a 'rottenness (*pourriture*)' out of which oozes culture qua *antiphusis*. The exemplar of this wounded nature from which denaturalizations 'bubble forth (*bouillonner*)' is nothing other than human nature as materialized by the incomplete *corps morcelé*, with Lacan introducing this body-in-pieces into his thinking already in the 1930s.

Earlier, I claimed that Lacan's anorganic barred corpoReal of the body-in-pieces provides a link perhaps missing between the Hegelian philosophies of nature and spirit/mind (*Geist*). I hence asserted that it would be both possible and productive to insert my anorganicist recasting of a certain Lacan back into Hegel's *Realphilosophie*. Fortuitously, Lacan himself, in his 1955 *écrit* 'Variations on the Standard Treatment', hints at this. Elaborating on the 'experiences' transpiring in the mirror stage (including those of a kind already described in Hegel's 1807 *Phenomenology of Spirit* in connection with the 'master/slave dialectic'), he maintains:

> But if these experiences – which can be seen in animals too at many moments in their instinctual cycles, and especially in the preliminary displays of the reproductive cycle, with all the lures and aberrations these experiences involve – in fact open onto this signification in order to durably structure the human subject, it is because they receive this signification from the tension stemming

from the impotence (*impuissance*) proper to the prematurity of birth, by which naturalists characterize the specificity of man's anatomical development – a fact that helps us grasp the dehiscence from natural harmony (*cette déhiscence de l'harmonie naturelle*), required by Hegel to serve as the fruitful illness, life's happy fault, in which man, distinguishing himself from his essence, discovers his existence.[54]

Characteristically, Lacan does not bother to furnish his readers with specific citations from Hegel's works. But, considering his indebtedness to Alexandre Kojève's version of the *Phenomenology* and his explicit mention of the dialectic between master and slave on the same page of the *Écrits*, Lacan probably is thinking here of the portions of this 1807 text's section on 'Self-Consciousness' preceding the subsection addressing 'lordship and bondage' proper. In the opening pages of this section, Hegel portrays natural desiring life as plagued by monotonous dissatisfactions and futile struggles.[55] That noted, Lacan's choice of the noun 'impotence (*impuissance*)' serendipitously echoes Hegel's motif of the impotence (*Ohnmacht*) of nature. For both authors, a natural clearing is held open for the arising of more-than-natural transcendences-in-immanence thanks to material nature's 'weakness' (Hegel) and 'rottenness' (Lacan). At the end of the above quotation, Lacan's allusion to Sartrean existentialism (itself influenced by the Kojèvian Hegel) indicates that, from a Lacanian perspective, there indeed is an essence that precedes existence (to contradict Sartre).[56] But, this essential (and yet not-One/non-All) nature is not all that natural in any standard naturalist, positivist, and/or presentist senses (the senses Sartre presumes as regards talk of essences in conjunction with the natural sciences). In fact, it is pervaded by negativities both materially real and experientially palpable, hence driving the initially biological being beyond a biology it finds unbearable ('man, distinguishing himself from his essence, discovers his existence').

Ex nihilo nihil fit – Less than something

Shifting back to a broader perspective I gestured at much earlier through reference to the concocted controversies surrounding evolution in America's absurd culture wars (when I spoke of 'the Jesus fish and the Darwin amphibian'), neuroscientist David Linden lays out an elegantly simple and utterly devastating argument against anti-Darwinian proponents of so-called 'intelligent design' with which my Lacan-inspired conception of anorganicity dovetails.[57] In his 2007 book *The Accidental Mind: How Brain Evolution Has Given Us Love, Memory, Dreams, and God*, Linden represents the human central nervous system as a 'kludge': 'the brain', he says, is 'a kludge ... a design that is inefficient, inelegant, and unfathomable, but that nevertheless works'.[58] Linden stresses that the human brain is, in fact, unintelligently designed ('poorly organized', 'a cobbled-together mess') insofar as it is the contingent by-product of countless uncoordinated evolutionary accidents in which, again and again, the relatively newer is tossed into an intricate but sloppy mix with the comparatively older.[59]

The human central nervous system would have to be 'Exhibit A' for those of America's culture warriors who still to this day desire to reprosecute the 1925 Scopes trial. As is common knowledge, the antievolution advocates of intelligent design rest their case on the move of emphasizing the complexity of organic beings and maintaining that such complexity is inexplicable on the basis of the blind, random mechanisms proposed by Darwinian models of evolutionary processes. They believe Darwin and his followers to be fatally unable to answer questions as to how highly functional and seamlessly organized organisms could arise from the unguided chaos of a physical universe of contingencies without teleologies. The human brain, if anything, would be the pinnacle of such stunning sophistication in the natural world; its networked assemblies of astronomical numbers of neurons and synapses come together to generate and sustain seemingly miraculous mindedness and everything this brings with it.

Linden's concise neuroscientific refutation of intelligent design consists of an additional move beyond just establishing the anorganic 'kludginess' of the anatomy and physiology of the central nervous system. This by itself already would be enough, since a demonstrable lack of functionality, organization, and so on – partisans of intelligent design manifestly assume the brain to be thoroughly organic qua cohesive, coordinated, frictionless, integrated, etc. – is sufficient to cast reasonable doubts on the claim that an intelligent designer intentionally built a marvellously elaborate and synchronized material seat suited for his human subjects. The further step Linden takes in driving home his critique is to assert, on the basis of ample supporting evidence, that the brain is endowed with its wondrous mind-making powers celebrated by proponents and critics of evolution alike specifically by virtue of its kludginess resulting from an absence of intelligent design:

The transcendent aspects of our human experience, the things that touch our emotional and cognitive core, were not given to us by a Great Engineer. These are not the latest design features of an impeccably crafted brain. Rather, at every turn, brain design has been a kludge, a workaround, a jumble, a pastiche. The things we hold highest in our human experience ... result from a particular agglomeration of ad hoc solutions that have been piled on through millions of years of evolutionary history. It's not that we have fundamentally human thoughts and feelings *despite* the kludgy design of the brain as molded by the twists and turns of evolutionary history. Rather, we have them precisely *because* of that history.[60]

In Linden's hands, the kludge model of the central nervous system – this is equivalent to, in my terms, an anorganic barring of the corpoReal of the brain in particular – elevates the lack/deficit of overarching harmony or synthesis therein to the ontological status of a privative cause at the level of biomaterial being in and of itself.[61] This perspicuous line of argumentation transforms the example of the human brain into a Trojan horse in relation to advocates of intelligent design; Linden turns the star piece of evidence appealed to in their case into the very thing refuting it most decisively. Furthermore, Linden's remarks in the above quotation can be read as subtly hinting at an implication of even greater radicality: the absence of God is the ultimate negative *Ur*-cause in a physical universe internally producing and containing human beings and their subjectivities (a thesis compatible with the One-less, detotalized ontologies of Lacan, Badiou and Žižek, among others).

The key principle behind anorganicity, with kludginess being one of its manifestations, can be stated through an inversion of a cliché: more is less (rather than, as the saying goes, 'less is more'). For instance, the kludgy *corps morcelé*, shot through and permeated with antagonisms, conflicts, deficiencies, fissures, gaps, splits and the like, is not a materialization of the factical (non-)givenness of a mysterious Void. The myth of the nongiven, with its mystical, metaphysical version of negativity, proceeds on the basis of a less-is-more logic, with the 'less' of a primal Nothingness giving rise to the 'more' of really-existing subjects. By contrast, my anorganic approach, substituting for this type of myth a nonmystical, physical version of negativity, proceeds on the basis of a more-is-less logic, with the 'more' of a contingent, nonteleological accumulation of material bits and pieces giving rise to the 'less' of discrepancies and discordances within and between these fragments. As indicated earlier, I adhere to crucial aspects of the letter of Lacan's teachings in positing such materially generated disharmonies as necessary objective conditions for the eventual emergence of fully fledged subjectivities. As per the more-is-less principle of the anorganic, surpluses of positivity, as unplanned, uncoordinated agglomerations of mute, idiotic entities and events, dialectically tip over into deficits of negativity. Put in terms familiar to government bureaucrats, computer programmers and tax lawyers, with the increasing complexity of organic systems, as with all systems (such as political institutions, software codes and bodies of laws), comes a proportional increase in the number of bugs and loopholes immanently generated within and through systemic complexity itself. In Lacanian parlance, both Symbolic and Real systems can and do succumb to (self-)barring.[62]

Lacan's crucial concept of the body-in-pieces and other ideas of his related to this concept, once plugged into the theoretical framework of transcendental materialism and its anorganicism, go from being dogmatically asserted givens always-already there out of thin air to becoming psychoanalytic and philosophical touchstones anchored in solid, science-consistent materialist thinking. Likewise, as regards the threshold between *Naturphilosophie* and *Philosophie des Geistes* in the more-than-logical *Realphilosophie* of Hegel's *Encyclopedia*, the dialectical dynamics of anorganicism permit speculating that the movement from animal to human organisms transpires when growth in the natural complexity of the animal organism crosses a certain tipping point. Past this point, animal organicism qua harmonious organization short-circuits itself in acquiring a critical mass of inner incompatibilities between its parts, thereby igniting the bursting forth of anorganic structures and phenomena. The 'more' of animal complexity leads to the 'less' of the negativities lying at the base of human being qua minded/spiritual humanity; the plus of positive natural additions transitions to the minus of denaturalizing subtractions.

As I have argued elsewhere, one of the major shortcomings of so-called 'speculative realism' is this loose movement's failure, at least thus far, to formulate an adequate, satisfying theory of the subject.[63] In fact, those factions within this movement relying upon either a Spinozism of eternally self-same '*natura naturans*' (as per Iain Hamilton Grant's *Philosophies of Nature After Schelling*) or the eliminative materialism of Paul and Patricia Churchland (as per Ray Brassier's *Nihil Unbound*) cannot or will not – given these philosophical commitments to Spinoza and the Churchlands – admit the existence of any robust version of irreducible subjectivity as I conceive it.⁶⁴ I have critiqued both this brand of Spinozism as well as eliminative materialism on other occasions.⁶⁵ In the present context, suffice it to say that my hybrid Hegelian-Lacanian-neurobiological anorganicity of kludginess makes possible a thoroughly materialist and realist account of the necessary conditions of subjects precisely through problematizing the flat, monochromatic, and deterministic images of nature underpinning such variants of speculative realism.⁶⁶

I will close by noting the French biologist and Nobel laureate Jacques Monod's indispensable refutation of an all-too-widespread misconstrual of evolution in biology in his 1970 book *Chance and Necessity*. Therein, he incisively observes that '*evolution is not a property of living beings*, since it stems from the very *imperfections* of the conservative mechanism which indeed constitutes their unique privilege'.⁶⁷ In other words, evolution does not unfold as a smooth, continuous succession of fluid flowerings in which unbroken sequences of clockwork living spheres blossom one out of another with placid balanced beauty, as imagined in the fantasies of organicist (w)holism. Instead, evolutionary changes happen if and when any number of things go terribly wrong for organisms in relation to their bottom-line strivings to perpetuate themselves as individuals and species (as in genetic mutations, environmental catastrophes, and so on – instances on the scale of phylogenesis of what Lacan, citing Hegel, calls 'the fruitful illness, life's happy fault' on the scale of ontogenesis). Hence, Monod justifiably concludes that evolution is antithetic to life – obviously, he undoes the standard equivocation between evolutionary and living processes – insofar as occurrences of evolution are moments when life as it is gets traumatically disorganized and truncated. He also later states that 'the accelerating pace of cultural evolution was to split completely away from that of the genome'.⁶⁸ However, the antinatural revolution of the immanent material genesis (as both phylogenetic and ontogenetic) of, in Hegelian locution, *Geist* out of *Natur* is nevertheless a trajectory internal to evolution in Monod's broadened sense. What is more, a precise parallel can be drawn between Hegel's treatment of war as a spiritual event with Monod's treatment of evolution as a natural event. For Hegel, periods of pleasing tranquillity (i.e. peaceful 'happiness') are historical 'blank pages' of sociocultural 'stagnation' punctuated by bracing, make-or-break episodes of disruption in the form of violent conflagrations.⁶⁹ For Monod, evolution is to life what war is to peace for Hegel.

If human beings are animal organisms 'sick unto death', this fateful derailment of the natural into the more-than-natural occurs by virtue of the real dialectical dynamics of the anorganic as the self-induced sickening of nature itself, a nature already weak and rotten on its own prior to its further de/in-completing of itself through belching out humanity. Advocates of the myth of the nongiven instantiate the gesture of adding a supernatural Nothing so as to explain away this enigmatic denaturalized transcendence that is nonetheless puzzlingly immanent to the natural world. An advocate of transcendental materialist anorganicism risks the step of subtracting from the natural world what these worshippers of a mystical negativity presumptively attribute to it such that they then feel compelled to have faith in a rigid, brittle antinaturalism threatened by the advances of the natural sciences. Interfacing the anorganic logic of the more-is-less principle with the life sciences and evolutionary theory is the key to the material (rather than mystical) negativity that is a cornerstone of a viable, nonreductive materialism.

Notes

1. This chapter builds upon and extends lines of argumentation I have elaborated on various prior occasions. See: Adrian Johnston, *Prolegomena to Any Future Materialism, Volume One: The Outcome of Contemporary French Philosophy* (Evanston: Northwestern University Press, 2013), pp. 59–77; Adrian Johnston, 'The Voiding of Weak Nature: The Transcendental Materialist Kernels of Hegel's *Naturphilosophie*', *Graduate Faculty Philosophy Journal* 33(1) (Spring 2012): 103–57; Adrian Johnston, 'From Scientific Socialism to Socialist Science: *Naturdialektik* Then and Now', in Slavoj Žižek (ed.), *The Idea of Communism 2: The New York Conference* (London: Verso, 2013), pp. 103–36; Adrian Johnston, *Adventures in Transcendental Materialism: Dialogues with Contemporary Thinkers* (Edinburgh: Edinburgh University Press, 2014), pp. 65–107; Adrian Johnston, 'Lacking Causes: Privative Causality from Locke and Kant to Lacan and Deacon', *Speculations: A Journal of Speculative Realism* (forthcoming); Adrian Johnston, 'This is Orthodox Marxism: The Shared Materialist *Weltanschauung* of Marx and Engels', *Quaderni materialisti* Special Issue: 'On Sebastiano Timpanaro' (forthcoming); Adrian Johnston, *Prolegomena to Any Future Materialism, Volume Two: A Weak Nature Alone* (Evanston: Northwestern University Press, forthcoming).

2. See Jacques Lacan, *Le Séminaire de Jacques Lacan, Livre X: L'angoisse, 1962–1963*, ed. Jacques-Alain Miller (Paris: Éditions du Seuil, 2004), pp. 357–8; *Le Séminaire de Jacques Lacan, Livre XVI: D'un Autre à l'autre, 1968–1969*, ed. Jacques-Alain Miller (Paris: Éditions du Seuil, 2006), pp. 280–1; Jacques Lacan, *The Seminar of Jacques Lacan, Book XVII: The Other Side of Psychoanalysis, 1969–1970*, trans. Russell Grigg, ed. Jacques-Alain

Miller (New York: W. W. Norton, 2007), p. 119. After their first citation, references to Lacan's seminars will be given as *Seminar* (or *Séminaire* to a French edition) followed by the Book number in Roman numerals.

3. Jacques Lacan, *Seminar of Jacques Lacan, Book VII: The Ethics of Psychoanalysis, 1959–1960*, trans. Dennis Porter, ed. Jacques-Alain Miller (New York: W. W. Norton, 1992), pp. 213–14; Jacques Lacan, *Le Séminaire de Jacques Lacan, Livre VIII: Le transfert, 1960–1961*, ed. Jacques-Alain Miller (Paris: Éditions du Seuil, 2001 [seconde édition corrigée]), p. 12; Jacques Lacan, 'Discours de Rome', in Jacques-Alain Miller (ed.), *Autres écrits* (Paris: Éditions du Seuil, 2001), p. 135; Jacques Lacan, 'Du symbole, et de sa fonction religieuse', in Jacques-Alain Miller (ed.), *Le mythe individuel du névrosé, ou poésie et vérité dans la névrosé* (Paris: Éditions du Seuil, 2007), p. 60.

4. Jacques Lacan, *Le Séminaire de Jacques Lacan, Livre IV: La relation d'objet, 1956–1957*, ed. Jacques-Alain Miller (Paris: Éditions du Seuil, 1994), p. 48.

5. Jacques-Alain Miller, 'Language: Much Ado About What?', in Ellie Ragland-Sullivan and Mark Bracher (eds), *Lacan and the Subject of Language* (New York: Routledge, 1991), p. 32.

6. Giovanni Pico della Mirandola, *On the Dignity of Man*, trans. Charles Glenn Wallis, Paul J. W. Miller and Douglas Carmichael (Indianapolis: Hackett, 1998), pp. 4–7, 10–11.

7. See Johnston, 'Voiding'; Johnston, 'Scientific Socialism'; Johnston, 'Orthodox Marxism'; and Johnston, *Prolegomena, Vol. Two*.

8. See Johnston, *Žižek's Ontology*, pp. 186–90, and Johnston, *Adventures*, pp. 139–83.

9. See Giorgio Agamben, *The Man Without Content*, trans. Georgia Albert (Stanford: Stanford University Press, 1999), pp. 65–72; Giorgio Agamben, *The Open: Man and Animal*, trans. Kevin Attell (Stanford: Stanford University Press, 2004), pp. 16, 21–2, 26, 29–30; Giorgio Agamben, *The Kingdom and the Glory: For a Theological Genealogy of Economy and Government*, trans. Lorenzo Chiesa (Stanford: Stanford University Press, 2011), pp. 245–6, 251.

10. See Alain Badiou, *The Century*, trans. Alberto Toscano (Cambridge: Polity Press, 2007), pp. 174–7; Alain Badiou, *Logics of Worlds: Being and Event 2*, trans. Alberto Toscano (London: Continuum, 2009), p. 114; and Johnston, *Prolegomena, Vol. One*, pp. 81–128.

11. Paul Ricoeur, 'Consciousness and the Unconscious', trans. Willis Domingo, in *The Conflict of Interpretations: Essays in Hermeneutics* (Evanston: Northwestern University Press, 1974), p. 97; Paul Ricoeur, 'Psychoanalysis and the Movement of Contemporary Culture', trans. Willis Domingo, ibid., pp. 143–7.

12. Daniel C. Dennett, *Darwin's Dangerous Idea: Evolution and the Meanings of Life* (New York: Touchstone, 1995), pp. 61–84, 521.

13. Badiou, *Logics*, pp. 399–401, 403–24.

14. Jacques Lacan, 'The Direction of the Treatment and the Principles of Its Power', in *Écrits: The First Complete Edition in English*, trans. Bruce Fink (New York: W. W. Norton, 2006), p. 514; Jacques Lacan, *Le Séminaire de Jacques Lacan, Livre XXI: Les non-dupes errent, 1973-1974*, session of 21 May 1974 (unpublished typescript); Jacques Lacan, *Le Séminaire de Jacques Lacan, Livre XXIII: Le sinthome, 1975-1976*, ed. Jacques-Alain Miller (Paris: Éditions du Seuil, 2005), p. 12; Jacques Lacan, *Le Séminaire de Jacques Lacan, Livre XXIV: L'insu que sait de l'une-bévue s'aile à mourre, 1976-1977*, sessions of 19 April 1977 and 17 May 1977 (unpublished typescript).

15. Jacques Lacan, 'Some Reflections on the Ego', *International Journal of Psycho-Analysis* 34 (1953): 13-15; Jacques Lacan, 'The Mirror Stage as Formative of the *I* Function as Revealed in Psychoanalytic Experience', in *Écrits*, p. 78; Jacques Lacan, 'Aggressiveness in Psychoanalysis', in *Écrits*, p. 92.

16. Sigmund Freud, *The Standard Edition of the Complete Psychological Works of Sigmund Freud, Volume I (1886-1899): Pre-Psycho-Analytic Publications and Unpublished Drafts*, eds. James Strachey et al. (London: Hogarth Press, 1966), p. 318; Freud, *Standard Edition Vol. 20*, pp. 154-5, 167; Freud, *Standard Edition Vol. 21*, pp. 17-19, 30; Jacques Lacan, 'Les complexes familiaux dans la formation de l'individu: Essai d'analyse d'une fonction en psychologie', in *Autres écrits*, pp. 33-5; Lacan, 'Mirror Stage', pp. 76, 78; Lacan, 'Aggressiveness', p. 92; Jacques Lacan, *Le Séminaire de Jacques Lacan, Livre VI: Le désir et son interprétation, 1958-1959*, ed. Jacques-Alain Miller (Paris: Éditions de la Martinière, 2013), pp. 27-30; Lacan, *Séminaire VIII*, p. 427.

17. Jacques Lacan, 'Guiding Remarks for a Convention on Female Sexuality', in *Écrits*, p. 616; Lacan, *Séminaire IV*, p. 254.

18. Adrian Johnston, 'Drive Between Brain and Subject: An Immanent Critique of Lacanian Neuro-psychoanalysis', *Southern Journal of Philosophy* Special Issue: Annual Murray Spindel Conference: Freudian Future(s) 51 (2013): 48-84.

19. Lacan, 'Complexes familiaux', p. 41.

20. Ibid., p. 44.

21. Lacan, 'Mirror Stage', p. 76.

22. Lacan, 'Aggressiveness', p. 92.

23. Lacan, 'Mirror Stage', p. 77.

24. Lacan, 'Aggressiveness', p. 94.

25. Lacan, 'Mirror Stage', p. 78.

26. Ibid., pp. 76-7.

27. Lacan, *Écrits*, p. 461.

28. Lacan, *Séminaire XXIV*, session of 19 April 1977.

29. Lacan, 'Direction', p. 514.

30. Lacan, 'Reflections on the Ego', p. 15.

31. Lacan, 'Direction of Treatment', p. 346.

32. Johnston, 'Between Brain and Subject', pp. 48–84.
33. Lacan, *Écrits*, p. 346.
34. Lacan, *Séminaire X*, pp. 253–4; Jacques Lacan, *Le Séminaire de Jacques Lacan, Livre XII: Problèmes cruciaux pour la psychanalyse, 1964–1965*, session of 10 March 1965 (unpublished typescript); Jacques Lacan, *Le Séminaire de Jacques Lacan, Livre XIV: La logique du fantasme, 1966–1967*, session of 7 June 1967 (unpublished typescript); Jacques Lacan, *The Seminar of Jacques Lacan, Book XX: Encore, 1972–1973*, trans. Bruce Fink, ed. Jacques-Alain Miller (New York: W. W. Norton, 1998), pp. 109–10; Lacan, *Séminaire XXI*, session of 20 November 1973; Jacques Lacan, 'Television', trans. Denis Hollier, Rosalind Krauss and Annette Michelson, in Joan Copjec (ed.), *Television/A Challenge to the Psychoanalytic Establishment* (New York: W. W. Norton, 1990), p. 6; Jacques Lacan, 'Aristotle's Dream', trans. Lorenzo Chiesa, in *Angelaki: Journal of the Theoretical Humanities* 11(3) (December 2006): 83–4.
35. Lacan, 'Aggressiveness', p. 101.
36. Lacan, *Mythe individuel*, p. 46.
37. Jacques Lacan, *The Seminar of Jacques Lacan, Book II: The Ego in Freud's Theory and in the Technique of Psychoanalysis, 1954–1955*, trans. Sylvana Tomaselli, ed. Jacques-Alain Miller (New York: W. W. Norton, 1988), pp. 322–3.
38. Lacan, *Seminar II*, p. 326.
39. Lacan, 'Complexes familiaux', pp. 33–5, 41–2; Lacan, 'Reflections on the Ego', pp. 13, 15; Lacan, 'On My Antecedents', p. 55; Lacan, 'Mirror Stage', pp. 76, 78; Lacan, 'Aggressiveness', p. 92; Lacan, 'Treatment of Psychosis', p. 461; Lacan, *Séminaire VI*, p. 159.
40. Lacan, 'Mirror Stage', p. 78.
41. Giacomo Rizzolatti and Corrado Sinigaglia, *Mirrors in the Brain: How Our Minds Share Actions and Emotions*, trans. Frances Anderson (Oxford: Oxford University Press, 2008), pp. xi–xii.
42. Jacques Lacan, 'Remarks on Daniel Lagache's Presentation: "Psychoanalysis and Personality Structure"', in *Écrits*, p. 545.
43. Lacan, 'Guiding Remarks', p. 611.
44. Lacan, *Séminaire VIII*, p. 117; Lacan, *Seminar XVII*, p. 33; Jacques Lacan, *Le Séminaire de Jacques Lacan, Livre XVIII: D'un discours qui ne serait pas du semblant, 1971*, ed. Jacques-Alain Miller (Paris: Éditions du Seuil, 2007), pp. 65–71; Jacques Lacan, *Le Séminaire de Jacques Lacan, Livre XIX: ...ou pire, 1971–1972*, ed. Jacques-Alain Miller (Paris: Éditions du Seuil, 2011), pp. 93–110; Lacan, *Seminar XX*, pp. 41–3.
45. Johnston, *Žižek's Ontology*, pp. 212–13.
46. Lacan, *Séminaire VIII*, p. 410.

47. François Ansermet, 'Des neurosciences aux logosciences', in Nathalie Georges, Jacques-Alain Miller and Nathalie Marchaison (eds), *Qui sont vos psychanalystes?* (Paris: Éditions du Seuil, 2002), p. 382.
48. Lacan, 'On My Antecedents', p. 55.
49. Jacques Lacan, *The Seminar of Jacques Lacan, Book XI: The Four Fundamental Concepts of Psychoanalysis, 1964*, trans. Alan Sheridan, ed. Jacques-Alain Miller (New York: W. W. Norton, 1977), p. 7; Johnston, *Prolegomena, Vol. One*, pp. 39–58.
50. Lacan, 'Mirror Stage', pp. 75–7.
51. Ibid., p. 77.
52. Lacan, *Séminaire XXIII*, p. 12.
53. Lacan, *Séminaire XXI*, session of 21 May 1974; Lacan, *Séminaire XXIV*, session of 17 May 1977. Quotes to the end of the paragraph are from this last reference.
54. Lacan, 'Variations on the Standard Treatment', p. 286.
55. G. W. F. Hegel, *Phenomenology of Spirit*, trans. A. V. Miller (Oxford: Oxford University Press, 1977), pp. 104–11.
56. Jean-Paul Sartre, *Existentialism and Humanism*, trans. Philip Mairet (London: Methuen, 1948), pp. 27–8, 42–3.
57. David J. Linden, *The Accidental Mind: How Brain Evolution Has Given Us Love, Memory, Dreams, and God* (Cambridge: Harvard University Press, 2007), pp. 235–46.
58. Ibid., p. 6.
59. Ibid., pp. 2–3, 5–7, 21–4, 26, 245–6.
60. Ibid., pp. 245–6.
61. Johnston, 'Lacking Causes'.
62. Johnston, *Žižek's Ontology*, pp. 167–77; Johnston, 'Brain and Subject', pp. 48–84.
63. Johnston, *Prolegomena Vol. One*, pp. 151–2, 167, 188–95.
64. Iain Hamilton Grant, *Philosophies of Nature After Schelling* (London: Continuum, 2008), pp. 8, 28–9, 36, 42–5, 53–5, 68–9, 77, 108–10, 137–8, 142–6, 149–50, 162, 168–71, 173, 180, 197; Ray Brassier, *Nihil Unbound: Enlightenment and Extinction* (Basingstoke: Palgrave Macmillan, 2007), pp. 3–31.
65. Johnston, *Žižek's Ontology*, pp. 269–87; Adrian Johnston, 'The Emergence of Speculative Realism: A Review of Ray Brassier's *Nihil Unbound: Enlightenment and Extinction*', *Journal of the British Society of Phenomenology* 40(1) (January 2009): 107–9; Johnston, *Adventures*, pp. 13–64.
66. Adrian Johnston, 'Points of Forced Freedom: Eleven (More) Theses on Materialism', *Speculations: A Journal of Speculative Realism* 4 (June

2013): 91–9; Adrian Johnston, 'An Interview with Adrian Johnston on Transcendental Materialism (with Peter Gratton)', *Society and Space*, 2013, http://societyandspace.com/2013/10/07/interview-with-adrian-johnston-on-transcendental-materialism/ [accessed: 21 January 2015]; Adrian Johnston, 'Interview About *Adventures in Transcendental Materialism: Dialogues with Contemporary Thinkers* with Graham Harman for Edinburgh University Press', Edinburgh University Press, April 2014, http://www.euppublishing.com/userimages/ContentEditor/1397840563624/Adventures%20in%20Transcendental%20Realism%20-%20Author%20Q%26A.pdf [accessed 21 January 2015]; Johnston, *Prolegomena, Vol. Two*.

67. Jacques Monod, *Chance and Necessity: An Essay on the Natural Philosophy of Modern Biology*, trans. Austryn Wainhouse (New York: Alfred A. Knopf, 1971), p. 116.

68. Ibid., p. 162.

69. G. W. F. Hegel, *Elements of the Philosophy of Right*, trans. H. B. Nisbet, ed. Allen W. Wood (Cambridge: Cambridge University Press, 1991), p. 361; Hegel, *History*, pp. 26–7.

CHAPTER 3
FOR A REALIST SYSTEMS THEORY: LUHMANN, THE CORRELATIONIST CONTROVERSY AND MATERIALITY
Levi R. Bryant

The political stakes of correlationist poststructuralism

Generally the debate between correlationism and speculative realism as well as new materialism has taken the form of whether or not and to what extent we are capable of thinking the absolute (that which is not correlated to a subject). Does everything have an intrinsic essence (strong realism)? By 'intrinsic essence' I mean that the properties of a thing truly belong to that thing themselves and do not arise from the cognitive or social agency that categorizes those things. This would seem to be what Harman's object-oriented philosophy (OOP) sometimes seems to defend with the claim that all objects have an essence, albeit withdrawn.[1] Are some properties 'by-products' and others 'connected' (weak realism)? This is the position I advocate, along with thinkers such as Lucretius and Ian Hacking.[2] Here, some entities and properties like value, gender, ethnic identities, social roles and so on would be constructed, while others would have independent existence. Or is it the case that all entities and properties are constructed or the result of correlations, such that there are no beings independent of observers?

In what follows I would like to reframe the rather academic debate between correlationism (or antirealism) and realism in terms of the political stakes that lurk behind these abstract positions. First I will outline the set of considerations that have led radical emancipatory political thought to favour the correlationist or antirealist framework and why, against the position of theorists such as Graham Harman, some variant of correlationist thought is worth preserving. I will then outline how Luhmann's theory of distinctions and systems theory, due to its abstraction and generality, provides us with the most thorough articulation of correlationist thought to date, allowing a wide body of diverse theory to be integrated according to a shared logic. Having developed this framework, I will then show how correlationist thought encounters difficulties dealing with the power exercised by material agencies that do not arise from correlations and that are crucial to understanding climate change, material features of environments and the impact of new technologies. Materiality acts not by virtue of signification, as correlationists contend, but by virtue of what it physically is. Correlationism tends to veil or render invisible these latter forms of agency. Finally, I conclude with a deconstructive reading of Luhmann, using his own theory of distinction and second-order observation to disclose the blind spot of correlationist thought and how this thought, despite itself, is led to realist claims. This deconstruction is not a destruction, but rather aims at a sublation that would allow us to retain what is best in correlationism when its proper limits are specified while also opening the way to the role played by material agencies in social assemblages.

It would be a mistake to think that there is anything like a unified philosophical position shared by those thinkers falling under the titles of 'speculative realism' (SR) and 'new materialism' (NM). The term 'speculative realism' arose as a compromise among participants at a conference devoted to realism and materialism held at Goldsmiths in April 2007.[3] While there was a shared commitment to realism and/or materialism by Ray Brassier, Iain Hamilton Grant, Graham Harman and Quentin Meillassoux, these positions differ from one another.[4] Each of these thinkers holds quite distinct positions that are in many respects opposed to one another. In short, there is a debate among speculative realists as to what constitutes the real and the material. As noted, like OOO, SR is a *genus* rather than *species* term, with debates among these thinkers as to just what the real is. The case is similar with NM, where thinkers such as Jane Bennett, Manuel DeLanda, Karen Barad, John Protevi and Stacy Alaimo, to name but a few, all share a commitment to exploring materiality while nonetheless proposing differing accounts of it.

What unites the speculative realisms and, to a lesser degree, the new materialisms – the plural here is crucial – is not a shared ontology but an opposition to what Quentin Meillassoux calls 'correlationism'. As defined by Meillassoux, correlationism is 'the idea according to which we only ever have access to the correlation between thinking and being, and never either term considered apart from the other'.[5] He continues:

[c]orrelationism consists in disqualifying the claim that it is possible to consider the realms of subjectivity and objectivity independently of

one another. Not only does it become necessary to insist that we never grasp an object 'in itself', in isolation from its relation to the subject, but it also becomes necessary to maintain that we can never grasp a subject that would not always already be related to an object.[6]

Meillassoux contends that it was Immanuel Kant who first inaugurated the correlationist turn. Although there were precursors, Kant announced the correlationist shift with his Copernican turn. As Kant remarks:

> Up to now it has been assumed that all our cognition must conform to the objects; but all attempts to find out something about them a priori through concepts that would extend our cognition have, on this presupposition, come to nothing. Hence let us once try whether we do not get farther with the problem of metaphysics by assuming that the objects must conform to our cognition.[7]

With Kant we get a deontologization of reality insofar as the thesis that objects conform to mind entails that we can never know what objects are in themselves, but only phenomena presented to mind. Phenomena are produced by the distinctions supplied by mind. Whether those distinctions correspond to reality apart from mind can never be known. Nonetheless, for Kant something like reality is preserved insofar as there is a universal structure of mind that we all share. The project of transcendental idealism consists in uncovering and articulating this structure.

What, then, should we understand by the 'deontologization of reality'? 'Deontologization' means that the properties we encounter in objects do not belong to the things themselves, but rather are contributed by mind. This is the core of the correlationist or antirealist position: what *appeared* to belong to the things themselves instead is contributed by *us*. Correlationism is not then the thesis that a subject must relate to an object to know that object. Every realist has advocated this claim. Rather, correlationism is either the thesis that (a) we can never determine whether the properties we attribute to things truly belong to the things themselves because we cannot determine what is contributed by our minds and what is contributed by the things themselves (weak correlationism); or that (b) it is, in fact, mind that structures reality such that properties are not contributed by the things themselves but rather things are the products of mind (strong correlationism). As Kant puts it, arguing for a rather strong variant of correlationism, 'the a priori conditions of a possible experience in general are at the same time conditions of the possibility of the objects of experience'.[8] For Kant, it is not just that the categories and forms of intuition structure our cognition but that they also *constitute* the objects of experience. In the B edition Kant will drive this point home, remarking that:

> [s]pace and time [and the categories] are valid, as conditions of the possibility of how objects can be given to us, no further than for objects of the senses, hence only for experience. Beyond these boundaries they do not represent anything at all, for they are only in the senses and outside of them have no reality.[9]

Here we have the core of the correlationist thesis. It is not merely that a subject must relate to an object to know it; rather, that subject actively constitutes its object such that the object has no being or reality apart from subject. There might, of course, be being or reality apart from the subject – what Kant calls 'noumena' – yet we can know nothing of this and our categories and forms of intuition certainly do not mirror this reality. There is only ever reality 'for us', never reality in itself.

In addition to strong and weak correlationism we can also distinguish between universalist and pluralist correlationisms. Universalist correlationism holds that while the mind is not a mirror of reality because, in fact, it constitutes beings through its cognitive activities, there is nonetheless a universal reality because the structure of mind is the same for all rational beings. The task of universalist correlationism would thus consist in uncovering this universal structure of mind. In Kant, for example, this would consist of the articulation of the twelve categories, the forms of time and space, as well as the various ways in which these elements are synthesized to produce reality. Similarly, Claude Lévi-Strauss's structural anthropology would be a variant of universalist correlationism insofar as it seeks to determine the universal structures of thought; while Husserl, under one reading, would be another. By contrast, pluralist correlationism would argue that there are no universal structures of mind but rather a variety of different structures. As a consequence, it would reject the thesis that there is one 'reality', for there would be no one way of constituting objects. Here the correlationisms would be called 'contingent' because, first, they would be the result of a history and, second, they would always be capable of being otherwise. Pluralist correlationism is the form taken by poststructuralist thought.

It is always, of course, possible to find exceptions, but Continental thought has largely been dominated by one form of correlationism or another.[10] However, whether reference is made to phenomenology or poststructuralism, correlationism is certainly the dominant or molar tendency within Continental thought.[11] Here it is likely that Heideggerians and poststructuralists will object, pointing out that *Dasein* is not the (Cartesian) subject, and that much poststructuralist thought describes, to use Althusser's famous phrase, process without a subject. However, it is important to note that it is not correlation to a subject that is crucial to Meillassoux's concept of correlationism. We can just as easily replace the term 'subject' with 'language', 'power', 'Dasein', 'body', 'sign', 'discourse', 'society', etc. Paraphrasing Meillassoux's descriptions of correlationism presented elsewhere, a position is correlationist if it argues that there is no X without givenness of X to Y, and no theory about X without Y positing X.[12] It matters little what we plug into the space of Y (the subject-function), so long as we make the claim that X cannot be thought without Y.

Correlationism ineluctably leads to some variant of idealism (of which social and linguistic constructivism are variants), for the claim is that we cannot speak of being independent of its relation to human being, whether in the form of a subject, a transcendental ego, a cogito, language, signs, power or economy. The practical imperative that arises from correlationism is the command to 'observe the observer'. I will have more to say in justification of this characterization in a moment, but what is important for now is that correlationism directs us to investigate how being or objects are given to a particular society, language, subject, configuration of culture, system of signs or subject. Correlationism calls us to investigate how the object is given to a subject (or whatever else appears in the position of Y).

Yet strangely, despite the thesis that we cannot think an object apart from a subject, the object quickly disappears in correlationism. For in directing us to observe how the object is given to a subject, to observe how an observer observes, we very quickly recognize, under pluralist correlationism, the sheer *contingency* of observers. Reality, we notice, can be structured in a variety of different ways and has, in fact, been structured in different ways at different points in history or by different cultures. As such, any particular version of reality is just that, a version, and therefore contingent. Other structures are always possible. We are thus led to suspect that perhaps there is no in-itself or object at all, but rather that the subject somehow constitutes or creates its object. What is given for one set of subjects, for example, might not *exist* for another set.

Put differently, correlationism leads us to conceive the in-itself, the absolute, or being *apart* from a subject as a sort of undifferentiated continuum that is then cut up or individuated by some form of human agency. Given that we saw above that language, society, etc. can be placed in the slot of 'subject' in the structure of correlationism, it might seem odd to suggest that pluralist correlationism inevitably argues that some form of human agency structures reality. However, to our knowledge, language and society only exist for and are only produced by humans. Thus, regardless of how antirealist a humanism might claim to be (as in the case, for example, of Althusser), it is still a humanism at the end of the day. From the correlationist standpoint, beings are what they are as a result of some form of human agency.

Here Marx's analysis of commodity fetishism in *Capital* provides a prototypical example. We begin by taking the value of the commodity as a feature or quality of the commodity itself – a realist stance with respect to value. We think that somewhere, within the diamond *itself*, dwells this property of being valuable, such that the diamond is *intrinsically* valuable. What Marx effectively demonstrates is the manner in which value is not a property of the diamond itself, but rather a feature that arises from social relations involved in producing the diamond:

> the commodity-form, and the value-relation of the products of labour within which it appears, have absolutely no connection with the physical nature of the commodity and the material relations arising out of this. It is nothing but the definite social relation between men themselves which assumes here, for them, the fantastic form of a relation between things.[13]

The value of the diamond is not something that resides in the diamond but rather something that only arises in relation to a subject – in this case, the socioeconomic system presiding over production. Put differently, value is not something intrinsic to the diamond itself. As an aside, the example demonstrates why, in my view, we should take care not to reject all forms of correlationism: there are phenomena for which correlationist accounts are perfectly appropriate, such as value in the case of the commodity. Diamonds have no value for cats, but only for humans.

Marx's critique of commodity fetishism and the correlationist thesis upon which it is based can be seen as the elementary schema of all critical theory. The basic gesture of critical theory and emancipatory political thought consists in showing that some property we took to be a feature of the thing itself is in fact a construction of social relations. As Lucretius wrote in the first century BCE:

> Whatever exists you will always find connected
> To these two things, or as by products of them;
> *Connected* meaning that the quality
> Can never be subtracted from its object
> No more than weight from stone, or heat from fire,
> Wetness from water. On the other hand,
> Slavery, riches, freedom, poverty,
> War, peace, and so on, transitory things
> Whose comings and goings do not alter substance –
> These, and quite properly, we call *by-products*.[14]

Lucretius here draws a distinction between properties that belong to the things themselves (real properties) and properties that arise from a correlation with a subject. It might initially seem difficult to see just why such an abstract distinction between types of properties and the debate between realism and antirealism would be crucial to emancipatory politics. However, it is important to note that defences of dominant power structures are always based on an ontology that asserts that oppressed groups are not oppressed at all because the real or intrinsic features of their being entail that they should occupy their allotted place within the social order. For example, in his defence of slavery, Aristotle writes that:

> where ... there is such a difference as that between soul and body, or between men and animals (as in the case of those whose business is to use their body, and who can do nothing better), the lower sort are by nature slaves, and it is better for them as for all inferiors that they should be under the rule of a master.[15]

Aristotle's thesis is that inferiority is an ontological, natural, connected or intrinsic feature of such persons and that therefore their status as slaves is both justified (by nature) and even desirable for these individuals themselves. The stakes of the debate over the status of these properties is thus quite clear. If these properties are 'connected', then the hierarchies we find in the social order are ontologically natural and therefore just. No doubt this is why so many critical theorists and poststructuralist correlationisms (PSCs) are suspicious of ontology. Far from being 'natural' or essential properties of persons, they take such properties to be historical social constructions and to represent unjust distributions of power.

The gesture of critical theory and poststructuralist thought will thus consist in the careful demonstration of the contingent, historical being of these predicates and how they are capable of being otherwise. For example, through exacting historical analysis, Michel Foucault will show how systems of power generate particular forms of subjectivity, while Judith Butler will show how gender, far from being a connected biological property of persons, is, in fact, performative or the result of the enactment of discursive systems inherited from the culture into which one is thrown.[16] Perhaps more dramatically, Jacques Derrida will show how the foundational concepts of philosophy, far from being founded on identity, instead result from a precarious play of differences that prevent univocal meaning (and therefore fixed reference) from ever being established.[17] Examples could be multiplied. Like Marx showing that the value of the commodity is, in reality, a product of social relations and Lucretius showing that predicates like slavery are by-products of correlations rather than intrinsic features of persons, the poststructuralists demonstrated the constructed nature of these predicates. If, then, it turns out that these properties are the result of correlations, it is possible for them to be otherwise and one can set about constructing new forms of life that would escape from these social hierarchies. We can thus see that the stakes of the issues surrounding the seemingly abstract issue of correlationism or the debate between realist and antirealists is quite high; and it is for this reason that SR's critique of correlationism and defence of realism has generated so much controversy within critically minded thought in the humanities.

Luhmann, second-order observation and the logic of correlationism

Throughout the foregoing I have sporadically referred to observers in my discussion of correlationism. Correlationism does not take observations at face value, but instead invites us to observe the observer and what the observer contributes to that which appears. It is here important to clarify the concept of observation, as this will help to shed light on the correlationist controversy and why there has been a renewal of realist and materialist orientations of thought. I draw the concept of observation from Niklas Luhmann, who retools the concept from Humberto Maturana and Francisco Varela's reworking of George Spencer-Brown's account of forms. It's important to note that 'observation' does not here refer to the five

77

senses, nor even to living beings, but rather to a highly formal operation that consists in drawing distinctions. It is not the possession of organs of sense that is crucial to observation, but rather the existence of a distinction. As Spencer-Brown puts it, 'we take as given the idea of distinction and the idea of indication, and that we cannot make an indication without drawing a distinction'.[18] Indication is the act of observation, while distinction is what renders the observation possible. Alternatively, we could say that distinction is the transcendental condition or condition for the possibility of indications or observations.

Spencer-Brown contends that 'a [world] comes into being when a space is severed or taken apart. The skin of a living organism cuts off an outside from an inside. So does the circumference of a circle in a plane.'[19] Each of these worlds has its own immanent logic, a logic of visibility and invisibility arising from the distinctions that have been drawn, rendering observation possible. Here it is crucial to note that the distinctions drawn are contingent or capable of being drawn otherwise. As Spencer-Brown puts it, 'the boundaries can be drawn anywhere [the observer] pleases'.[20] Different worlds will come into visibility as a result.[21] In a phenomenological register we could refer to observation as 'phenomenality' or 'givenness', while distinction would be that which gives the given. My thesis is that Luhmann's theory of distinction allows us to articulate a common frame or logic belonging to a wide variety of different correlationisms. However, as we shall see, Luhmann's theory of distinction, despite his own intentions, also allows us to critique correlationism.

Spencer-Brown represents the distinction that renders observation possible with the following symbol:

Figure 1

That which falls under the bracket is what can be indicated as a result of drawing the distinction. However, it is important to note that the distinction has two sides, which are referred to as the marked and unmarked spaces of the distinction.

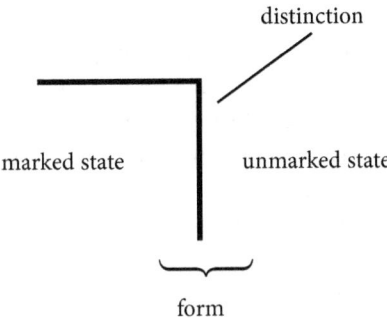

Figure 2

The two sides of the distinction – the marked and unmarked space – taken together are referred to as a 'form'. To reiterate: the observer just is the *distinction* – not an organism or organs – whether that observer be an animal, human, social system or computer technology. Already we see a posthuman twist in Luhmann's theory of distinction, for a wide variety of entities can deploy distinctions and be observers.

Spencer-Brown's point is that to observe or indicate anything at all a distinction must be drawn that *excludes* or places other beings, events, lines of thought, etc., in an unmarked space. Being or the universe as such cannot be indicated; or rather, the attempt to observe the universe as such would present only pure chaos. Thus, for example, when zoology observes horses there is a prior distinction that renders this indication possible – a distinction that delineates horses – and there is necessarily an exclusion of everything else that is not indicated by this distinction. In this context, it is crucial to note that it is *zoology* (not the scientist) that is the observer. In other words, there is a social system, a discursive system, that draws the distinction allowing horses to be observed. The distinction is itself contingent, such that it could be drawn differently. For example, while zoology might draw distinctions so as to indicate shared biological features among different species of equines, the discursive system of the preindustrial American military cavalry might have drawn distinctions to indicate the suitability of horses for war. These different distinctions cause very different things to appear.

The real value of Spencer-Brown's theory of observation lies not in his account of indication but rather in how it draws attention to what is *not* indicated. Every form is haunted by two blind spots. There is, of course, the unmarked space of the distinction or that which is excluded from observation.

However, more profoundly, what is also unobserved in observation is the observer or the *distinction itself*. As Luhmann puts it, drawing on Michel Serres, 'the observer is the nonobservable. The distinction he uses to indicate the one side or the other [of the form] serves as the invisible condition of seeing, as blind spot.'[22] It is as if distinction, in allowing something to appear, creates a sort of optical illusion where that which appears is encountered as identical to that which is rather than being an effect of the distinction (observer) that brings it into relief. As a consequence, Luhmann will constantly remind us that the observer 'cannot see what it cannot see', and that 'reality is what one does not perceive when one perceives it'.[23] If we cannot see what we cannot see, then this is because the distinction that constitutes the indication withdraws in the act of being used. By contrast, if we do not perceive reality when we perceive it, then this is because the distinction only exists for the system that observes reality and does not exist in the environment of the system without the act of observation. Thus Luhmann will remark elsewhere that for the system drawing the distinction, 'the world as it is and the world as it is being observed cannot be distinguished'.[24]

Far from merely presenting an account of how indication or observation takes place, Luhmann's theory of observation invites us to engage in *second-order observation* or to 'observe the observer'. While an observer is not able to observe itself as operating with distinctions to make indications, *another* observation (deploying a new distinction) or observer *can* observe the first observer to discern both how the observed observer draws its distinctions and what its blind spots are. Investigating the distinctions that constitute and produce givenness for these systems is what takes place in second-order observation. Of course, in observing the observer a new distinction will be drawn with its own blind spots: one can operate with distinctions by making indications, or observe distinctions, but cannot do both at once:

> All observation (including the observing of observations) presupposes the operative deployment of a distinction that at the moment of its use must be employed 'blindly' (in the sense of 'non-observably'). If one wants to observe the distinction in its turn, one has to employ a different distinction for which the same is true.[25]

For example, the United States cavalry can either indicate horses suitable for war or observe the criteria it has formulated (distinctions) to indicate war-horses, but it cannot do both at once. If it indicates war-horses, the distinction it uses to make that observation becomes invisible; while if it observes those distinctions, war-horses become invisible. The distinction that renders the observation possible always goes unobserved, even as it functions as the condition for the observation. For the cavalry, horses just are what its distinctions have predelineated.

Here, then, the value of Spencer-Brown's and Luhmann's theory of observation becomes apparent. As Luhmann remarks, observation 'can claim no extrawordly, privileged standpoint'.[26] Furthermore, there is not *an* observer but observer*s* – as many observers as there are distinctions. As a consequence, second-order observation 'destroys [the] "one observer – one nature – one world" assumption' characteristic of philosophy.[27] No longer can we presuppose the existence of a universal *cogito* as in the case of Descartes, nor a transcendental unity of apperception as in the case of Kant, nor a transcendental ego as in the case of Husserl. In each case, these universal – or monotonously first-order – observers function to ground a shared and identical world. However, second-order observation reveals that there are as many observers as there are distinctions and that these observers need not at all be human (and on this basis the assumption that all humans draw distinctions in the same way or that there is even a universal set of features shared by all humans is highly questionable). Other animals, social systems and artificial intelligences are also observers.

Luhmann thus argues that second-order observation presents us with a theory in which there is no distinct reality out there,[28] and that therefore second-order systems theory brings about a deontologization of reality.[29] They do so because, as we saw earlier, systems cannot distinguish the world as it is and the world as it is observed. Luhmann will go even further and remark that 'there are no correlates in the environment of [a] system ... even for distinctions and designations'.[30] As he continues, 'all distinctions and designations are purely internal recursive operations of a system'.[31] I hope to show in a moment why this is a questionable thesis, but for now it is sufficient to point out that if Luhmann is right, if it is the case that it is distinctions that allow beings to come forth and that distinctions do not exist in the environment of a system – and therefore that the entities that come forth do not exist in the environment of systems – then we can no longer speak of a reality out there apart from systems of observation. There is only that which presents itself to systems as a consequence of the distinctions deployed by that system; and because there are many different distinctions there will be many different realities.

Luhmann's twist to Kant's correlationist revolution consists in undermining the universality of the structure of correlation, showing how the drawing of distinctions is capable of producing a variety of different structures of phenomenality or givenness. It is here that we encounter his poststructuralist dimension. Luhmann doesn't hesitate to characterize deconstruction as second-order observation or the activity of showing how distinctions produce different worlds or fields of phenomenality.[32] In works like *The Order of Things*, Foucault can be thought as demonstrating the manner in which various systems of knowledge discursively produce their objects in different ways at different points in history through the distinctions they deploy.[33] The uncanny effect of Foucault's archaeologies lies in revealing the contingency of these systems of knowledge, or how they are contingent and lack a one-to-one correspondence with reality. Judith Butler does something similar with gender, showing how gender is discursively and performatively produced through the deployment of a contingent set of distinctions. In the case of Jacques Lacan it has shown how the fundamental fantasy functions as a frame or set of distinctions for the unconscious subject, structuring its relation to the Other and reality. While it would be a mistake to characterize Gilles Deleuze and Félix Guattari as correlationists, they do, following Jakob von Uexküll, develop a posthuman correlationism that explores the world of nonhuman organisms through a second-order observation of how these organisms observe that they call 'ethology'.[34] In addition to providing a formal framework for comprehending commonalities among these diverse thinkers through his formal theory of observation, Luhmann also contributes to the poststructuralist framework by developing a posthumanist account of how systems themselves are observers deploying their own distinctions (e.g. economic, political, religious and other systems) independent of humans. With qualifications when it comes to Deleuze and Guattari, and the later work of Foucault, each of these thinkers can be thought as engaging in a form of reflexive or second-order observation that reveals the contingency of a set of distinctions and their accompanying objects while also investigating the blind spots that haunt these systems.

Observing correlationism: Why realism and materialism now?

Correlationism invites us to engage in second-order observation of systems, of how these systems observe, revealing: (a) the contingency of the distinctions they deploy in the production of phenomena, the 'given', or objects; (b) the blind spots of these systems; (c) the reality-effect these systems produce; and, finally, (d) that these systems have no direct relationship to reality.

In doing so, the second-order observation or correlationism common to poststructuralism presents a compelling critique of representationalist realist accounts of truth wherein systems conform to a reality that exists independent of that system.

Given the persuasiveness of poststructuralist correlationism's critique (hereafter PSC), we might ask why we are witnessing a resurgence of realism? Why has realism not been safely buried and become a curious relic of intellectual history? It is likely that there is no single answer to this question. However, much of the resurgence of realism probably has to do with the material circumstances within which we find ourselves today: in our current circumstances the environment has increasingly forced itself to the attention of observing systems in ways that are not easily susceptible to correlationist or constructivist analysis. This intrusion of the environment into observing systems has taken place first and foremost with respect to climate change. However, it has also arisen from the new technologies that have transformed both the face of the globe and how we live, as well as the centrality of energy in sustaining our social systems. In all of these instances we must think a form of causal agency that doesn't result from distinctions, but from the physical or material properties of entities *themselves* independent of whatever distinctions a system happens to draw.

To see why PSC has difficulty handling these sorts of material agencies we can engage in a second-order observation of correlationism itself, asking both what correlationism observes and what its blind spots are. Paradoxically, it is Luhmann's theory of observation, which purports to deontologize reality, that allows us to critique PSC. With notable exceptions, such as Deleuze and Guattari and the later Foucault, it would not be amiss to say that PSCs predominantly observe meaning, signs, signification, narrative and discourses, demonstrating how entities and identities are effects of the distinctions drawn by these agencies. As Lacan formulates the thesis, 'there's no such thing as a prediscursive reality. Every reality is founded and defined by a discourse'.[35] More dramatically yet, he remarks that '[t]he universe is the flower of rhetoric'.[36] Within this framework, reality, then, is an effect of discourse or rhetoric. In his own work, Luhmann will argue that reality is an effect of communication. Yet climate change and the powers of technology are not effects of discourse, signs, signifiers or communication, but rather result from powers that belong to material entities themselves.

As a consequence of this thesis, it is discourse in some form or another that falls in the marked space of poststructuralist, correlationist thought.

The referent of discourse and that which is outside of discourse but that does not appear in discourse falls into the unmarked space of PSC. While poststructuralism, as a variant of correlationism, claims to think the relation between system and object, it in fact reduces the object to signification. As Stacy Alaimo puts it, '[m]atter, the vast stuff of the world and of ourselves, has been subdivided into manageable "bits" or flattened into a "blank slate" for human inscription'.[37] Materials, entities, are treated as blank slates that are carriers of human inscriptions or embodied forms of rhetoric. As a result, the object becomes a text to be deciphered and interpreted like a novel or film. One of the clearest examples of this would be Baudrillard's *System of Objects*, where we are shown how commodities embody unconscious meanings that reinforce everything from class divisions to patriarchy;[38] but also Slavoj Žižek's *The Plague of Fantasies*, where we are presented with an analysis of French, German and English toilets, showing how each embodies a different national ideology (German reflective thoroughness, French revolutionary haste and English utilitarian pragmatism).[39]

While it seems to be the object that is indicated under PSC, it is in fact rather signification or discourse that comes to the fore. The blind spot of PSC is therefore materiality, things, or what Bruno Latour calls 'actants'. Matters or things introduce differences into the world not by virtue of how they signify within a discourse but by virtue of what they are and the powers or capacities that they possess.[40] Carbon emissions do not raise temperatures leading to the melting of polar ice because of signification but by virtue of how they prevent heat from escaping the atmosphere. Likewise, smart phones do not link people globally allowing for coordinated action across the world by virtue of the signifier but because of a system of radio towers, satellites, data bases and so on allowing for linkage via the internet. These are material differences, not signifying differences.

There is, to use Jane Bennett's language, a force of things, a productive power of things, which does not arise from signification but which is a feature of these things themselves.[41] Yet this power of things is precisely what becomes invisible under PSC because this formation of thought deploys a distinction that calls us to *not* investigate what powers things possess, but rather how they are carriers of meaning that systems have constituted. In observing the blind spot of PSC we are able to shift attention away from signification so as to draw attention to this power of things by virtue of what they are. In other words, through a second-order observation of PSC we cross its line of distinction and enter its unmarked space so as to observe from the standpoint of materiality. Furthermore, it is not merely that PSC prevents us from discerning the power of matters necessary for understanding things such as climate change, it is also that discursive power is not the only form that power takes. As Latour has so persuasively shown, for example, power is not simply exercised discursively but also nondiscursively through the agency of things and how they afford and constrain various social relations.[42] While it is indeed the case that systems of signification exercise all sorts of power by virtue of how they sort, categorize and define us, material features of environments exercise power in all sorts of subtle and dramatic ways as well. Here we might think of different suburban home designs. To be sure, the architecture of homes reflects signifying assumptions regarding families, relations between men and women, relations between parents and children, the activities with which people occupy themselves, etc. However, power here is not exercised merely at the level of signification, but rather also involves physical features of the home. For example, a kitchen that is separated from the general living and dining area exercises a power of segregation from partners and children not merely by virtue of signification but by virtue of plaster, stone, sheet rock and wood that creates real physical separations between those who dwell in the home. It is not the signifier alone that exercises power, but also these material agencies. Indeed, as Foucault taught us in his discussion of the panopticon, the material features of architecture can exercise a power of its own independent of signification. A home, in its material being, could be thought as a sort of machine that separates and relates living bodies – let's not forget animals that dwell in homes – both within the home through walls and hallways, as well as with respect to the outside world through openings, doors, and windows. These material channels and walls play a key role in how living bodies relate, yet all of this becomes invisible if we attend to signification alone.

Observing machines

It would be a mistake to abandon PSC for it has shown us, in a compelling way, how the identities we take as having being in their own right are, in fact, contingent constructions of social relations functioning as supports for unjust power. In demonstrating this, PSC opens a space for emancipatory politics; for where identities are constructions rather than natural beings it becomes possible to construct different identities and to contest systems of categorization that organize social relations and segregate living bodies. However, we have also seen that things exercise a power of their own, independent of signification, and that certain things such as climate change or the role that infrastructure, geography and technology play simply cannot be properly understood as long as we remain within the theoretical framework of PSC. These things require a realist framework that does justice to the power and agency of things. Although I cannot address the epistemological complexities of the issue here – in this context I advance my argument on pragmatic grounds – what is needed is some way of distinguishing those elements that are constituted by systems such that they do not exist in the environment of the system in which they appear from those that have independent existence in their own right.[43]

What is needed is, then, a framework powerful enough to capture both of these orientations without abandoning the gains of poststructuralist critique nor reducing things to carriers of signification and products of systems. While I can only sketch an outline of such an account here, it turns out that Luhmann's thought ironically contributes many elements to such a theory. If such a move is surprising, then this is because Luhmann was so insistent in claiming that his thought deontologized reality and spelled the ruin of any notion of independent reality. Here everything spins on reading Luhmann against himself and in raising the question of whether he can coherently maintain the position he claims to defend. In other words, we must ask whether Luhmann's thought does not harbour hidden realist resources that, in a sort of *Aufhebung*, allow us to both retain the contributions of PSC while also imagining a new form of realist thought.

We have already seen how Luhmann's theory of distinctions and observation can be turned against itself to observe the blind spots of PSC, thereby paving the way to an observation of the contributions of material beings. However, it is also worth noting that Luhmann's own thought, despite its avowed rejection of ontology, is itself dependent on a variety of ontological theses.[44] As he remarks in *Social Systems*, 'it is crucial to distinguish between the *environment* of a system and *systems in the environment* of this system'.[45] That is, Luhmann's sociological project of observing social systems cannot get off the ground without positing the existence of systems. Systems do not merely constitute beings through the distinctions they deploy, *they are beings*. Yet if we grant the existence of systems independent of other systems, why should we not grant the existence of other beings that are not of the order of observing systems but independent of them?

While I cannot here go into all the details of his complicated theory of systems, Luhmann draws a distinction between the environment that systems constitute and systems that exist independent of a system. Luhmann argues that 'the point of departure for all systems-theoretical analysis must be the *difference between system and environment*.'[46] His thesis is that systems constitute themselves by distinguishing themselves from an environment, but also that they constitute their environment. As he remarks, 'the environment receives its unity through the system and only in relation to the system.'[47] In other words, there is not one environment, but as many different environments as there are systems. The point here is quite simple: take the bee as an example of a system; bees constitute their environment and give it a unity in the sense that they are only selectively open to their environment in terms of what they can sense and what they attend to as relevant to their existence (flowers, the hive, other bees, certain predators, and so on). Luhmann contends that 'elements are elements only for the system that employs them as units and they are such only through this system.'[48] For example, for the bee, flowers are not flowers but sources of nectar. Similarly, what interests the capitalist is not the commodity as a physical object but only what it is as a unit in exchange. The biology of trees only interests capitalism insofar as it affects that system of exchange and otherwise falls into the unmarked space of capitalism. It is in this sense that systems constitute their own elements. Nonetheless, there are also *other* systems that exist in the environment of a system that may or may not belong to the environment the system constitutes. In the environment of the bee there are all sorts of micro-organisms that do not belong to the bee's environment; and leaves exist in the environment of the lumber market but are not elements in that system of exchange.

It is clear from the foregoing that a sleight of hand is at work in Luhmann's thought, for he uses the term 'environment' in two quite different senses. On the one hand, there is the environment that systems *constitute* as a set of selections from the chaos of the world that are relevant to its ongoing operations. Let us abbreviate this environment as E_c to denote the constituted environment that the system observes through its distinctions. On the other hand, there is the environment that exists *independent* of the system regardless of whether the system observes it. We can call this environment E_i to denote the independently existing environment. Luhmann remarks that the constitution of E_c always involves risk in that

> establishing and maintaining the difference between system and environment ... becomes the problem, because for each system the

environment is more complex than the system itself. Systems lack the 'requisite variety' ... that would enable them to react to every state of the environment ... There is ... no point-for-point correspondence between system and environment.[49]

Clearly, when Luhmann refers to risk and an environment more complex than the system he is referring to E_i rather than E_c; an environment more complex than a system is one that is not registered by that system. Because of the constraints of time or acting on the one hand, and the overwhelming complexity of E_i on the other, the system is forced to select in constituting E_c. This selection involves risk, since that which it ignores in selecting might ultimately spell the demise of the system. For example, in failing to monitor asteroids in our solar system we risk the destruction of the earth due to a catastrophic impact, but one cannot monitor everything in real time and still operate.

We thus see that Luhmann's position compels him to adopt a tempered form of realism along three fronts. First, Luhmann must posit the existence of other systems for his sociological project of observing systems to be coherent. These other systems can't merely be constituted by the observing system if his sociology is to be informative. Other systems must themselves exist as entities independent of the system that observes them. We might have a distorted understanding of these systems as a result of our own distinctions but that doesn't undermine their existence. Second, he must posit the existence of an environment external to a system (E_i) independent of the environment that the system constitutes (E_c) to account for what might be called the 'perspectivism' of systems theory and his account of risk, selection and complexity. Third, building on his commitment to systems theory, while systems might constitute their own elements, these elements cannot be constituted *ex nihilo*. They must draw on some sort of matter that is then formed as an element of the system. For example, an organism as a system constitutes its cells as elements of its own system, but it must draw on all sorts of materials to do this. Likewise, social systems must draw on all sorts of materials to constitute their elements (identities, roles, hierarchies, communications, etc.). Indeed, as Luhmann's thought develops, we find that he increasingly discusses material phenomena such as writing and communications technologies that are not strictly of the order of observing systems constituting their own objects or elements, but which nonetheless play a key role in how social systems evolve and develop.[50] These technologies contribute to the evolution of society not by virtue of what they communicate but by virtue of how they *allow* communications take place. As McLuhan famously put it, here 'the medium is the message'.[51]

To be clear, the aim here is not one of abandoning Luhmann and PSC so as to defend a naive realism, but rather one of creating a space in which the resources of PSC can be preserved. While he is not often associated with the poststructuralists, it is my view that Luhmann provides the most sophisticated and, due to its formalism, the most integrative theory of PSC available – and it also allows us to think the contributions of materiality to social assemblages. Luhmann's theory of systems and observation allows us to see how systems constitute fields of selective relevance (E_c), characteristic of how a system constitutes its elements, while also providing the means to think environments independent of systems (E_i) that nonetheless contribute to the form social assemblages take. Where many strains of PSC tended towards a sort of imperialism of language, signification or the outside, Luhmann's systems theory shows the limits of constitution in E_cs, allowing us to think an outside while also giving us the means to explore the variety of ways in which systems constitute their environments and subject these constitutions to emancipatory critique.

Notes

1. There is a great deal of confusion surrounding the term 'object-oriented ontology' (OOO), treating it as synonymous with the ontology proposed by Graham Harman. I coined the term 'object-oriented ontology' in July 2009 to distinguish ontologies committed to the existence of substances, entities or objects from Harman's specific ontology and its commitments, or 'object-oriented philosophy' (OOP); see Graham Harman, 'Series Editor's Preface', in Levi R. Bryant, *Onto-Cartography: An Ontology of Machines and Media* (Edinburgh: Edinburgh University Press, 2014), p. ix. OOO is thus a *genus* term like 'rationalism', 'empiricism', 'idealism', 'materialism' or 'poststructuralism'. It refers not to a unified ontology, but to a variety of *different* ontologies committed to the thesis that being is composed of substances. While these thinkers might not themselves accept the label, examples of object-oriented ontologies would be Aristotle, Thomas Aquinas, Leibniz, Whitehead, Deleuze (under one reading), Bruno Latour, Isabella Stengers, Jane Bennett, Stacy Alaimo, etc. Clearly there are heated debates among these thinkers regarding just what constitutes a substance, just as there were debates among the rationalists, among the empiricists, and among the idealists. While often sympathetic, my onticology and machine-oriented ontology, developed elsewhere in *The Democracy of Objects* (Ann Arbor: Open

Humanities Press, 2011) and *Onto-Cartography*, are proposed as materialist and Deleuzian alternatives to Graham Harman's ontology of nonrelationality, vicarious causation and withdrawal.

2. See Ian Hacking, *The Social Construction of What?* (Cambridge: Harvard University Press, 2000). Such positions argue that there are some features of entities that are intrinsic, while there are others that only exist for an observer.
3. Personal correspondence with Graham Harman in 2010.
4. Graham Harman has been a vocal critic of materialism. As a consequence, it should be noted that while all materialisms are necessarily realisms, not all realisms are materialisms.
5. Quentin Meillassoux, *After Finitude: An Essay on the Necessity of Contingency*, trans. Ray Brassier (New York: Continuum, 2008), p. 5.
6. Ibid.
7. Immanuel Kant, *Critique of Pure Reason*, trans. Paul Guyer and Allen W. Wood (Cambridge: Cambridge University Press, 1998), Bxvi.
8. Ibid., A111.
9. Ibid., B148.
10. In the world of philosophy and theory, it is not uncommon for one to find an exception to a generalization and triumphantly declare that the generalization is ill-founded. For example, Gilles Deleuze certainly does not fit the model of correlationism, nor, as Harman has argued, does Latour easily fit this model; see his *Prince of Networks: Bruno Latour and Metaphysics* (Melbourne: re.press, 2009). Harman, of course, shares the thesis that correlationism or philosophies of access dominate Continental thought. The issue here is not whether or not exceptions exist – they always do – but rather what view *dominates* within a discursive community. Within the discursive community of Continental thought defined by its presses, journals and graduate programmes, correlationist thought certainly defines the majoritarian or prevalent trend of philosophy.
11. Another name for 'correlationism' is antirealism. For a brilliant account of how antirealism or correlationism has dominated contemporary Continental philosophy, see Lee Braver, *A Thing of This World: A History of Continental Anti-Realism* (Evanston: Northwestern University Press, 2007).
12. Quentin Meillassoux, 'Presentation by Quentin Meillassoux', in Robin Mackay and Dustin McWherter, *Collapse III: Unknown Deleuze [+ Speculative Realism]* (Falmouth: Urbanomic, 2007), p. 409.
13. Karl Marx, *Capital: Volume 1*, trans. Ben Fowkes (New York: Penguin, 1990), p. 165.
14. Lucretius, *The Way Things Are: The* De Rerum Natura *of Titus Lucretius Carus*, trans. Rolfe Humphries (Bloomington: Indiana University Press, 1968), p. 33.
15. Aristotle, *Politics*, trans. Benjamin Jowett, in Jonathan Barnes (ed.), *The Complete Works of Aristotle: The Revised Oxford Translation: Vol. 2* (Princeton: Princeton University Press, 1984), 1254^{b}15–21.

16. For Foucault, see *Discipline and Punish: The Birth of the Prison*, trans. Alan Sheridan (New York: Vintage Books, 1977). For Butler, see *Gender Trouble: Feminism and the Subversion of Identity* (New York: Routledge, 2006).
17. See for example Derrida, 'White Mythology: Metaphor in the Text of Philosophy', in *Margins of Philosophy*, trans. Alan Bass (Chicago: Chicago University Press, 1986).
18. George Spencer-Brown, *Laws of Form* (New York: EP Dutton Publishing, 1979), p. 1.
19. Ibid., p. xxix, modified.
20. Ibid., modified.
21. Throughout what follows I distinguish between 'universe' and 'world'. 'Universe' denotes what is independent of all distinctions. It would be there regardless of whether or not distinctions were drawn. 'World' denotes that which appears as a consequence of a system drawing a distinction.
22. Niklas Luhmann, *Theory of Society: Volume 1*, trans. Rhodes Barrett (Stanford: Stanford University Press, 2012), p. 35.
23. Niklas Luhmann, 'The Cognitive Program of Constructivism and the Reality that Remains Unknown', trans. Peter Germain et al., in William Rasch (ed.), *Theories of Distinction: Redescribing Descriptions of Modernity* (Stanford: Stanford University Press, 2002), pp. 129, 141.
24. Niklas Luhmann, *The Reality of the Mass Media*, trans. Kathleen Cross (Stanford: Stanford University Press, 2000), p. 11.
25. Luhmann, 'Constructivism', p. 135.
26. Luhmann, 'Identity – What or How?', in *Distinction*, p. 114.
27. Luhmann, 'Deconstruction as Second-Order Observing', in *Distinction*, p. 96.
28. Ibid., p. 108.
29. Luhmann, 'The Program of Constructivism', p. 132.
30. Ibid., p. 135.
31. Ibid.
32. Luhmann, 'Deconstruction'.
33. Michel Foucault, *The Order of Things: An Archaeology of the Human Sciences*, trans. uncredited (New York: Vintage Books, 1994).
34. Gilles Deleuze and Félix Guattari, *A Thousand Plateaus: Capitalism and Schizophrenia*, trans. Brian Massumi (Minneapolis: University of Minnesota Press, 1987), pp. 256–65.
35. Jacques Lacan, *Encore: On Feminine Sexuality, The Limits of Love and Knowledge, 1972–1973*, trans. Bruce Fink (New York: W. W. Norton, 1998), p. 32.
36. Ibid., p. 56.
37. Stacy Alaimo, *Bodily Natures: Science, Environment, and the Material Self* (Bloomington: Indiana University Press, 2010), p. 1.

38. Jean Baudrillard, *System of Objects*, trans. James Benedict (New York: Verso, 2005).
39. Slavoj Žižek, *The Plague of Fantasies* (New York: Verso, 1997), pp. 4–5.
40. While I cannot develop it in detail here, elsewhere I argue that entities are defined not by their qualities or properties but rather by their *powers* or capacities; see especially Bryant, *Democracy*, chapter four, and *Onto-Cartography*, pp. 40–6. In this, I follow Spinoza's account of affect as well as the ontology developed by George Molnar.
41. Jane Bennett, *Vibrant Matter: A Political Ecology of Things* (Durham: Duke University Press, 2010).
42. See, for example, Bruno Latour, *Pandora's Hope: Essays on the Reality of Science Studies*, trans. Catherine Porter (Cambridge, MA: Harvard University Press, 1999).
43. In *Democracy*, chapter two, I draw on Roy Bhaskar's earlier work to develop a transcendental argument showing that experience and inquiry can only be coherently understood if the world (not mind, as Kant would have it) is a certain way and that entities independent of mind exist.
44. See Luhmann 'Identity' for his critique of ontology, which is a constant throughout all of his work.
45. Niklas Luhmann, *Social Systems*, trans. John Bednarz Jr. and Dirk Baecker (Stanford: Stanford University Press, 1995), p. 17.
46. Ibid., p. 16.
47. Ibid., p. 17.
48. Ibid., p. 22.
49. Ibid., p. 25.
50. Luhmann, *Theory of Society*, §§2.5–2.8.
51. Marshall and Eric McLuhan, *Laws of Media: The New Science* (Toronto: University of Toronto Press, 1988), p. 5.

CHAPTER 4
DELEUZE: SPECULATIVE AND PRACTICAL PHILOSOPHY
Sjoerd van Tuinen

Speculative philosophers who seek to revive the classical opposition between empiricism and rationalism maintain a tormented relation to Gilles Deleuze. On the one hand, they are themselves the bastard children of a Deleuze reception which reassures us of his rationalistic credentials. Ever since Alain Badiou's *The Clamor of Being* (1997), the aim of this (mainly Anglo-American) tradition has been to establish an image of Deleuze as a bona fide (academic) philosopher who relieves us from decades of analytical and phenomenological relativism. This is the Deleuze of the great theoretical theses of immanence, the univocity of being, the externality of relations, the dice-throw, the syntheses of time, and so on. On the other hand, those very same speculative philosophers tend to reject the vitalist image of Deleuze that has dominated the earlier reception, which emphasized the empiricist, that is nonphilosophical and practical aspects of his work. It is these aspects which are now considered hippie and indiscernible from what Quentin Meillassoux has labelled the 'sceptico-fideist' position. On this account, the absolute and the nonhuman for Deleuze are a question of 'belief' in the micropolitical event and not in the major powers of rational thought.

The problem with sceptico-fideist discourse, according to Meillassoux, is that it argues from a point of view of consequences evacuated from all truth-content and in this way constitutes a convergence of rational critique and religious piety: 'thought no longer provides an a priori demonstration of the truth of a specific content of piety; instead, it establishes how any piety whatsoever enjoys an equal and exclusive right to grasp the ultimate truth.'[1] Thus fanaticism is usually condemned as being wrong not because it is based on false principles but because it has 'irrational' consequences. Instead, Meillassoux wants to save enlightenment rationalism from the risk of its own moralization and consistently opposes truth to belief and principles to consequences. By strictly separating the intelligible from the sensible he takes up the Kantian attempt at an immanent criticism of reason, but now in a reverse sense: a critique of the pious self-limitation of reason by reason itself. Unsurprisingly, the price is an almost total loss of any practical orientation. Theoretically speaking, Meillassoux sets out to define the conditions of possibility for a rational critique of our various beliefs and ideologies. But from the point of view of practice, should we not repeat Nietzsche's question 'how far, he too, is still pious'?[2] Or ask with Deleuze whether this classical critique of pure reason is really capable of going beyond 'the humble recognition of the rights of the criticized' and thus of bridging the 'opposition between project and results' inherent to Kantian criticism?[3] Does the speculative denunciation of correlationism not remain practically inconsequential?

The aim of this chapter is to argue, first, that it is practically impossible to disconnect the rationalistic and the empiricist aspects of philosophy, and secondly, that the return of speculative reason and the critique of correlationism become necessary and interesting only in the context of a transcendental empiricism that experiments with conditions of real instead of possible experience. The red thread of my argument is constituted by what I consider as Deleuze's reinvention of the principle of sufficient reason (PSR). Inheriting a long-standing rationalist tradition which seeks to either reduce or subordinate the PSR to the principle of noncontradiction (PNC), Meillassoux abolishes the PSR altogether as the principle of both dogmatic metaphysics and correlationism, as its sole function would be to guarantee that whatever exists, including first of all the correlation between being and thinking, does so necessarily. By contrast, Deleuze is the inheritor of an empiricist tradition which is not so much opposed to the PSR, as rationalists such as Kant, Hegel and Meillassoux make it seem, but rather uses it for the virtual interpretation and evaluation of our actual becomings.[4] More than in the theoretical domains of epistemology and ontology, then, the PSR is a speculative principle valid for all sorts of practical problems, including those of politics and art. In what follows, I will explore this pragmatic (re)orientation of speculative thought with and through five central concepts of Deleuze: naturalism, structuralism, univocity, immanence and materialism. While I agree with Meillassoux's diagnosis that, until now, the Copernican revolution of thought in science has in fact been answered by a 'Ptolemaic counterrevolution' in philosophy, I will conclude by proposing a new, Deleuzian image of thought, namely that of a speculative practice in which elasticity and plasticity constitute the elliptic poles of a Keplerian revolution.

Principles and consequences: Naturalism

While Deleuze is an immediate progenitor of the speculative turn in Continental philosophy, we can distinguish at least two divergent branches of Deleuze-inspired speculative thought: speculative realism (Meillassoux, Brassier, DeLanda, Bryant, etc.) and speculative constructivism (Massumi, Stengers, Latour, Debaise, etc.).[5] The two branches correspond to the speculative and practical aspects that Deleuze, in his earlier works, identified as belonging to a single philosophy: *naturalism*, or the multiple and the principles of its production.

Writing about Lucretius, Deleuze argues that '[n]ature is not attributive, but rather collective: it expresses itself through "and", and not through "is".[6] From the speculative point of view, naturalism is the affirmation in thought of nontotalizable compositions and combinations of atoms (the distinction of 'true' from 'false infinity' in nature). From the practical point of view, naturalism is the pleasure in the diversity of finite compounds (the defence of a positive sensibility against the images of sadness in man). But the two viewpoints converge in the determination of the idea of philosophy as opposed to myth:

> The speculative object and the practical object of philosophy as Naturalism, science and pleasure, coincide on this point: it is always a matter of denouncing the illusion, the false infinite, the infinity of religion and all of the theological-erotic-oneiric myths in which it is expressed.[7]

Atomism is the necessary means of ethics, while joy is the necessary orientation of thought: a double, joint affirmation of a differential multiplicity of events without place and time (the so-called *eventa* or necessary/absolute contingencies) that makes naturalism move between what cannot but be thought (the *clinamen* as quasicause below the minimum of the thinkable time of atoms moving through the void) and what cannot but be felt (the simulacra as quasicause below the minimum of the sensible time of perceived images).[8]

Similarly, Deleuze never ceases to emphasize that Spinoza's great theories of a single substance – the univocity of its attributes, immanence, universal necessity, parallelism and so on – are inseparable from the three practical theses of materialism, immoralism and atheism, each of which consists of a joyous liberation: of the unconscious from consciousness, of ethics from transcendent values, and of desire from its confusion with sad passions.

> The *Ethics* is a book written twice simultaneously: once in the continuous stream of definitions, propositions, demonstrations, and corollaries, which develop the great speculative themes with all the rigors of the mind; another time in the broken chain of scholia, a discontinuous volcanic line, a second version underneath the first, expressing all the angers of the heart and setting forth the practical theses of denunciation and liberation ... Ethical *joy* is the correlate of speculative affirmation.[9]

More specifically, Deleuze warns us not to overlook the practical sense of philosophy in favour of its speculative content. If learning proceeds through the formation of common notions, which, once given, acquire a varying degree of generality, their empirical or propositional function continues to be constrained by the necessarily contingent encounters to which they respond. There is no speculation without risk and experiment, whence the empirical order of learning: our passive joys enable us to gain common notions with a very limited content-value, but from the active joys that follow from what we understand we form ever more general common notions, such that finally we may learn to pass to the universal/univocal knowledge of the absolute (beatitude): the intellectual intuition or love of God/Nature, in which theory and practice, intelligibility and sensibility, content and expression, proposition and sense coincide.[10]

It is with Friedrich Nietzsche (and by reclaiming speculative philosophy from Hegelian dialectics) that Deleuze most completely articulates his naturalism. Nietzsche's empiricism privileges the concrete 'feeling' of difference, affirmation and enjoyment over the abstract thought of negation, opposition or contradiction.[11] On the level of Nietzsche's 'speculative teaching', this means that becoming, multiplicity and chance do not lack any being, that difference is pure affirmation, and that the eternal return excludes all negativity. On the practical level, Nietzsche exposes all the mystifications which disfigure philosophy:

> the apparatus of bad conscience, the false marvels of the negative ... turn multiplicity, becoming, chance and difference itself into so many misfortunes of consciousness itself and turn misfortunes of consciousness into so many moments of formation, reflection or development. Nietzsche's practical teaching is that difference is happy; that multiplicity, becoming and chance are adequate objects of joy by themselves and that only joy returns.[12]

Hence Deleuze's reinterpretation of the principle of the univocity of being, according to which 'being is said in a single and same sense of everything of which it is said, but that of which it is said differs'.[13] If, with Spinoza, univocal being lost the theoretical neutrality it still had in Duns Scotus and became expressive and affirmative, Nietzsche would effectively realize it by way of his concept of the eternal return: 'Being is said in a single and same sense, but this sense is that of the eternal return or repetition of that of which it is said.'[14] Repetition is being, but it is the being of becoming or the necessity of contingency – in other words, the repetition of difference. As a consequence, the speculative content of the eternal return – the physical or cosmological doctrine which defines the same not analytically as the nature of that which returns but, on the contrary, as the synthetic fact of returning for that which differs – simultaneously carries out a practical selection among differences according to their capacity to continue transforming themselves and changing into one another.[15]

At first glance, the speculative and practical principles of the event as discontinuity of time, of the constraint of the unforeseeable encounter and of the eternal return as perpetual throw of the dice that gives rise to its own necessity suggests a Mallarméan mode of thinking common to Meillassoux and Deleuze. For the latter, however, the intuition of the *necessity* of contingency means first of all the end of the belief in (classical) reason and all first principles. If we can still refer to this intuition as a principle, then it is as 'a plastic, anarchic and nomadic principle'[16] – that is, not as an unconditioned principle, but as a 'principle without a prince'[17], a principle that cannot be separated from its consequences and that is no more generic than they are. Put differently, for Deleuze the relation between thought and nature, the principle and what it grounds, is not analytical but synthetic. The implications become clear as soon as we take a look at the philosophical principles upheld by Meillassoux and Deleuze. Meillassoux simultaneously abolishes the PSR and derives the PNC as the *inverse* of the necessity of contingency.[18] He thus never leaves the transcendent domain of logic and safely holds on to necessary essence, as becomes clear from his critique of the ontological argument and his proof of the 'divine inexistence' or *peut-être* of God, according to which nothing that exists necessarily can possibly exist.[19] Deleuze, by contrast, subordinates the PNC to the PSR at the same time as he reinvents the latter as the *reverse* of the necessity of contingency. He thus turns thought into *onto*-logy again, but instead of returning to the classical metaphysics of necessary existence, he reclaims the PSR for an immanent belief in the world instead of in reason alone, a belief that is both necessitated and challenged by contingent existence.[20] Every true thought, even one that is strictly 'logical', is inseparable from its 'milieu' or 'ground', from the 'problematic disparition' of the aleatory and the dependent that constitutes a new type of real necessity.[21]

As this chapter aims to demonstrate, the naturalist attempt to reclaim the PSR neither compromises the speculative power of rational thought with ontotheology nor subordinates it to the correlationist 'always already', because rather than a question of the external *conditioning* of possible objective knowledge about possible nature, thinking is a question of the intrinsic and subjective *genesis* of real thought and real nature, under the strict constraint that one is intrinsically heterogeneous from the other. Speaking from the perspective of those who have taken up the task to discover and criticize correlationism wherever they can, one might even argue that if Meillassoux's speculative logic is closer to Kant than is commonly assumed, Deleuze's naturalism more adequately fits the mask of speculative materialism. Meillassoux follows Kant's turning away of thought from a given experience of nature (e.g. the capacity of experimental science to produce a knowledge of the ancestral) to the conditions of possibility of this experience and ultimately finds these conditions in a place that is even further removed from nature, namely in the speculative object of reason alone. Deleuze, by contrast, starts 'by the middle', that is, from the immanence of experience and nature, including the experience of thought. Immanence, however, does not mean identity. The necessity of contingency is not the positive content of a priori knowledge and the objectivity it grounds, but a practical ordeal by which thought learns to think against established reason itself and against the transcendences that are given with it.[22] Instead of the rational principle of 'unreason' or of the 'lack of reason' (*irraison*), itself inseparable from the sad passion of a rational but anxious and spectral hope for redemption as indicated by Meillassoux, the universal breakdown (*effondrement*) of all first principles may then be experienced as joyful and positive effect of ungrounding or deterritorialization (*effondement*) of reason itself.[23] It becomes the very force of 'madness' (*déraison*) insisting in all naturalist appeals to speculative principles.[24]

Logic and existence: Structuralism

Rather than looking for a general foundation on the basis of which we can neutrally speak in the name of a generic nature, Deleuze's naturalism constantly asks how we acquire the right to speak at all. What is the nature/power proper to reason? For Deleuze, the question of right (*quid juris*? as opposed to *quid facti*?) is not a general and abstract question, like the questions of classical metaphysics (why?) and classical critique (how?), but a universal and concrete 'cry'.[25] It arises when reason is confronted with, and forced to overcome, its own limitations. As a speculative question, it is inseparable from the determination of a ground (*fond*) and of the principle according to which this ground must be distributed: the image of thought, or the partitioning of the empirical and the transcendental. In Plato, this ground is the Idea and its image of thought is that of representation (the resemblance of models and copies enables us to distinguish true from false pretenders to the ground). In Deleuze's reversal of Platonism, the ground is still the Idea but the principle of its distribution is repetition (the play of *simulacra* that raises thought to the *n*th power of the false).[26] Thus, while for Plato the principle transcends all consequences and refers back to a stable ground, for Deleuze we have only 'effects' and a constantly shifting principle of their evaluation. Difference rather than identity is therefore Deleuze's name for the Idea, and repetition is the ordeal of difference: 'difference is behind everything, but behind difference there is nothing'.[27] Or to put it in terms of modern philosophy: the PSR neither analytically descends to the ultimate identity of the *species infimae*, the things in themselves of Leibniz, nor is it grounded in the synthetic activity of the understanding dominating the other faculties in the Kantian subject. In fact, Deleuze circumvents both the Kantian analytic (correlationism) and the Hegelian dialectic (the idealist absolutization of the correlation) by arguing that whatever presents itself to reason as that which cannot but be thought (difference or the Idea), presents itself as something sensed. As Salomon Maïmon argued, the PSR leads us towards a transmonadical milieu of infinitesimal differences that constitutes the transcendental limit of all faculties, including those of reason and understanding. Whatever the PSR grounds is inseparable from this plastic milieu of the groundless ground and hence 'to ground is to metamorphose'.[28] Deleuze is thus not interested in general conditions of possibility of particular but ordinary facts. Only in those singular and perplexing cases in which the groundless ground rises up in sensation and an act of thought distributes it anew do we speak not just by fact (objective representation of what is) but by right (subjective evaluation or selective redifferentiation of our actual becomings). In the case of these 'events', the post-Copernican philosopher finally becomes a legislator and thought acquires the reflective 'power of arranging cases'.[29]

One does not speculate at will; rather, speculation depends on the action of the groundless on/in us. Thought becomes speculative only when its normal or empirical exercise becomes impossible and the search for a ground poses a 'dialectical' or 'structural' problem.[30] It then acquires a new zeal, having to lay out a new 'plane of consistency' stretching along a volcanic line of infinite becoming, unconstrained by any fixed principle or boundary. Speculation is the moment of what Deleuze and Guattari call geophilosophy, or the disjunctive unity of being and thought: the earth is deterritorialized by thought no less than thought is reterritorialized by the earth. Or in other terms, speculative logic coincides with transcendental or structural genesis itself. Logic is not the mediation of being by identity, but the critical affirmation of 'difference in itself' and its clinical 'repetition for itself'. As Jean Hyppolite had argued before Deleuze, the productive tension between existence and logic, or experience and thought, means that there is no ontology without a specific logic and no logic without a concrete ontology.[31] Thus while Deleuze's *The Logic of Sense* is a book on the genesis of reason (*logos*) or 'sense' and *The Logic of Sensation* is a book on the genesis of sensation, these two types of genesis themselves are not very 'logical' or 'sensible' at all. Rather, as David Lapoujade has shown, they are the aberrant movements of the earth whose reason or 'sense' is to be rendered by logic. Aberrant movements constitute the highest power of existence just as irrational logics constitute the highest power of thought.[32] If Deleuze is a vitalist and empiricist, this is not because he opposes life to logic, but because the powers of life ceaselessly produce new logics that subject thought to their irrationality.[33] Further, a genetic movement is all the more logical if it escapes from rationality. The speculative power of logic is all the higher, the deeper it is immersed in the problematic or paradoxical element of the Idea that subsists and insists in itself at the limit of what is empirically intelligible or sensible to us. Life, for Deleuze, is precisely this milieu of the problematic as such, the element of what 'matters'. And since life/the Idea is never separable from madness, we must always inquire into the legitimacy with which reason speaks, especially when it speaks of its opposite.

This is the challenge that Meillassoux does not even remotely touch upon. Deleuze himself maybe still fails to adequately meet it in *The Logic of Sense*, where he defines the (non-)relation of immanence between thought and being in terms of the famous topology of surface and depth, the surface of sense and the depth of corporeal mixtures. Exterior to language and beings, he defines sense as the condition of reality both for the structural relations and for the distinction between signifier and signified, words and things. It is therefore not what language denotes, manifests or signifies, but the structural event of language itself insofar as, like the wound cutting through the body, it cuts through corporeal states of affairs and reveals the autonomy of the surface where it takes place. All sense, in other words, emerges from nonsense. However, it does not always emerge with the same right, and this is why Deleuze distinguishes two kinds of nonsense. On the one hand, propositional language distinguishes itself from physical depth and constitutes a metaphysical surface by producing its own speculative object: for example, the logical paradox of a set that is included in itself as a member, such that the member divides the set that it presupposes; the free indirect speech of Gustave Flaubert in *Madame Bovary*; or the nonsense of Lewis Carroll, such as the smile without the cat in *Alice in Wonderland*; the event of growing by which Alice becomes both larger and smaller than she is in the present; and the displacement of the basic oral duality of eating and speaking into speaking of food or eating words. In each case, logical nonsense, by upsetting the empirical distribution between words and things, liberates sense from the ontological regime of identity and the PNC. It necessitates the production and distribution of a new consistency of the event as it is expressed in words and attributed to bodies. On the other hand, it is not certain that the non-sense of paradox is sufficient to ground the genetic pretences of logic. The well-articulated and well-formed nonsense of Carroll is little more than an 'ideal game', a pastime speculation with little real consequence. It pales in comparison with the nonsense of Artaud, in whose work the difference between corporeal depth and incorporeal surface breaks down, such that words lose their syntax and regress to the inarticulate language of sighs and cries. Here the PSR is immediately confronted not only with inexplicable and incomprehensible nonsense (the unintelligible which cannot but be made intelligible), but first of all with insupportable and intolerable sensations (the insensible which cannot but be sensed). Should we not reserve the concept of speculation only for this irrational and truly risky genesis in which a corporeal affect (the voice) learns to rise up again and produce its own superficial effect, an aberrant becoming expressed in a linguistic act unlimited by the actions and passions in the depth of bodies?

Language and being: Univocity

What Artaud demonstrates is that thought can disintegrate into madness but that it is nonetheless possible to endure this process of disintegration.

His screams do not belong to the world of schizophrenia only, but also reveal a power of the unthought in thought, 'that schizophrenia in principle' of the body without organs in which the continuous demolition of the body and reason is speculatively transformed even if its surface remains partial and cracked. Beyond the empirical ego of thought and speech, which is hardly put to the test by Carroll and thus continues to mediate between words and things, Artaud discovers the fractured subject of the thinker whose faculty of thought is raised to its transcendental exercise by 'an infinite nonself within the finite self'.[34] Only at this point, where the death drive acquires its 'speculative form' and produces the involuntary and unconscious genesis of thinking within thought, do we discover a real becoming, whence '[w]e would not give a page of Artaud for all of Carroll'.[35] Moreover, the very impunity of his comparison between Carroll and Artaud, surface and depth, reveals that Deleuze himself inhabits none of the two dimensions of nonsense and instead still thinks by proxy rather than by right.[36]

Notwithstanding Deleuze's own shame of being a philosopher, however, the interest of *The Logic of Sense* is not just to account for the genesis of good and common sense from non-sense, as they consist only of the constant factual 'reeffectuation' of a present sense (e.g. the representational reason of psychoanalysis, for which bodies and language share the same structure of symptoms). By showing that the transcendental distribution of words and things does not resemble the empirical content of propositional language, Deleuze's aim is to arrive at 'the speculative univocity of being and language', in other words, the immanence of body and thought or of practice and speculation.[37] Their relation is univocal as soon as we understand language as pure being, that is, as pure event (*eventum tantum*), and it is speculative, because univocity is effectuated only when it is no longer limited by any present state of affairs in depth but constitutes an infinite or absolute becoming. The task of philosophy is not to legitimate the established image of thought, but to become worthy of the potentialities of the event and all that it puts at risk. Thus in order to acquire the right to 'speak the event' and determine and distribute its virtual consistency, its concepts must express a real movement of the ground at the surface ('intensity') and not merely remain a linguistic surface effect.[38] Only with Artaud does philosophy really become capable of going beyond the anticipation of current practice and of 'countereffectuating' the present state of the world and the established image of thought. Counteractualization is the highest power of the PSR, because it enables the PSR to finally turn against the PNC. It is here that the PSR marks the reversal of the traditional sense of ontology, such that we move not only from depth to surface (dynamic genesis), but also from surface to depth (static genesis), that is, from thought to being and from effect to quasicausality.[39] Thus life's pathological intensities constitute both the origin of sense or onto-logy and the risks of a speculative life which converts organic life into a spiritual and critical force. Materialism does not mean the priority of the body over thought, but the expressive power of the body to pass from silence to the production of sense beyond the established image of thought: being as voice and vital clamour.[40]

If *The Logic of Sense* still marks an impasse, this is because it is not clear if genesis is due to a paralogical quasicause or due to a real intensity. Artaud's schizophrenia is the power of thought, but Carroll's perversion is its exercise in thought. Only perversion seems capable of delivering thought from the impotence in which it always risks falling back. It is the ideal double of schizophrenia.[41] Simultaneously, *Difference and Repetition* had already described in 1968 the genesis of thought from the body's vicissitudes: 'on the path which leads to that which is to be thought, all begins with sensibility'.[42] Deleuze's subsequent books, both with and without Félix Guattari, therefore move the whole concept of becoming from the surface-depth division to that of intensities on the body without organs. 'Artaud will belong at the ground of our language, and not at its rupture.'[43] Language and philosophy are no longer based on the primacy of sense (structure and genesis) but on a radicalized pragmatism or functionalism in which language no longer says anything but has asignifying usages which make it all the more real. From here on, the concept of speculation disappears entirely from Deleuze's work: materialism ceases to be a speculative idea and becomes a *practice*.

Reason and ground: Immanence

A radical enactivism does not exclude a speculative orientation, even if it is the practical aspect that contains the ultimate meaning – or rather, sense – of speculation. Rather than delegitimizing speculative propositions or limiting his relevance for the contemporary 'speculative turn', Deleuze's practical turn should instead be understood as the condition of a new sense of speculation based on a new use of the PSR. 'The only possible theory', he writes, 'is a theory of practice.'[44]

Reminiscent of Heidegger's critique of ontotheology, Meillassoux argues that dogmatic metaphysics is based on the ontological argument and culminates in the PSR.[45] But whereas Heidegger continued to believe in strong ties between thought and being, or reason and ground, such that he saw an analytical necessity binding philosophy to Greece as sufficient ground for its identity even if this origin contained its own groundlessness, Meillassoux argues that the only legitimate intuition philosophy has of being is that of a hyperchaos or complete groundlessness (as well as the PNC and the necessity for the existence of something). With the deduction of the 'principle of factiality' – the necessity of facticity or historicity – he transforms Heidegger's strong correlationism into its opposite: the absence of any correlation between thinking and being.[46] As a consequence, Meillassoux sees only two options: sheer contingency or sheer necessity.[47] But in this way, does he not reinstal the metaphysical opposition par excellence, an opposition made possible by a strange transcendence of thought disconnected from all territory?

If Heidegger and Meillassoux circle around each other, the one emphasizing the transcendence of being and the other the transcendence of thought, then perhaps Deleuze teaches us how to break the circle (which is only ever that of theory) and subject it to immanent practice. When Deleuze and Guattari point out in *What is Philosophy?* that any synthesis of ground and reason remains contingent and is not valid for every age, they accept a disjunctive synthesis between thought and being and thus a modified version of the PSR – not in the epistemological sense of Graham Harman, who has recently pleaded for loose or accidental ties between thinking and being based on a return to weak (Kantian) correlationism and the necessary existence of the 'thing in itself', but in the pragmatist or empiricist sense of Leibnizian philosophy. The function of the PSR in Leibniz is to mediate or follow the aberrant movements of contingency and excavate their irrational logic. For as soon as we leave the domain of good and common sense ruled by the PNC, Meillassoux's intellectual intuition of the necessity of contingency becomes trivial. For contingency, if it is real, implies the necessary absence of all reason. Or as Mallarmé says: nothing rather than something. But, as we have seen in Deleuze's deduction of madness as the condition for reason, the necessary absence of all reason is also the transcendental problem of reason, its very motivation and limit, where we pass from exclusive disjunction under the auspices of the PNC to inclusive disjunction under the auspices of the PSR. Contingency or difference is thus the Leibnizian name for the immanence of the ground to the groundless, the virtual Idea, and the PSR is the principle of its distribution on a plane of organization (Leibniz) or consistency (Deleuze). If being (difference) is both ground and abyss, it is precisely what makes the movement of reason (repetition) necessary and real. Sense must be made; it is never given. Its logic is based on AND and not on IS. The immanence of speculative and practical philosophy in Leibniz (and his followers from Baumgarten and Herder to Whitehead and Deleuze) means that the Idea always remains vague and morphic, an abyssal flashing of obscure but distinct forces, among which thought bears an immanent potency of selection and integration. Again, rationalism and empiricism are less opposed than some speculative realists like to think. The groundless ground is neither a known unknown nor an unknown unknown, but a felt unknown. Reason is always already involved in the depth of an unconscious and infinite murmuring. The conceived combination, the finite and clear but confused explication of a nontotalizable, compossible world on the surface, is a living hypothesis that emerges from, and feeds back into, implicitly felt virtualities: '*concepts* are inseparable from *affects*, i.e. from the powerful effects they exert on our life, and *percepts*, i.e. the new ways of seeing or perceiving they provoke in us'.[48]

Thought and body: Materialism

The immanence or univocity of thinking and being means that difference both binds and separates them, both grounds and ungrounds them. Between them there is only the disjunctive synthesis of an 'instantaneous exchange' or 'weaving'.[49] Thought relates to being like a sealed car speeding down a dark highway, while being relates to thought like a receding horizon.[50] Thus while thought's relationships to being remain extrinsic to being itself, they define the intrinsic genesis of the thinker for her- or himself.[51] For this reason, the 'logic of sensation' is not based on impressions of sense perception, but rather on immediate impressions of self-perception. Similarly, the nonsense word is the only type of word by which language expresses both itself and its sense. In both cases, genesis is a matter of 'folding' or 'autoaffection'. The fold is the sign of a pragmatics of a finite thought that stays immanent to being because it retains the movement of the infinite to which it gives consistency, yet at the same time remains radically different from it.[52] With Deleuze no less than with Leibniz or Spinoza, the fold is the autopositing of the infinite. It is what makes the infinite actual: infinity in action, or, practical philosophy.

If we subscribe to Meillassoux's understanding of materialism, namely the lack of all codetermination between being and thought, then any philosophy that upholds their equality and reversibility – indeed, any naturalist philosophy – is not materialist. Pure immanence, moreover, is immanent only to itself and therefore does not make thought immanent to the body. There are nonetheless reasons for calling Deleuze a materialist. If the milieu exterior to thought is teeming with indeterminate forces and their differential relations that constitute matter (the groundless ground), while thought is the distribution and determination of their forms (reason as the return of active forces), then the latter needs the body as determinable content (passive material of expression). At the interface between forces and thought, the body as capacity of affecting and being affected enables a real experience of the Outside of thought (ungrounding) all the while this Outside is folded into thought and made relative to its grounding movement.[53] When the individual body cracks up, all sorts of nonhuman forces rise up to its crystalline surface, such that the consistency of our immediate relations to the environment may be redistributed. The body is thus the very site of the fold where thinking and being coarticulate to produce a plane of immanence. Between order and chaos, it is the actual limit that enables thought to believe in its exterior milieu, in other words, its virtual potential of counteractualization.[54] From Spinoza to Bergson to Deleuze, the body is the foundation or existential territory of the thinkable and the symptom of that which can only be thought. Together, thought and the body constitute a psychophysics of being, the double becoming of being as always already thought-being.[55]

The body without organs, then, is the fold of the thought of the Outside. Speculative philosophy has nothing to do with some fundamental metaphysical truth about matter, but with the expressive activity of/on the body without organs when it passes from silence to the production of sense, in other words, when philosophy begins to matter and have effects. The difference between thought and body, in other words, is a matter of *how* one thinks, not of *what* one thinks. The body without organs is the ordeal of the soul: it is not just vibrant matter but also a passionate manner. Deleuze challenges philosophy to take an authentic stance to its grounding, to enact its own orientation in thought and thus learn to speak by right, even if it remains only the logical double external to the ground.

Whereas the question of authenticity is usually interpreted as a modern, Cartesian question (How do I relate to...?), this Ptolemaic reflex is now subject to a Copernican revolution that reorients the sense of our propositions or statements towards their pragmatic effect on the world. "'Give me a body then': this is the formula of philosophical reversal."[56] This is a turn from realism to constructivism. However, it is so not because it makes everything relative to us, but because it demands us to make our reasons relevant for the ground. Hence the mantra of Deleuzian speculation: 'we do not yet know what a body can do'. The ordeal of grounding forces us to take into consideration thought itself as a sense-effect producing a virtual force among other actual forces. It is an ascesis that liberates the implied intensity of thinking (a life) from representation and crystallizes it with what it is not. Beyond our individual reasons, we discover a communal ground or body politic that obtains outside the speculative act that intervenes in it. How to inhabit your body or participate in that of others? The habitat is never a natural given, but always constructed in its continuity and variation by the contemporary independent ways of inhabiting it.

Elasticity and plasticity: The Keplerian revolution

How to conceive of these ethical and political folds between thinking and being outside factuality or throwness? From the legislative image of thought to that of geopolitics, the critical moment for speculative philosophy is the moment when existing relations between thought and being are ruptured and history becomes disoriented. These relations can vary on a scale of strength from possibility to probability, but in each case, they describe the mode in which the body relates to that groundless or horizonless milieu that we have previously termed the speculative Idea.[57] From the perspective of its relations, the body has neither inside nor outside. Rather, it is the power or potential of accidental becoming: *plasticity*. What a body is capable of depends on its interstices, even if no interstice has in itself the power to cause anything. It is in its interstices that the ground rises up to the surface and subjects the body to a metamorphosis under the constraint of the unforeseeable. Interstices are ideas: they generate new questions and preclude any general response. Where does an interstice stop? Where does one encounter the indifference of the body to what pushes through it? There is no general response. But while it is up to thought to determine (i.e. provide the principle for) how the body will actually become, the body continues to condition the act. For as Spinoza explains his version of the PSR, not every thought has an equal right: 'if, for example, I say that I have the right to do whatever I like with this table, I am hardly likely to mean that I have the right to make this table eat grass'.[58] Thought, in other words, is the faculty of relations, just as potentiality lies in the interstices between what something is made of and what it actually does. All speculation implies a willingness to learn and experiment with the body and its interstices: *elasticity*, or the power to 'double the outside with a coextensive inside'.[59] As a power of contraction and dilation, elasticity is the weak tie whereby an exterior force is folded over by an interior resistance or passivity such that some kind of continuity is returned to a dynamic field of discontinuity. If plasticity describes the transformability of being, elasticity describes the flexibility of the surface of sense or the Artaudian athleticism of thought in relation to the nonsense it encounters. Taken together, elasticity and plasticity define the powers of folding by which thinking develops being (asymmetrically producing its own version of the outside) while being (the intensity which forces thinking) remains enveloped in thinking.

Speculative thought derives its legitimacy from a cultivation of interstices.[60] Its aim is to turn strong links between thought and body into weak links and demand for sufficient reason where previously there was only necessity. Like the Lucretian void, interstices reveal the body's composedness, its synthetic constructedness and its discontinuous or transfinite relations to other bodies in the succession of bodies. The risk of a breakdown of the body is not the total loss of reason; on the contrary, it is thought's detachment from the groundless ground, its incapacity to be affected by the Outside. Plasticity is therefore a potential for thought, but it is not its model.[61] With the discovery of the strength of weak links, the ultimate question for speculative thought becomes: How to become more elastic in order for the possible (distinguished from the probable, the repression of interstices) to fill us up? How to turn thought from mere speculation on the void into a mediator between intensities? How to raise our conditions of thought to the nth power?

For Deleuze, the passage of the PSR from conditioning to genesis and the asymmetry between right and fact constitutes the Copernican revolution of transcendental philosophy.[62] Even Spinoza's version of the PSR based on the exclusion of all contingency becomes subject to the 'principle of contingent reason' of a 'Copernican revolution', such that identity no longer comes first and substance is made to reverse around its modes.[63] However, because Deleuze upholds the inseparability of thought and being, which is not to be confused with a functional dependence, perhaps we should indeed not speak of a Copernican revolution, as Meillassoux has suggested. Instead, the production of weak links in a bipolar system of thought-being reminds us more of what Michel Serres has called a 'Keplerian revolution', as Kepler was the first, in the history of modern science, to break with the conviction of the unity between the powers of reason and the reasons of the world.⁶⁴ Contrary to what Meillassoux calls 'Galileism', which still accepts as self-evident that to the regular and eternal movement of the planets there should correspond the geometrical figure of perfection, the circle, Kepler divested mathematics of this power of a priori rational judgement and used it instead as an empirical tool, thereby arriving at a figure that was for him just one among others, the ellipse. By stretching the circle, Isabelle Stengers writes, he speculated 'on the *relevance* of mathematics to describe the world of phenomena, against the *power* of mathematics to judge this world in the name of a normative ideal'.⁶⁵

From the perspective of classical rationalism, this stretching of the circle can easily be explained – as Stengers does – as a break with the PSR. From the perspective of transcendental empiricism, however, the circle of sufficient reason moving from ground to grounded has always been a 'tortuous circle', a rendering of reason without this rendering itself being founded on stable grounds.⁶⁶ In the Keplerian image of critique, a point of view which 'has never been modern', the essence of speculative thought is that 'wisdom functions elliptically'.⁶⁷ Precisely to the extent that the PSR integrates difference qua contingency, empiricism and rationalism are no longer opposed, but reciprocally reinvent one another through their inclusive disjunction. The ellipse is, in other words, the image of a concrete speculative thought that distributes the world according to its interstices and contributes itself to it by the eternal return of feedback loops.

Notes

1. Quentin Meillassoux, *After Finitude. An Essay on the Necessity of Contingency*, trans. Ray Brassier (London: Continuum, 2008), p. 47.

2. Friedrich Nietzsche, *The Gay Science*, trans. Josephine Naukhoff, ed. Bernard Williams (Cambridge: Cambridge University Press), §V:344.

3. Gilles Deleuze, *Nietzsche and Philosophy*, trans. Hugh Tomlinson (New York: Columbia University Press, 1983), p. 89.

4. Deleuze follows Heidegger in tracing the PSR beyond the principle of identity and the renunciation (*fondre*) of any foundational ground (*fond*), but instead of plunging into the abyss of ontological (in)difference (there is nothing outside the correlation of thinking and being), he discovers, through Bergson, a moving depth or chaosmos of productive differences (duration). See Sjoerd van Tuinen, 'Difference and Speculation. Heidegger, Meillassoux and Deleuze on Sufficient Reason', in Alain Beaulieu, Edward Kazarian and Julia Sushytska (eds), *Deleuze and Metaphysics* (Lanham, MD: Lexington Books, 2014).

5. Matthijs Kouw and Sjoerd van Tuinen, 'Blinded by Science? Speculative Realism and Speculative Constructivism', in Anna Longo and Sarah De Sanctis (eds), *Breaking the Spell. Philosophy in Pursuit of the Real* (Milan: Mimesis, 2015).
6. Gilles Deleuze, *The Logic of Sense*, trans. Mark Lester and Charles Stivale (London: Continuum, 1990), p. 267.
7. Ibid., p. 278.
8. Ibid., pp. 266-8, 274-7.
9. Gilles Deleuze, *Spinoza Practical Philosophy*, trans. Robert Hurley (San Francisco: City Lights Books, 1988), pp. 28-9; Gilles Deleuze, *Expressionism in Philosophy: Spinoza*, trans. Martin Joughin (New York: Zone Books, 1997), p. 272.
10. Deleuze, *Expressionism*, pp. 287-8, 281.
11. Deleuze, *Nietzsche*, pp. 9-10.
12. Ibid., p. 190.
13. Gilles Deleuze, *Difference and Repetition*, trans. Paul Patton (New York: Continuum, 2001), p. 36.
14. Ibid., p. 42.
15. Deleuze, *Nietzsche*, pp. 48, 68.
16. Deleuze, *Difference and Repetition*, p. 38.
17. Levi R. Bryant, 'The Ontic Principle: Outline of an Object-Oriented Ontology', in Levi R. Bryant, Nick Srnicek and Graham Harman (eds), *The Speculative Turn: Continental Materialism and Realism* (Melbourne: re.press, 2011), p. 266.
18. Meillassoux, *After Finitude*, p. 71.
19. Quentin Meillassoux, 'The Immanence of the World Beyond', in Connor Cunningham and Peter Candler (eds), *The Grandeur of Reason: Religion, Tradition, and Universalism* (London: SCM Press, 2010), pp. 444-78.
20. On the intimate relation between belief and speculative rationality, see Sjoerd van Tuinen, 'Speculating with Established Sentiments. The Empiricist Conversion and the Problem of *Ressentiment*', in *Theory, Culture and Society* (forthcoming).
21. Gilbert Simondon, *L'individuation à la lumière des notions de forme et d'information* (Grenoble: Jérôme Millon, 2005).
22. Deleuze, *Nietzsche*, p. 93.
23. On *irraison*, see Meillassoux, *After Finitude*, p. 60. The reclamation of a rational divine redemption is presented in Quentin Meillassoux, 'Spectral Dilemma', trans. Robin Mackay, in Robin Mackay (ed.), *Collapse IV: Concept Horror* (Falmouth: Urbanomic, 2008), pp. 408-99. On the joy of unfounding or deterritorialization, see Deleuze, *Logic of Sense*, p. 263.
24. Deleuze, *Difference and Repetition*, p. 352.

25. David Lapoujade, *Deleuze, les mouvements aberrants* (Paris: Éditions de Minuit, 2014), p. 27.
26. Deleuze, *Logic of Sense*, pp. 260–6.
27. Deleuze, *Difference and Repetition*, p. 57.
28. Ibid., p. 154.
29. Gilles Deleuze, *The Fold. Leibniz and the Baroque*, trans. Tom Conley (Minneapolis: University of Minnesota Press, 1993), p. 23. On the philosopher-legislator, see Deleuze, *Nietzsche*, p. 91.
30. The speculative and the practical are discussed by Deleuze as the two aspects of structuralism. They do not correspond to the transcendental and the empirical, but to the virtual and the actual, which communicate in a 'mutation point [that] defines a praxis, or rather the very site where praxis must take hold' (Gilles Deleuze, 'How Do We Recognize Structuralism', in David Lapoujade (ed.), *Desert Islands and Other Texts, 1953–1974*, trans. Mike Taormina (Los Angeles: Semiotext(e), 2004), p. 191). On the search for grounds as a dialectical problem, see Deleuze, *Difference and Repetition*, p. 160: 'Whereas Analytics gives us the means to solve a problem already given, or to respond to a question, Dialectics shows how to pose a question legitimately.'
31. Deleuze, *Desert Islands*, pp. 15–19.
32. Lapoujade, *Deleuze*, p. 13.
33. Deleuze's empiricist logic, Lapoujade shows, is not a philosophy of ordinary man and the regularity of association of ideas or the regulation of the passions: habits and norms. Instead, it is a superior or transcendental empiricism in which only the extreme cases count. This is why Deleuze never draws on examples from ordinary life, but only on the aberrant movements of those who legitimately reveal the illegitimacy of all foundations (*Deleuze*, pp. 14, 49). But in this movement of singularization, Deleuze simultaneously passes from law to politics, or from geophilosophy to geopolitics. By giving a right to all the minoritarian voices, beyond the groundless foundations of capitalism, he raises the question of Grand Politics: who has the right to occupy the earth? And who has the right to raise and answer the question, what is (speculative) philosophy?
34. Deleuze, *Difference and Repetition*, p. 58. He later adds that 'questions and problems are not speculative acts, and as such completely provisional and indicative of the momentary ignorance of an empirical subject. On the contrary, they are the living acts of the unconscious, investing special objectivities and destined to survive in the provisional and partial state characteristic of answers and solutions' (ibid., p. 106).
35. Ibid., p. 93. On the 'speculative form' of the death drive, see Deleuze, *Logic of Sense*, pp. 209, 238–40.
36. Deleuze, *Logic of Sense*, p. 114.
37. Ibid., p. 248.

38. On the right to speak the event, see Gilles Deleuze and Félix Guattari, *What is Philosophy?*, trans. Hugh Tomlinson and Graham Burchell (London: Verso, 1994), p. 21.

39. A cause is not a reason. The PSR claims that everything that happens, including causation in empirical time (*Chronos*), has a reason. While it is true that everything is an effect, not everything therefore necessarily has a cause. The actual can always be understood as an indeterminate, intensely present yet enigmatic process of emergence in which effects are events with an intrinsic value (to the extent that they belong to the transcendental time of *Aion*) and cause and effect can exchange places. Given a certain situation, a singularity may always be unfolding amid ordinary activity and eventually turn against the laws that governed it. Rendering the reflective (as opposed to regressive) logic or sense of such an event is necessarily a speculative or fictional project, even if fiction now becomes the form of a real – that is genetic and synthetic (as opposed to analytical) – explanation, a power of the false: 'starting from the effect we determine the cause, *even if through a "fiction"*, as the *sufficient reason* of all the properties we conceive the effect to possess' (Deleuze, *Expressionism*, pp. 134, 137). Besides Spinoza, Schelling and Bergson are necessary parts of this reverse ontology of the PSR. For all of them, the eternal insistence of the ground or the past of existence in whatever presently exists explains why yearning, imagining and speculation can have material effects all the while history is necessarily contingent.

40. Deleuze, *Difference and Repetition*, p. 35.

41. Lapoujade, *Deleuze*, pp. 129–30.

42. Deleuze, *Difference and Repetition*, p. 144.

43. Gilles Deleuze and Félix Guattari, *Anti-Oedipus. Capitalism and Schizophrenia*, trans. Robert Hurley, Mark Seem and Helen R. Lane (London: Continuum, 2003), p. 157.

44. Gilles Deleuze, *Empiricism and Subjectivity: An Essay on Hume's Theory of Human Nature*, trans. Constantin V. Boundas (New York: Columbia University Press, 1991), pp. 32–3.

45. Meillassoux, *After Finitude*, p. 33.

46. Ibid., p. 80 on the necessity of facticity or historicity.

47. In his recent criticism of Meillassoux, Graham Harman equates Meillassoux's understanding of the PSR to that of Leibniz, for whom sufficient reason would come down to sheer determinism. In his own account, by contrast, Harman argues that 'what is really most interesting about the principle of sufficient reason is that it allows for a looser connection between things than ironclad necessity, and a tighter connection than absolute contingency'. Yet this is also, precisely, the way in which Leibniz himself explains the PSR. See van Tuinen, 'Difference and Speculation'.

48. Gilles Deleuze, *Two Regimes of Madness: Texts and Interviews 1975–1995*, trans. Ames Hodges and Mike Taormina (Cambridge, MA: MIT Press, 2006), p. 238.

49. Deleuze and Guattari, *What is Philosophy?*, p. 38.
50. Deleuze, *The Fold*, p. 137.
51. According to Harman, Deleuze 'rudely airbrushed' Leibniz's Aristotelianism of essences in order to replace it with a mannerism that defines individuals only by their modal, i.e. external relations; see Graham Harman, *The Quadruple Object* (Winchester: Zero Books, 2011), p. 17. While manners are indeed relata external to the matter they synthesize, Deleuze is however clear that they are internal to the soul (essence) that contemplates them. It is precisely through this synthetic function of the soul that Deleuze follows Leibniz's *New Essays* in reconciling rationalism with Lockean empiricism. See Deleuze, *The Fold*, p. 4.
52. Deleuze and Guattari, *What is Philosophy?*, p. 38.
53. Guillaume Collet, 'Bodies-Language: Immanence in Gilles Deleuze's *Foucault*', in K. D. Martin and A.-C. Drews (eds), *Inside. Outside. Other. The Body in the Work of Gilles Deleuze and Michel Foucault* (Bielefeld: Transcript Verlag, forthcoming).
54. See Gilles Deleuze, *Cinema 2: The Time-Image*, trans. Hugh Tomlinson and Robert Caleta (Minneapolis: University of Minnesota Press, 1989), p. 173: 'We must believe in the body, but as in the germ of life, the seed which splits open the paving-stones, which has been preserved and lives on in the holy shroud or the mummy's bandages, and which bears witness to life.'
55. On the psychophysics of being, see Deleuze, *The Fold*, p. 96.
56. Deleuze, *Cinema 2*, p. 189.
57. Gilles Deleuze and Félix Guattari, *A Thousand Plateaus*, trans. Brian Massumi (Minneapolis: University of Minnesota Press, 1987), p. 469.
58. Baruch Spinoza, 'Tractatus Politicus', §IV.4, in *The Complete Works*, trans. Samuel Shirley (Indianapolis: Hackett), p. 697.
59. Gilles Deleuze, *Foucault*, trans. Seán Hand (Minneapolis: University of Minnesota Press, 1988), p. 118.
60. See Daniel W. Smith, 'Concepts and Creation', in Rosi Braidoitti and Patricia Pisters (eds), *Revisiting Normativity with Deleuze* (London: Bloomsbury, 2012), pp. 144–5: 'If being produces the singular under conditions that constantly reduce it to the regular or the ordinary, then the task of creation amounts to a resistance against its established image in order to extract singularities that it extends into one another.'
61. See Catherine Malabou, *Avant Demain. Epigénèse et Rationalité* (Paris: PUF, 2014), chapter thirteen. For a critique of Catherine Malabou's concept of plasticity, see Sjoerd van Tuinen, 'Elasticity and Plasticity: Operable Man and the Crisis of Repetition', in Andrej Radman and Heidi Sohn (eds), *Critical and Clinical Cartographies: Embodiment / Technology / Care / Design* (Rotterdam: nai010 Publishers, forthcoming).
62. Deleuze, *Difference and Repetition*, p. 162.
63. Ibid., pp. 50, 377.

64. For Serres, the Keplerian revolution describes 'the planets as circulating in an elliptical orbit with two centres – the sun, brilliant and fiery, and a second, dark one that is never spoken about. Indeed, knowledge has two centres; by its gigantic movement the Earth shows us the double pole.' See Michel Serres and Bruno Latour, *Conversations on Science, Culture and Time*, trans. Roxanne Lapidus (Ann Arbor: University of Michigan Press, 1995), pp. 162, 185.
65. Isabelle Stengers, *Power and Invention: Situating Science*, trans. Paul Baines (Minneapolis: University of Minnesota Press, 1997), p. 24.
66. Deleuze, *Difference and Repetition*, p. 128.
67. Serres and Latour, *Conversations*, p. 185.

PART II
LANGUAGES OF SPECULATION

CHAPTER 5
ITERATION, REITERATION, REPETITION: A SPECULATIVE ANALYSIS OF THE SIGN DEVOID OF MEANING

Quentin Meillassoux

Translated by Robin Mackay and Moritz Gansen

Correlation and subjectalism

For several years now, my principal concern has been the capacities of thought: What exactly can thought do?[1] The apparently classical thesis that I put forward comes down to saying that thought is capable of the 'absolute', capable of producing something like 'eternal truths', and all this despite the various destructions and deconstructions that all traditional metaphysics have undergone over the last century and a half. I began to develop this position in 2006 in *After Finitude*, in a form which, to my mind, made possible an original reactivation of materialism; and it is this investigation that I would like to continue to pursue here.[2]

Let us first recall the strategy I followed in order to try to assert the 'absolutizing' capacity of thought: My idea was to propose the most economical and most rigorous possible model of deabsolutization. Indeed, a profusion of critiques have been directed against philosophy's claim to the absolute, but it seemed to me that these critiques all rested upon core arguments that could be distilled into a general model. I cannot claim to reconstitute the richness and complexity of these various antiabsolutisms, but my hope was to develop an adversary rigorous enough that any argument capable of refuting this model objector would also then be capable of refuting any historically existing critique.

I thus forged a typical antiabsolutism which I called 'correlationism', reducing it down to two arguments called the *correlational circle* and *correlational facticity*.

I will briefly review them in this order, which is the only logical order in which to do so.

If metaphysical materialism seemed fundamentally untenable since Berkeley, this is for a reason perhaps as simple as it is decisive.[3] The materialist seems always to commit a 'formulatory contradiction' when he claims to know a reality independent of his thought, since the reality of which he speaks is precisely one that is given him to be thought.[4] When I claim to accede to a thing in itself, I accede in truth only to a datum, from which I cannot abstract the fact that it is strictly correlated to the access I have to it, and which has no conceivable meaning outside of this access. If I say or simply think (formulate to myself) that something exists absolutely, that is to say independently of me (the *ab-solutus* is first of all the separate, the non-relative), then this is a thought content linked to the speech and/or thought I have just produced. In this sense, it seems pointless to ask what things are, since no mind can ever apprehend them.

So by correlationism I mean, in a first approximation, any philosophy that maintains the impossibility of acceding, through thought, to a being *independent* of thought. According to this type of philosophy, we never have access to any intended thing (understood in the most general sense, not necessarily in the phenomenological sense) that is not always-already correlated to an 'act of thinking' (understood, again, in the most general sense). Consequently, correlationism posits, against all materialism, that thought can never *escape from itself* so as to accede to a world not yet affected by our subjective modes of apprehension.

I thus call the 'correlational circle' the argument that consists in vindicating that vicious circle, formulatory in essence, which is inherent to any materialism that posits the absolute existence of a reality outside of all representation. The contradiction takes place not between one sentence and another (between two meaning-contents), but between a sentence and its formulation, which is not a second sentence, but just the actualization of the first sentence. Let us suppose that on a blackboard there is the sentence: 'I have access to an absolute independent of the thought that I have of it'. This sentence, not formulated, is no more contradictory than the sentence 'I do not exist' written on the same blackboard but not formulated by anyone. Indeed, in both cases, there is no internal, logical contradiction between the sentences, as there would be in the sentence 'I exist and I do not exist', which is structurally contradictory whether one formulates it or not. Just as the truth of the sentence 'I do not exist' only collapses on condition that it is formulated by someone, so the 'realist' sentence 'I accede to a nonthought reality' only collapses if it is effectively thought – that is, if the 'nonthought' as such is produced as its precise contrary: as a content that is effectively thought, by an intentional act.

Logical contradiction takes place between two *logoi*: 'I exist' and 'I do not exist'. Formulatory contradiction takes place between one single *logos* and its effectuation, which is not a second *logos*. It is not literally logical in essence, because the *logos* is not present in both terms of the opposition. This time we are dealing with an inconsistency between two heterogeneous terms: a sentence, which in itself could subsist without being enacted (in the form of an inert writing); and an act that is itself not a new sentence, for if, to formulate – or enunciate – a sentence, I had to formulate or enunciate it at the same time as a second sentence, then all my speech would echo like a cacophony in which it would seem that I cut myself off every time I spoke.

It seems that this argument of the formulatory contradiction is the final deadlock in which any materialism so defined will always end up: How can we claim to think what is when there is no thought, without seeing the manifest formulatory contradiction that this involves? Correlation itself can be conceived in many ways: subject-object, consciousness-given, noetico-noematic correlate, being-in-the-world, language-reference, etc. But in each case, correlation will be posited as a primordial fact rendering null and void the belief in the thinkability of an 'in itself' that transcends all thought.

Correlationism cannot however rest upon this one decision *alone* – at least if it is to respond to the definition I have given: namely, that of an enterprise of the deabsolutization of thought. Although the correlational circle suffices to disqualify the materialist absolute, it does not suffice to disqualify every form of absolute, nor every form of realism. There is, as we well know, a nonmaterialist form of absolutism, whose principle consists no longer in claiming to think a noncorrelational absolute, but in making correlation *itself* the absolute as such.

Before continuing, let us propose at this point a clear denomination of the positions in play. I call 'correlationism' any form of deabsolutization of thought that, to obtain its ends, argues for the enclosure of thought into itself, and for its subsequent inability to attain an absolute outside of itself. I call 'speculative' any philosophy that claims, on the contrary, to attain such an absolute. I call 'metaphysical' any philosophy which, on top of maintaining, like speculative philosophy, the thinkability of the absolute, does so with the aid of some use of the Principle of Sufficient Reason.[5] The Principle of Sufficient Reason always consists in establishing that things *must be* thus rather than otherwise. Every philosophy whose absolute is presented in the form of modally privileged beings or modes of being, insofar as they are given as necessary, is a metaphysics. A metaphysics might establish that atoms or the void are necessary (rather than aggregates of atoms, or incorporeal, fictive gods). It might just as well establish that only a perfect God is absolutely necessary, or on the contrary that only a Becoming reigns perpetually over all things. The metaphysical mode of the absolute, always of the order of being-thus (where *this* rather than *that* is necessary), I call *absolutism*. I distinguish this from the speculative approach – my own approach – which, as we shall see, posits an absolute that does not depend on the Principle of Sufficient Reason, a position that I call *absolutory (absolutoire)* rather than *absolutist*. This nonabsolutist absolute will no longer take the form of a necessary being (for example God) or of a necessary mode of being (for example becoming), but that of the contingency of all beings and all modes of being – the corollary of which will be a rationality freed from the Principle of Sufficient Reason, and which therefore maintains that there is no reason for anything to be as it is rather than otherwise.

We thus have two possibilities for opposing correlationism: an *absolutist metaphysics* and an *absolutory speculation*. But the second position is not the one that was, in previous centuries, opposed to correlationism. Instead, correlationism has been combatted by a metaphysical adversary, but not just any type of metaphysics. Two major possibilities of metaphysical opposition to correlationism were possible in principle but the first one has, as we have said, been rendered impossible from the outset by the correlational circle: metaphysical materialism. I call 'materialism' any thought that accedes to an absolute that is at once external to thought and *in itself devoid of all subjectivity*. For example, Epicureanism is a materialism, insofar as it claims to accede to the absolute reality of atoms and the void, where the latter are not characterized by any subjective – thinking, psychological, egoic, sensible or vital – traits. This type of position, as we have said above, was destroyed by the circle, since the subjectivity denied in the absolute always resurfaces in the thought of the materialist who exposes its attributes. It is thus not this kind of adversary – this kind of metaphysics – that has been able to seem a threat to correlationism, but an entirely other type which, far from denying the subjectivity in the absolute, makes it an intrinsic characteristic of the absolute.

There is a second form of absolutism, this time *non*materialist: this absolutism is historically the only one to have survived the correlationist critique, for it consisted not in disputing the enclosure of thought into itself, but in confirming it in the name of the absoluteness of thought itself (or of certain remarkable traits of thought). The thesis consisted in interpreting the enclosure of thought unto itself not as a symptom of its finitude, but as a consequence of its ontological necessity. If thought cannot exit from itself this is not because it runs up against its gnoseological limits, but because it discovers a form of existence that is intrinsically necessary: *the subjective*. Of course, the most elementary form of this belief would be solipsism: I can believe that the absolute subjectivity is my subjectivity, as a psychological individual, and dream that I am alone in the world. But in the history of philosophy, no one has ever sincerely taken this path, and the metaphysical reply to correlationism consisted in absolutizing the subjective in general – according to a transindividual modality in which every human, and indeed every living or inorganic being, participates at its proper level. This absolutism has taken various forms, leading each time to the absolutization of one or several determinate forms of subjectivity, if not of the subject in its totality. It has been possible to absolutize perception (Berkeley, where the perceptions of the mind do not confront any perceived matter since they are themselves the matter of the perceived), sensation (Maupertius's and Diderot's hylozoism),[6] reason (Hegelian idealism), will (Schopenhauer), wills plural, in their mutual conflict (Nietzsche's will to power), freedom (the Bergson of *Creative Evolution*, where the very genesis of space from duration is the analogue of a liberty which, contracting from its past, relaxes in a dreamlike scattering of the self),[7] the self in its initial germinal state (Deleuze's 'passive I' or 'larval subject' in *Difference and Repetition*),[8] and so on. There was thus a proliferation of subjectivizations of the real, sometimes in conflict with each other, in particular between the vitalist pole (from hylozoism to Deleuze and perspectivism, via Nietzsche and Bergson) and the idealist pole (dominated by Hegel). But such conflicts disguised *a fundamental agreement*: that after Berkeley, there could be no question of returning to the totally asubjective reality of Epicurean materialism.

What we might call 'The Era of the Correlate, or of Correlation', opened up by Berkeley – and which, in my opinion, continues to dominate Continental philosophy today – can thus be described as consisting in *two opposite movements* in regard to the absolute: on the one hand, correlationism, which, in the form of scepticism (especially), transcendentalism, phenomenology or postmodernism has denied thought all access to the absolute. And on the other hand, a new metaphysical tendency which, given its importance, I shall from now on designate with a neologism that aims to specify it in terms of what it is at its deepest level: *subjectalism*. Subjectalism always consists, beyond its many variants, no less numerous than those of correlationism, in absolutizing subjectivity or certain of its traits, so as to maintain post-Berkeleyan antimaterialism without renouncing the speculative status of philosophy. Why this term 'subjectalism'? Because we need a term that allows us to encompass at once all forms of idealism and all forms of vitalism, so as to contest the apparent opposition between these two currents, in particular during the twentieth century, and instead emphasize their essential kinship in an antimaterialist convergence.

I shall return to this point shortly. But first I would like to go back to the terminology adopted in *After Finitude* so as to emphasize the terminological modification proposed here, which, without changing anything fundamental, may perhaps lend itself to misunderstanding. In *After Finitude*, I already argued for the same opposition, which is essential to my project, between correlationism and subjectalism; but for the latter theoretical gesture I chose the name 'subjectivist metaphysics'. The advantage of this expression is that it explicitly contains the term 'metaphysics' – which is characteristic of all subjectalism – but its drawback is that the adjective evokes a 'subjectivism' that is generally associated with a refusal of any universal position. Therefore I now opt for a neologism which must be understood as *always* designating an anti- or amaterialist metaphysics of Correlation, one in which certain subjective traits, or just one, are raised to the rank of an absolute that colours being with its particular psyche, and which in consequence installs a difference of degree (or as some say, intensity) between the inorganic, the organic, and the thinking being, individual and then collective.

So here are the terms I shall use from now on: I call the 'Era of Correlation' the antimaterialist, post-Berkeleyan era that has shut us up inside correlation, *either through an antispeculative gesture* – which *alone* I call correlationism – *or through a speculative gesture* – which I call subjectalism – that absolutizes the correlation of thought and the world through the choice of various traits, all of which are present in human subjectivity. It is indeed an Era that we are dealing with here, *since it crosses many epochs* of philosophy, allowing us to discover in it the perenniality of the intracorrelational opposition between subjectalism and correlationism: the late Renaissance and the Classical Age (from Montaigne to Leibniz); the Enlightenment (Diderot/Kant); the turn of the eighteenth and nineteenth centuries (early Fichte/Hegel); the turn of the nineteenth and twentieth centuries (neo-Kantianism and Husserlianism on one side, Bergsonism on the other), the second part of the twentieth century (Ruyer and Deleuze, faced by certain variants of postmodernity), etc.

Iteration, Reiteration, Repetition

I will speak of *Correlation* with a capital 'C' when I intend to evoke this Era and the fact that the essence of correlation, in modern thought, has consisted in *doubling itself* between metaphysical and antispeculative adversaries – themselves principally divided in their turn between vitalists and rationalists on the subjectalist side, and between transcendental and postmodern thinkers on the correlationist side. This polemical proliferation has occupied the whole terrain of philosophical struggle, and overshadowed the necessity of not in turn participating in this confrontation, but of changing the terrain. I would thus qualify as correlation*al* any thinking in the grip of the era of the Correlational – whether correlation*ist* or subjectal – and of its subsequent conflicts; this correlational thinking seeming to saturate the philosophical possibilities through the distribution of oppositions according to a dominant line of antagonism.

Correlation thus means the opposition of the correlational with itself: of absolutist, metaphysical and antimaterialist correlation with deabsolutory, antispeculative, and antimaterialist correlation. And it is precisely because the Correlation is a relentless battlefield between its component parts that it is so difficult to defeat it: just as the militants of an emancipatory politics are never so oppressed as when they are taken up in a ferocious war between two powers that are equally destructive for them, like a corrupt militarized state mercilessly confronting a fanaticized religious opposition, the two camps being in their turn run through with violent rival factions.[9] What may however escape such a confrontation we can clearly see from the very forces taken up in it: it can only be a materialism (against both parties); a speculative materialism (specifically against correlationists); and a nonmetaphysical materialism (specifically against subjectalists). What will be at stake will be to develop a nonmetaphysical speculative materialism so as to counter *all* forms of correlational thought, and thus to prove that they do not constitute all of philosophy, but only a delimited zone of conflict that we can fight against en bloc or just leave peacefully.

Let us now come back to subjectalism and to the advantages of this denomination. With this term, as I have said, I wish to emphasize *the antimaterialist unity of metaphysical vitalism and metaphysical idealism*. This basic agreement between idealism and vitalism – against the 'old' materialism – has given rise to some strange arguments on the part of vitalism. For vitalism ostensibly sought to make itself the radical enemy of idealism, when it did not claim to be taking up the heritage of materialism in the name of this much-touted struggle. Hylozoism is thus the entirely 'subjectivized' form of the (supposed) materialism of the eighteenth century; that is to say, it is no longer a materialism at all, since it identifies all reality with a sensible mode of subjectivity realized in all things. The strangest moment was reached when various vitalisms – Nietzsche, Deleuze – participated in the radical critique of consciousness and of the Cartesian subject, which were identified with an eminent form of objectivist idealism. But in what did this 'antiidealist' critique consist? It consisted in critiquing, no doubt, a certain mode of subjectivity that had been placed in a foundational position (consciousness, reason, freedom – the *Cogito* being the favourite target); but only so as to simultaneously hypostasize one or several traits of human subjectivity by imbuing all reality with them – even inorganic reality. This enterprise thus produced typically subjectal concepts such as the 'will to power', 'the degree of contraction of duration', or the 'inorganic life of things'.[10] Which is why this antiidealism was fundamentally compatible with spiritualism – Bergson's in particular, as is explicit with Deleuze.

So was it *this* that was paradoxically called the 'critique of the subject', of the humanist subject? Critiquing the primacy of the rational subject so as to put in its place the subjective everywhere; setting against a certain type of subjectivity (consciousness, freedom, objective knowledge), housed only in the human, another type of subjectivity (will, life, habit, contraction of duration), this time housed everywhere? And it was also *this* that was readily called the 'deanthropologization' of nature? Refuting the final causes (which are intentional, the mark of human subjectivity) hypostasized in nature, but only to hypostasize, this time in everything, in every dynamism, another aspect of our humanity (sensation, habit, creation, life defined as the resolution of problems, and so on)? From this point on, between the human and the nonhuman (including the inorganic) we only see *a difference of intensity*, with all of reality participating to its own degree, even if only minimally, in a willing, larval or sensible subjectivity.[11] Certainly, this anthropologization could be held at a distance by the abundant insistence upon the *quasiequivocity* of the subjective terms employed: it was a question, so we are told by commentators aiming to justify what we read, of subjectivity, of will, of creation – but *not at all* in the sense of their human and conscious instance. Given this radical distance, it was not at all a matter of a naive animism. Very good – but in that case, why use the *same words*? Why would Nietzsche have used the expression 'will to power' if he did not mean to speak of something that had some relation to the will that we experience in ourselves? Why else except because that supposedly radical difference between the human instance of the subjective and its organic and inorganic instances was, from the subjectal perspective, only a difference in degree, and not a *difference in nature*?

But the most singular form of this denial of a metaphysics of hypersubjectivation (known as 'critique of the subject', or 'materialism', or 'philosophy of suspicion') was perhaps this other argument, typical of such a subjectalist hypostasis, this other way in which it could claim to be antihumanist, or 'counter-anthropological': it was a question, so we were told, of breaking with the derisory *anthropocentrism* thanks to which the human proudly believed itself to be the sole repository of the subjective faculty that is to be absolutized (conceited man believes that he alone is composed of volitions, of appetitions, of creations, and so on). It was therefore a question of showing that the human was but a particular representative, misguided by the prejudices of its consciousness, of a sensibility, of a life, that overflowed it on every side, even into the inorganic. He believed himself an individual in possession of its attributes, whereas he was himself only the accidental – almost anecdotic – attribute of his Attributes elevated into supreme Powers and deployed everywhere; man as a predicate of his Predicates that have become the properties of all things. Not sensible man, but a Sensibility that is sometimes human but very often something else. We must hence, so it was insisted, step off our laughable pedestal and instead go back down within ourselves to an infraconscious level in order to fully participate in this ahuman subjectivity whose flux must transpierce us in every part, coming from the innermost depths of the Universe to reveal to us that we are part of it, and thus that we do indeed have something in common with it. And we must discover that the refusal of certain philosophers to believe in this expansion of the subjective to the very limit of worlds – that this refusal was but the consequence of their retrograde admiration for man as 'master and possessor of nature'; or of their narcissism wounded by the idea of not being the *unparalleled* centre of Creation; or of their 'retreat' before the difficulty of this intuition so rare and so bitter (thus Bergsonian duration, so strenuous to identify for a consciousness modelled on space, according to the imperatives of action); or finally of their fright before the abyss of what has been glimpsed (thus the Nietzschean will to power, so terrifying in its ultimate consequences). Those commentators who spoke to us in this manner thereby seemed to suggest their grave heroism, which would no longer let itself be deceived by any supposed preeminence of the human over nature, conscious as they were of having come as close as possible to these unheard-of thoughts, assuming a duration that powerfully escapes ordinary consciousness, the idea of a will to power fating us to the supreme ordeal of the Eternal Return, the inorganic life whose dangerous intensity they knew to be such that it will destroy whoever would find himself traversed too closely.

But first, and above all, one might remark that this *refusal of anthropocentrism* in fact led only to a most startling *anthropomorphism* that consisted, following the most classic illusion, of seeing in every reality (even inorganic reality) subjective traits whose origin is in truth all human; for it goes no further than, by means of a human imagination, to vary the experienceable traits of our always human existence by degree and in this way place the result of this doubly anthropomorphic operation in all things, and all that according to a scale ranging from most to least.[12] And thus the hubris – if this poor moral accusation is to be adopted as an argument – was just as much on the side of those who saw themselves everywhere in the Universe, and what is more, in a mirror that sent them back a most flattering compliment: for these subjective qualities, according to the universal gradation, very often crowned humans as being among their most remarkable, if not the highest, intensive supports. If there was ever a way of placing oneself at the summit of all things, it was surely to place oneself in all things in a most diluted state.

Would there not be more modesty, then, in considering that the Universe has nothing to do with our subjective qualities, that it could very well do without them at any degree whatsoever, and to say, more soberly, that there is no absolute scale that makes our properties superior (because more intense) to those of nonhuman living creatures or inorganic beings? When it comes to free will or baroque musical composition, we surely have a certain advantage over the moon, but when it comes to the moving geometry of its orbit, its unequalled capacity to reflect sunlight and its engendering of tidal rhythms – in all these respects we lag far behind, far behind this power that is dead through and through. The world is far too diverse to be reduced to one single intensive scale, one that will always end up with a hierarchy of values in the name of life from which nothing escapes (in the world of intensities, even anarchies are crowned).

We should instead reinstate to that which is dead, totally deprived of life, its proper status, irreducible to our value judgements that fall back on the categories of the living. That which is dead has many lessons to teach us and, if we really must make such evaluations, can very well prevail over the living. When, in 2011, the Musée des Beaux-Arts de Pau suffered an attack of microscopic fungi (*acremonium penicillium*) which created patches of moisture on about thirty old paintings stocked in their reserve collection, they responded with the use of fungicide and the control of hygrometric controls. And, as far as art is concerned, it is not only the inert that must be saved from the living, but even cadavers: the piece created by Jan Fabre in 1996 entitled *Vleekskomp (Meat)* takes the form of a side of beef suspended from a hook, covered entirely with dead beetles. Over the years this piece turned out to be inhabited by destructive insects, which had to be opposed by eliminative measures ('curative intervention'), by fumigation and anoxia, and then by containing it in a hermetically sealed vitrine ('preventive conservation') to avoid a new invasion.[13]

For our part, we are not content with mere metaphors: the paintings for the preservation of which one has killed *are* entirely lacking in life. Every masterpiece is a *dead splendour* – we only call it 'living' because of the obsessive axiology that would have it that the living always wins out over the dead in value, and that since art is an intense experience its works must consequently, according to our criteria of value, be alive. But no, masterpieces are dead – yet how these strange things grip us! And the same goes for the dead that is not of man's doing, such as the lunar landscape, made of ancestral minerals shattered into craters where no wind has ever blown. The dead seizes the living, to our great joy.

With the childish prejudice against death that would give life to that which is not alive – on the pretext that it *pleases* us – we unscrupulously metaphorize life. And not so as to understand what life really is, but as a value judgement which, seeing it wherever our approbation roams, becomes incapable of understanding it for what it is. When a reality becomes a norm, in truth it ceases to be respected, its rich and unique being is diluted in the uniform current of our estimations: in qualifying the highest realizations as living, we remove all precise, correct meaning from real life, any meaning that would be capable of helping us deepen its meaning. Placing life at the summit of our axiology is the most effective way to bury it for our ontology: as its extension becomes maximal (because as wide and disparate as our successive admirations) so its comprehension becomes impoverished to the same degree, and thus becomes a legal code for our appreciation of everything and nothing. Life was a cosmically very rare phenomenon, of unprecedented complexity; here it is as respectable as the verdict of a court of justice repeated, sentence after sentence, with a rap of the same mallet.

But for a materialist, life in general – whatever we might understand by this catch-all term – 'Life' is not an axiological summit; we are surrounded by interesting works without life, which neither grow nor reproduce, or by stars that light up the night sky with their erratic distribution but are incapable of fleeing when panicked by a predator. Dead matter, inhuman splendour. And nothing is ever at stake in the hierarchy between the dead and the living in general; everything is at stake each time between *this* living being and *this* dead one – case by case, depending on the situation, when we are compelled, by force of circumstance, to choose. We will save this child in danger at the expense of the destruction of the door that separates us from him, however well-crafted it might be; but, once more, we prefer the destruction of a swarm of mites (very much alive) to the destruction of the seventeenth-century lace that was their dinner, and which spreads out delicately for our eyes its lack of life, woven in a thousand ways.[14]

So don't speak to us of a hubris of the subject in relation to the universe: certain of our qualities are ours alone, but what could be more banal than having specific qualities? And who would inflate this into a general hierarchy regarding what we possess and what inhuman things possess? We are inferior to so many living things in many respects: flight without cumbersome technical artifice; uninterrupted life in abyssal undersea crevasses; the weaving of a web without the mediation of any instrument in order to capture prey; flowering. If we are startled by the rupture *without continuity* between the different orders – matter, life and thought – this is not because we want to build general hierarchies, but because novelty here strikes us as the mark of a becoming that is capable of the most radical irruptions. And in this way we discover that we belong to a thinking species capable at once of admiring the splendour of other kingdoms (we participate in them, as a being made of matter and of life), while acceding (we shall come back to this) to the absolute contingency of our condition – the absolute contingency of everything. We are characterized by our grasp of ourselves as fragile thinkers of the absolute, with no ontological support superior to that of any other being, and acceding in this way to what this same status affords us: an awareness of the distressing contrast between the eternity that we think (itself without any superior value, the 'stupid contingency of all things') and the precarity of those who accede to that ultimate stopping point of what there is.

It is this appeal of a suffering between the thought of eternal contingency (that is given in each of us as an obscure sentiment of the nonmeaning from which we emerge, all the more violent in that it is denied, 'reinvested' in the unbridled belief in Meaning) and the precarious contingency of the thinking of this eternity; it is this that makes us act in favour of humans before any other being. But ontologically, precisely nothing distinguishes us: stone, fly or man – contingent beings, no more and no less.

Iteration, Reiteration, Repetition

As for the refusal met with by subjectalism, there are no grounds for blaming it on the extreme difficulty of the thinking at stake (Bergson is no more difficult than Kant; on the most decisive points of his arguments, he even possesses a jubilant limpidity that borders on aggression the sharper it gets); no reason to see in it an effect of unconquered terror (Nietzsche is too violently interesting to succeed in frightening us – he just makes us impatient to turn the page); no more are there any grounds to discover in this refusal our love for the Cartesian humanism that all our masters taught us to disdain with such consistency that its refusal became, for our generation, second nature, a conformism that is too powerful for us to envisage extracting ourselves from it without a powerful feeling of guilt. And finally, as for the refrain, since Freud, of our wounded narcissism, a supposed source of the refusal to accord a continuity between us and the living or the Universe, to tell the truth, we have accumulated so many of these wounds of all kinds solemnly inflicted upon our ego by Copernicus, Darwin, Marx and cognitive science, that those of my generation, and the following generations too, have become pretty much immune to them. If these wounds burdened us, this is because there were so many of them that we no longer knew how to put them in order – especially when they were in contempt of one another.

One must seriously fantasize the world in the image of one's own desire to be transgressive to believe that there still exist, somewhere, in reasonable number, some young princes with such an exacerbated sensibility that they still need salt for the wounds left by such vexatious attacks on the metaphysical vanity of their own egoity.

All of this rhetoric of trembling before the obstacle, or the wound-too-terrible-to-be-assumed, is entirely artificial, for it feels that its 'ghost train' might be empty – along with the racket of the magician who explains that no one visits his attraction because everyone is so terrified of it, whereas in fact they are simply disinterested, because they no longer find credible or thrilling these pasteboard skeletons and sorcerers operated by precarious workers expelling their lugubriously repetitive cries in ennui.

Nothing is at stake at this level of supposedly horrific depths which ennoble their partisans with a courage that is supposed to arouse our admiring respect: in truth, everything comes down to the fact that *it just doesn't add up*, quite simply; that nothing in these subjectal philosophies proves that in acceding to our most obscure depths we accede to the most universal depths of the world. Given this, nothing convinces us in these philosophies, however thrilling they might otherwise be. This is not the question – what is a philosopher worth who does not *violently* admire the philosophies he disagrees with – but once more, nothing any longer convinces us in these theoretical configurations; and if we wish to discover something that inspires our adhesion, we will go and look elsewhere.

For a consequent materialist, the human finds in itself, either at the level of consciousness or at the level of infraconscious life, only its own subjectivity; and indeed it seems to the materialist that there is no reason for the Universe, *entirely inhuman because entirely asubjective*, to fill itself up, intensely or infinitesimally, with all the sensible titillations, impulsive volitions and diverse modalities of our psyche; all this to please the subjectal philosopher who hopes, through the speleological exploration of himself, through his successive descent into his infinitely ramified crypts, to get out of himself to the point of running through the real in all its dimensions. Whatever may be our admiration for these thinkers for having plunged into the depths of themselves, we have no reason to believe that they have plunged anywhere else. It is not because the subjective contains hidden dimensions that the latter take us out of ourselves, any more than we might suppose a wardrobe to reveal the Universe to us just because it turns out to have a false bottom.[15]

No, we decidedly do not believe in this operation: *to critique the subject only so as to subjectivate everything*. To dismantle the subject once more, only to swim in the abundant waters of the oceans of micropsychisms. To free oneself from the human, in this strange denied humanism, all too obviously amounts to disseminating the human everywhere, even into stones and particles, according to the entire scale of intensities. The destitution of the human just makes us encounter it, in more or less diluted form, on every street corner – or rather in every paving stone of every corner, of every street. As for us, we no longer inhabit these places so full of life, which are supposed to frighten us or fill us with a superior dilation, and this is why we think that *today we are less in need of a critique of the subject than of a critique of the subjective*. Less need to suspect the responsibility of the subject in respect of its acts, its utterances, the nothingnesses it confronts, gripping it with every breath it takes, than to grow a desert around such a subject that, owing to the lack of the vital drops of a seasonal rain, would put paid once and for all to all these charming wills, warring and implacable, and these delicious creative durations that set consciousnesses, living beings and melting sugar cubes in motion – these intensities that promised us that, once our existence was over, we would still survive a little – barely, but a little – *at home* among these perennial, nodular, querulous, divergent lives,

Iteration, Reiteration, Repetition

and laying out the thousand perspectives of their richly disharmonious creations.

And inversely, we are convinced that a materialist subject is possible – but it will only be possible if it is encircled by a 'matter=X', that is to say a matter which has no common term with our subjectivity, but which nevertheless will have nothing enigmatic about it, but just a whole network of hypotheses constituted by ever more complex scientific paradigms: probability waves, gravitational fields, an expanding Universe, rendered mathematically, if necessary in terms of variables x, with the required precision. A matter of which it is vain to ask *on top of this* what 'it is like' to be such a thing, so as to seek some kind of empathy with such realities by projecting one's own sensations to their infinitesimal limit. By twisting my joints – but *just a tiny bit* – I do not gain a better comprehension of what might be meant by the local curvature of a relativist space-time by a given mass. I am far more likely to achieve this goal by using, within my means, physics and mathematics, by plunging into their harsh writings like the description of a lethal real – in this sense authentically terrible.

The materialist subject, if she arrives one day with the rigour she merits, will forever live in Hell, surrounded by the dead of different types: the dead who were her equals, loved or unknown (humans she grieves for, in her conscious thoughts, or in her sole survival), surrounded by the cycle of destruction of animals and plants (living in perpetual disappearance), but also surrounded by that type of dead thing that never had the opportunity to die (inorganic matter that has never lived and could never lose its life), and finally confronted with the death that is proper to her (her near future). These are the deathly declinations in which she will feel herself authentically in the world. And such will be her '*orphic* explanation of the Earth' (Mallarmé). The Book open to her gaze ranging over the differentiated orders of the nonliving.

The materialist proposes to cease replaying again and always the same subjectalist argument (subjectivity in all things because nothing conceivable outside of subjectivity) so as to render the world far richer than in these models. For these models are basically monist, even when they seek to be pluralist: in them, everything is uniformly sensation, habit, infinitesimal self, life, will, creative duration, and so on – and nothing is distinguished in them except according to a difference of degree, or an intensive difference. A mode of difference that prohibits things from not having anything in common with each other. I believe that on the contrary we must accede to the *pure heterogeneous that breaks with all differences of degree or intensity* in favour of differences *in nature* – the only authentic differences, those which do not underhandedly lead back to identity (an identity of nature) in an alterity (of degree). We do not need a monism – or a monopluralism, a monism of difference that seeks to be a pluralism (*the magic formula*: 'monism=pluralism') but ends up reabsorbing all things into one and the same Whole (albeit an open Whole) to a greater or lesser degree (*the tragic formula*: 'pluralism=monism'). On the contrary, what we need are *dualisms everywhere*: pure differences in nature, with no continuity whatsoever between that which they make differ, between the many regimes of the real – matter, life, mind, society, etc. – whose possible coordination does not at all allow us to think their rapprochement, unless in a crude mode of blind fact. *Not a monopluralism, but a polydualism.*[16] We need fractures that render impossible any reductionism from one regime of beings to another (life reduced to matter, mind to life, etc.) and permit the entities of our world to escape all attempts to reduce them to one unique nature (whether we call it nature or not, denials are of little consequence). *The heterogeneous turned against the intensive, difference in nature turned against difference in degree; the eternally possible polydualism of Hyperchaos against the pseudonecessary monopluralism of Chaosmos.*[17]

But, as we shall see, this cannot be achieved by figural derivation. It requires another approach, to which we shall return.

Let us come back to the term 'subjectalism'. The critical advantage of this term is to place into *the same camp* these currents that claim to be radically opposed, to arrange them all together around a common decision – Hegel, Nietzsche and Deleuze included – and to place them all in the wake of Berkeley himself. For Berkeley, inventor of the argument of the correlational circle, was not a correlationist, but a subjectalist: a philosopher for whom there exists only the subjective – minds and their ideas, human spirits or divine spirits.[18] Once we reopen the materialist struggle against every form of hypostasis of the subjective (not only, once again, of the subject in a limited sense, as consciousness, reason, freedom, but of the subject in all its modalities – will, sensation, preconscious life, and so on), we see only *declinations* where we had been told that there were radical, supposedly abyssal *ruptures*. All subjectalisms reveal themselves to us as oscillations, sometimes of tremendous amplitude, of the Berkeleyan decision, yielding each time a new, reinvented way of inhabiting its formidably effective antimaterialist gesture. Berkeley, Hegel, Nietzsche, Bergson and Deleuze prosecuted, following strategies as diverse as possible, *a combat that supposed the same originary victim*: a combat that took as given the impossibility of taking seriously the possibility of a desubjectivated matter. From this point of view, there is *no* essential difference between these thinkers. All are content to traverse the subjectal continent according to the erratic trajectory of their own genius.

But if there is to be a true critique of the subject (whether constructive or destructive), it must above all consist, as we have said, in a critique of the subjective and of its hypostasis. Such a critique thus cannot *but* be materialist, since only the materialist absolutizes the pure nonsubjective – the x with neither consciousness nor perception nor will nor life nor creative intuition to any degree whatsoever. This real 'in pure death' (as one says of a fabric that it is 'pure silk') is that which represents the state of inorganic matter – that is to say matter anterior to, and independent of, all subject and all life. Our – neomaterialist – project can thus be formulated as follows: how to escape both correlationism and subjectalism, and all their historical and even conceivable variants? How to operate the combined recusal of scepticism, criticism, transcendental and existential phenomenology, of postmodernism (so many correlationisms); but also of idealism, spiritualisms, vitalisms and perspectivisms (so many subjectalisms)? How to go beyond the Era of Correlation?

Before recalling the strategy that makes this twofold recusal of modern and contemporary antimaterialisms possible, I should like to make a final lexical remark. This time it concerns the difference between materialism and realism. I call 'realism' any position that claims to accede to an absolute reality – thus any speculative position in the wider sense. In this sense, every true materialism has to stand the charge of realism; because it is indeed a realism. But inversely, one can see that not every realism is necessarily a materialism: for anticorrelationist realism can be materialist as well as subjectalist. Realism, in the latter case, is fully a part of the Correlation – it is correlational although not correlationist. And in fact, he who founds the Era of Correlation – Berkeley – is a true realist: the partisan of a world whose absolute components (in itself and not only for us) are made of minds and ideas, from man to God. 'Speculative realism' can thus designate a movement whose identity supposes an exit from the correlationist sphere of influence – but not a movement that moves outside of the *correlational* sphere. For in designating itself as a 'realism' rather than as a 'materialism', this sphere gives itself as being in principle compatible with any subjectalism whatsoever, old or renewed.[19] The term 'speculative realism' thus does not designate *as unambiguously as possible* what we seek to do: to exit from Correlation en bloc. This only a *speculative materialism* is capable of doing, by pointing the arrow of thought toward the very heart of all that is dead.

Let us return now to our demonstration. I said that correlation succeeds, with the help of its first argument (the 'correlationist circle'), in destroying all materialist realism. But it is powerless to combat subjectal realism with the same argument, since the latter also affirms that one cannot, without contradiction, extract oneself from subjectivity, but draws the inverse conclusion from this: no longer that thought cannot think the absolute; but that thought thinks thought *as* the absolute.[20] Confronted with this second form of nonmaterialist absoluteness, the correlational circle is of no help, and we must mobilize against it another decisive argument, namely what I call *correlational facticity*.

To understand this second argument, let us reformulate the meaning of subjectalism, proposing a version of the latter that is modelled in the most rigorous way possible. In this new defence of the absolute, the reasoning is as follows: since the very idea of an in-itself independent of thought is inconsistent, it makes sense to posit that this in-itself, since it is *unthinkable for us*, is *impossible in itself*. If we know only that which is given to thought, this does not mean that we are separated from the absolute by being trapped within our subjective limits, but that, *in an absolute sense*, there can be nothing that is not correlated to a subjective act. The strict necessity with which correlationism demonstrated that we can never think anything outside of subjectivity is transmuted into the thought of an ontological necessity: we always experience subjectivity as a necessary, and hence eternal, principle from which no one can escape. We shall thus define as subjectalism any metaphysics that absolutizes the correlation of being and thought, whatever sense it attaches to the subjective and objective poles of such a relation. Hegelian idealism is obviously the paradigm of such a metaphysics of the Subject thought as the Absolute – but vitalism can in principle obey the same logic, if we model it in a similar way: all supposed exit from thought outside of the will is but the latter's experience of its own willing – in this case, of its will to accede to this kind of escape, etc.

We can see that correlationism, in order to counter the subjectivist absolute and not just the materialist absolute, must mobilize a second argument, capable of deabsolutizing the correlate itself, capable of prohibiting its becoming-necessary qua perennial structure of that which is. This second argument is that of 'correlational facticity'.

For correlationism to be able to undertake a deabsolutization of thought, it must in fact maintain that correlation *is not absolutely necessary*, and that this absence of an absolute necessity of correlation is accessible to thought – that one can justify it through an argument and that it needs not simply be posited as an act of faith. This *thinkable* nonnecessity of correlation is precisely what I call 'correlational facticity'. The thesis of correlational facticity is thus as follows: thinking can think its own absence of necessity, not only qua personal consciousness, but qua supraindividual structure. It is only on this condition that correlationism could think the very *possibility* of an *unknowable entirely-other* of correlation. How could we justify this thesis?

In one way only: by emphasizing the *absence of reason* for correlation itself, in whatever sense this correlation is understood. To what act of thought does this absence of reason (which I shall call '*unreason [irraison]*') refer? To an observation that is not empirical but of a more fundamental order: we mean that order of facticity that characterizes, for example, the a priori forms of the transcendental, and which belongs to a dimension other than that of the mere contingency of a phenomenon (the facticity of modal categories belongs to a modal dimension anterior to that of these categories, in particular that of modality). It is a question of acceding to a *Faktum* of the Correlation that is more radical than that of an empirical fact and that conditions givenness itself, since it involves the whole of our relation to things, of our relation to representations, of our whole being-in-the-world, of the historico-linguistic conditions of a context of social and cultural life, etc. For if the Correlation is unsurpassable, it is not given in the manner of a necessary foundation: nothing in it indicates its own necessity, even though we cannot think its being-otherwise, even though we do not know how to escape from it to accede to its radical outside. *That there is* language, consciousness, being-in-the-world – this is, in each case, a matter of an originary 'there is' – of a primary fact beyond which thought cannot reach.

We must distinguish here between three notions: the *contingent*, the *fact* and the *arche-fact*. We shall call 'contingent' every entity, whether thing or event, that I *know* is capable of not being, or that could have not been, or could have been other. I know that this vase could have not existed, or could have existed otherwise; I know that this dropping of the vase onto the floor could have or could have not happened.

On the other hand, we shall call 'fact', in the strict sense, every type of entity whose being-other I can conceive of, but of which *we do not know* whether it could have effectively been other than it is. Such is the case with the laws of physics of our Universe:[21] for I can, without contradiction, and without it being invalidated by any past experience, conceive of these laws changing in the future (this is the principle of Hume's critique of causality); and therefore I cannot prove that they are necessary. But I do not know, for all that, whether these laws are indeed contingent, or whether on the contrary they are actually necessary, even if this cannot be proved. In this sense, we shall say that these laws belong to 'facticity' – but not that they are 'contingent' as a vase or its falling.

Finally, we shall call 'arche-fact' any fact which I cannot, in any way, conceive of as being other than it is, or as not being, and whose necessity I nevertheless cannot prove – in which regard we must say that it is a fact, in broader and radicalized sense. Now, it is precisely with regard to the notion of the arche-fact thus defined that subjectalist absolutism and correlationism diverge.

For what does the subjectalist say? That I cannot think the other of correlation: I may be able to think that the given world could have been otherwise, that its laws might fail – I indeed can think, and even imagine, a world governed by other laws. But I cannot think the very abolition of correlation and all its possible invariants, since to think their abolition is, once again, to think it as a correlate of my current thinking, and thus to commit a formulatory contradiction. Now, if the other of correlation is unthinkable, for the subjectalist this means that it is impossible: the noncorrelated is, according to her, a notion that is just as absurd, and thus just as inexistent as that of the square circle. Correlation therefore is not, according to the subjectalist, a contingent reality: it is an absolute necessity. Whereas the thesis of the correlationist is, on the contrary, as follows: certainly, she admits, I cannot think the other of correlation, and thus correlation is not a fact in the same way that physical laws are; but neither, she adds, can I found the supposedly necessary being of correlation in reason. I can only *observe* correlation and my enclosure within it through the exercise of my thought. Now, an observation is always a relation to something that is given, ultimately, as a pure *factum*. If I cannot think the other of correlation, this actually only designates the factual limit of my thought; but it cannot be proved that this subjective unthinkability of noncorrelation corresponds to the absolute impossibility of the existence of such a noncorrelational reality. We cannot prove that the unthinkable for us is impossible in itself without begging the question – without presupposing what is to be proven, namely that every experience of unthinkability corresponds to an absolute impossibility – to a truth in itself and not to a truth not for us.

Correlation thus also constitutes a certain type of fact: a fact whose other is unthinkable but can nevertheless not be posited as absolutely impossible. *Correlation, in this sense, is an arche-fact.*

What I then call the 'principle of factiality' consists in absolutizing no longer correlation – the first decision of correlationism – but correlational facticity – the second decision of correlationism. It is a matter of showing that the ultimate thesis of this deabsolutizing thought harbours a hidden absolute: facticity, indeed, archefacticity. Why does facticity constitute an implicit absolute of correlationism? Because the latter must admit that we are capable of thinking our possible nonbeing, so as to stave off the subjectalist absolute that declares it unthinkable. But the possibility that we should cease to exist – this possibility is by definition independent of our thinking, since it actualizes our nonbeing.

We can therefore only think our possible nonbeing, and thus our facticity (as individual *and* as correlational structure) on condition of being able to think the *absolute* possibility of our no longer being – a possibility that is independent of our thinking, since it consists precisely in the annihilation of that thinking. *There is thus indeed an effectively thinkable absolute, by the very confession of the correlationist*; one that the latter can no longer refute since she presupposes it – namely, the possible nonbeing of every thing, including correlation; an absolute that we have designated as the mark of a 'hyperchaotic Time'. In order for the event of the abolition of correlation to be thinkable, it must be possible to think an event that, by definition, has no need of correlation to be effective. In this case, contingency, facticity and archefacticity become one for us: we know that what is could not be, and that what is not could be. Things, people, events, physical laws, correlation itself: to be is to be determinate – to be this or that – and thus to be able to change without any reason whatsoever, perfectly contingently, within a Time capable of destroying every entity, whatever its mode of being. What we took to be a limit of thought – facticity – is an absolute and thinkable property of that which is.

What we call *factiality* is *facticity*'s property of not itself being factual. Factiality designates the nonfacticity (that is to say, the absolute necessity) of facticity *and of facticity alone*. We shall therefore call 'principle of factiality' the speculative statement according to which only facticity alone is nonfactual – or (what is the same thing) according to which only contingency is necessary. Such is the principle – that of the necessity of contingency alone – that governs the idea of the speculation that I call 'factial'.

The idea that I pursue is then as follows: I maintain that it is possible to derive nonarbitrary conditions from the necessary facticity of all things – absolute properties of that which is, whether or not we exist to think them. For I propose – and the whole interest of the thesis lies herein – that to be contingent, an entity (be it a thing, event, law or structure) cannot be just anything whatsoever. For example, if we define the inconsistency of an entity as its capacity to be universally contradictory, then – as I believe to have established – this entity is absolutely impossible, because it would always already be what it is not, and would exist at the same time as not existing. Inconsistency is impossible not because it is absurd, but because it would permit its bearer to be absolutely necessary – incapable of changing since it would already be what it is supposed to become; incapable of ending, since for it, to be is not to be.[22] On this basis, we must refuse the possibility of an inconsistent, universally contradictory entity, not because it would be illogical (this would be begging the question), but because it would be absolutely necessary – the only property that is absolutely prohibited to any reality whatsoever, even God. I thus attempt to maintain two theses at once: every determinate reality can be other than it is (and is thus contingent); but contingency implies nonarbitrary and necessary properties, which I call *Figures*. In essence, my work thus consists in deriving from the principle of factiality various Figures qua absolute invariants of the maximal variance accorded to every entity.

Let us recapitulate our preceding discussion, projecting ourselves into perspectives that would partially contest their results.

The reign of the Correlation is dominated by an asymmetric antagonistic structure: correlationisms dominate subjectalisms through the intervention of the argument of the facticity of correlation. If we left these two correlational instances to themselves, the first would carry the day against the second. Within subjectalisms we have, however, opened up a specific contestation bearing on the fact that subjectalism, in its turn, has an internal line of division: infraconscious subjectalisms (Diderot, Nietzsche, Bergson, Deleuze) against conscious subjectalisms, taken up in the structure of the subject of objective knowledge – perceptual subjects (Berkeley) or rational subjects (Hegel). We have opened up an offensive against infraconscious subjectalism because it has been able to arrogate, in a correlational period, the antiidealist ethos of materialism: this latter having become 'impossible', the place of a 'privileged opponent' that satisfied the struggles against the rationalist side of the Correlation – transcendental and metaphysical alike – was up for grabs. Our aim was, on the contrary, to show that only materialism can confront all forms of idealism (Kant or Hegel), but also all forms of vitalism and spiritualism (from Diderot to Ruyer, via Bergson).

But it is now time to critique, in turn, this front that we have opened up against subjectalism. For the very fact that we have extracted materialism from the Correlation reminds us of its change in status: *it is no longer metaphysical, but speculative* (in the strict sense). Which means that the very way in which it opposes itself to that which it is not is going to change fundamentally.

Let us first recall the aim that we pursued in *After Finitude*, and which we will approach once again in the second part of this text. Our wish was, and remains, to establish the following: the condition of the meaning of the natural sciences – which, after Jean-Claude Milner, we call Galileanism – can only be found in a materialism capable of founding the thinkability of a nature that is indifferent to our existence and fully mathematizable. Metaphysics having irremediably obsolesced, this materialism must yield an ontological basis for Galileanism without the intervention of the Principle of Sufficient Reason, by founding not the necessity of some determinate reality (this or that nature) but the necessity of real possibles whose structural invariance is as follows: whatever world may be actualized by Hyperchaos, it must be describable in its proper determinations by an adequate set of mathematicized renderings. What we must derive from the principle of factiality is not that our actual world is mathematizable but that any possible world, any portion of any possible world, is mathematizable. On the other hand, scientific *theories* regarding an actual world – in this case, ours – have nothing to tell us. It is in this sense that we diverge most clearly from a metaphysics which, speaking of what there is, necessarily crosses the path not only of theories but also of facts responsible for the theory of the sciences of its time.[23] And since these theories and their constitutive facts never stop evolving because of the evolution of science itself, they will always ruin the metaphysical constructions that have staked (whether they like it or not) their existence on these scientific complexes – whether the latter are peripheral or central to their own construction (for any metaphysics that is rigorously systematic will collapse unless some point, albeit a peripheral one, of its structure is drawn from the movement of science).[24] By collapse, we mean to say that this theory will no longer have any disciples delving in their turn into the mass of scientific knowledge of their times to demonstrate that the philosophy of their master remains valid despite the revolutions that happened after it – but that this philosophy will only have commentators who discuss it as a *corpus*, in search of its 'textual truth'.

Scientific theories are extraordinarily dynamic powers – and saying this does not imply any kind of relativism. For it is science that, from victory to victory, inflicts defeat after defeat on its own theories, in its most extraordinarily interesting moments. To the point where each of us can expect in their lifetime to know such shifts, such as that which (in all probability, since no theory has ever been eternal) will one day devastate cognitivism, rendering it just as obsolete for our offspring, near or far, as behaviourism is for us today.

This is why a theory, even the most contemporary theory, carries with it the pleasant scent of its epoch, like those old things found in our grandparents' attics, and their madeleine-effect: at best, it dominates several centuries and conserves the aura of its eighteenth- and nineteenth-century mastery, like Newtonianism; at worst, it disappears after a few decades, marked with the seal of desuetude, just as behaviourism spreads an ambience that is not so much that of the years during which it developed (the 1910s) as of those of its rise to prominence and its acme (for me, behaviourism remains full of the imaginary sombre fragrances of the Unites States of the 1950s). But whether the philosopher adopts a scientific theory, or a part of it, to make it a perennialized condition of knowledge (Newton's absolute three-dimensional space and linear time become a priori forms of sensibility in Kant), or believes himself obliged to discuss at length a theory that contravenes his thesis (Bergson's discussion of Eimer and French's neo-Lamarckism's law of orthogenesis in the first chapter of *Creative Evolution*), it is always, without exception, at these moments when she crosses over with scientific theories, that she writes those of her pages that will be the first to yellow and fade.

What is captivating and perennial in Science is that it always destroys the naivety, itself renewed with each generation, of those who believe they have the unprecedented privilege of being born at the moment when, in a fabulous coincidence, the ultimate theory, the theory that will not one day become the object of a history of the sciences, the theory that will forever remain in the present, has just arrived. This ideology of the perennial theoretical present – of the theory that will never know the fate of becoming something past – masks the fact that the only perdurance, the only eternal

Iteration, Reiteration, Repetition

fact of Science, is its mathematization. Which, tied down to the experimentation that allows it to put its finger on the contingency of the actual (one does not deduce contingent determinations a priori), turns it into a Chronos that will, no doubt, in centuries future, devour its own children, even if they have the eminence of Newtonian dynamics.

This is why every metaphysics becomes impossible through its claim to perennially render what is: for in them it is always a matter of a meta-*physis*; and this physis will always be already bound up in a meshwork of theories and facts themselves saturated with theories, that is to say accessible by instruments which are materialized theories. Thus a theory will be gripped in the movement of the devouring of its progenitor who, sooner or later, will no longer be the last word in science, but the most recent casualty of science: the memory of an epoch now offered up as an object (as we say offered up for sacrifice) to the discipline of the history of sciences. And all this according to a theoretical becoming whose unpredictability is the most complete of all, for there is no science of the future of science (if this science existed, it would have completed science at the very moment of its appearance).

The factial does not at all tie its fate to the theories of the moment, as burning as they may be, crying out that *this time here it is*, that the aim is achieved, that nothing will move again except the ever more triumphant improvement or the ever more confirming correction of the ultimate, finally complete Theory. Or even to prophesy that the last aim is *almost* attained, that we are on the edge of triumph – for *imminence* is the very pathos of a 'positivist' ideology that maintains that everything, or the essential, in a department of knowledge is *on the way to* the radical resolution of its problematic field, but which, having to work with the fact that, of course, this is not the case, must rant that everything is nevertheless on the verge of such a resolution, and that it is only *a question of time*. But there comes a day when the time, decidedly, will have to wait.[25]

The factial links its fate only to the Galilean gesture – the mathematization of the sciences – and not to the theories engendered by this gesture. It intends to show, against correlationism, that a real that is independent of thought is thinkable as reducible to a mathematicized science, regardless of the succession of theories. In this way, it escapes from the predestined obsolescence of all metaphysics (their becoming a corpus that is merely commented on); at the same time, it avoids the dogmatic effects inherent to them.

Speculative materialism is indeed both unusual with regard to the content of its theses on being, and, because of this, remarkably 'nonintrusive'. It is first unusual in that it does not absolutize any determinate material reality: atoms, void, molecules, forces, classical waves, probability waves, the spatiotemporal continuum, and so on. These so-called 'material' realities (or at least 'physical' realities) are theories that not only are revisable, but above all, even if they were to constitute definitively proven facts (something that is impossible), are absolutely contingent, just like the laws that govern them. What I have resolved to call 'Hyperchaos' can destroy them without cause or reason, since they are modes of reality deprived of any necessity.[26] I am thus not at all dogmatic in regard to what our world actually is – and this because I refuse to depend, like a 'positivist', on this or that contemporary state of science in order to yield propositions judged to be the sole true ones.

My approach is entirely different. I affirm that the only point of absolute exteriority encountered by thought is that of contingency: its own contingency, and that of its world. Given this, the radical consequence is as follows: since we speculate on the absolute, *we prohibit ourselves from speaking of what is* – that is to say of what is *actual* – and speak only of that which *could really* be. After all, what is, is entirely contingent – and this in a sense far more vast than empirical contingency or transcendental facticity, which are both hampered in so many ways by the physical laws or the a priori categories and forms of sensibility. Any figural event whatsoever (any event that conforms to Figures) may come to pass – any world whatsoever may succeed any other one. Now, the only thing that should interest the speculative philosopher is not what is contingent, but what is necessary. But since nothing that exists is necessary, speculation must not in any case speak of it – except as an *elucidating mediation* aiming to bring out a determinate question. Thus, in *After Finitude*, I only spoke of the science of dating and of the archefossil so as to awaken the reader's consciousness to the following fact: the correlationism that was then largely dominant in contemporary philosophy had as its rigorous consequence to make the discourse of science meaningless. The paradox culminated in the following proposition: the first condition of the thinkability of science turned out to be the abandonment of the transcendental – a transcendental whose vocation was to investigate the conditions of possibility of science. We thus discovered that, far from being an intrinsically transcendental concept, the notion of 'condition' could be the act of obsolescing the transcendental, and could be put to work within a speculative regime of knowledge (the search for the nonarbitrary conditions, or *Figures*, of absolute contingency). But to obtain this result, the effective results of the sciences of dating that we set out with were of little importance (whether the Universe precedes or does not precede the emergence of the living has no bearing on the proof sought); the future evolution of these sciences and their recusal to come by other, more effective systems matters little, and even the critical reinterpretation of the temporality of the Universe through a certain understanding of general relativity has no importance. What was important was to put our finger on the fact that science is meaningless unless it is *capable* of describing a world that is really independent of us – a condition of meaning and an ontological condition that no correlationism can put back together again.

We thus intended, by this method, not to depend – in the absolutory statements that we tried to extract from factiality – upon any scientific theory coming out of the experimental sciences, as eminent and dominant as it may be today. Because so long as there is science, every theory now accepted remains forever at risk of being replaced by a 'superior' theory.

Do not deduce from this that we ourselves are not captivated by the contemporary theories of this or that scientific discipline: but we simply like them for what they are according to all plausibility. We believe too much in science than to idolize one of its theories, which is never anything more than one of its stopping points. And these points cannot (with the exception of a didactic usage indicated above) concern us as philosophers. For as philosophers, we have to deal with the sense of our existence, and a philosopher deals with this sense on the level of an eternal truth, not that of the 'state of the art'. We do not intend to share the heartbreaking destiny of a young nihilist ravaged by her belief in the negation of all freedom in the name of a determinism that she believes to be perennial, and this because a certain nineteenth-century Laplacian science, now outmoded, presented itself to her as an indubitable reality. No scientific theory will have any influence on our conception of being and becoming, because our vision of being does not cross with any fact, and consequently any theory of any fact. 'Let us first distance ourselves from all facts', said Rousseau;[27] let us task ourselves with trying to do so more radically than he – for it is then that a philosophy rich in new content may come into view.

Speculation does not deal with existents: it must only speak of certain Figures (no doubt rare) that belong to a contingency delivered from all constraint other than that of its own eternity. This is the eternity that we seek, because it alone gives meaning to the act of wagering the meaning of one's existence in its name, outside of everything that only lasts for a certain time, whether a passing fashion or a scientific paradigm of the first order.

From now on, speculative philosophy guarantees to all other disciplines of thought *that they alone are in a position to describe and explain* (in a nonnecessarist form) *the world in which we live.* My materialism is so far from being hostile to empiricism properly understood (not identifiable with a determinate empiricist doctrine) that it attempts to found its absolute necessity: my only disagreement with *the true empiricist* is that I affirm that he is absolutely right. But in what does this 'true empiricism' consist? In this: if you want to know or think what is, you must pass by way of a certain regime of the empirical understood in a broad sense: scientific experimentation (the natural sciences), research (the human sciences), but also literary experience and artistic experience (the experience of pure singularity), and so on. And my approach is here to refuse any particular philosophical regime the right to contest the sovereignty of these 'disciplines of experience' that I have enumerated. Now, what contests the sovereignty of these disciplines is not just any philosophy whatsoever: it is *metaphysics* insofar as it, by definition, always leads back to the Principle of Sufficient Reason. The latter, as we have said, in its minimal form always consists in affirming that existing things have a reason to be as they are rather than otherwise. If you accept this principle, the metaphysician will always have the right to dictate what is as being that which must be, and to dominate the nonabsolutist disciplines with his knowledge, claiming to be the only one with access to the necessary reason that makes the world as it is. A position which I call 'dogmatic' or 'absolutist', and to which I oppose a strictly speculative position: that of the factial, which maintains the absolute falsity of the Principle of Sufficient Reason, and thus renders illegitimate any intrusion of necessary reasons into the sphere of what actually exists.

So in this sense our materialism is neither dogmatic nor intrusive: it does not say what the ultimate elements of our world are (this is the role of fundamental physics in each epoch), nor does it claim to demonstrate in general that there is necessarily what there is (such and such a substantial body or perpetually creative becoming). On the contrary, it defends the exclusive right of experience to describe the inexhaustible intricacies of the real that make up our world, and to do so by way of disciplines which not only are taken up in theoretical revolutions unpredictably within themselves, but are separated from each other over the course of any given epoch according to the heterogeneous regimes of experience (from the natural sciences to literary theory, by way of various human and social sciences).

We thus accord a major ontological significance to the fact that academic knowledges are given in organigrammes, in distributions of separate disciplines in which none of them are able to claim to encompass or underwrite all the others. The organigramme is a mode of assembly without fusion of knowledges, which endows it with an original mode of unity different from the system, whose function is the faultless unity of a particular doctrine. Distinct from systematics, 'organigrammatics' is, beneath its dull administrative appearance, an original ontological fact that defends against every phantasm of total knowledge. Its value comes from the fact that its constitution is always contrary to its denomination: every real organigramme fails to unify knowledges like an organism. Insofar as this is the case, the essence of the organigramme is to be reformable by a later administration, in view of a rationalization which, once more, will not take place. The actual being is given in the depth of its union without unity.

And we accord at least as primordial an importance to the second fact that there are productions that exclude themselves from these organigrammes (literature and art, in particular). Not only does the organigramme refuse the idea of a knowledge of knowledges, but it is itself particularized by the separation of external practices from its institutional field. The 'fissured real' is given magnificently in this separation of disciplines, in this sketch of arborescences that in truth are ill-formed, in these flimsy coordinations that are always to be revised, in this centrifugal force that distances knowledges and practices ever further from one another, and makes calls for interdisciplinarity ring ever more hollow. This fact is so strong that each attempt to reduce one discipline to another will have every chance of failing forever – not only for corporatist reasons, whose evidence is not in question, but for powerful ontic reasons. There will always be disciplines in the plural, even if their configuration is modified profoundly from one epoch to another; and this not only, in vague terms, because of the 'domains' separable as surveyed lands, all of the same nature, but, we suspect, because there are in fact in our world fissures of beings *as such*, which resist unification by means of a superior knowledge that would traverse all the others in order to give their ultimate reason.

The fissured real is given above all in the irreducibility of the world of contents and qualities of sensible life, to that of the natural sciences, strictly mathematized. To seek to reduce the first to the second at any cost, or to seek to inject the second at any cost into the first, these are two attitudes which in truth are symmetrical and which do not give a chance to the irreducible, to the fissure that runs through the actual (the world that is in fact ours). To affirm that sensible content – whether conceptualized as *qualia*, or as secondary qualities, or in some other way – are but epiphenomenal lures, and that the real is entirely a matter of the mathematizable basis of physical, chemical or neuronal sciences, is only the inverted version of the thesis according to which there are already infinitesimal contents, sensations, volitions in matter as mathematically rendered by science. These are two inverse reductionisms which tend to have little or no interest in anything that persistently resists their monism.[28]

Our materialism is, on the contrary, an antireductionism. Indeed, it is via *anti*reductionism that we wish to give every chance to the *reduction* of the physical world to its possible mathematization. Now, rather than concluding from this that everything is reducible to this mathematizing gesture, we conclude from it that, since life and human practices overflow this being-mathematizable on every side, there is manifestly an emergence *ex nihilo* of life from matter, and of thought from life. In this case there would indeed be not creations (taken up in the continuity of the virtual, of the Bergsonian past) but irruptions (pure ruptures with no link to the ripening of a past).[29] So many local destructions of the Principle of Sufficient Reason. In this way, every time that a domain of being proves irreducible to another – every time that a discipline takes hold of it that cannot be the prey of any other, what we see is the 'scar' on the real left by this emergence *ex nihilo*.

Speculative materialism thus has as a first consequence, contrary to its metaphysical version:

1. That it does not explain to science what are the true components of matter; of the actual, we say nothing (or almost nothing, as we shall see).

2. That it does not reduce disciplines to a fundamental discipline that would be in a foundational position, or even abolish them in favour of the 'mother-science' that it claims to constitute. Philosophy has its territory – Hyperchaos and its Figures – which in return guarantees for every nonphilosophical discipline that its experience of the actual cannot be dethroned by any philosophy whatsoever.

3. To continually relaunch the inquiry into irreducibilities, for the latter are so many possible irruptive scars fissuring the actual world; inquiries that will never arrive at certain results (the speculative can demonstrate nothing certain about the actual, it is content to track possibilities), but only at more or less faded traces wherein the staunch materialist, with her thirst for an only approximate coherence of being, distributed into broken spheres of beings, indexes the falsity of the Principle of Sufficient Reason. It is notably in these inquiries that materialism allows itself to speak – but only just – of the actual: for such inquiries confirm the pertinence of the organigrammatism of knowledges.

Iteration, Reiteration, Repetition

These fissures are neither *fractures* too wide (which would destroy any coherence of the world), nor *cracks* too fine (which would allow a knowledge to bridge them so as to alone speak the whole of what is): they are *fissures*, gulfs, but narrow enough not to destroy the terrain upon which they occur: telling us at once of the irreducibility of x to y, and of their coarticulation in fact. In exactly the way in which thought saturated with perceptions, sensations and qualitative affects is coordinated with a body that is determinable in its internal movements by strictly mathematical parameters. A union without unity that would make of us at once more than one and less than two – and this in an arithmetic of whole numbers that does not admit of such intermediaries.

Let's now reflect on the consequences of the thesis according to which materialism must be speculative, and not metaphysical, and must therefore prohibit itself from speaking of what is, limiting itself to speaking of the contingency of what is. We are materialists insofar as we obey both of the two principles proper to every materialism:

1. Being is not thought.
2. Thought can think being.

That being is not thought can be seen first of all in the fact that being is the contingency of beings, which is not itself a being – and is thus not a thinking being. Being is Hyperchaos doubled with its unlimited possibilities, of which thought is just one case. Secondly, in chapter three of *After Finitude*, I try to demonstrate (this is the 'materialist ontological proof') that if contingency is eternal, then there must, for all eternity, exist contingent beings – and not nothing. For contingency is nothing beyond that which is contingent – it is not a principle 'floating in the air', but the property of beings that are always determinate. I thus establish that something must exist – and not a pure nothingness – and that this something is not necessarily thinking. This something which is not necessarily thinking is matter in general. Actualized determinately, this matter contains the principle of factual consistency, that is to say the physical constants proper to a given world. Matter is thus thinkable in principle insofar as it is deprived of thought, of subjectivity, and, in a determinate actual world, it could be that it is described fully by a mathematized physics whose referent 'feels nothing' of being what it is.

Here is the thesis of speculative materialism – for the moment incompletely established, for I have not yet demonstrated that all matter, of any world whatsoever, is essentially describable in mathematical terms.

This materialism is thus essentially compatible with Galileism, whatever may be its theories of the moment. Certainly such a doctrine, not being metaphysical, extricates itself from the Principle of Sufficient Reason, insofar as this principle urges us to seek the necessary reasons for what is. But moreover – and this should go without saying – the principle of factiality does not for all that prohibit practitioners of science from explaining the empirically given by means of causes and laws. If we are in fact governed by determinate physical laws, it is entirely legitimate to seek the factual causes and reasons that explain everyday reality. I reject the metaphysical Principle of Sufficient Reason which seeks an absolute reason for the given, but not the various *heuristic principles* that would explain our everyday facticity.

We must, however, take an extra step in this direction, to broach once more the thesis of subjectalism: that of a universal subjectivity of reality. I have rejected this thesis insofar as it claimed to found the absolute necessity of the subjectivation of the real, in the name of the correlational circle invented by Berkeley. But this defence was too strong, leaning on a metaphysical reason, and ending up in apodictically upholding the subjectivity of what is. I have also critiqued the other side of the justification, not of subjectalism in general, but of 'infraconscious' subjectalism, which is directed against all idealism, against every subject of representation: here the defence was too weak, too easily identifiable as an anthropomorphic rhetoric in denial, seeking, by means of a biased self-presentation, to take a place that had been left empty – that of a demystificatory materialism.

But if I have called the first defence too strong, this is because it was general, like the correlational circle – not adjusted to each particular subjectalism. We characterized the era that favoured all subjectalism but did not so much enter into the proper justification of each of them. And if I say that the second defence was too weak, this is because it was imbued with an argument whose aim was rhetorical, one which, held by the philosopher or by her epigones, would permit to dress up certain subjectal modes of thought (those of the gulfs of subjectivity leading to the being or the becoming of all things) in the critical rags of defunct materialism, but would not allow any basic justification of the philosophy considered (subjectalism was not so much admitted for its rigour as in the name of the – idealist – enemies it gave itself).

However, we must add that the treasures that subjectalism offers us, particularly infraconscious subjectalism, may in principle find their place

Iteration, Reiteration, Repetition

in contemporary philosophy *from the very point of view of a materialism become speculative.*

It is here that we must understand the very particular nature of an approach that works at saying nothing about the actual world. Let us first specify the meaning of this ascesis, dealt with so far in a much too undifferentiated way. If we place the actual world outside of our limits, this is because we only derive the general conditions of the possible. Thus, as we have said, we will not derive, in the second part of this text, the conclusion that *our* world is *in fact* mathematizable, but rather that *any possible world whatsoever*, any regime of the real, can *necessarily* be seized through mathematicity. As to the way in which our (actual) world is submitted to mathematicization (what are the laws, constants, etc.), we cannot but leave the job to the disciplines concerned (physics and others), being careful not to overlap any of our results with the 'chronogeny' of one of these theories.[30]

But we have already seen that we could, this time abandoning the strictly demonstrative figural approach, pass into a regime of enquiry – a matter of gropings, hesitations, and perhaps discoveries – interesting ourselves in actual and factual elements – (f)actual, we might perhaps say – whose existence concerns our general approach in a privileged fashion.[31] Here, the figural method is of no use to us, and we have to forge our instruments depending on the type of research mobilized, and on a case-by-case basis. Three types of actual facts have interested us in this way or have been briefly evoked:

1. Those which make possible an elucidating mediation – like the problem posed by the science of dating in the first chapter of *After Finitude*. This type of investigation must allow us to throw away the ladder once it has been climbed. We must use a (f)actual configuration (ancestral dating does in fact exist) and then show, once the demonstration is made (it was a question of establishing that correlationism taken seriously leads to the removal of all signification from the experimental sciences), that this (f)actual complex was useful, but not in principle indispensable to the demonstration: it only allowed us to give, in a first stage, a more accessible and clearer version of it. This is the sphere of (f)actual didactics.

2. The hypothetical traces of ontic fissures prohibiting a same regime of explanation from applying to different domains of the real. We will call these fissures, as 'fossil traces' of irruption *ex nihilo*,

irruptive fulgurites. Fulgurites are 'lightning stones', quasicylindrical tubes produced by the impact of lightning on a rock, or even sometimes on the sandy ground of a desert. By this metaphor I designate a solution of radical ontic discontinuity between two domains of the world: for example between the sensations that the living being feels and its material basis made of nonsensing entities (particles and forces). It is a question of the fulgurite of an irruption *ex nihilo* that cannot be explained by the Principle of Sufficient Reason, and whose existence it is unnecessary to deny by reducing the living to matter or by saturating inorganic matter with life, so as to rediscover a hidden continuity concealed under the manifest discontinuity. Something struck what there was with a pure supplement, which is not a sign of a supernatural action but of the higher absurdity of hyperchaotic contingency. It is not a calculating God who in one single fulguration creates what is supposedly the best of all worlds. It is Hyperchaos that strikes without necessity, and possibly for eternity, any actual world whatsoever, through the production of whatever supplement irreducible to what existed up to that point within it.[32] The absurdity being doubled by the fact that these supplements are articulated with the very thing to which they are irreducible: here is the secret, once more, of the paradoxical duality of soul and body that obsessed classic philosophers, faced with a two that could not be reduced to one (irreducibility of the soul to the body), nor give rise to a separate two (the substantial union of soul and body).[33] We would thus find a trace of it each time that a knowledge had refuted with all the required force the reductionist will of another knowledge against it.[34]

It is these unions without unity (of the mind and the body, of irreducible sciences united in the same world), these fulgurites, that the materialist obstinately seeks: they are so many buried treasures produced by all-powerful nonmeaning having struck the compact, or less cracked, mass of what there was before. We know that natural beauty was a marvel for Kant because of its contingency in regard to mechanical laws – as the trace of an archetypal Intelligence introducing the gratuity of a purposiveness without purpose into the dryness of a causal nature, a flower or the splendour of a sunset that cannot be deduced from the categories of the understanding. In the same way, irruptive fulgurites are a marvel for us because nothing makes them necessary in our world

– which could be saturated with life (if the subjectalist were right) or reducible to a pure mathematicity (if we were no longer there). They offer themselves up to our discovery through philosophical investigation, as one discovers a treasure or a ruin. This is enough to show our radical hostility toward any materialism that would tip over into reductionism.[35]

3. I would add a third (f)actual investigation, which I have evoked before and which I will not broach here, but which it is clear we could ultimately not do without: namely that *there exists in fact a thought* of the necessary contingency of things. This factual existence is that of the *materialist subject*: a contingent and thus underivable subject, and precisely because of this a *materialist* subject – making of its own existence an irruption without necessity in nonthinking being, condemned, in the actual world, always in fact, to precariousness – that is to say, to annihilation, sooner or later. To think the categories of the *subject* thus framed by the conditions of its irruption is the indispensable counterpoint of a critique of the omnipresent *subjectivity* defended by subjectalism. For to say that the subject is not omnipresent demands saying what it is precisely, so as to show clearly that it does not saturate being or becoming. And what is more, there would be no factial ethics if there were no thought of the subject who must face up to this ontology of contingency. And such an ethics is necessary because, as we have said elsewhere, the subject is that which, from our point of view, must confront the impossible mourning of the spectral dilemma.[36] But here again, the very mode of thought with which this problem can be approached will not be pregiven by figural derivation, since here we are dealing with a fact, and not with facticity.

Let us now come back to our initial approach: we said that our offensive against subjectalism aimed at two things: 1) the justification via the Correlation; 2) the subjectivation of the real as the medium of an antiidealist polemic. What we have shown is that the most decisive critique of these positions sets out from the terrain of the Correlation itself: if we leave subjectalism and correlationism face to face, it will always be the second that carries the day by way of emphasizing the facticity of any correlate whatsoever.

However, we have disqualified this second argument, favourable to correlationism – and this in return modifies our position on subjectalism, or at least on a subjectalism properly understood. After all, since the argument of the facticity of the correlate is destroyed in favour of the absoluteness of facticity, and since this type of absolute brings about a speculative philosophy that ceases to decree the definitive truths regarding what is, *nothing prevents the factual possibility of a subjectivity that is omnipresent in the real*. If we do say nothing, or so very little, as to what is, then the statement that there could not be a cosmic subjectivation (i.e. one present in every last corner of the world) falls outside of our purview.

We could then *rehabilitate the theses of subjectalism not qua metaphysical truths* (necessary and founded on the Correlation), *but qua postulates* of a 'possible project for the description of our world'. Postulates that are opposed to the (f)actuality that we are investigating, but postulates whose now hypothetical character makes them compatible with a thinking of unconditioned contingency: for *nothing prevents Hyperchaos from producing a world that would bear no trace of its capacity for fulguration – a world where everything would be held in the continuity of intensities, with no pure rupture indexical of its power to produce that which is without past*. Nothing prohibits Hyperchaos from producing Deleuze's Chaosmos, making of the thinking of the latter a correct rendering of what, in fact, is. Not only is the factual not the principal enemy of the thinking of intensity, it actually frees it from its true principal adversary – correlationism. The fundamental discord between the factual and subjectalism would only intervene in two cases: a) if the subjectalist were to consider that the world must necessarily be as she describes it (falling back into metaphysics); b) if the subjectalist were to consider that the subjectivated world that she renders constitutes an ultimate factum, and that there is no unconditioned principle beyond that archi-fact (falling into antispeculative thinking). But this disagreement does not at all prevent the possibility that we maintain for Hyperchaos to have engendered a world *(f)actually adequate* to that of the wills to power, of durations, or of inorganic life.

So nothing prohibits *the hypothesis* that our world is *in fact* – contingently – shaped by intensively graded subjectivities. This hypothesis, certainly, is no longer indispensable, and doubly so: it is not indispensable to science – it is not necessary, as Deleuze believes, in order to think causality – since science's mathematicization of nature does not appeal to such a subjectivist interpretation of the world;[37] and it is not indispensable to speculative philosophy, for which a nonsubjective real is perfectly thinkable. This hypothesis can nevertheless be advanced according to a heuristic principle that would go 'beyond' the scientific explanation of our world, without touching on the speculative absolute of materialism.

One would thus pose the hypothesis of the subjectivity of the real no longer as a metaphysician (*métaphysicien*) who in doing so claims to establish an absolute truth, but – according to the term I propose – as a 'cryptophysicist (*crypto-physicien*)' conscious of the contingent nature of the subjectivity thus investigated. I call 'cryptophysics' a metaphysics that has become postulatory and is no longer dogmatic. I could speak of a postulatory metaphysics, but in *After Finitude* I identified all metaphysics with a thinking of the absolute mediated by an absolutized use of the Principle of Sufficient Reason. All metaphysics is thus, according to me, dogmatic, and I need a new term to describe a discourse which, even though its rendering of the world proceeds beyond constituted knowledges, in particular scientific knowledges, does not claim to seat its description of the real upon a necessary foundation, limiting itself to a revisable postulate that it tries to verify by applying it to the reality of its times. If I employ the expression 'cryptophysics' this is, on one hand, because this regime of thought is a quasiclandestine physics – a second physics, but not one endorsed, like true physics, by physicists themselves: a 'speculative physics'. And on the other hand, because this clandestinity supposes a 'physics from below': it is generally deployed as an infraconscious immersion reversed out onto the world.

Here we see the advantage of the factial: whereas a metaphysical subjectalism excludes the possibility that the principle of factiality should have some truth, the principle of factiality includes the possibility that the real might conform to some kind of subjectalism. The chaosmos excludes the possibility of Hyperchaos; but Hyperchaos includes the possibility of the Chaosmos.

Nevertheless, it is not a matter of falling into irenicism here, but of redefining the terms of a confrontation. What we are saying is that we cannot derive from the principle of factiality Figures that involve an actual reality – and thus that we cannot, by means of figural derivation, prohibit the possibility that a determinate subjectalism might be an accurate rendering of the actual world. Yet the factial nonetheless incorporates, as we have said, another theoretical regime than that of the sole demonstration of Figures: that of an enquiry, within the bare actual, into the facts that retain a 'trace' of the irruptions of Hyperchaos in *our* world. Subjectalism saturates the world with its graded continuities, but as for us, we are interested by everything that resists this intensificatory model of things.

And, as I have said, these enquiries into the (f)actual are linked to positive knowledges, on the one hand insofar as they resist their absorption by one sole knowledge among them, and on the other hand insofar as they multiply the counterexamples against all metaphysics – or any cryptophysics – that would claim to underlie them. Every cryptophysics will be a globalizing thought, and by virtue of this fact it will enrich philosophy with its heroic brio: but it will also always have to contend with the fact that the least crossing over between its positions and a portion of the real treated by a disciplinary knowledge will bring about the risk of a destabilization of its approach insofar as Science will transform itself. Every fact of an actual real is like the crest of a wave illusorily fixed by a photograph: for a certain time, it seems sufficiently fixed and solid to provide a seat for a theoretical position, but suddenly, or gradually, the photograph reveals itself to be an image from a film that had been freeze-framed; the rolling of the sea, that is to say Science, takes over again; and there is no longer a crest. Here cryptophysics will encounter the same difficulty as metaphysics: the most powerful of cryptophysics are immersed in the mass of scientific facts of their times (by exigency of precision in the strong sense), and once the facts upon which they depend are modified or vanish, they will no longer have any disciples, but only commentators. Or, at best: disciples affirming that a recent theoretical advance renews the actuality of a cryptophysics that was thought obsolete. Thus a new crest of the wave is described as the shore of salvation.

For my part, I proceed differently: I observe the mathematization of the real, without entering into its theories; and I observe the irreducibility of knowledges and arts one to the other. I observe on the one hand (and will soon demonstrate the status of this observation) a mathematizable material world: in this sense my materialism is a 'materialism'. And I observe on the other hand that no mathematical reduction of the disciplines that deal with the subjective contents of our humanity can be conceived of. I thus observe that our world allows us to glimpse, through the very multiplicity of its regimes of knowledge and experience, the presence of fulgurites between irreducible fields. I cannot demonstrate this division, but I show its adequation to the very organization of disciplines, to their resistance when faced with an attempt at impoverishing them (one knowledge reduces the others to itself), or to subordinate them (one cryptophysics traverses all knowledges to show them what they have in common). My position is never dependent on a 'theory of the moment', on a particular fact. I show only the perfect thinkability of the very idea of the organigramme as a defective putting-into-organism of disciplines.

It could be that the actual world is so meagre as to only comprise a single nature infinitely creative of new and unforeseeable forms. A world of intensities heavy with their past and never-endingly amassing new configurations without anything escaping their innovative and subjectivating causality. Not one sole irruption (a pure supplementary discontinuity), but a world of continuist creation. Everything would be growth, nothing would be fulgurance, irruption without any attachment to the past, without any link with the context in which it arrived. Not a gram of pure death would be allowed to us there, not a single entity without relation to that living and open Whole would be offered to us – not one negligence, in sum (*neglegere* as contrary of *relegere*, from which religion plausibly comes). Intensities, relations everywhere; the linked linked to the linked. Not one sole *ravishing negligence*: not one sole difference of nature irreducible to relational conformity. No exception, no entirely nonsubjective instance, only, again and again, returning from afar, and implacably, novelties full of the past that they at once contain and overcome. And this world, if it were our world, we would certainly have to accept.

But what we would lack in this creative saturation would be this hollow tube of the fulgurite, this infinite and local break, capable of not curling up into these complex lives, fabricated of complicit lives, within which we swim to the point of suffocation. A breakage which, offering us the spectacle of a world traversed by the silent seism of a secret unlinking, would articulate the Universe with itself through the mediation of the trace of a lightning strike frozen as soon as it happened. Difference in nature ceasing to be vanquished by difference in degree. Difference fissuring nature beyond any degree. Creation and intensity almost everywhere, we can concede this; but *what is more*, some ruptures offering to the world the discrete reminder of its mad origin.

Essay on the derivation of Galileism

I now come to the principal subject of this paper: the attempt to obtain a factial derivation that would legitimate *the absolutory capacity of modern science* – that is to say, *Galilean science*, which proceeds via the mathematization of nature. It is my project to rediscover a Cartesian rather than a Kantian conception of experimental science. Instead of arguing that mathematics and physics only bear on the a priori forms of our experience, I am convinced – for reasons that I cannot fully explain here and which pertain to the 'aporia of the archefossil' discussed in chapter one of *After Finitude* – that one must maintain, like Descartes, that mathematics and mathematized physics give us the means to recover the properties of a world that is radically independent of thought. Of course, we must admit – this time against Descartes – that every theory of the experimental sciences is revisable. But it is a matter of establishing that it at least makes sense to suppose that a scientific theory can identify a true property of reality, independently of whether we exist to think that reality. In this way, unlike the correlationist (whether Kantian or not) who affirms that the world is but the obverse of human (or animal) representation, we would no longer have to perform ever more intellectual acrobatics to account for the scientific description of the Universe anterior to the appearance of terrestrial life. As the modern natural sciences are characterized by their mathematization, it is reasonable to suppose that their capacity to speak of a 'world without us' stems from mathematics itself.

My plan is thus as follows: I will try to show a minimal condition, modest yet fundamental, of the various contemporary formal languages – logical as well as mathematical. This minimal condition, as we shall see, has to do with our capacity to *think a sign devoid of meaning* (abbreviated as 'sign *dm*').[38] I will then derive this capacity to think a sign empty of meaning from the principle of factiality, by showing that there is an essential link between this kind of sign and absolutized contingency. I therefore will have to show in what way this factial derivation of the sign *dm* allows us to argue that physics (or any other natural science) must be based upon this absoluteness of the empty sign in order to produce hypothetical (revisable) descriptions of the present world, capable, in turn, of being true in an absolute sense – that is to say, independently of our existence.

But in order for this last proposition to be clear, one must distinguish between two senses of the word 'absolute'. In the first, 'absolute' refers to a necessary property of every being; this is the absolute in the speculative sense. Thus facticity, and the logical consistency derived from it, are absolutely necessary and infrangible properties of every being. This type of properties, absolute in the first sense of the term, I call *primoabsolutory* properties. But I also identify a second sense of the word 'absolute', which here concerns the reference of the natural sciences: here, then, 'absolute' designates properties of the world that I do *not* posit as absolutely necessary, but as facts which, as to their existence, are *radically independent of thought*. To say it more clearly: the laws and constants described by the natural sciences are not, for me, necessary – like every thing, they are subject to that superior regime of Time that I have called Hyperchaos. But I would like to show that these laws and constants are not, for all that, mere correlates of thought; that they are – presuming they are described by a true theory – absolute in the original sense of *absolutus*: *separate* from us, independent of the thought that we have of them. Contingent, of course, but independent of our existence for their perdurance. These properties of the world, absolute in the second sense of the word, I call *deuteroabsolutory*: properties independent vis-à-vis the human, implying no ontological necessity.

How is this articulated with what we have said above on the perishable nature of scientific theories? A figural derivation is eternal: it is valid for any possible reality, and in this sense it is primoabsolutory. What I am going to derive is thus not the fact that *our* world, the actual world, is describable in mathematical terms – but that *every possible world* can be mathematized and can conserve in itself these mathematical characteristics, whether or not there is any thinking to formulate them. I will thus legitimate the deuteroabsolutory practice of the experimental sciences, which strive to propose a determinate series of mathematized descriptions of the real. The actual world reproduced by the sciences is thinkable, against the correlationist thesis, in terms of a world independent of our intention. In this way, the theories put forward by science – whatever they may be – could always, qua *hypotheses*, be thought as *true in themselves* and not only 'for us'. And if this set of theories is superseded, it will be in favour of another new set of theories and/or experimental facts, which in their turn, as every time, could be posited as absolutely true, of a deuteroabsolutory truth.

My objective can therefore be stated as follows: to prove the capacity of the experimental sciences to produce deuteroabsolutory statements, and to do so by means of an appropriate factual derivation. To demonstrate that mathematics permits physics to produce revisable hypotheses pertaining to the contingent givens of a world independent of us as regards its factual existence. Thus we will have arrived at an understanding of the remarkable capacity of the sciences to describe the Universe as it existed anterior to man and to living beings, and as it will without doubt exist after they have gone.[39]

The stakes, in more graphic terms, can be formulated as follows: can we found the capacity of mathematics to grant us access to the Kingdom of the dead, and then to return so as to recount to the living the discoveries of such a journey? The principle of materialism, as I have said, is infernal: it supposes that the Hells of the inorganic world – those deep, subterranean realms where life and subjectivity are absent – can nevertheless become the object of human knowledge. For the materialist, this pure other of ourselves that is death is available to us before death, in the form of a knowledge of what we shall be when we are no more. In *After Finitude*, the factial began to open this breach towards the without-life, in the form of universal derivations – such as those of the contingency and the noninconsistency of every existent, whether subjective or nonsubjective. But nothing has been said, in these primoabsolutory statements, of the factual determinations of our world, or of that which is characteristic of its dead matter. To do so one must accede to statements capable of describing determinate realities. This is the task of Galilean science: not to tell us what is the universal property of every existent, but to tell us what the dead looks like in our world. To found this exploratory power is indeed to found the deuteroabsolutory capacity of mathematics.

The resolution of the problem was first formulated in a discouragingly general way, but inevitably so: I needed a specific criterion of logicity and of mathematicity. Not a criterion of rationality in general – like consistency, derivable from factiality, which is a criterion of all rationality, in formal as well as natural languages – but a criterion for formal languages alone. A criterion at once general – and thus modest – enough to belong to the logico-mathematical as such, yet specific enough to apply to it alone, to the exclusion of natural languages. If one had to find this differentiating criterion that characterizes formal languages alone, then it would have to harbour, if one were on the right track, a use of language that rests in some notable way upon the absoluteness of contingency. This specific dependence upon contingency would then have to be capable of founding the absolutory character of mathematics, and consequently of the experimental sciences formulated by means of mathematics.

In other words, before verifying whether the logico-mathematical does indeed rest upon an implicit intuition of eternal contingency, one would have to discover the criterion by which natural and formal languages differ decisively.

Now, the solution appeared to us precisely in the name given to modern logic and mathematics: they are called, as I said, *formal* languages – that is to say, languages that originate in the formalism that took hold in logical and mathematical writing from Hilbert onward. Hilbert's formalism has been much discussed, along with its potential limitations – particularly the well-known failure of Hilbert's programme in view of Gödel's proofs regarding systems capable of containing arithmetic (the impossibility of a proof of consistency, incompleteness). But, as we will observe, I take up only a very small part of this formalism, albeit what seems to me the most

Iteration, Reiteration, Repetition

interesting part – a part that has never been seriously contested by later mathematics.

In what does formalism in mathematics generally consist, if we limit ourselves to its most elementary expression?

Let's begin with an example, which will accompany us throughout the discussion, since it is the easiest one for me to explain: that of set theory in its standard axiomatic form, so-called Zermelo-Fraenkel set theory. (However, I would add straight away that the same considerations apply to category theory, which is in many ways more powerful than set theory, and which finds more favour with certain contemporary thinkers.)

This axiomatic is formulated in a first-order logic, that is to say in a logic whose quantifiers ('For every' and 'There exists') bear only upon terms ('individuals') and never upon properties. Thus, it uses five types of sign: variables (which are placeholders for individuals of the predicate calculus), logical connectives (negation, conjunction, disjunction, implication, equivalence), quantifiers (universal, existential), relations (equality and belonging), and punctuation (parentheses, curly brackets). It is with these signs alone, and those that can be defined with them, that set theory formulates its axioms (which are eight in number, if we include the axiom of choice and the axiom of foundation) and its theorems. Set theory, as we know, 'has progressively become the general axiomatic framework in which mathematics is written'.[40] For this is a theory capable, notably, of constructing both numbers (ordinals and cardinals) and functions (which are a certain type of set, a set of ordered pairs) – and thus a theory that is 'foundational' for mathematics in this simple sense that it constructs its two principal objects: numbers and functions.

On first sight, set theory consists of an axiomatic in the sense inherited from Euclid's geometry: a minimal set of statements on the basis of which all others can and must be logically deduced. But this axiomatic differs from Euclid's insofar as it is a formal axiomatic, in a sense that principally stems from the revolution that Hilbert set off. In what does this formalism consist, and in what way are contemporary axiomatics characterized by it?

In the following way: in the axiomatic as inherited from Euclid, *the definitions of terms precede postulates and axioms*. For example, the three first definitions of Euclid's *Elements*, with which Book I opens, begin by defining the point, the line, and the limits of a line: the point is that which has no parts, the line is a length without breadth, and the limits of a line are points (which have already been defined). It is only once these definitions have been made that we get the postulates, unproven or unprovable principles that in their formulation make use of the terms previously defined, and the axioms, unprovable principles concerning the relations of the whole and its parts.

Before stating the principles – statements posited as true – a Euclidean axiomatic thus puts forward the definitions of the terms used in the proofs or in the postulates. Now, what is specific to a formal axiomatic, that by way of which it breaks with the Euclidean-type axiomatic, on the contrary bears upon the fact *that one does not begin with any initial definitions*. In the axioms, one immediately posits relations between terms which themselves are not defined. Consequently, I would argue that we must clearly distinguish two types of signs, which I shall call 'base-signs' and 'operator-signs'.

Let us explain this difference, still with reference to set theory. The base-signs in set theory are the individual constants and variables, generally designated by Greek letters: α, β, γ, etc., or the letters of unknowns: x, y, z, etc. These terms are *named* as sets; but to name them, we cannot insist strongly enough, is not to *define* them. In set theory, we never get mixed up in defining what a set is: we limit ourselves to designating with a nondefined sign what an interpretation of the system might designate with this name – without this nomination at all influencing the formal system under consideration.

It is hence this that we call a 'set': a sign, itself devoid of signification, and a fortiori of any reference. And this is the initial object of mathematics, insofar as the latter is 'founded' upon set theory: the pure and simple sign that refers only to itself.

The second type of sign, which I have called the operator-sign, designates the various operations that will be able to be carried out on the base-signs: these are signs already used in logic (implication, conjunction, disjunction, equality) just as well as properly mathematical signs. In fact, set theory adds nothing to the logical calculus but the signs of membership ($\in$) and non-membership ($\notin$).

It is through the intermediation of the operator-signs – in particular of the membership sign and the axioms that prescribe its usage – that one can intuitively rediscover certain properties that are actually reminiscent of those of ordinary sets. For example, the axiom of extensionality gives the condition of the identity of two sets: a and b are identical sets if they have the same elements. This is a rule of substitution of one set for another, once they are both entirely determined by their elements alone. But this axiom does not define what a set is any more than the others. It only exhibits the condition of the identification of two sets, without giving any meaning to what is thus identified. Moreover, such a definition is, for one simple reason, impossible in set theory: a set is nothing other than that which can have other sets as its elements (an element of a set is in fact always another set), or that which can be a member of another set. As we can see, what characterizes a set cannot give rise to any definition – except a circular definition supposing in its formulation that which is to be defined.

It is therefore very much as if the base-signs progressively acquired properties that (more or less) conform to their initial nomination. But they do not do so through an initial definition; they do so through the *effect* that the operations they support can have upon them. The base-signs – which are signs dm – acquire an 'apparent density' that is but the effect of the froth of the ever more complex operations that they can support, without ever themselves departing from their originary absence of signification. In a formal axiomatic, one must thus avoid being led astray by the appellations that only give names to the base-signs: names, and not meaning.

The axioms are thus not definitions – not even 'definitions in disguise', as is often suggested. They are not at all definitions: it is an entirely different matter, a matter of the substitution of a *relation* for a definition. Coming back to set theory, we observe that the predicate 'to be a set' simply does not exist, whereas sets, on the other hand, can receive numerous predicates (ordinal, cardinal, empty, infinite, etc.). The base-sign hence never acquires the meaning of the word 'set' as formulated in natural language. But the remarkable point here is that mathematics turns out to be capable of producing statements that *are* very rich in signification, on the basis of operations upon such signs that remain void of meaning. For if it always remains impossible to define what a set is, it is perfectly possible, in the ZF axiomatic, to differentiate between sets, and thus to construct remarkable sets: for example, the empty set, defined as the set of which no other set is a member, and on the basis of which one can construct the whole succession of ordinals, the source of all numeration.

From what we have said so far, we can then draw a precise principle of distinction between a natural language and a formal language:[41] for we can decide *to differentiate them according to the role that signs devoid of meaning play within them*. We shall therefore say that a formal language, unlike a natural language, accords a structural role to the sign devoid of meaning – at least on a *syntactical* level. For alphabetical natural languages do indeed make rule-governed use of letters and syllables that are, in themselves, devoid of signification – but they do so at the morphological level of the constitution of words, and not at the syntactical level of the constitution of sentences. At the syntactical level, a natural language can certainly also use words devoid of meaning – for example Mallarmé's 'ptyx', if we agree that this word means nothing – but there is no rule that *imposes* this type of word upon natural languages. Their propensity is, on the contrary, to avoid them, so as to fulfil their ordinary function of communication. Consequently, what is proper to a natural language is to grant, at the level of syntax, a contingent (and generally marginal) role to the sign *dm;* whereas what is proper to a formal language is to grant it an essential and structural role at the very same syntactic level.

These two usages of the sign *dm* allow me to distinguish between what I shall call *formal meaning* and *ordinary meaning*. What is proper to formal meaning, in my definition, is hence the rule-governed use of syntactical units that are devoid of signification (or non-signifying). What is proper to ordinary meaning in natural languages is the *absence* of a rule-governed use of syntactical units devoid of meaning.[42] My object becomes thus more precise, for I can make the following hypothesis, which can be formulated very concisely: my aim is to show why *formal meaning is capable of producing deuteroabsolutory truths* that are inaccessible to ordinary sense.

Before tackling head-on the problem of the status of the nonsignifying sign, we must have in mind a sufficiently current idea as to the relation between philosophy and formal languages. A widespread thesis claims that to conceive formal languages as the operating manipulation of empty signs is to grant licence to all kinds of philosophical speculation, and, more specifically, to all kinds of ontological considerations. This thesis is found as much among mathematicians as among philosophers. On the side of mathematicians, Jean Dieudonné, for example, says that when the mathematician is attacked by philosophers with their paradoxes, he rushes to hide behind formalism, maintaining that 'mathematics is just a combination of meaningless symbols'.[43] It is thus implicitly understood by the mathematician that the empty symbolism of mathematics is a way of neutralizing any ontological question or intention.

Faced with this reaction of the mathematician, the philosopher seems to have the choice between two options. Either she agrees with the definition of mathematics as 'combination of meaningless symbols' and resigns herself to the fact that it is futile to seek an ontology underlying mathematics, since mathematics is identified with a pure manipulatory technique of

Iteration, Reiteration, Repetition

empty signs. Or she tries, on the contrary, to break through the mathematician's formalist defence by uncovering an ontology hidden beneath the appearance of empty signs – and does so by contesting the absence of real signification for these base-signs: by discovering their hidden meaning and referent.

We see the alternative: either mathematics is the pure manipulation of empty signs and excludes itself from all ontological consideration; or it supports an ontology and does not ultimately rest upon a network of signs *dm*, but on signs whose hidden meaning must be discovered. For example, one will say, with Alain Badiou, that the signs called 'sets', however nondefined, do indeed designate that remarkable ontological referent that is the 'pure multiple', the set all of whose elements are themselves sets.

But I maintain a third thesis that refuses the alternative held up by the two previous positions: instead of considering the manipulation of empty signs (*dm*) an exclusion from ontology, I seek to constitute *an ontology of the empty sign* – and I affirm that the singular ontological import of mathematics proceeds precisely from the fact that, unlike ordinary meaning, it makes systematic use of signs that are effectively devoid of signification.

In other words, I propose to examine the ontological import of mathematical formalism as such: precisely insofar as it exhibits what is doubtless an essential characteristic (or such is, in any case, my hypothesis) of (logico-)mathematicity itself.[44] I am convinced that an essential part of the enigma of mathematics – In what does mathematics consist? What does it speak of? – turns upon the elucidation of the following question: How *can we* think a sign devoid of meaning? And what exactly do we do when we mentally produce such a notion? My thesis will be that we fulfil an eminently ontological aim when we do so.

Let us therefore pass on to the central question of our discussion: What is a sign devoid of meaning? The first thing that, to my mind, must be clearly maintained – for it does not go without saying, even today – is that a sign devoid of meaning *is* still a sign. I mean to say that a sign void of meaning is an authentic sign: it is no less a sign than a sign that signifies something. This simple remark, which I shall justify in a moment, is enough to distance us from most modern analyses of the sign, which, setting out from the linguistic sign or the indexical sign, do not conceive of the sign outside of its capacity *to refer to something*: to a meaning, an object, a reference. The linguistic sign, in Saussure, cannot be thought outside of the indissociable correlation of a signifier and a signified. The sign, in Peirce, is thought as referring to an object through the intermediary of an interpretant. If we hold strictly to such an obligatory correlation of sign and meaning, one will refuse to maintain that a sign empty of all meaning is really a sign – above all if its role is syntactical (if it has the rank of a word and not that of a letter).

And yet what mathematical formalism teaches us is that there does indeed exist a form of sign – one whose function is essential – that refers to nothing other than itself as sign: neither icon nor index nor signifier. A sign that is not the index of any reality outside of itself – whether a reality that it resembles (icon), the trace that allows us to infer an animal's path (index), or the word articulated to a signification (signifier). A sign that neither signifies nor denotes anything; that refers to nothing other than itself; and which, at the limit, *is therefore no longer a reference* since nothing other than itself, in its given presence, is in play. But what the formalist revolution must also convince us of is that a rigorous theory of the sign *dm* must not only incorporate the empty sign into semiotics, but that it must in fact *begin* with the examination of this type of sign. For the sign *dm* is the most elementary and thus the most fundamental form of the sign: that of the pure sign, brought to our attention in person, *as* sign, *before* the intervention of meaning. The empty sign, qua true sign, uncovers for us the remarkable fact *that meaning is contingent in the constitution of the sign*, that the sign has no need for meaning in order to be a sign – and that semiotics (the study of signs) comes before semantics (the theory of meaning), and is independent of it: the former covers a domain that is autonomous from the latter, the domain of the nonsignifying sign.

By affirming that the sign devoid of meaning is indeed a sign, I wish to break with a widespread philosophical conception that denies the sign the capacity to remain a sign if it has no meaning. This conception is both very general and vague, but it is detectable any time a philosopher thinks that it goes without saying that *a sign, if it is devoid of meaning* (or of signification, there is no difference here), *is reduced to its material support*: a trace of ink on paper, a sound wave, or, we might say today, liquid crystals visible on a screen. The very expression *flatus vocis* to designate an expression or a word devoid of meaning translates this presupposition: for *flatus vocis*, the 'breath of the voice', is nothing more than a sound. Remove the meaning, it is suggested, and all that remains is the sound and not the sign. In other words, such a conception suggests that the immaterial part of the sign resides wholly in its meaning, and that if this meaning is removed from the sign, the latter is reduced to its physical part alone – like a body deprived of its soul.

Against all reduction of this kind, of the sign devoid of meaning to its material basis (sound or mark), we must indeed maintain *that there exists in the very sign itself a stratum of immateriality* that not only *has nothing to do with meaning* but that precedes it, conditions it, and can exist independently of it. But what, then, does this immateriality independent of the ideality of meaning consist in? This nonsemantic stratum of semiotic immateriality is indeed known to linguists – and there is abundant literature on the subject. The way it is spoken of therein allows us to understand that there exists in the sign a duality that is not that of the signifier and the signified, but another more fundamental duality that precedes it: that *of the type and the token*. A sign – for example, a written sign – is never just a mark on paper that you have before your eyes; for when you see a mark *as* a sign, this mark ceases to be only a mark, that is to say a singular material thing, and becomes *a token of a type-sign*. When I write the letter 'a' three times onto the board, I write three tokens of a type that itself is unique: the letter 'a' in general, as instantiated in the tokens proposed, without, however, being reducible to them. In other words, when you see a mark as sign, you see *the limitlessly reproducible token of an intangible type-sign*. If I take the 'a' as a mark, I am only dealing with an individual trace of ink; if I take it as a token, I see in it the essentially unlimited number of its possible reproductions under the aegis of a type that is, itself, always identical to itself. Now, this *potentially* unlimited reproduction of the token obviously does not concern anything material in the latter. If we ask a factory manager to reproduce, in a given time, a standard part that we present to her, she will evaluate the material quantity she can produce, and the possible rate of production given the technical and human means at her disposal. But faced with a token, the envisaged possibility of its reproduction is not at all linked to the technical and energetic capacity of humanity. I have no need to evaluate the stock of material 'a's that humanity could produce so long as it survives in order to see the tokens of 'a' as being reproducible 'at will'. It is thus an essentially immaterial possibility of reproduction that constitutes the duality of type and token. *There is indeed in the 'signifier' – independently of the 'signified' – an immaterial internal articulation (type/token) that allows it to differentiate itself from the sole material support of the sign, without for all that appealing to the immateriality of meaning.*

This distinction, as I have said, is not at all new; it is well known, in fact – at least since Peirce, who thematizes it in the form of the distinction between 'sinsign' and 'legisign' – and, as I said, there is considerable literature on the subject. But, although I cannot claim to have been able to exhaustively review this corpus, I have not found within it the two points to which I would like to draw your attention. The type has given rise to many theories concerning its status:[45] Does it belong to the universals – that is to say, is it a property? Or is it rather an abstract object, like a number or a class? Or is it perhaps a genus? This is the kind of discussion that the notion provokes – without any definitive agreement having been reached on the subject, as we might expect. Now, what I find unfortunate in this type of debate is that it speaks of the type-sign *in general*: that is to say, without making the prior distinction between the sign provided (*pourvu*) with meaning and the sign devoid (*dépourvu*) of meaning. But to my mind, if one wishes to speak of the type under the best possible theoretical conditions, then it must be treated 'in the pure state'; one should hence begin by divesting it of every other form of immateriality within the sign – that is to say, one should examine it in a sign empty of semantic content. It is there that one will have the chance to understand what is going on.

I thus propose a neologism to distinguish the type that interests me and which I am going to discuss, that is to say, the type in its pure form: the type of the sign void of meaning. Drawing on the Greek adjective 'kenos', meaning 'empty', I call this type of empty sign the *kenotype*. And so my question will be: How can we grasp a kenotype; or: How can we grasp, within a mark itself, the duality type/token of an empty sign?

The second aspect that I do not find, or find insufficiently treated, in these kinds of discussion is what I consider the major theoretical interest that there is in bringing together the problem of the ontological status of the type with the question of formal languages.[46] For me, this convergence of problematics seems a priority, and in fact in it are concentrated the entire stakes of the question of the type in general. The sign empty of meaning constitutes the junction point between the formalist refoundation of mathematics and the philosophical discussions on the ontology of the type-sign. For this crossover of problematics – a crossover of the theory of the type/token and of mathematical formalism – allows us to exhibit the possibility of an ontology of the sign *dm*, and thus to combine the upholding of an ontology of mathematics with the definition of the latter as the manipulation of empty symbols; two theses which are usually, as we have said, considered mutually exclusive.

Let us then take up our analysis of the empty sign once more. The grasping of a sign *dm* implies, as we said, its division into (keno)type and token.

Iteration, Reiteration, Repetition

I argue that this division of the empty sign into a material part – the ink mark, the sound – and an immaterial part, also distinguishes it (at least in our conception) from an individual thing. But an objection emerges right away. Could I not identify this type/token duality with that banal duality that runs through every thing, the duality between its individuality – this chair, here and now – and its *concept*: the immaterial concept of chair? In that case, the kenotype would be nothing other than the concept of a sign considered as a mark, as a material and individual thing pending its designation.

Let us formulate this objection more precisely. When I direct my attention to a material chair qua chair, I certainly grasp a certain duality: this chair here, that I perceive here and now, and at the same time the concept of chair, which contains an indefinite number of possible chair-instantiations. When I consider a sign devoid of meaning, one might hence think that its type/token duality is nothing more than the banal duality between an individual material form, perceived here and now – the form of the 'a' made of ink that I perceive on the paper – and its concept (the concept of 'a', considered as a certain type of loop form characteristic of a certain type of letter). The kenotype would then be nothing more than a concept: the concept of 'a' that is instantiated by this or that material *a*.

And yet we can easily demonstrate that the relation of the type to its token is not that of a concept to its objects.

The letters of an alphabet, hieroglyphs, calligrams certainly have their concept: *a* can have for its concept 'first letter of an alphabet common in languages of European origin'. More generally, to qualify a sign as a 'letter', an 'icon', a 'calligram', etc. is indeed to make it fall under a certain concept. But the type does nothing of the sort: with the type we can mentally grasp an 'a' written on paper as the token of a type that is only this same 'a' insofar as it can be iterated in the course of one and the same reading (whether in 'giraffe' or in 'Paris'). The type is nothing more than the iterative use of a sign, which is its minimal condition. You can recognize two 'a's, two hieroglyphs or two calligrams identically – and thus inscribe them in an iterability – but for all that you will not necessarily learn the difference between the concept of a letter and the concept of a calligram.

We can verify this immediately through the following imaginary situation: suppose that, through mere fantasy, I think about developing a secret code, and that I begin by putting down on paper the signs – whether already existent or not – of which it is composed, and this before even determining what language these signs will allow to cipher. The sole fact that my

167

marks are intended as signs means that I grasp them as iterable. The result of my idea of my first signs could therefore be as follows:

$$$, etc.
✦✦✦, etc.
༃༃༃, etc.
¶¶¶, etc.

These signs are properly speaking signs of *nothing*: I do not yet know what I am going to use them for. And yet, I can already grasp them as the signs of my new code – identical in terms of their type, iterated in terms of their token. I can decide to make them the letters of an alphabet – if I decide to cipher an alphabetical language – but just as well make them the ciphers of calligrams or of any other kind of sign. I can also decide that one series will in fact be constituted *of the same type* as another series: that the '$', for example, will be the same 'letter' as the '✦', the latter being only another typographical version of the former (the '✦' would become the capitals or italics of the "$").

All of this demonstrates well enough that I can make use of the type/token difference without yet using the concept/object difference, and that the two couplets are not at all reducible to each other. Everything depends at this stage on the simple arbitrariness of my decisions as to the form of the signs, the language chosen, and the identity or not of the series. We can even imagine a language made of fanciful signs that aims not to reproduce any real language: the pure fancy of a pseudolanguage, or a lure designed to fool an enemy by making him believe that one is intensively exchanging coded information whereas there are really just simple sequences devoid of meaning.[47] Inversely, the cryptographer who needs to decipher a coded language will be obliged to discern distinct iterable signs before determining in which case these differences are meaningful and in which they are not: the couple type/token will thus precede the conceptualization of the elements of the language being analysed.

In short, as we see, the type exceeds the sphere of the concept because it introduces distinct series (to be differentiated or identified later), outside of the sphere of meaning – whereas the concept itself is not capable of navigating outside of the domain of signification.

What we also encounter here, of course, is the *arbitrariness of the sign*. The expression is a famous one, apparently well-known, but in this case the

Iteration, Reiteration, Repetition

familiarity is deceiving. Because by this expression, I do *not* mean arbitrariness in the Saussurian sense. In Saussure, the arbitrariness of the sign designates, as we know, the *unmotivated* character of the sign *with regard to its meaning*. In other words, the 'arbitrariness' of the sign in Saussure means that there is no 'internal' (natural or necessary) bond between a signifier and its signified: '[t]he idea of "sister (sœur)"', writes Saussure, 'is not linked by any inner relationship to the succession of sounds s-ö-r which serves as its signifier', and could thus be represented by any other series of sounds – as we can very well see from the example of words outside of French that express the same idea.[48]

But for my part, I am interested in the signifier *before* its link to the signified; and therefore, I am interested in a *pre-Saussurian* arbitrariness of the sign defined independently of its relation to meaning. In short, I am interested in an arbitrariness *anterior to the couple signifier/signified*, since the two elements of this latter couplet are indissociable; in an arbitrariness that is more fundamental than 'unmotivation' (this is what I call arbitrariness in the Saussurian sense: the nonnecessary link between sign and meaning). This arbitrariness is that which, as above, allows me to posit signs before even having determined their usage; or even to posit signs in order to produce a language which, in truth, is not a language. But this arbitrariness is decisive for any use of the sign: for it alone allows me to grasp a mark like ✽ no longer as a (unique) trace of ink but as an (iterable) sign. It is once I have recognized that a mark can be indefinitely replaced by any other mark (in a process of ciphering of the language to which it belongs) that I can recognize that this mark is indeed a sign. It is once I have recognized that a language is cipherable that I have recognized a language as a language. *The pre-Saussurian arbitrariness of the sign is the essential condition for the recognition of a sign as a sign.*

Perhaps one could still make the following objection: that the marks ✦✦✦, etc. or ✽✽✽, etc. are indeed grasped through a concept – that of the sign *in general* anterior to its division into letter, calligram, and so on. It will then be said that it is the very concept of sign itself that allows me to mentally iterate it identically: thus the very meaning of the word 'concept' would be responsible for the iterative power of the mark – the 'etc.' would mean: ✦ is a sign, ✦ is also a sign (and the same sign), and so on.

But, once more, this is impossible. For the concept of sign equally identifies *every* sign as being, in the same way, a sign in general. In particular, in the present case, it is a matter of signs empty of meaning, since I have not yet decided on how they will be used – and thus I cannot append any other status to them apart from that of sign: I have no conceptual instrument to differentiate them. Now, I can perfectly well produce a multiplicity of *distinct* empty signs – I can produce series of *distinct type-sign* tokens. I can decide that the ✦✦✦, etc. or ✺✺✺, etc. will be distinct signs in my future cipher, without yet having determined what their difference will be.

To take another example, in set theory, a series of tokens of the type-sign α is not necessarily identical to a series of tokens of the type-sign β (so long as the set α is not posited as identical to the set β), even if both were posited as equally empty signs at the beginning of an axiomatic. Now, if the iterability of α and β depended solely on the *concept of sign* – in this case that of *empty* sign – *then it would be impossible to think a difference between α and β, reduced to being instances of one and the same concept*. I cannot, through the concept of sign, think two distinct series of empty signs, since the two series present no difference as to the concept under consideration: they are equally multiplicities of empty signs. The differentiated iterative power which I confer upon these two series hence does not come from the conceptual sphere that one applies to them, but from elsewhere – an elsewhere that remains enigmatic.

The enigma becomes yet more precise: an empty sign possesses an immaterial force of identical reproduction. But since it is arbitrary, no concept can capture its essence – it is in principle infinitely variable with regard to its form, and this form has no necessity in itself. And since I can posit distinct types of empty signs, its iterable identity is no longer that of the general concept of 'sign' (or even the concept of 'sign devoid of meaning').

Does this mean that the sign is a pure convention that rests only upon the arbitrary identification of various marks? Does the 'etc.' that qualifies the series of a token originate simply in my sovereign decision to identify empty marks with each other? Just as I decided, just now, that in my cipher in formation this series of signs could be identical to this other series (making the two series typographical variations on one another), could we not say that *within* each series I decide by convention that one token is identical to the following one? The 'etc.' would then be only the mark of my unlimited sovereignty as to what is posited as identical or not. But the word 'convention' only masks the problem; for either the convention identifies distinct *signs*, and in this case presupposes the notion of the sign and its iterability – instead of constituting it. Or the term 'convention' signifies that I identify two distinct *things*, and in this case the *unlimited* iterability of

Iteration, Reiteration, Repetition

tokens is not given by this identity of *two* terms. Two things that I identify by convention – for example, two objects held to be substitutable in a game – does not necessarily call for the idea of infinite reproducibility. I can perfectly well envisage that a convention posits as equivalent two unique realities, but limits its import to that strict duality.

To conventionally identify two (material, individuated, unique) marks yields two marks identified as one – and nothing more. To identify two marks grasped as *tokens*, on the other hand (the ink trace 'a' grasped as a *letter*, and another similar *letter* 'a', or a dissimilar 'A'), supposes that we add to the identification an 'etc.' that is lacking in the convention reduced to itself.

The unlimitedness of the 'et cetera', the condition of the grasping of a sign as a sign, therefore cannot come from (a) the concept, which fails to capture the empty sign and its kenotype; nor from (b) convention, which does not contain in itself the power of iteration. *So from what capacity of the mind does this 'etc.' come?* This is the question that we must continue to close in on.

Among the solutions that we can draw from familiar categories, there does, however, remain one last track: that of simple empirical and conceptless resemblance, of the simple sensible recognition of a same form. We can observe a resemblance between two entities without necessarily knowing their concept – as when we observe the similarity between two pictorial motifs in an abstract painting. Is it not an experience of this kind to which the recognition of a mark as the token of an empty sign corresponds?

But here again, empirical resemblance is insufficient to constitute the iterability of the sign: to observe a resemblance does not imply that we make replicas of the beings thus resembling one another, in a series posited as potentially unlimited. When we observe the resemblance between twins, we do not make of them tokens in principle of a same type-sign signified by 'twin'. This is what we do, however, when we read the word 'twins' twice upon the same page – and *a fortiori* when we recognize the tokens of a base-sign in a formal language.

But we must be yet more precise. For it is certain, on the other hand, that we cannot completely disregard all relation to the sensible recognition of forms in the perception of the sign: a sign must indeed be seen or heard, and one must perceive in its matter a form more or less similar to that which one knows, in order to apprehend it as a sign (or, if you prefer a structural formulation: I must *perceive* a set of sensible differences in order to recognize a system of distinct signs). *Empirical* recognition is thus *necessary* for the grasping of the sign – necessary, but not sufficient. We must therefore conclude that two empirically similar marks carry with them *two types of sameness*: the sameness of sensible similarity, and the sameness of iterative identity. How can we think the coexistence and the articulation, in the same material reality, of these two regimes of the same?

It is essential to elucidate this point in order to implement our derivation of the empty sign. To formulate it more precisely and clearly, I have made up a little fable, which I call the fable of the 'overjoyed palaeographer', and which will allow me to bring to your attention a mental experience that I believe to be very instructive as to the nature of the sign.

The Fable of the Overjoyed Palaeographer

Imagine a young archaeologist, working on an excavation site belonging to a civilization of which, as yet, very little is known, but which it is believed had no writing. Our researcher in the field is working at digging up a tablet; now, when this artefact begins to come to light, she discovers upon it, suddenly, two superposed lines each made of similar marks:

§§§§§§§§
+++++++++

At first she believes that these are but the similar *motifs* of the *frieze* decorating the edge of her tablet. But suddenly, her heart leaps: for she has the intuition that she might have encountered, not a frieze, but two *lines* of signs. She thinks that she might have found the equivalent of a child's school notebook, in which one learns how to correctly write a character. She now grasps what appeared to be motifs as tokens reproducible at will:

§§§§§§§§§, etc.
+++++++++, etc.

The question, then, is as follows: what happened when her apprehension changed – from the grasping of the marks as motifs, to the grasping of marks as tokens; from seeing a frieze to seeing a double line? From whence, in her mind, came that which totally changes the vision of a civilization yet is not engraved on any tablet: our 'etc.'?

We must make several preparatory distinctions:

I call *similarity* the perfect empirical resemblance of two empirical entities, and I call *dissimilarity* an empirical difference that can be distinguished at the level of ordinary perception (between red and yellow, between a circular and a polygonal form, and so on.). I thus suppose, for the sake of the simplicity of this demonstration, that the marks on the same line on the tablet are *similar*.

My thesis is as follows: there is a difference in kind between the two ways of seeing the marks, that of marks as motifs, and that of marks as tokens. But above all, I will show that this difference can be isolated *without needing to mobilize from the outset the unlimited proliferation of tokens, as opposed to the finite grasping of the frieze*. To say it more clearly: I will show that even between two *finite* series – of motifs and of tokens – one can extract a fundamental difference of 'grasping', without, consequently, appealing to the 'etc.' that however punctuates every 'grasping' of the sign. We can even go further in the analysis *by going back to the very source of the unlimited proliferation of tokens* – by going back to their *raison d'être*. We shall come closer to the enigma of iterability, and with this, as we shall see, closer to the essence of Number as power of reiteration; and we shall do this by understanding whence precisely comes the difference between the apprehension of the frieze and the apprehension of a line of writing.[49]

To do so, we must begin by remarking that, within the two ways of seeing – without taking account of the 'etc.' of the tokens – a *sensible* difference is generated. The frieze, even though constituted of similar marks, still produces a *sensible* difference that is, however, *not a dissimilarity*. This nondissimilar sensible difference, produced when the marks are seen as motifs, I call a *repetition*, or a *monotony*. It is this differentiating effect of repetition that is *annulled* when the marks are seen as tokens – and, as I will show, *it is precisely because seeing them as tokens annuls all difference owing to repetition that it allows one to grasp an unlimited iteration*.

Let us explain what is meant by 'repetition' or 'monotony'. We can distinguish two principal modalities of repetition: an auditory modality, which produces what I call a *monotonous-chant effect*, and a visual modality that produces what I call a *frieze effect*. Let's begin with auditory repetition. It is Bergson's 1889 *Time and Free Will* that will set us upon the way.[50] For Bergson, as we know, there are two types of multiplicity: that of material objects juxtaposed in space – quantitative multiplicity, which can give rise to a count and a summation; and that of the facts of consciousness interwoven in duration – qualitative multiplicity that must rather be thought of in the mode of a melody. For in a melody, the notes are heard successively but not separately. On the contrary, they are fused together, so that a same *do* will not, in truth, have the same qualitative resonance when concluding this or that melodic sequence. Each note is tinged with the unity to which it belongs, so that the same *mi* that enchanted us in one passage will sound like a false note when it appears in another. As a result, similar sounds *acquire a differential significance from the sole fact of their being repeated*: if I reproduce the same sound, or if I hear the same chimes of the clock, a sentiment is produced in me of a qualitative and original organic totality that will give to the last repeated term – although it may be perfectly similar to the one that preceded it – a different and singular subjective effect. To take up the melodic example again: if I repeat the same *do* five times, the last will truly be different from the first, because it will be freighted with the repetitive sequence that it brings to a conclusion and which is as if contracted within it, giving rise to an original totality that the first *do* of the same sequence did not contain at all. The remarkable point is that the monotony of the chant produces a different sensible effect with each new repetition of the same term: *each time*, the same note becomes different, and *differently* different from its predecessors. This is why it makes no sense to think of the infinite proliferation of a monotonous chant: for one must hear each new note to perceive its originality, and the effect proper to it. The grasping of a monotonous chant is thus essentially perceptual and finite, not mental and unlimited; it gives meaning to an aesthetic judgement bearing upon the choice of note and the finite number of repetitions proposed, in view of the global effect of the sequence.

There is thus a differential effect inherent to empirical sounds stemming from the sole fact of repetition – one that even affects perfectly similar sounds. There is, in other words, *a sensible differential effect that cannot be identified with a dissimilarity*. It is the pure passage of time – at least of conscious, sensible time – that produces this difference that I call repetition or monotony.

But whereas Bergson claims that only duration, and not space, presents to us such an effect of monotony, I believe that sensible (visual) space in fact no less presents the differential effect of repetition. This point is strategically important for the rest of this demonstration – we will see why – and I shall therefore dwell on it for a moment.

Let's take an architectural example: the Bibliothèque François Mitterand, designed by the architect Dominique Perrault as part of the Bibliothèque nationale de France. Since this project is artistic as well as functional, it makes sense to pass an aesthetic judgement as to the repetitions – that is to say, the monotonies – planned by the architect: the repetition of the four corner towers, but also that of the streetlights, the safety grilles over the central garden, the caged trees, or the slats of the plaza. One can be enthused, irritated, or depressed by it; but it is always possible and legitimate to make a judgement on both the form of the chosen motifs – their dimensions, their colour, their materials – and the finite number of repetitions of them that the architect decided to employ. A spatial repetition, just like a melodic repetition, is a finite sequence producing 'a nondissimilar sensible differential effect'. An artistic success or failure is thus always possible, a possibility which in turn makes an evaluation possible. According to the same logic, one can appreciate the success or the failure of a work by Daniel Buren such as his 'Peinture acrylique blanche sur tissu rayé blanc et rouge (White Acrylic Painting on White and Red Striped Fabric)' (January 1970), made of twelve identical vertical red stripes, 8.7 centimetres wide, alternating with white strips of the same width. This appreciation would have no signification without the effect of repetition, which assures the produced totality its proper differential unity.

There is thus a *qualitative* aesthetic effect of spatial repetitions of which contemporary art and architecture have made us aware – more so today, no doubt, than in Bergson's time. This is why it is false to say, as Bergson does, that space must be the foundation of a *quantitative* summation of the same, as opposed to duration, the domain of qualitative repetition. For if the two dimensions of the sensible (space and time) are equally qualitative, they are *equally incapable of explaining the pure iteration of the sensible sign*, which escapes the differential effect of repetition (since otherwise, it would not surpass the qualitative perception of a finite series). And because of this alone, neither space nor time can explain the human capacity to produce a quantitative count rather than sensing a qualitative differentiality; for, as we have seen, quantitative summation itself depends upon the iterability of the sign.

Before going on to clarify these theses further, let us make our terminology a little more precise:

– Every reproduction of a same mark will be called a *recurrence*.

– A *repetition* (or *monotony*) is a *differential and finite* recurrence: a frieze (spatial), or a monotonous chant (temporal). A repetition is thus spatiotemporal in nature, with space and time understood in conscious, perceptual terms – and not as a physical and measurable continuum. A repetition is therefore a recurrence producing a sensible difference not of the fact of the dissimilarity of its motifs, but of the sole fact of the reproduction of similar elements. Temporal monotony creates a '(differential) monotonous-chant effect', spatial monotony a '(differential) frieze effect'.

– On the other hand, I call *iteration* (and no longer 'repetition') *a recurrence that is nondifferential and hence unlimited, because it produces a pure identity of marks*. This iteration is precisely implemented in the grasping of identical tokens of the same type. In such a case, I come to see in the mark itself that which is neither sensibly dissimilar nor different in any way from one mark to the other. There is no difference in type between one mark and another of a same sign – regardless of the possible differences between the marks (one 'a' written a little differently from another 'a'), but, above all, regardless of the inevitable differential effects that belong to similar (perfectly resembling) marks. Beyond any explanation by way of conventions, I end up being able to recognize certain marks as tokens that are perfectly identical as to their type, and can *for this reason alone* think them as iterable at will. Because, thought as rigorously identical as to their types lines of such signs escape the differentiating-finitizing effect of repetition, and instead open me up to the universe of writing, beyond that of design or music.

Iteration thus escapes the effect of repetition. Now, since the effect of repetition is none other than the effect of sensible space-time (and not of a dissimilarity), iteration finds in the mark itself a property=x which is not dependent upon time or space, *and which therefore is, in the strict sense, atemporal and nonspatialized*, even though, *paradoxically*, it is indexed to a determinate material thing.

The iterative way of seeing the mark grasps something eternally identical in a multiplicity of empirical marks, whether similar or not. We see in the marks – taken as tokens and not as motifs – something that is *eternal without being ideal* (since the marks are devoid of meaning and essence – of *eidos*, *idea*, or form).

Now, let us note the following point, which for me is essential: the access to this unprecedented regime of identity is also the condition of access to an equally unprecedented regime of difference: a difference that is neither dissimilarity nor the effect of repetition. In other words, the empty sign allows us a foothold *in another language of difference* – one that is no longer dependent upon sensible space-time – and which thus, as eternity, may be a candidate for a possible absolutization via contingency.

To understand this point, let us set out from a naive enumeration: we begin with signs that are simple bars devoid of meaning, which we iterate according to an identical kenotype: I, I, etc.

Suppose that we were to allow ourselves, in this elementary symbolic writing, as well as the base-sign *dm*, an operator-sign corresponding to ordinary addition: '+'.

Iteration, Reiteration, Repetition

Here, then, we are able to produce a differentiated sequence whose condition is the iteration of the sign:

Reiteration	I	II	III	IIII, etc.
Iteration		+I	+I	+I

It is only because the '+' signs (given an operatory meaning), and the (dm) 'I' signs are *identically iterable*, that I can *produce an augmentative succession* (II is superior to I by a single unit, etc.), in which each term *differs from the preceding term in a nonqualitative sense* (dissimilarity or monotony).

But if a differential effect (a repetition-effect) were ever to come about in iteration, no quantitative progression would be thinkable, because from one term to the other the operation would be modified, and its result with it:

I	II	III'	IIII" etc.
	+I	(+I)'	(+I)"

With iteration, I am no longer involved in the *indefinite* (which supposes an indefinite augmentation), but in the *unlimited* (always the same, reproduced identically); and I now have access to a third type of recurrence that is neither repetition nor iteration. This third type of recurrence is differential like repetition, but differential in a different way than the latter, since it is conditioned by iteration and opens onto the indefinite:[51] I call it *reiteration*. We have thus obtained a difference which is neither that of dissimilarity nor that of repetition: a third difference, genesis of every 'quantitative' difference, as opposed to qualitative or sensible difference.

Iteration is nondifferential and unlimited, repetition is differential and limited, and reiteration is differential and unlimited – and more precisely, indefinite (its unlimitedness engenders a term each time differing from its preceding term). Reiteration is the foundation of 'potential infinity' and the source of all naive arithmetic. It is involved in mathematical practice not only as a privileged object, but also as a method, namely in mathematical recurrence. Reiteration is the entry into the differential territory of iteration: the possibility of thinking differences outside the field of sensible repetition. This point is essential for our undertaking: for sensible plurality (let's say *diversity*) does not escape the correlation (I cannot absolutize it, it belongs to the sphere of our relation to the world),[52] whereas mathematical plurality (reiterative plurality, which we shall call *multiplicity*) opens us up to a world of difference that I hope to derive from the principle of factiality, by way of the empty sign that makes it thinkable. The first characters and derivations proposed in *After Finitude* were strictly primoabsolutory: they concerned *every* being indifferently (every being is contingent and consistent, and beings exist, whatever they may be); here, it could be that we accede to a world of *deuteroabsolutory differences*: describing some existent characterized mathematically in such and such a fashion, as opposed to some other existent characterized otherwise (the universe of distinct inorganic existents measured by science). Since there is reiterative multiplicity, this imposes upon us the very idea of a differentiated measurement of the actual (of the dead world separated from the correlation) that exhibits, by way of reiterative differences, the specificities of our world rather than those of any possible world in general. If we were to derive the absolutory capacity of reiteration, we would obtain: (a) as primoabsolute, the thesis that *every possible world* can be measured by mathematical multiplicities; (b) the fact that an actual, determinate world (deuteroabsolutory, contingent but independent of us) can thus be the object of such measurements and can be known for what it is specifically (in opposition to any other world), by way of operations inherited from the remarkable property of every world: measurability (access to deuteroabsolutory differences). We would then have derived the absolutory scope of Galileism, and the legitimacy of the mathematicized sciences to draw from our world measurements, laws and constants. But for the moment these are just anticipations that formulate the task that we have yet to take on: (a) to derive from the principle of facticity the sign dm and to make of facticity the condition of thinkability of mathematicity insofar as it rests upon the rule-governed use of such a sign for its most elementary operation (reiteration); (b) to establish that reiteration thus derived can be applied to the givens of the actual world so as to yield differentiated measurements of it.

To pose the question of the conditions of possibility of iteration – in a speculative, not a transcendental sense – is thus to pose the question of the origin of reiteration, and therefore of the very idea of a count and of number in their most original sense; but also that of space in its geometrical and no longer sensible sense, or of mathematical induction. In all of these cases, I mentally reiterate a sensible mark, or a portion of sensible space, and I make it escape the limits of perception in order to give it an intelligibility that only the indefinite captures. Each time there is indefiniteness (of geometrical space stretching out without limit, of the elements of a proof by induction), there is a nonsensible and thus reiterative plurality. Now, it is thereby a matter of the prerequisites for all ulterior mathematical or logical theorization: there can be no arithmetic, no geometry and no proof by induction without the thinkability of reiteration.

We can now understand why Bergson cannot help us in understanding the source of iteration and reiteration: because we have extended his idea of the qualitative multiplicity of duration to perceptual space. For Bergson, number comes from space: 'every clear idea of number implies a visual image in space', he writes in *Time and Free Will*.[53] Number, according to Bergson, has its origin in the visual image of units juxtaposed in space – units, consequently, that are separated from each other, and potentially in turn divisible into smaller spatial units. He thus reserves the qualitative difference of repetition for duration, which qualitatively interweaves its successive units; and the nonqualitative reiteration of numbers is blamed by the philosopher upon a space devoid of the capacity to link together what it juxtaposes. But since we have, for our part, emphasized the capacity of sensible space to produce a qualitative difference just as time can, we must seek the source of the iterative power of the sign elsewhere. Elsewhere – that is to say, *in a derivation of the empty sign operated on the basis of the principle of factiality*.

Final derivation of the kenotype

The challenge now is to establish the existence of a factial derivation of the kenotype – and thus of the sign devoid of signification. Where could it come from, this capacity of thought to iterate a sign, independently of the ideality of meaning? Is this a primary fact that cannot be explained – or can we infer this 'iterative' capacity of thought from a deeper principle? The thesis we intend to demonstrate is as follows: *it is because I can intuit in every entity its eternal contingency that I can intuit a sign devoid of meaning*. How do we obtain this result?

We have already established three characteristics of the sign *dm*: it is (a) *arbitrary* (which means that it escapes the unity of conceptual/ideal meaning); (b) *iterable* identically (this is what constitutes the unity of the type); and (c) *inseparable from its empirical basis* (this, importantly, is what permits the recognition of series of distinct tokens with regard to their type, by way of their nonsimilarity – α and β). In highlighting these three properties we aimed to prepare the essential requisites for the derivation we seek.

I have supposed it granted that the sole eternal property of every thing is its facticity – now identified with a contingency (since from now on correlated with a knowledge), but a speculative, not an empirical, contingency (one that concerns every entity – not only things, but also physical laws). It is thus clear that I can intuit any reality whatsoever in two distinct ways:

as a contingent thing – the ordinary way of seeing things and events as facts; or as a carrier of eternal contingency – the speculative way of seeing the necessary contingency inherent to every entity. But at the same time, *the contingency of a thing always belongs particularly to this or that thing*: contingency is not *beyond* the particular things, since it constitutes, on the contrary, the perishable character of all reality. In particular, contingency is inseparable from the concrete, empirical determination of a thing – since it is because things are like this or like that (red, round, and with an individual redness or roundness) that they could be other, or that they could be no more. It is this determinacy of things – their being only this or that – that was negated by inconsistency, which is indifferently everything and its contrary; which was why we decreed its impossibility.

Given this, I can account in one single movement for the two properties of the sign:

a) When I see in a thing its contingency, this contingency is iterable identically from mark to mark *without any differential effect of repetition*. For that which, in any sensible substrate, escapes the differential effect of space-time is indeed contingency qua eternal. *Whence the effect of the unlimited iteration of tokens*. Because the contingency of one mark is eternally the same as the contingency of another mark, I can identify them without any parasitic interference from a sensible differential effect that might exist elsewhere (dissimilarity and/or repetition).

b) But since contingency is always contingency *of* such and such an empirical particularity, I am free to *index* contingency – in itself always identical – to this or that series of replicas, and to thus differentiate, by convention, the contingency of one particular series of marks (for example the series '$\alpha\alpha\alpha\alpha$, etc.') from another series (for example the series '$\beta\beta\beta\beta$, etc.'). In other words, I can, by convention, index an equally eternal contingency to one series of marks, or to another that is dissimilar to the first and posited as distinct. Whence the possibility of producing distinct series of signs all equally void of sense.

Empirical particularity serves at once as the support of the identity of tokens within the same type and of the difference of the series of replicas between one another.

c) There remains the arbitrariness of the sign: in what way can this be derived from contingency?

The relation between contingency and arbitrariness is less immediate than it appears, and it is all the more interesting for this. Recall that by the notion of arbitrariness we do not mean the Saussurian unmotivation of the signifier in relation to the signified, but the more profound possibility for every sign – and this before even being freighted with any meaning – to be recoded by another sensible mark charged with the same function. In a formal language, the same base-sign can, without any problems beyond purely pragmatic ones, be named, renamed, by series of α, of β, of γ, etc.; and this property of signs *dm* has repercussions for signs provided with meaning, insofar as it belongs essentially to every signifying message to be able to be rewritten or cyphered (encrypted) using a new set of characters.

Now, what is the precise relation between this arbitrariness of the sign and factial contingency? The sign is arbitrary – that is to say, recodable. It is also, like every existent, eternally contingent. What relation is there between these two properties? First of all, the contingency of the sign does not signify its perishability in the physical sense, since in that case contingency and arbitrariness would no longer coincide; even if – in a world where precious stones abound – I were to choose a supposedly infrangible, physically indestructible diamond for the mark of a sign, that would not prevent the diamond-sign from being recodable by another mark. The contingency of which we speak is speculative, not physical: it designates the possible being-otherwise of every entity, even entities that we cannot modify by human means. Physical laws are unmodifiable by humans – but they are nonetheless factual, devoid of metaphysical necessity: the uncontrollable (by man or any other entity) is not synonymous with the necessary, for it remains destructible by Hyperchaos (whether an infrangible solid or a physical constant).

But the remarkable point about the sign is that it must be seen as being able to be otherwise, even if its basis is physically indestructible for us. Even a Spinozist cannot 'see' a sign as a sign without grasping it as being able to, in principle, be otherwise – replaceable by another. A sign can only appear as a sign in the form of its arbitrariness: a Spinozist who believed that everything is the necessary result of causality could only grasp a sign as such in denying it, for he would have to grasp it as a nonnecessary result of a causal series, given that every mark could have been other than it is – which is a condition of the givenness of a language as a language. A language is given to thought for what it is only on condition of being given as capable of giving rise to an indefinite string of secret codes, of 'doubles' that attest to its contingency at the level of marks. It is thus essentially given as nonnecessary, striking with contingency the very causal series that engendered it, even when the latter might have been of the order of uncontrollable constraint. It is this level of speculative facticity (and not physical destructibility) that allows the thinkability of a sign through its arbitrariness.

Here appears the true singularity of the sign *dm*: whereas normally we grasp things through their properties, and secondarily through their contingency, we are constrained to grasp these same things through their speculative contingency (their arbitrariness) once they are seen as signs (any sensible reality whatsoever being able to serve as a mark). In ordinary perception, we are gripped by the thing itself, and it is only secondarily that it is given to us as that which it is: a fact. I perceive the veranda, and, secondarily, as its shadow, *the fact* that there is a veranda. The veranda encounters our grasp before the facticity of the veranda that surrounds it like its diffuse aura. The thing is necessary to its own facticity in the precedence of its vision. But the sign boasts this remarkable peculiarity of only being accessible *by way of the exhibition firstly of its facticity*. A seashell is first of all a seashell for us, and only then, potentially, a factual seashell – and even this point will be contested by a Spinozist who will make it the necessary effect of an absolutely necessary causal series. Yet the same seashell, if I decide to use it as a sign in a language of my invention, becomes from the outset and *primarily* factual – fabricated from the arbitrariness of the sign that is the condition of its being grasped as a sign. It is only secondarily that this semiotic arbitrariness is *indexed* by the material form of the seashell that represents its token. Arbitrariness is the essence of the sign, whose sensible form is only a replaceable materiality.

Now, it is precisely at the moment when we flip from the grasping of contingent things to the grasping of the contingency of things (from empirical things perceived through their determinations to empirical marks perceived through their arbitrariness) that we immediately iterate them without limit. *We then understand the intimate ontological link between these two characteristics of the sign: arbitrary, iterable* – contingent and eternally the same, since contingency is eternal and escapes any conscious, repetitive effect of sensible space-time.

Whereas the sign provided with meaning is forgotten in favour of its meaning and its reference, the sign *dm*, giving itself ultimately for itself, as pure sign, makes me accede to its pure gratuitousness, to its pure absence of necessity, to the fact that anything whatsoever could fulfil its task just as well as it does. So that it is indeed the nonfoundation of all beings, and not of the sign alone, which discreetly reveals itself in this asignificance. Through the intuition of the sign *dm*, I leave the physical world, where everything seems to have a cause, in order to penetrate the pure semiotic world – where nothing has a reason to be, where nothing has meaning – and where everything, in consequence, breathes the air of eternity.

Here, then, is what the factial derivation of the sign dm consists in. To recapitulate the three elements of this derivation, I would say the following: the grasping of the sign proceeds *from a switching of our mode of apprehension* – from the ordinary mode of apprehension that grasps certain contingent things, I switch to the semiotic mode of apprehension that grasps the eternal contingency of this or that thing. This grasping of a facticity other than the empirical (arbitrariness, the unreason of every thing) makes it possible for me to identically iterate marks brought together conventionally as replicas of distinct type-signs.

The referent of asignificance

In producing this derivation, I have not, however, succeeded in reaching the final goal of my demonstration. I have only given a part of it. For what is it that we have established? We have shown that the sign dm has an ontological import. But in what sense? In the sense that we have emphasized that the grasping of the sign dm has as its *condition* an ontological truth: the necessary contingency of all things. But this derivation of the kenotype is far from being sufficient to establish the thesis that we had primordially in view: that of the deuteroabsolutory import of mathematics. For all we have demonstrated is that, in order to produce an empty sign, one must have access to the eternity of contingency. But we have not at all shown that the empty sign allows, in turn, the description of a world independent of thought. We have only established that one must accede to eternal contingency in order to produce a mathematics *capable of not speaking of anything – since it is founded upon signs devoid of signification*. The new puzzle that appears before us is thus the following: How can a sign empty of meaning allow us to describe the world without becoming once again a sign *provided* with meaning, hence capable of reference outside of itself? How, through what paradox, can we hope that a sign void of meaning could not only have a referent, but a (deutero-)absolute referent, more radically separate from us than every correlational apprehension?

In resolving one problem, we find yet another, which seems even more difficult than that which preceded it. Such is the philosophical journey *par excellence*, where 'thinking we had reached port, we are carried back into the open sea'.[54] But in truth, in our case, things do not wear the Odyssean grandeur of the anger of the gods blowing our boat toward waters of dangerous ancestral splendours. We rather hope to manage to plunge, by way of mathematics, into the whirlpool of the inhuman Universe that confronts us, and instead here we are, becalmed in a port, within a writing incapable of exiting from itself, incapable of making of a world indifferent toward us the referent of its symbols elegantly voided of any encumbering content.

This solution however is not so distant, and in conclusion I will sketch out the direction, without formulating it with all the required rigour.

This time what is at stake is the following: I have reflected upon the most elementary form of counting, that which takes place through the accumulation of lines:

I, II, III, etc.

Let us posit that this is the writing of a count in someone who has not mastered Arabic numerals – or any other complex system of numeration.

How can we get from this elementary counting to the counting *of* something: how do we pass from the verbal expression 'I count' to the expression 'I count this or that'? What happens when someone who counts on their fingers suddenly counts fingers? Let us suppose that this elementary system of lines allows me to count the alstroemeria of a bouquet that I am making, according to the following procedure: I make a line on the paper each time I add a flower, and I stop once there are a dozen. Let us symbolize with 'A' the flowers thus counted; we have thus a term-by-term correspondence that can be schematized as follows for the beginning of the sequence:

I, II, III, IIII, etc.
A + A + A + A

How can we understand the nature of this correspondence? Let us begin with the most spontaneous interpretation: we shall say that each line ('I') has as its referent each flower ('A') that it allows me to count. Since the lines have a referent, then the lines, obviously, have a meaning given to them by such a referent: the 'alstroemeria' counted by the line. But obviously, this thesis falls as immediately as it is formulated: a number never has as its meaning that which it counts. If, following the dismantling of a clandestine zoo, the police count three clouded leopards, three grey gibbons and three black goshawks, the number three has not changed in meaning, passing from one species to the other depending on how it is applied. The theory of the reference of number is thus corrected as follows: the number refers not to the thing, but to its unity. What the 'one' repeated by the lines refers to is the intrinsic unity of the thing, which seems to be its property just like the colours or the deciduous leaves of the alstroemeria. The thing thus becomes the referent of a number by way of its 'unitary property' alone, which the count grasps exclusively.

However, this solution is hardly any more satisfying than the preceding one, very simply because it only puts the 'one' of the count (I, II, III, etc.) in relation not with the thing itself, *but with that which is already implicitly a counting* of the thing itself. To grasp the unity of a thing is in truth to already be able to count it: the unity of an object comes down to grasping it as one, as already counted-as-one. In this way, one does not put a one-line into relation with a one-thing, but a one-line with a one-line already drawn out of the thing. Unless, perhaps, we have a nonnumerical theory of unity as the individuating singularity of the thing. In this way every unity will be inherent to the concreteness of the counted thing because it will contain in itself the set of its finest characteristics, rendering it irreplaceable by the unity of another thing. Thingly unity will thus be unicity and not numericity – and it will be this singular unicity that will be counted-as-one.

But then we fall into aporia once again: for this unicity will be none other than the concrete thing – its individual substance with all the properties that singularize it and ultimately make it unique. We will rediscover the concrete thing of which we had said that it could not be the referent of our line, for the line becomes the name of the unique thing in question, and has no meaning other than being the common name of this thing (or even its proper name). But the name of the thing is not the number of the thing. Numbers, as we have said, are indifferent to the singularity of the things that they count, and if we make of the unity of the counted thing the very thing itself, we fall back into our original impasse: each count-for-one will change its meaning each time we change the thing we are counting: 'one' would signify this singular black goshawk, unique and irreplaceable by another, and thus could not sum it with another 'one' whose meaning would be entirely other, grasping another member of the same species, but slightly different: a fortiori it would be impossible to sum the one-lines whose referents would be really distinct (like it is impossible to add an Amaryllis to an autographed copy of *Capital*). Names do not number; and the ontological unities of things are either masked names, or masked numbers.

We believe that every theory of the semantization of number thus risks falling between Scylla and Charybdis: avoiding the risk of giving the number as its referent a concrete reality that would make the number a name for the counted thing (which is absurd in regard to the functioning of the count), at risk of giving the number simply itself as referent, incorporated into the thing as its unity, a pseudoproperty among an object's other properties, when it is only a matter of an implicit count already made of the thing. If number is semanticized, if it has a meaning, either this meaning bears no relation to the procedure from which it results (common or proper name), or this meaning, passed as if 'under the skin' of the numbered thing (ontological unity of the thing) in order to make us believe that quantity had a referent that would not itself already be presupposed, is only itself but the prelinguistic property of the quantified.

Faced with this dilemma, we propose a different solution: *the lines* of our example above *do not have as their referents the flowers as things, but as typographical variants the flowers themselves grasped as signs devoid of meaning.* For let us remember that we can make a sign, and a sign *dm*, from just anything whatsoever: I can see a chair, a pet, and thus also a flower as so many marks become signs mentally identically iterable. For I can accede to the type of any sensible mark, I can mentally iterate and even reiterate it at will. This means that, when I count flowers or goshawks using lines, what I do becomes very clear: *I see the flowers and the goshawks as signs as devoid of meaning as my lines.* The correspondence is thus not that of lines that would have as their meaning, and as their referents, flowers or birds of prey; the correspondence is between equally empty signs which are in a reciprocal relation of typographical variation.

A and *a* are two signs void of meaning, which do not resemble each other, or barely, but which do have a correspondence that allows the association of one and the other, and their substitution according to the established rules. In any case, *a* is not the name that would have as its 'meaning' and 'reference' *A* – or vice versa. *Their correspondence is not semantic but graphical.*

To count something, to associate one-line to any things whatsoever functions in the same way: *there is no semantization of signs but only semiotization of things.* And thus, the numerical sign will conserve its emptiness in mathematizing the Universe, having voided the Universe of its meaning to the point of making it the typographical variant of its operation. The eternal silence of infinite spaces through which the way of the count wends. The whole world can be numbered not by giving meaning to the signs of numbers, but by proposing a rewritten version of their absence of meaning. And this correspondence implies no fusion: the world is measured without fusing into its measure, insofar as its deuteroabsoluteness remains thinkable.

Iteration, Reiteration, Repetition

To conclude, there appears here the entire importance that we have accorded to, and derived from, the possibility of producing distinct series of signs *dm* (*ααα*, etc; *ββββ*, etc.) as well as of reidentifying them, without exiting the sphere of the sign *dm*. We do the same here in, this time, placing in connection the two series (IIII, etc.; AAAA, etc.), and in reiterating the first in order to make it carry the reiterative use of counting (I, II, III, etc.) and the weight of the numbering sign, not of the numbered thing.

Such is the way that we must take in order to resolve the ultimate difficulty of the kenotype: a way that brings with it yet more difficulties, which I cannot go into here.

Notes

1. This text originates from a workshop (at Freie Universität, Berlin, 21 April 2012). An electronic version of the original paper was circulated, against my wishes, which now passes for a published text attributed to me, when in fact it was only a set of notes aiming to stimulate discussion with the students. The only valid version is the following one. However, I have tried to maintain the 'direct' style of the workshop, and I have also conserved its spirit: rather than rigorously justifying each of my assertions (I reserve this for forthcoming works), I indicate here a general direction of research.

2. *After Finitude: An Essay on the Necessity of Contingency*, trans. Ray Brassier (London: Continuum, 2008).

3. Berkeley is one of the very rare thinkers to have succeeded in changing the course of philosophy in its entirety with an argument whose fundamental nature is expressed in *just a few lines*; see *A Treatise Concerning the Principles of Human Knowledge* (Indianapolis: Hackett, 1982), §§4–10, pp. 24–7. A rigorous reading of these pages will arouse in anyone who seriously considers them the impression of a collapse of all metaphysical materialism, a collapse to which no serious response has been given in the course of the following centuries. It is in part from this conviction, patiently consolidated, that *After Finitude* proceeds: any materialist who believes that Berkeley has been surpassed, or who dismisses him, reducing him to his mere caricature, simply does not know what she is talking about when she invokes the name of 'materialism'. To respond to Berkeley, without disdain or dilatory manoeuvre – to respond to him as simply, directly and straightforwardly as he 'executed' materialism – this was one of the deepest ambitions of *After Finitude*.

4. I speak of a 'formulatory contradiction' rather than a 'performative contradiction', since the latter concerns only an act of enunciation, of public utterance: an act said aloud and, what is more, to an interlocutor (the performative is by nature social and communicational). An example of a performative contradiction would be the phrase 'I am not speaking' addressed

to an interlocutor capable of hearing and understanding it – and thus of hearing and understanding that someone is speaking to them and saying that they are not speaking to them. But the contradiction I am referring to – that of the correlational circle – can obtain even in a mental act. I need only think 'I do not exist', without saying it, for this phrase to be contradicted by the mental act that produced it. The same goes, according to the 'correlational circle', for the proposition 'I think an in-itself independent of thought', which has no need to be uttered but only needs to be formulated mentally, to be falsified. It is thus a 'formulatory' contradiction (a meaning-content contradicted by the act of formulating it in the mind), and not a performative contradiction (which only intervenes at the level of actual speech, but does not concern the mental act reduced to itself). Thus, the Cartesian *Cogito*, the deep source of correlationism, could not be understood in performative terms, because it is not utterable, despite the apparent expression of it given in the 'Second Meditation': 'this pronouncement "I am, I exist" is necessarily true every time I utter it or conceive it in my mind'. See René Descartes, *Meditations of First Philosophy*, trans. Donald Cress (Indianapolis: Hackett, 1993), p. 25. For at the stage when she formulates it, the subject of the *Cogito* does not know whether she has a body, and thus lips, a tongue, teeth – all of which are necessary for the pronunciation (which is physical in nature) of the phrase. The subject of the *Cogito* thinks this in the mode of conception (via the understanding), or she thinks that she says it, but no longer knows whether she really says it, whether she utters it (to herself or to another). Note that even if we were to admit that a performative can be produced in solitude (such as a promise made to oneself out aloud), this could not be the case for an act that prohibits us from supposing any utterance.

5. I understand 'speculative' in two senses: (a) a broad sense that includes metaphysics, since any thinking of the absolute is speculative; and (b) a restricted sense that only includes philosophies that accede to the absolute without recourse to the Principle of Sufficient Reason. In this sense, a strictly speculative philosophy is thus nonmetaphysical. Hopefully it will in each case be clear from the context in which sense I am using the term.

6. On Maupertius's and Diderot's hylozoisms, see Denis Diderot, *Thoughts on the Interpretation of Nature and Other Philosophical Works*, ed. David Adams (Manchester: Clinamen Press, 1999), pp. 224–6. Diderot there discusses Maupertius's *Dissertatio inauguralis metaphysica de universali naturae systemate* (1751), itself published under the pseudonym of Doctor Baumann. On Maupertius's response to Diderot, see his *Essai de cosmologie, système de la nature: Réponses aux objections de M. Diderot* (Paris: Vrin, 1984). On Diderot's own variant of hylozoism, see 'Conversation between D'Alembert and Diderot' and 'D'Alembert's Dream', trans. Jacques Barzun and Ralph H. Bowen, *Rameau's Nephew and Other Works* (Indianapolis: Hackett, 2001), pp. 92–165.

7. Henri Bergson, *Creative Evolution*, trans. Arthur Mitchell (Mineola, NY: Dover, 1998), pp. 210–17.

8. Gilles Deleuze, *Difference and Repetition*, trans. Paul Patton (New York: Columbia University Press, 1995), pp. 78–9.

9. Obviously I do not see correlational philosophies in this light: the analogy is intended to express the saturating structure of a myriad of confrontations traversed by a dominant line of antagonism – it targets not the status of the combatants but their general configuration, taken up in a conflict that is ever more separated into successive divergent sheaves and thus gives the impression that it exhausts all possibilities.

10. See Gilles Deleuze and Félix Guattari, *What is Philosophy?*, trans. Hugh Tomlinson and Graham Burchell (London: Verso, 1994), pp. 212–13: 'But, if nerve connections and cerebral integrations presuppose a brain-force as faculty of feeling coexistent with the tissues, it is reasonable to suppose also a faculty of feeling that coexists with embryonic tissues and that appears in the Species as a collective brain; or with the vegetal tissues in the "small species". Chemical affinities and physical causalities themselves refer to primary forces capable of preserving their long chains by contracting their elements and by making them resonate: *no causality is intelligible without this subjective instance. Not every organism has a brain, and not all life is organic, but everywhere there are forces that constitute microbrains, or an inorganic life of things*' (emphasis mine).

11. As we readily admit, each of these elliptical assertions should be complicated insofar as it concerns a particular philosophy: but such complication, we believe, does not stand as a recusal of our thesis. In Bergson, for example, duration is part of consciousness, of evolutionary life and of the Universe in its entirety, not of the partial systems of matter that we isolate artificially. But if we must 'wait while the sugar melts' and if, in that case, we are dealing, according to Bergson, with the experience of the incompressible duration of the Universe which escapes its mathematical descriptions, then an isolated system (the glass of sugar water that he speaks of) does indeed participate at its own level in the duration of the whole Universe. It is thus legitimate, in truth, to say – as Bergson himself moreover maintains – that no part of the Universe is ever totally isolated from the Whole, and that every part thus participates to its degree in its global duration. See Bergson, *Creative Evolution*, pp. 10–11.

12. This anthropomorphism has for a long time been denied – although it is nothing but the direct consequence of any thought that thinks relation in terms of degree or of intensity. It fell to Hans Jonas to have had the integrity to finally let the cat out of the bag, a decision relayed in Pierre Montebello's fine book: 'Why go via oneself to get to nature? Why pass via our instinctive life (Nietzsche), our effort (Ravaisson), our psychic life (Bergson), our self (Tarde) in order to then spread out over the entire universe? Very simply because we are the summation of physical, organic and psychic strata, and because these strata must communicate since we exist. […] There are certainly differences in nature. But are these differences of nature? Are we sure that everything is essentially and substantially separate? If one does not separate, it is often objected, then one anthropomorphizes. […] The extension of desire and of force is a hypothesis, but, and here is the whole difference, it is the

only hypothesis that holds, precisely because is entirely anthropomorphic. It is a hypothesis to which the facts are not opposed and which, in this sense, is less contradictory than pure psychologism or pure materialism. Hans Jonas has developed this essential argument: my epistemological position, he says, "*confesses the so decried sin of anthropomorphism*". [...] But perhaps [...] the human is effectively the measure of all things, certainly not through the legislation of its reason, but through the paradigm of its psychophysical totality, which represents the maximum concrete ontological accomplishment we know of (emphasis added)'. See Pierre Montebello, *L'autre métaphysique. Essai sur Ravaisson, Tarde, Nietzsche et Bergson* (Paris: Desclée de Brouwer, 2003), pp. 12–13, and Hans Jonas, *Evolution et liberté*, trans. Sabille Cornille and Philippe Ivernel (Paris: Rivages, 2000), pp. 31–2.

13. See Alain Fraval and Ingrid Wydler, 'La pièce de viande et la vermine', in *Insectes* 156(1) (2010): 19–22.

14. Here again metaphorization would have us say that a work of art contains, sedimented but still palpitating, the life of the artist or of the labour that formed it. And we remain intrigued by this persistence in refusing the harsh banality of the truth: that *poiesis* produces dead objects that get worn out, not newborns who will grow old. It is fascinating that our scorn for dead things, but also our disdain for *real* life, constrains us to repeat the obvious so as to counter the extension of life beyond its real frontiers. Insofar as 'living' stands as a compliment, the living will be as nothing.

15. It matters little that subjectalism abandons the language of depth for that, valorized, of the surface, as in Deleuze's *Logic of Sense*. In doing so one makes pivot a space of the living which it is still just as impossible to escape from: one slides rather than flows, but one still remains in movement – because one always remains there.

16. The complete citation from Deleuze and Guattari on mono-pluralism clarifies the distance that separates them from us: 'Arrive at the magic formula we all seek – PLURALISM = MONISM – via all the dualisms that are the enemy, an entirely necessary enemy, the furniture we are forever rearranging' (Gilles Deleuze and Félix Guattari, *A Thousand Plateaus*, trans. Brian Massumi [Minneapolis: University of Minnesota Press, 1987], pp. 2–3). We much rather believe that a philosopher's job is not to absorb a pure and thus true (=heterogeneous) pluralism into a monism, even one of intensive difference; and we also believe that the enemy dualism mentioned by Deleuze has the merit of being always rearranged very simply because monism, of whatever form, is powerless to destroy it and never ceases to 'find the furniture again' in a new place, in a new form. This dualism is indestructible because it is part of the truth, and it is none other than the precious ally of a properly understood materialism. A speculative (and no longer metaphysical) materialist is thus a resolute partisan of the dualism of soul and body, as a trace of the higher, hyperchaotic absurdity of what is. Certain of the dualisms of metaphysics are transmuted into meaningless breaks in intensive continuity, this latter remaining basically subject to the Principle of Sufficient Reason (necessity

Iteration, Reiteration, Repetition

of a common nature between cause and effect, the principle and what it applies to).

17. In Deleuze, chaos is certainly itself composed of 'infinite variabilities' which are 'without nature or thought'. But it is still deployed according to a line of life that makes it culminate in 'composed' chaos, a chaosmos, where chaotic variability is transformed into a 'chaoid manifold'. Under the regime of Hyperchaos, on the other hand, nothing prohibits a world setting out from immobile natures, then degrading through successive destructive irruptions into a more and more unbridled becoming. These are just possible worlds – natured natures (Chaos(mos), immobile then degraded natures), and not naturing nature (only Hyperchaos is this). On Chaos(mos), see Deleuze and Guattari, *What Is Philosophy?*, pp. 201, 204 (translation modified).

18. Berkeley thus did not 'found' correlationism, but, as we have said, the 'Era of Correlation'; he did so by giving subjectalist form to the argument of the 'correlational circle'. It is Hume, in my opinion, who inaugurates the properly correlationist form (a sceptical form, in fact) of the 'correlational circle': from the circle, he no longer deduces that all reality is spirit but that we can no longer extract ourselves from the sphere of impressions and ideas, and that the thing in itself must remain irreducibly unknown to us. On Berkeley's decisive texts against the thinkability of materialism see *Principles*, §§3–10. On the correlationist turning of these theses, see David Hume, *An Enquiry Concerning Human Understanding* (Indianapolis: Hackett, 1993 [2nd edn]), §12.

19. I thus see Graham Harman as a paradoxical subjectalist – hypostasizing *between* things the relation that humans maintain with them insofar as they partly *withdraw* from him in their very manifestation. A subjectivity surpassing all humanity or all organic life, become omnipresent as a failing or caricatured relation to another subjectivity. This friendly divergence takes away nothing of my admiration for someone I take to be one of the major philosophers of this new century: his metaphysics, luminous with originality and intelligence, constitutes to my knowledge one of the greatest theories of the object being developed today, along with that of Tristan Garcia.

20. We understand 'thought' in two distinct but complementary senses, whose context should normally allow determination. Thought is, first, in a restricted usage, the speculative faculty of the relation to the absolute via which the subject exits or fails to exit from himself. In this sense, it is that part of subjectivity that sanctions, by its theoretical success or failure, the exit from all subjectivity. Thought in the broader sense (which is closer to the Cartesian sense) is, second, the whole of this subjectivity whose destiny is linked to the demonstrative power of its restricted occurrence. No doubt we will be reproached for this equivocity, but we do not believe that the systematic univocity of the philosophical lexicon is indispensable for its clarity. The contextual determination of the words used can make things clearer: 'to think thought as the absolute' obviously means to think (in the restricted sense, that of a demonstrative capacity) thought (as subjectivity in the broad sense) as the absolute. It is to the movement of the text, not to a dictionary of notions, that

21. I speak of *physical* laws, those which govern the regularity of natural processes: I am not speaking here of *theories* made concerning these laws, which are always revisable.

22. The complete demonstration of this derivation is formulated in chapter three of *After Finitude*.

23. Obviously, a metaphysics cannot claim to speak of what there is without *ever* coming across a 'fact' of which science speaks: what would it be talking about, otherwise? All metaphysics is submitted to the imperative stated by Bergson at the beginning of *The Creative Mind* – to speak of a world with sufficient precision that it can be our world and no other possible world: 'What philosophy has lacked most of all is precision. Philosophical systems are not cut to the measure of the reality in which we live: they are too wide for reality. Examine any one of them, chosen as you see fit, and you will see that it could apply equally well to a world in which neither plants nor animals have existence, only men, and in which men would quite possibly do without eating or drinking, where they would neither sleep nor dream not let their minds wander; where, born decrepit, they would end as babes-in-arms; where energy would return up the slope of its dispersion; and where everything might just as easily go backwards and be upside down.' See Henri Bergson, *The Creative Mind*, trans. Mabelle L. Andison (New York: Dover, 2007), p. 1. It goes without saying that it is enough to understand a little of the works of, say, Aristotle or Hegel, to consider that the imperative of precision is not a Bergsonian novelty but an imperative of all great metaphysics.

24. This in fact is what has happened with Bergson, who founded the superiority of his 'true finalism' over neo-Darwinism, in the first chapter of *Creative Evolution*, on a fact which, as he believed, was established by the science of his time: the structural similarity between the human eye and the eye of the scallop (the coquille Saint-Jacques), a similarity that goes as far as the inverted structure of the eye. This eye, coming from two independent creations of life and not one common ancestor, proves, for Bergson, an originary 'psychological' project, which could not be due to the chance of variation that Darwinism promotes. It is nothing less than *élan vital*, as the unique explanatory factor of the evolution of the living, that was deduced from such a proof. But it turned out that the scallop had two retinas and two optical nerves, and also that the inversion of its eye proceeded from a system of optical reflection absent in the human eye. Such discoveries attest to a spectacular anatomical difference between the eye of the scallop and the human eye, and bring down the whole regime of argument of the first chapter of *Creative Evolution*. The mollusc's double retina stopped the *élan* of the proof in its tracks. On this point, see Bernard Balan, 'L'oeil de la coquille Saint-Jacques: Bergson et les faits scientifiques', *Raison presente* 119 (1996): 87–106; and Armand de Ricqlès, 'Cent ans après: *L'Évolution créatrice* au péril de l'évolutionnisme contemporain', in A. Fagot-Largeault and F. Worms (eds),

Annales bergsoniennes, IV. L'évolution créatrice 1907–2007: épistémologie et métaphysique (Paris: PUF, 2008), pp. 118–21.

25. I use 'positivism' in a sense that is my own: by this word I understand any belief in the definitive truth of a determinate scientific theory – a truth that implies not the statism of a completed discourse, but the overactivism within this theory alone, in view of its maximal extension bordering on the ultimate discovery (the components of matter, the nature of the mind, etc.). I call 'scientism', on the other hand, the thesis (to which I do not adhere) according to which truths are ultimately of a scientific nature, but which identifies science with the general movement of its successive theories: a 'scientistic' thinker is far less naive than a 'positivist' and is a far more interesting adversary: he believes in the supremacy of science, but preserves his scepticism in the face of the enthusiasms of the 'positivist' for the theory of the moment. For him, it is not science's job to get bogged down in the detour of an endlessly pondered theory, but to pass from one theory to another that is superior in explicative valence, being unfaithful to each one. The structure of 'scientism' is polyrevolutionary rather than monotheoretical – which is precisely what makes it eminently interesting. I always place these terms ('positivism', 'scientism') in quotation marks to differentiate them from their current or differently theorized usage. Let us add the condition that will always allow a 'positivism' to be reborn from its ashes: namely that it is not logically impossible (or ontologically impossible, from our point of view) that a definitively true theory should in fact be discovered one day. But the irony that makes 'positivist' ranting vain is that *even if a theory were definitively true, we would never know it*. As far as the sciences are concerned, one can only know what is known (definitively) even if one knows (definitively): for one can never exclude the possibility of a theory – even the truest theory – being refuted in the future by a series of unprecedented experiments. Even if a fully complete science were to come about one day, no one, including those in science, would ever know it. This is why the attentive reserve of the 'scientistic' thinker (remaining on the lookout when faced with the apparently best-confirmed theory) *will always be superior in principle* to the triumphalist clamour of the 'positivist'.

26. I hesitated, on this point, over the lexicon: after having used the term 'Hyperchaos' in *After Finitude*, for a while I used the term 'Surchaos' (as I said in an interview with Graham Harman) because the first term seemed to me to wrongly suggest a chaos that is more disordered, more absurdly frenetic than those that had preceded it in the various philosophical systems (the prefix 'hyper-' having acquired, wrongly, an intensificatory connotation in current language). But the Chaos that I envision can produce either a frenetic disorder or an impeccable order – whence the idea of Sur-chaos, overlooking the old metaphysical order as well as the old chaotic disorder which it renders indifferently possible one and the other. But I could not bear to commit the barbarism of mixing a Latin prefix with a Greek name – whence the return to 'Hyperchaos', whose meaning, after all, can be posited clearly enough to avoid any equivocation.

27. Jean-Jacques Rousseau, 'Discourse on the Origins and Foundations of Inequality among Men', trans. Donald A. Cress, in Donald A. Cress (ed.), *The Basic Political Writings, Second Edition* (Indianapolis: Hackett, 2011 [original French publication 1754]), p. 46 (translation modified).

28. The variants of vitalism nevertheless differ from the variants of reductionism in that they are not immediately absurd: to say that our mind can be reduced to a physico-chemical complex is to affirm that the sensible contents that we believe we experience do not exist. It is to say that it seems to us that something appears to us, but that in truth, nothing appears to us – an absurdity aping a paradox. To insert the living into all things, however, remains a coherent philosophical project, of which we will even maintain, going against our presentation above, that it is legitimate, however difficult.

29. Since to create (*creare*) comes from to grow (*crescere*), the act always supposes a continuous process at the source of new formations. Our enterprise, made up of irruptions, seeks to secondarize creation: creation may be effective, but in this case, it is only the fact of a possible world become actual – a creative world itself produced by emergence *ex nihilo*.

30. Science is a 'chronogeny' insofar as it is the history of a lineage where Chronos devoured his progeny (his theories), being helped with each generation by a descendent who was spared (the accepted theory of the moment), before devouring him in his turn, with the help of a descendent of that descendent (a later theory maintained against its elder).

31. Facticity comprises existent facts (existing or actual), as well as inexistent facts (virtual or potential facts, possibilities). I thus call, in need of an abbreviation, actual or existent facts '(f)actual'. This should not be confused with factiality, which is the nonfacticity of facticity in general, or with (f)actuality, which is just the set of actual facts.

32. Let us note that there is no necessity that a fulgurite should denote a succession in time: the sensible contents doubtless appeared after inorganic matter, but irruption can in principle designate two domains at once radically separate yet contemporary.

33. Coarticulation is not a preestablished harmony in the Leibnizian sense. It is rather the solution to an enigma of preestablished harmony invoked by Hume in his *Enquiry Concerning Human Understanding*, in the mode of a residual enigma, between the course of our ideas and that of nature. In Hume, that causality has no seat in nature and yet responds to our expectations takes on the allure of a startling agreement (albeit advanced in an ironic manner, it is nonetheless maintained) that makes him adopt the Leibnizian expression. Now, the Hyperchaos capable not only of breaking every physical law but also every law of chance gives us the truth of it: it is a matter not of a preestablished harmony in the mind of a calculating God, but of a fulgurated articulation beyond all necessity and all reasonable probability alike. An accord established at the very moment of its fulguration, and on the absence of any principle of reason, not a harmony preestablished in the ruminations of a God submitted to the

principle of the best. That our world remains in spite of such ruptures 'surpasses understanding' – reasonable understanding (the calculation of probabilities and determinisms) but not a demonstrative and figural rationality. Here is the passage of Hume in question: 'Here, then, is a kind of pre-established harmony between the course of nature and the succession of our ideas; and though the powers and forces, by which the former is governed, be wholly unknown to us; yet our thoughts and conceptions have still, we find, gone on in the same train with the other works of nature.' See Hume, *Human Understanding*, §5, p. 36.

34. For example, the brilliant refutation inflicted by the anthropologist Marshall Sahlins on the dubious pretensions of Edward O. Wilson, who aimed to reduce all social study of man to a sociobiology: see Marshall Sahlins, *The Use and Abuse of Biology: An Anthropological Critique of Sociobiology* (Ann Arbor: University of Michigan Press, 1977) and Edward O. Wilson, *Sociobiology: The New Synthesis* (Cambridge, MA: Harvard University Press, 1980).

35. Our personal maxim has long been that 'reductionism is the materialism of imbeciles'. But we now know that there is a diabolically intelligent use of it: that made by Ray Brassier in his critical commentary on Churchland; see *Nihil Unbound: Enlightenment and Extinction* (Basingstoke: Palgrave Macmillan, 2010), chapter one. However, from our point of view, the interest of this analysis lies essentially in the way in which Brassier reads and instrumentalizes Churchland in view of his luminous nihilism, and far less in the way in which Churchland thinks his eliminativism.

36. 'Spectral Dilemma', trans. Robin Mackay, in Robin Mackay and Damian Veal (eds), *Collapse IV: Concept Horror* (Falmouth: Urbanomic, 2008), pp. 261–76.

37. For an illustration of a nonsubjectal thinking of causality, see *After Finitude*, chapter four.

38. Translator's note: Following Ray Brassier's translation of *After Finitude*, the French *sens*, denoting both 'sense' and 'meaning', but also 'direction', is here consistently rendered as 'meaning'.

39. I here insist on the difference between this and the subjectal hypothesis: subjectalism can only *postulate* the effective influence of subjectivity in the world. I on the other hand will derive, in a necessary fashion – we will see at the price of what difficulty – the absolutory capacity of all mathematicized science. It will thus be *proven*, according to the factial regime of proof, and not postulated, that the deuteroabsolutory real that composes the actual world (and any other world) is accessible to Galileism.

40. Jean-Louis Krivine, *Théorie des ensembles* (Paris: Cassini, 1998), p. 1.

41. What I say here is, to my mind, valid for every formalism, whether logical or mathematical. In this way, we could easily rediscover the difference between the base-sign (dm) and the operator-sign in category theory: the latter is written using arrows (the equivalent 'operator-signs') applied to 'point' signs, which are devoid of meaning (named by letters: equivalent of the 'base-signs'). These 'points' are but the supports for arrowed operations that give them all

their properties 'from the outside', and they are in themselves so perfectly devoid of signification that they can even be eliminated in certain notations: the arrows are thus simply 'named' by letters at each extreme and seem to be deployed between 'empty points'. Instead of saying that an arrow goes from point a to point b, we seem to simply say that this arrow 'ab' is oriented according to its own nomination. This is the ultimate – and logical – degree of the voiding of the base-sign.

42. It will be remarked that in these two definitions of 'natural' and 'formal' meaning, it is the first that is *negative and the second that is positive*: it is not in formal meaning that something is lacking (the 'concrete' meaning that allows us to make reference to the world), but in natural meaning: the regulation of the sign pure of all meaning. Moreover, it will be remarked that we are not saying that formal meaning draws its negativity from the sign *dm*, since there are also signs devoid of meaning in natural language. The difference comes from the presence of a rule of the sign *dm* in the first case and the lack of any such rule in the second case. Just as, for the classics, against the usage in natural language, infinity was the true positive reality and the finite was a negative reality, in the confrontation formal/natural negativity is not found where we might think.

43. Jean Dieudonné, 'The Work of Nicolas Bourbaki', trans. Linda Bennison, in *American Mathematical Monthly* 77 (1970): 145.

44. I do not make any fundamental distinction between logic and mathematics from the ontological point of view (but, I emphasize: only from this point of view). The fundamental gesture, for me, resides in the formalism of the notation common to both. We observe, moreover, with category theory, that the demonstrations of these two regimes of proof ceaselessly cross over one another (categorical Universes being able to unify logical and mathematical decisions); and I have no need, unlike for instance Alain Badiou, to posit a *philosophically* essential difference between them.

45. On this subject, see Linda Wetzel, 'Types and Tokens', *Stanford Encyclopedia of Philosophy*. Available from www.plato.stanford.edu/entries/types-tokens [accessed 15 January 2015]. And above all, by the same author, *Types and Tokens: On Abstract Objects* (Cambridge, MA: MIT Press, 2009).

46. We should nevertheless emphasize Linda Wetzel's analysis of the Hilbertian theory of the sign in her doctoral thesis: *On Numbers* (Cambridge, MA: MIT Press, 1984).

47. As would be the case for the Voynich manuscript, which has long been believed to contain a ciphered language, whereas it would seem that in fact it contains a pseudolanguage, which in consequence is pseudociphered.

48. Ferdinand de Saussure, *Course in General Linguistics*, trans. Wade Baskin (New York: Philosophical Library, 1959), p. 68.

49. One might consider that I dally excessively over the question of empirical resemblance given that it is quite evident that the unlimited iteration of a

token could not come from a sensible similarity between marks or motifs, whose series is always finite. But my intention is to identify, as I have said, the *source* of the iteration, to show whence it comes and, as we shall see, an effective way of doing so consists in going by way of certain remarkable properties of sensible resemblance; above all, not similarity but what I shall call 'repetition'.

50. Henri Bergson, *Time and Free Will: Essay on the Immediate Data of Consciousness*, trans. Frank Lubecki Pogson (New York: Dover, 2001), chapter two and 'Conclusion'.
51. I distinguish the indefinite from the infinite according to the traditional difference between the potential infinite and the actual infinite. The indefinite is the endless augmentation of the finite (1, 2, 3, etc.); it is the indispensable, but not sufficient, preliminary to the thinkability of an actual infinity whose existence set theory guarantees via an axiom. I cannot explain here how I derive actual infinity factially, on the basis of the derivation of the indefinite.
52. Affirming its deuteroabsoluteness can only lead, as we have seen, to a cryptophysical position that can only be authorized by itself, and whose retrospective value depends upon the effectiveness of its descriptive scope. But we have also seen that the weakness of this project is due to the dependence upon a body of scientific knowledge that it cannot but widely cross while it is plausibly in perpetual evolution and also, on the other hand, owes to a unificatory will, whereas the knowledge of the actual world is perpetually torn apart by the organigrammatic structure of knowledges.
53. Bergson, *Time and Free Will*, p. 79.
54. To paraphrase G. W. Leibniz, 'New System of the Nature of Substances', in R. S. Woolhouse and R. Francks (eds), *Leibniz's 'New System' and Associated Contemporary Texts* (Oxford: Oxford University Press, 1997), p. 17.

CHAPTER 6
LANGUAGE ONTOLOGY
Armen Avanessian

A hypothesis concerning a relational ontology of language

The renewed interest in realism and materialism in contemporary Continental philosophy comes with a polemic – sometimes explicit but most often implicit – against the main trends of twentieth-century philosophy. The recent *speculative turn* is supposed not only to go beyond various strands of French poststructuralism or Anglo-American analytic philosophy, but, so we are told, it directly opposes or objects to the theoretical projects of the *linguistic turn*.[1] Ontology, it would seem to follow, is inaccessible to any kind of philosophical endeavour anchored in a philosophy of language or in linguistics.

In what follows, I propose a somewhat different thesis, which is also one of the basic assumptions of an ongoing research project on *Speculative Poetics*, that language always already contains an ontological thesis: the world that language mediates is made up of relations, not of objects.[2] Language therefore has an *immanent* knowledge and can thus claim for itself a higher degree of realism than our perception, which presents us with things alone. A supplementary thesis holds that language leads us right into the world if only because the world (the world we have, see, or think) develops, to a degree that is difficult to overestimate, in parallel with language, without being its correlationist product. In order to justify such a language-ontological speculation – which is to say, a speculative ontology of language – we need to determine how language relates to our thought and our perception of the world. To this end, I will articulate the interface of semiotic and language-ontological speculation in terms of a materialism and realism of language. My general (*poietic*) claim is that every attempt to play off the reality content of knowledge instituted by the perception of things (*aisthesis*) against the reality content instituted by semiotic or recursive part-to-whole relations risks a self-dissolution of thinking (*noesis*). The relational ontology I have in mind can be understood as a realism of relations. That is, we do not see things themselves but rather see things in their relations. What language gives us to see is the existence of relations – as Novalis wrote in the late eighteenth century:

> If only one could make people understand that it is the same with language as with mathematical formulae. These constitute a world of their own. They play only with themselves, express nothing but their marvelous nature, and just for this reason they are so expressive – just for this reason the strange play of relations between things is mirrored in them.[3]

An unnecessary split in philosophy

To overcome the split between twentieth-century philosophy after the linguistic turn and contemporary philosophers of the speculative turn, we have to connect the language-based poststructuralist and analytical philosophies of recent decades with the contemporary interest in ontology. The premise here is that language, literature and thought are part of the world. Historically, speculative philosophy from Leibniz to Hegel to Whitehead and after has always called for experimentation with language. Every use of words that takes them to be ready-made for use – as if both language and the world preexist one another and each only needs to be adequately or 'truly' adjusted to the other – must fail. I claim that *thinking literature* consists in situating natural language, literary artefacts and poetic thinking on a single plane. To investigate literature as a laboratory of language, for example, we must break with a key assumption of twentieth-century philosophies of language, of linguistics as well as post-Saussurian theories of language, namely the idea that language is nonreferential or simply arbitrary. Language, on the contrary, is *not* arbitrary. It evolves recursively, that is, language further develops the world in ever-new referrals back to itself. An ontology of language corresponding to this premise helps not just to overcome the split between current speculative realisms or materialisms and earlier philosophical positions. Beyond that, as I will show, the speculative realm also clears up various misunderstandings or even overcome long-standing oppositions within twentieth-century philosophy itself. It cannot but be in the interest of any speculative or ontological philosophical adventure today to build on philosophies of language, all the while aiming to overcome the nominalism that usually characterizes them.

I want to show that a speculative ontological approach to the capacities and mechanisms of language can capture its realist ontological dimension.

Central here is the concept of recursion, which belongs to a different conception of language than that of structural linguistics built as it is on equivalence, difference and reflexivity. To think a reality that lacks necessity and is instead based on necessary contingency, to think the possibility of nonarbitrariness and to come to a different understanding of referentiality, I will later turn to Quentin Meillassoux's groundbreaking thoughts on the sign devoid of meaning that – given his mathematical and logical focus – he unfortunately limits to formal languages, thereby disregarding the recursive capacities of natural language.

A holistic semiotics

In order to address the above-mentioned misunderstandings between postlinguistic-turn philosophies of the twentieth century, I propose to analyse them against the foil of the famous semiotic triangle by asking which of its three angles (referent, signified, signifier), and which moves from angle to angle, a particular philosophical tradition emphasizes. Even if there is not the space here for a detailed analysis of the differences and even contradictions in labelling and interpreting the triangle, a brief comparison already shows discrepancies within the 'language is arbitrary' camp itself. In the Continental tradition, for example, the most common labelling of the semiotic triangle goes signifier/signified/referent; another one is expression/meaning/referent. While philosophical accounts typically focus on the 'truth'-relation between signified and reference and thereby ignore the relevance of the third angle, Umberto Eco criticizes this schema in favour of a semiotic triangle of symbol/reference/referent. It therefore becomes evident that while these authors share an apparently common ground in referring to semiotics, they are actually speaking of very different semiotic triangles. It's then no surprise that the individual accounts have difficulties understanding each other. Speaking the same (semiotic) language led – and still leads – to fierce polemics between the camps. Here, however, I am concerned with the somewhat opposite effect: the fact that they tend to misunderstand each other even where they seem to agree. It is quite possible that a certain agreement – for example, in our context, an agreement on the arbitrariness of signs or language – concealed and therefore prolonged the underlying theoretical failure of communication based on semiotically different (and opposing) philosophies of language. It seems, for example, that there has actually never been any agreement or sufficient discussion on whether the alleged arbitrariness is based on the arbitrary relation between signifier and signified, or signifier and reference, or any of the other fundamental structuring distinctions.

Introducing a generalized semiotic theory might help to describe our common practice of constituting the world as we are interpreting it, while we are interpreting it. Far too often, linguistics has been content with its insight that language always already exists and changes, thereby dispensing with the idea of objective truth. Philosophy, in turn, in the past has all too often demanded that language objectivize truth and nothing but a truth it sees as external to language; that is, that language objectivize truth with regard to the 'referent'. That is why analytical philosophy especially – even while it relies heavily on often exotic thought experiments – has had great difficulty coping with fiction, understood as a dangerous shifting of the (deictical) meaning, and has had to condemn the *écriture* of so-called 'French Theory' as an uncontrolled production of signifiers.

By contrast, from the point of view of what I call a 'holistic semiotics', signifiers can acquire (significant) meaning only thanks to their constant differential movement, a metonymic movement of chains of signifiers that always takes place. It is of decisive importance not to understand this as (only) an abstract *reflexive* procedure. This metonymic slide takes place in *recursions* of always different magnitudes, in which parts and wholes integrate each other in new part/whole-relations. These recursions incessantly shift the signification of the parts they integrate. Contrary to what is commonly, and falsely, assumed in philosophical criticisms of deconstruction (be it hermeneutics or analytic philosophy), the sliding of the signifier does not destroy sense. That such a sliding precludes the idea of a fixed sense easily obscures its incessant production of sense through the shifting of sense. Indeed, there could be no sense without such sliding (as Jacques Derrida pointed out in various texts, notably in *Of Grammatology*).

From this perspective, such differences (or seemingly unbridgeable oppositions) between philosophy and linguistics or between differently oriented philosophies arise necessarily when semiotic relations are reduced to serving particular discursive interests. Against such reductions, I insist that semiotic relations always have to be thought in all three dimensions (of signifying expression, signified meaning, and referent) and that they form a relational whole.

Referential alternatives

My suggestion, then, is to take into account not just the relation (of signification) between referent and signified exclusively, as philosophers often do, implicitly or explicitly, but all three elements of the semiotic triangle initially introduced by Charles Sanders Peirce's speculative grammar (Peirce's own term, adopted by those who followed him, was *speculative rhetorics*). From a semiotic point of view, Derrida and Paul de Man, for example, describe a very different semiotic movement than philosophical hermeneutics does. This common yet disparate semiotic ground caused a fundamental misunderstanding and resulted in some unnecessarily harsh debates between the two camps. Put in the more formal terms of a thesis: unlike traditional philosophy and hermeneutics, which was heavily invested in the perspective of meaning, deconstruction was increasingly interested in a way of labelling the semiotic triangle that starts from the angle of expression or the signifier. Deconstruction's obvious focus on the signifier does not, however, imply a non- or anti-referential philosophy, which is how it had to appear for any established philosophical position whose semiotics took the signified or meaning as its point of departure. Instead, there is 'simply' another direction leading away from the signifier, namely towards the referent (and not just the apparently solipsistic relation between signifier/signified – Derrida's misunderstood *il n'y a pas de hors-texte*). Such a deconstructive change of direction opens up the possibility of thinking about referentiality and reality in a new way: not following Gottlob Frege and, to a certain extent, Ferdinand de Saussure, via *symbolization* (the relation of signifier and signified) or via *signification* (the relation of signified and referent or of meaning and object), but via the relation between signifier and referent (*denotation*).

Iconoclasm and the implicit language philosophy of SR

The introduction of the Peircean tripartite model can help us understand speculative realism or materialism as a linguistic or lingual relationalism. Quentin Meillassoux and Ray Brassier, for example, have both engaged with semiotics or the (analytical) philosophy of language. On the other hand, a new linguistics of universal grammar prefers finalistic or functional explanations to describe the makeup of language. I think it is important for both to resist the thesis that language is arbitrary, which would yet again create a rift between language and the world. And it is precisely such a rift that led to an epistemological and linguistic immanentism cut off from phenomenological cognition and confined the subject to a correlationist hall of mirrors.

When we look at the relationship between symbolic relations based on what Peirce calls 'Thirdness'[4] and relations between things and at the same time consider that indexical semiotic relations can (and, if they want to be meaningful, to a certain degree must) be negative, we understand how most contemporary speculative philosophy can be a realism that (like all philosophical writing) is a practice of language without, however, possessing a theory of language (at least during its 'first phase'). I believe contemporary speculative philosophy can and should be accompanied by a realist or materialist linguistics, a poetics or a theory of language that reflects the unavoidable relation of thought, language and the world. Only then can there be a meaningful justification – thanks to poiesis: the opening up of the world in language – of the realist project of anticorrelationist thought. From the perspective of noesis, constructions of language and of cognitive capacities go hand in hand.

The practice of triadic semiotic relations can be helpful here to describe an economization of language, overcoming explanations such as Augustine's (criticized at the beginning of Wittgenstein's *Philosophical Investigations*), in which every real entity calls for an individual word to denote its signification. This would necessitate an excessive vocabulary and completely overburden our capacities. Only the relationalism of the symbolic system can account for many more objects (tools) than would ever be possible with indices. Here lies another decisive lesson from a holistic semiotics: we acquire grammar in the construction of triadic semiotic relations. This construction can only be achieved in what can be called an iconoclastic procedure. Primates, for example, cannot learn our languages because they cannot renounce producing indexical relations, which they can very well be trained to establish.[5] This boundary seems to remain insurmountable. There is no indication that even an ever-expanding appropriation of indexical signs like *banana* and *hammer*, *orange* and *knife* would enable them to distinguish between food and tools in general. Even when they are shown boxes that contain food at one time, tools at another, they usually do not form complex symbolic semiotic relations. At most, they appropriate one more singular token, one for boxes. For relations between things and relations between signs to be produced, the relations between signs and objects have, at first, to be severed in an iconoclastic act. It is this *relationalism* of language – which must not be confused with a correlationism – that gives language its unique ontological capacities and makes it a direct and real element of the world, an object in the same dimension as other objects.

Analytical philosophy of language

Paraphrasing Descartes, we can summarize the enthusiasm that drives analytic philosophy as follows: 'I think things, therefore they are', or, more elaborately: 'I think things truthfully, therefore they are. If, then, I translate my thinking into propositions that follow the rules of logic, I can identify things.' But within the project of analytic philosophy, the capacity to identify things by means of propositions is lost time and again. Even though they develop a theory of truth as a theory of meaning, such theories time and again lose their relation to the things of the world, to what linguistics call the referents. For (semiotic) reasons already touched upon, analytical philosophy – very broadly speaking, of course – has a tendency to connect language with referents by way of a theory of truth. In such cases, language consists of a lexicon and logic, with logic more or less replacing grammar (or syntax). The signified is seen as a 'semantic property', that is, as a predicate of the signifier, and a concept is satisfactory when it links sentences to referents or things. The pathos of a theory of language in which language assumes the place of the transcendental subject of knowledge consists in the utopian conception that a perfect language, cleansed of all contingency, would designate all things and would therefore also allow for the identification of each and every particular thing on the basis of its description or its name. However, such a language is robbed of its productive function – of what can also be called its poietic function. And would such an ideal language (or such an ideal of language) actually be a language at all? The more a (theory of) language approximates an ideal language, the further it moves away from the things to which it owes its reality until, finally, such a total separation or eradication of reference lets things be things without language (or lets things do their own thing).

Pushing the argument to the extreme, we could ask whether we are confronted here with another surprising proximity between two strands of postlinguistic-turn philosophies that on the surface are strongly opposed to one another: analytic philosophy and poststructuralism. Does not this respectful separation of language from the real paradoxically coincide with the accounts of deconstruction and its affiliates within modernist literature, literary theory and aesthetics?

True analytic philosophy

The project of analytic philosophy can thus roughly be described as follows: its movement through the semiotic triangle outlines (i.e. circumscribes and goes around) the relation of referent and signified, placing this relation under criteria of truth. The expressive signifier, accordingly, comes into view only within the perspective of its concordance with or deviance from logical principles. Its task is limited to living up to criteria of truth and thereby guaranteeing reference. This is also the origin of the tendency toward standardization that every interpretation of language as a (deficient) logical system entails. With notable exceptions such as Robert Brandom's work, the goal of attaining referents with a theory of truth presupposes an absolute discipline of language.[6]

Let's have a quick look at two classic examples. For Willard Van Orman Quine, an unbridgeable abyss opens up between meaning and referent, between 'physical phenomena as a physical phenomenon, and our scientific imaginings as activities within the world that we imagine'.[7] We encounter a similar scenario in Donald Davidson's reflections on the status of translation manuals, in which sentences lose the function of referring to referents and only refer to sentences in (another) language:

> a translation manual is only a method of going from sentences of one language to sentences of another, and we can infer from it nothing about the relations between words and objects. Of course we know, or think we know, what the words in our language refer to, but this is information no translation manual contains. Translation is a purely syntactic notion. Questions of reference do not arise in syntax, much less get settled.[8]

Despite (or precisely because of) the reduction in such accounts of syntax to a logical calculus or the transformation of the signified into a predicate, the relation to the referent turns into a mystery.

Another attempt to preserve the relation of referent and signified from the dissolution that threatens it in an ever more precise differentiation is made by Saul Kripke. Kripke thinks the idea of reference in terms of chains, and the question of how reference is transmitted is of central importance to him.[9] Interrupting this process of transmission would undermine the realist potential of language. Truth that refers to this relation (*adequatio rei et intellectus*) cannot be had as a semiotic relation. And yet it drives the discourse; it leads to the continuous differentiation of this relation and thus also to what we know as an ever more approximate description of the referent. What emerges in Kripke is the fascinating idea of an articulation of reference with metonymy, that is, with (recursive) part-to-whole relations. Against the common understanding of reference, either via the relation of unity and opposition or via the relation of identity and difference, reference would then be created via operations of partitioning and the recursive formation of a whole. The question, then, is how one would have to think a corresponding metonymic or contiguous reality, one that lacks necessity, disrupts the common (onto-)logic of non-contradictory propositions, and is instead based on necessary contingency.

Contingency and reference

What theory of language or semiotics, what kind of sign would correspond to an absolutely contingent world(view) that fundamentally challenges every philosophy aiming for 'unity' and 'identity' (and their dialectical counterparts 'opposition' and 'difference')? In contrast to all earlier attempts at making contradiction disappear, Quentin Meillassoux's philosophy makes it a fundamental ontological category. He assumes a contradictory factuality (the absolutizing of contingency), which replaces the demand for coherent facticity:

> Why can't physicists demonstrate the necessary determination of a law by reason alone? Because these are *facts*, not necessities ... I call 'facticity' the lack of reason for any reality; that is, the impossibility of giving an ultimate ground to the existence of any being.[10]

With regard to our question concerning (the possibility of) a speculative ontology of language, this means that we either give up the ability to identify referents (and, in its wake, our belief in the existence of facts as well) or we maintain our faith in factuality and give up the principle of causality in favour of a generalized principle of contingency.

Meillassoux himself has taken up these considerations in some recent reflections on the *signe dépourvu de sens* (sign devoid of meaning). For him, an

> empty sign possesses an immaterial force of identical reproduction. But since it is arbitrary, no concept can capture its essence – it is in

principle infinitely variable with regard to its form, and this form has no necessity in itself. And since I can posit distinct types of empty signs, its iterable identity is no longer that of the general concept of the 'sign' (or even the 'sign devoid of meaning').[11]

The 'empty sign' conceived by Meillassoux is the foil against which it is possible to outline the necessary properties of any concrete sign. The concrete sign derives its semioticity from its diverging, in a significant manner, from the determinations of the empty sign: the arbitrariness, iterability and variability of the concrete sign are already limited by the requirement that it must at the same time be a real thing (and part of the world to the same extent as other objects). Every concrete sign, in other words, can only be a sign because it differs from the empty sign – if only because as a real thing, it entertains a certain (but contingent) relation with other real things. We could also say that the sliding of signifiers, which we saw was a necessary property of any (real) sign, presupposes real change-ability. Every (real) sign – insofar as it is (at the same time) a concrete thing – fulfils this precondition.[12]

Natural and/or formal language

There is an obvious objection to adapting Meillassoux's attempt at formulating an 'ontology of the empty sign' for my purposes: Meillasoux clearly states that he is talking only about formal language and not about the signs of natural language.[13] His argument starts with a distinction between pure or simple base-signs and operator-signs. A *signe dépourvu de sens* is one 'devoid of any signification, and a fortiori of any reference'. It is a sign that 'refers only to itself'.[14] As such, for Meillassoux this sign devoid of meaning is what he calls an initial object of mathematics: it acquires meaning only as an effect of mathematical operations. And this is where he sees the necessity of a

> distinction between a natural language and a formal language: for we can decide *to differentiate them according to the role that signs devoid of meaning play within them.* We shall therefore say that a formal language, unlike a natural language, accords a structural role to the sign devoid of meaning – at least on a *syntactical* level. For alphabetical natural languages do indeed make rule-governed use of letters

and syllables that are, in themselves, devoid of signification – but they do so on the morphological level of the constitution of words, and not at the syntactical level of the constitution of sentences.[15]

Now, in order to justify the claims of a nonmetaphysical but materialist and realist ontology, that is, a noncorrelationist but speculative ontology (also) of natural language, we have to scrutinize Meillassoux's own implicit philosophy of natural language. It has a very refreshing effect in his interpretation of literature, notably of Mallarmé, whom he reads quite differently than does an entire modernist, post-Saussurian tradition in literary theory that is mostly obsessed with what one could call *syntactical estrangement* (that is, meaning undermined by an aesthetical use of syntax). But Meillassoux's opposition or juxtaposition becomes problematic when it leads to a quasiontological difference between natural and formal language. The problem here is that, given his focus on logic and mathematics (set theory) and his understanding of language as a primarily syntactical construct, Meillassoux refers to exactly the kind of linguistics he disagrees with, namely Saussure and his (false) dogma of arbitrariness.[16] In order to guarantee the (ontological and speculative) primacy of formal language, Meillassoux then argues via a separation of syntax and morphology. He thereby inadvertently accepts and continues the Saussurian tradition he opposes. Time and again, the distinction between syntax and morphology equals the one between logic and grammar – with grammar dealing with morphology rather than syntax. In Meillassoux's case, this leads to a primacy of logical and mathematical formal languages, apparently the only ones able to deal with empty signs (on the syntactical level).

However – and this is my central point – there exists a grammar that is capable of breaking up this binary relation of formal or natural language, syntax or morphology, logic or grammar, syntax or grammar.[17] Picking up on the work of the linguist Elisabeth Leiss, Anke Hennig and I have tried to demonstrate how these distinctions disappear in Noam Chomsky's linguistic theory precisely because the order of speaking is or has the order of sentences.[18] One of the hallmarks of the Saussurian tradition, in contrast, is to understand 'speaking' as a social phenomenon that remains beyond the reach of linguistics. And the same goes for sentences: understood as communications or utterances, their analysis is relegated to subdisciplines such as socio-, psycho-, or textual linguistics. It is exactly these separations that disappear with Chomsky and especially with Leiss, for whom only a whole sentence makes for a complete sign.

Genealogies of Speculation

Leiss's argument is built on Peirce's tripartite semiotics, which allows me to reformulate my thesis in the terms of the semiotic triangle: to make sense or have a reference, a sign needs to run through or traverse the whole triangle. This metonymic understanding of signs sees them not as being empty or full, but as being more or less complete. The 'empty' sign is a thing; it is operative or applicable only because of its relational existence as a thing among other things in the world. Furthermore, the meaningless signs of natural language are all-purpose signs. From the point of view of a *poetic grammar*, a grammar such as Roman Jakobson's that is informed by literary devices, this leads to the demand that the separation between language (*Sprache*) and speech (*Sprechen*) be broken down. It is not even sure whether this difference even exists, or – as one could argue with the great counter-Saussurian linguist Gustave Guillaume – whether the poietic capacity of language isn't exactly based on the following: in speaking, we not only actualize an existing paradigm of language, we also always potentialize a not-yet-existing paradigm of language and our understanding of the world.[19] While using language in speaking we change, in infinitesimally small steps, not just language as such but our being in the world. Hence my call for a poietic understanding of language and its recursive operations, always integrating speakers, language as such and the world in order to produce (ontologically) new meaning.

Speculative mereology

Natural languages are organized and develop via recursion both on a morphological and a syntactical level. It is typical of recursive structures in language that their structures become ever more complex.[20] As I have already mentioned, it is due to the recursive development and use of language – both on the morphological level (*see, seen, seeing*) and syntactical level (*I see, You don't know that I see, You don't know that I see you reading this*) – that language, while referring back to itself in producing new meaning, further develops not just itself but the world and its relations within that world. This also explains how recursion in language heightens the realism of language and expands the possibilities it contains to describe and understand the world. It is a process that is completely different from the deadlocked modernist (or avant-garde) concepts of self-reflexivity based on relations of equivalence. Such equivalence-based self-reflexivity may obscure reference, but recursivity – which is based on metonymic part-to-whole relations – certainly does not.

We can see now that correlationism, which Meillassoux famously makes out to be the antagonist of any realism or materialism, presupposes a very specific and reflexive theory of language. From a linguistic point of view such a theory could be named a relationism of equivalences in which the paradoxes, mirroring effects and equiunivocities produced in circles by relations of equivalence, necessarily turn against realism. But again: only a (self-)reflexive account of language remains necessarily correlationist. A recursive one does not.[21]

The recursive structure of language and thinking (the world)

Recursion is the only universal most linguists agree is shared by all languages. According to Chomsky,

> [the] critical formal contribution of early generative grammar was to show that the regularity and unboundedness of natural language syntax were expressible by precise grammatical models endowed with recursive procedures. Knowing a language amounts to tacitly possessing a recursive generative procedure.[22]

Based on theories of cognition, the greatest later achievement of a universal grammar, increasingly understood to be extralinguistic, is the new sense it gives to finding syntactic recursive structures. The fact that language returns to itself evinces its productive or speculative function: the parallel development of language and thought.

Recursive structures in syntax are not merely the play of language in which it mirrors itself. They also hint at the fact that sentences do not only refer to sentences in other languages and at how, in Meillassoux's words, 'a sign empty of meaning allows us to describe the world without becoming once again a sign *provided* with meaning, and hence capable of referring outside of itself'.[23] A realist or materialist ontology of language – unlike a correlationist or metaphysical one – has to reject the sceptical poststructuralist commonplace that language merely forms the world or creates images of the world. From the point of view of a speculative linguistics or a speculative poetics, language both changes the world of which it is a part and, at the same time, optimizes human cognition by means of recursive structures. Language in its referentiality relates to the object to be known by recursively forming the matter of knowledge. To this extent, as Leiss remarks in reference to Derek Bickerton, language makes

> specifically human cognition possible in the first place ... According to this approach, language is the interface between the world and a material brain, which otherwise isn't very exciting. Language thus optimizes a primate's brain and produces cognition that is specifically human.[24]

Aesthetic philosophy of language: Equivalence versus poiesis

As I hope has become clear by now, the movement of linguistic recursion cannot be thought as purely immanent to language. It presupposes a combination of language and reality. Such an understanding of recursion allows us to go beyond modernist conceptions of language in at least four ways. It is against: (i) ideas of metalanguage; (ii) the principle of equivalence; (iii) a total nonreferentiality of language; and (iv) a basically aisthetic and correlationist understanding of language (at the expense of language's poietic qualities and its material dimension). The opposition between a model of language based on relations of equivalence (and their reflexivity) and a model in which language consists of recursive part-to-whole relations can thus also be understood as the difference between an aesthetic and a poetic model of language. On one side, we have a correlationist theory of language and, corresponding to it, an aesthetics of literature that wants to trace the event character of the literary back to an effect of withdrawing reference from the subject. The literary work and language in general do not appear to be the result of a poiesis; they are merely the result of a practice in which they are produced for a reflexive aisthesis. This aesthetic conception of language as reflexive rather as recursive fails to acknowledge the materiality or reality of language. My goal in arguing against it here is to provide some first insights into an understanding of language that is both speculative and poetic, 'the central experience of poiesis' being, according to Giorgio Agamben, the 'pro-duction into presence, ... the fact that in it something passed from nonbeing into being, thus opening the space of truth (α-$\lambda\dot{\eta}\theta\varepsilon\iota\alpha$)'.[25]

What does language look like when it becomes the object of aesthetics instead of poetics, as it so often does? What deformations must it be subjected to in order to be understood as a manifestation or model of sense knowledge? An aestheticized understanding of language tends toward reflexivity on the one hand and a void of sense on the other. While the first property results from the cognitive character of language, the second derives from its sensibility: the sensibility of language obscures its meaning, and its self-reflexivity obscures its reference. We find such an aestheticist view of language even in Jakobson, who sees only reflexivity when he is talking about the poetic function. In his conception, the poetic function reflects itself and thereby produces a specific economy of attention. Here, the function's *poietic* element is replaced (or completely ignored) by an aesthetic one. It is limited to having created the object of a reflexive perception. We can generalize this moment of (self-)reflection, and we can discern in it an aesthetic model of language.

For Jakobson the poetic function of language obscures its referential function, and most aesthetic conceptions of language go even further than he does in this regard. What is striking here is the connection between a theory of reflection and a theory of a language without reference. Literary language that refers to itself – especially the language of classical modernism – is not only reflexive; in closing in on itself it also cuts itself off from its reference to the world. The correlate of reflexivity is then referencelessness, both on the level of a theory of language and on the level of a theory of literature (where referencelessness is usually designated as a sublime 'void of meaning').

Conclusion

What I have tried to outline here is an understanding of language that banks on a seemingly paradoxical referentiality rather than considering reference to have been refuted by (Saussurian) arbitrariness. The early Romantics already aimed for a conception of (non-)meaning or (non-)reference, which has to be distinguished from a reflexive philosophy of language after the linguistic turn dominant in the twentieth century. In this light, the latter is *not* a linguistic turn *strictu sensu* and might be better called an *aestheticized linguistic turn*, or be considered part of a more general *aesthetic turn* since around 1800. We find similar thoughts in Derrida,[26] and recently, we have seen in Meillassoux a quest for 'an arbitrariness more fundamental than "unmotivation"' (this is what I call arbitrariness in the Saussurian sense: the nonnecessary link between sign and meaning)'.[27]

Natural language, I have tried to show, is indeed similar to the case of mathematical formulae; or, to quote from Novalis, it is 'by expressing nothing other than their wonderful nature' that natural language 'mirrors in themselves the curious play of relations in things'. I have provided a similarly paradoxical answer to Meillassoux's central question:

> How can a sign empty of meaning allow us to describe the world without becoming once again a sign *provided* with meaning, hence capable of reference outside of itself? How, through what paradox, can we hope that a sign void of meaning could ... [have] a referent, more radically separate from us than every correlational apprehension?[28]

In the spirit of what has been called the *semontology* of early Romantic philosophy, I have attempted to push further the semiotic ontology Meillassoux has started to develop. I have just cited from Novalis because only where 'the sign provided with meaning is forgotten in favor of its meaning and its reference' does the sign devoid of meaning, 'giving itself ultimately for itself, as pure sign, mak[e] me accede to its pure gratuitousness, to its pure absence of necessity, to the fact that anything whatsoever could fulfill its task just as well as it does. So that it is indeed the nonfoundation of all beings, and not of the sign alone, which discreetly reveals itself in this asignificance.' That, one last time, was Meillassoux and not Novalis.[29]

Notes

1. Levi Bryant, Nick Srnicek and Graham Harman, 'Towards a Speculative Philosophy', in Levi Bryant, Nick Srnicek and Graham Harman (eds), *The Speculative Turn: Continental Materialism and Realism* (Melbourne: re.press, 2011), pp. 1–18.
2. This project as well as the thoughts in this essay take up key themes of *Metanoia: Spekulative Ontologie der Sprache* (Berlin: Merve, 2014; English translation forthcoming), a book I wrote with Anke Hennig. Beyond my drawing on central passages from that book here, my thanks go to her.
3. Novalis, 'Monologue', trans. and ed. Margaret Mahony Stoljar, *Novalis: Philosophical Writings* (Albany: SUNY Press, 1997), p. 83.
4. In Peirce the triadic dimension of 'Thirdness' has the dimension of representation and mediation, in contrast to the categories of 'Firstness' (or the Quality of Feeling) and dyadic 'Secondness'.
5. See also Elisabeth Leiss, *Sprachphilosophie* (Berlin: de Gruyter, 2009), p. 258.
6. For, to the extent that signifieds or signifiers avoid correct predication they also endanger the success of the truth-loving subterfuge – 'subterfuge' in this

context referring to the movement through the semiotic triangle – that leads from meaning via expression (or from the signified via the signifier) to the referent.

7. Willard Van Orman Quine, *Word and Object* (Cambridge, MA: MIT Press, 1960), p. 5.
8. Donald Davidson, 'Reality without Reference', in *Inquiries into Truth and Interpretation: Second Edition* (Oxford: Oxford University Press, 2001), p. 223.
9. Saul Kripke, *Wittgenstein on Rules and Private Language: An Elementary Exposition* (Cambridge, MA: Harvard University Press, 1982).
10. Quentin Meillassoux, 'Presentation', in Robin Mackay and Dustin McWherter (eds), *Collapse III: Unknown Deleuze [+Speculative Realism]* (Falmouth: Urbanomic, 2007), pp. 428, 442.
11. Quentin Meillassoux, 'Iteration, Reiteration, Repetition: A Speculative Analysis of the Sign Devoid of Meaning', trans. Robin Mackay and Moritz Gansen, this volume, p. 170.
12. On this point, compare Avanessian and Hennig, *Metanoia*, pp. 57–130.
13. Meillassoux, 'Iteration', pp. 161–2.
14. Ibid., p. 160.
15. Ibid. pp. 161–2. Meillasoux continues: 'At the syntactical level, a natural language can certainly also use words devoid of meaning – for example Mallarmé's "ptyx", if we agree that this word means nothing – but there is no rule that *imposes* this type of word upon natural languages. Their propensity is, on the contrary, to avoid them, so as to fulfill their ordinary function of communication. Consequently, what is proper to natural language, at the level of syntax, a contingent (and generally marginal) role to the sign [devoid of meaning]; whereas what is proper to a formal language is to grant it an essential and structural role at the very same syntactical level.'
16. Meillassoux aims for 'an arbitrariness that is more fundamental than "unmotivation" (this is what I call arbitrariness in the Saussurian sense: the nonnecessary link between sign and meaning)' ('Iteration', p. 169).
17. What we have in Chomsky's *Universal Grammar* is, basically, a grammar *of* syntax (and not a morphological grammar), a sentence-grammar, a syntax, and finally an operative grammar that clearly targets and transcends the distinction between grammar/morphology and syntax.
18. Avanessian and Hennig, *Metanoia*, pp. 227–32. See also Leiss, *Sprachphilosophie*, pp. 277f.
19. Gustave Guillaume, *Temps et verbe. Théorie des aspects, des modes et des temps suivi de L'architectonique du temps dans les langues classiques* (Paris: Honoré Champion, 1984 [first published 1929]).
20. I am not talking here about recursion in computation in which it is mainly a problem-solving procedure. The repetition of items in computation precisely

does not aim for difference or a new meaning the way linguistic recursion does.

21. Once again, Meillassoux allows us to articulate a criticism of the generalization of relations of equivalence and its effects is the congruent with the philosophical criticism of a correlationist understanding of language: 'Correlationism takes many contemporary forms, but particularly those of transcendental philosophy, the varieties of phenomenology, and postmodernism. But although these currents are all extraordinarily varied in themselves, they all share, according to me, a more or less explicit decision: that there are no objects, no events, no laws, no beings which are not always-already correlated with a point of view, with a subjective access. Anyone maintaining the contrary, i.e. that it is possible to attain something like a reality in itself, existing absolutely independently of his viewpoint, or his categories, or his epoch, or his culture, or his language, etc. – this person would be exemplarily naïve, or if you prefer: a realist, a metaphysician, a quaintly dogmatic philosopher' ('Time Without Becoming', trans. Robin Mackay, *Spike Art Quarterly* 35 [Spring 2013]: 88).

22. Noam Chomsky, *On Nature and Language* (Cambridge: Cambridge University Press, 2002), p. 3.

23. Meillassoux, 'Iteration', p. 183.

24. Leiss, *Sprachphilosophie*, pp. 125–6.

25. I am referring solely to Agamben's reminder of the ancient understanding of *poiesis*, not his philosophy of language according to which 'the central experience of poiesis, pro-duction into presence, is replaced by the question of the "how", that is, of the process through which the object has been produced. In terms of the work of art, this means that the emphasis shifts away from what the Greeks considered the essence of the work – the fact that in it something passed from nonbeing into being, thus opening the space of truth (α-λήθεια).' (*The Man without Content*, trans. Georgia Albert [Stanford: Stanford University Press, 1999], p. 70).

26. See for example the first chapter of his *Grammatology*. For a systematic discussion of the close similarities between the early-Romantic and deconstructive philosophy of language, see Winfried Menninghaus, *Unendliche Verdopplung: Die frühromantische Grundlegung der Kunsttheorie im Begriff absoluter Selbstreflexion* (Frankfurt am Main: Suhrkamp, 1987).

27. Meillassoux, 'Iteration', p. 169.

28. As Meillassoux asks, 'How, through what paradox, can we hope that a sign void of meaning could not only have a referent, but a (deutero-) absolute referent, more radically separate from us than every correlational apprehension?' ('Iteration', p. 183).

29. Meillassoux, 'Iteration', p. 182.

CHAPTER 7
THE REALIST NOVEL AND 'THE GREAT OUTDOORS': TOWARDS A LITERARY-SPECULATIVE REALISM
Arne De Boever

The map

This chapter takes its cue from what Quentin Meillassoux has rather playfully called 'the great outdoors'. In his words, the great outdoors is

> the *absolute* outside of precritical thinkers: that outside which was not relative to us, and which was given as indifferent to its own givenness to be what it is, existing in itself regardless of whether we are thinking of it or not; that outside which thought could explore with the legitimate feeling of being on foreign territory – of being entirely elsewhere.[1]

As such, the great outdoors poses a challenge to what Meillassoux calls correlationism, or thought that is caught up in the relation between reality and its perceiver, leaving us unable to think either one independently from the other. In Meillassoux's work, the great outdoors becomes the terrain of what has been called a speculative realism, which thinks a mathematizable reality that exists independently from the human being (that is, without thought, 'subsisting without being given') but to which the human being, through mathematics, nevertheless has access (for it is a reality that can be thought).[2] Meillassoux's philosophical question is: how is this kind of thought, this access to the absolute, possible?

In what follows, I explore the relation of the great outdoors to language, representation and specifically literary realism. My central question is: can there be a literary realism of the great outdoors? Meillassoux shows there is a philosophical realism of the great outdoors, and he calls it speculative. One way to rephrase my central question is: what might a literary-speculative realism (LSR) look like? I intend to approach this question following two distinct but in my view related paths. I begin by showing how this question is anticipated in debates about literary realism, developing out of structuralism and poststructuralism and the aesthetics of realism, modernism and postmodernism – debates that, as I see it, largely take place within what I understand to be a representationalist and biopolitical framework. To think LSR means to move away from such a framework towards what I characterize as a deathly, linguistic approach to literature, one that leaves the narration of novels and films behind and moves us toward what contemporary French novelist Michel Houellebecq has referred to as the 'juxtaposition' of poetry and painting.[3] This will also mean, as will become clear, to leave behind what some consider to be realism's humanism. In short, the first path is about pitching LSR against a traditional realism that I understand to operate within a representationalist, biopolitical and humanist framework (RBH).

Secondly, I take up Meillassoux's own and neglected discussion of literary fiction – his discussion of Mallarmé's poetry has received more attention[4] – in order to ask whether it accomplishes the deathly, linguistic LSR that I propose in the first part of this article. I argue that it does not: in his literary examples, all drawn from the genre of science fiction, Meillassoux paradoxically remains too constrained by the framework of realism to pull off this other, deathly and linguistic realism. In closing, I turn to the work of the contemporary French novelist Michel Houellebecq to consider how his struggle with realism's aesthetic and the attempt to write the great outdoors give way in Houellebecq's realist novel *The Map and the Territory* to a deathly and linguistic realism that, within the parameters that I have laid out, can be characterized as speculative. From within the genre of realism itself Houellebecq thus goes further than any of the science fiction examples Meillassoux offers.

First path: Literary realism

If one accepts realism's programme to be to give an account of the world, and specifically a representation of the living, it is clear that such a programme is both representationalist and biopolitical. Take, for example, Tom Wolfe, who polemically defends such a programme against postmodernist trends in narrative fiction. In his 1989 essay 'Stalking the Billion-Footed Beast: A Literary Manifesto for the New Social Novel', Wolfe called for a renewed commitment to a realism that would be able to write 'the life around us'.[5] As

The Realist Novel and 'the Great Outdoors'

an example, he offers his own novel *The Bonfire of the Vanities*, which tried to '[cram] as much of New York City between covers as you could'.[6] Chastising young novelists for feeling helpless before an actuality that, as per Wolfe's recollection of Philip Roth's statement on this issue, 'is continually outdoing our talents', he questions their abandonment of the real and proposes a 'detailed realism based on reporting, a realism more thorough than any currently being attempted, a realism that would portray the individual in intimate and inextricable relation to the society around him'.[7] 'American society today', he writes, 'is no more or less chaotic, random, discontinuous, or absurd than Russian society or French society or British society a hundred years ago, no matter how convenient it might be for a writer to think so. It is merely more varied and complicated and harder to define.'[8] When confronted with reality's 'billion-footed beast', Wolfe writes, 'the answer is ... to do what the journalists do': 'to wrestle the beast and bring it to terms'.[9] We need a realism that would tame the beast of reality to let it live in realist fiction.

One can characterize such a vulgar understanding of realism as both representationalist and biopolitical. The first term probably does not require too much explanation: Wolfe's realism is representationalist, in the sense that it seeks to give an account of the world. I propose the second term – biopolitical – on the basis of some of my own work on the politics of the realist novel.[10] There, I have uncovered a biopolitical theory of realism in the work of the contemporary novelists J. M. Coetzee, Kazuo Ishiguro, Paul Auster, Tom McCarthy, and others. This theory asks one to take seriously the historical coincidence that the modern genre of the novel, which programmatically seeks to write the lives of ordinary human beings into their most intimate details (as opposed to the lives of mythical or legendary figures represented in the tales of yore), emerges at the same time that, in Michel Foucault's analysis, the transformation of Western power from sovereignty into biopolitics takes place. In the realist novel, as Ian Watt already pointed out, characters do not only have names that sound like yours or mine, they also have birthdates, birth-times even (or, for that matter, death-times: we know that Richardson's 'Clarissa died at 6:40pm on Thursday, 7 September', as Watt recalls).[11] This biographical trait is staged in the diary-writing that makes up a significant part of what is often considered to be the first English-language novel, Daniel Defoe's *Robinson Crusoe*, a novel whose full title – *The Life and Strange Surprising Adventures of Robinson Crusoe, Mariner* – reveals better its biographical drive.[12] In the modern novel, characters are so full of life 'they practically need birth certificates', as Yann Martel puts it in his contemporary rewrite of the Crusoe tale, *Life of Pi*.[13]

Now, in the famous fifth chapter of the first volume of *The History of Sexuality*, Foucault suggests there has been a shift in the history of Western power from the old, classic power of sovereignty, defined by the right to kill (a power of death) to a new, modern power of life.[14] He makes a distinction between anatomopolitics, which is focused on individual bodies and rules through disciplinary techniques, and biopolitics, which is interested in the biological life of the population (the human being as species) and governs through interventions and regulatory controls. Biopolitics tries to make (produce, foster, optimize) life rather than take it: to keep life alive to the point of near-death, if needs be. While several novel theorists had already considered the relation between the novel and anatomopolitics, specifically the disciplinary power that rules individual bodies, I tried to show that some contemporary novelists through their intertextual engagement with certain classic examples of the novel-genre (the already mentioned *Robinson Crusoe*, but also Mary Shelley's *Frankenstein*, and others) invite one to investigate the relation between the novel – specifically, the realist novel – and biopolitics. The programmatic attempt to write life through the novel is then complicit with the shift in the history of Western power that Foucault theorizes. If Wolfe's rather pompous summary of the realist aesthetic is that it would 'tame the billion-footed beast of reality', then his realism is biopolitical through and through. As Peter Sloterdijk already suggested in 'Rules for the Human Zoo', reading is breeding.[15] Writing is, too.

As I indicated earlier on, Wolfe wrote his manifesto in response to postmodernist trends in narrative fiction. Those trends, which he traces back to modernism (Samuel Beckett, for example), arguably developed out of, or at least in some relation to, structuralist and poststructuralist approaches to realism and its representationalist and biopolitical project. One can think, for example, of anthropologist Claude Lévi-Strauss's structuralist understanding of myth, which posited that myth offers an imaginary, symbolic resolution for a real social contradiction that thus always remains at some remove from the myth.[16] Extended to all narrative, this means that any narrative (and not only the mythical one) seeks to resolve within its coherent form real, material problems that remain at some remove from that coherence, and in fact risk to disrupt it. Indeed, in *The Political Unconscious*, Fredric Jameson uses Lévi-Strauss's theory for his understanding of all narrative, and not just myth, 'as a socially symbolic act'.[17]

Structuralism offered what could be characterized as a 'weak' solution to this problem by laying bare this situation within its theoretical narrative.

Poststructuralism – one can think of deconstruction, for example – applied structuralism's insight to structuralism itself, a move that is famously anticipated in Roland Barthes's structuralist treatise *S/Z*, which ends in poststructuralist 'suspension', or with the structuralist project breaking under its own weight.[18] For Wolfe, the modernist and postmodernist literature that developed out of, or at least in relation to, these philosophical positions ultimately removed us from realism's programme to give an account of the world. And indeed, we have become used to a distribution of the sensible that separates modernism and postmodernism from realism due to their rejection of the realist aesthetic.

As I see it, however, there is a realism that *continues* in modernism and postmodernism, and in the structuralist and poststructuralist philosophical approaches with which they are associated. Indeed, from the perspective of realism, it would seem that both structuralism and poststructuralism can be interpreted as attempts to arrive at the real, material contradiction that any socially symbolic act, and specifically narrative, excludes. In their attempt to undermine the realist project of giving an account of the world, and to show that such a living representation of the living is always impossible, they are arguably also approaching a reality that they emphatically claim cannot be 'written'. Deconstruction would be the most advanced name for such a reality, even if it is a reality that is perpetually displaced, more of the order of the performative than the descriptive. When it comes to the realist programme of giving an account of the world, the conclusion is the same for realism, modernism and postmodernism: it can't be done. 'Deconstruction' is the closest that we are going to get to it. The billion-footed beast cannot be tamed; the best that can be done is to expose taming's *différance*. That's as real as it gets.

Let me consider just one example of how this debate continues today. In 2001, literary critic James Wood proposed – with reference to Tom Wolfe's manifesto – the genre of what he called 'the big, ambitious novel' to refer to novels like Zadie Smith's *White Teeth* (he also mentions other novels by Salman Rushdie, Thomas Pynchon, David Foster Wallace, and others).[19] In Wood's view, these are novels that pursue their account of the world, their living representation of the living, 'at all costs', trying to capture (perhaps) something of the extreme acceleration that is characteristic of 'the life around us' in the digitized late twentieth and early twenty-first centuries. As Wolfe already pointed out in his manifesto, such acceleration is of course not new and one can debate whether the acceleration we are living through today is indeed unprecedented. The point is, however, that Wood seems to wonder whether the realist novel can hold together at such high speed, amid this explosion of information. He suggests that the contemporary realist novel is groaning under everything it is trying to contain: driven on by what he refers to as the 'grammar' of storytelling alone, it no longer tells any actual stories. Its supposed extreme vitality, while seeming to borrow from realism, actually evades reality in his view and lacks the human element. It is here that we can add to my characterization of the realist novel as representationalist and biopolitical; it is also, in Wood's view, humanist – hence, RBH. While such a hysterical, histrionic realism may have originated in Dickens, Wood considers it to lack the 'very passionate and simple sentences' that makes Dickens's big, ambitious novels human. In writers like Smith, 'information becomes the new character'. It is this particular use of a Dickensian style that, in Wood's view, ties authors as 'distinguished' as Don DeLillo and as 'cinematically vulgar' as Wolfe together.

Zadie Smith, for her part, agreed, as evidenced by a response published shortly after Wood's criticism came out.[20] As I have suggested elsewhere, Smith's more developed response to Wood's criticism arguably appeared in a review article 2008, in which she laid out two paths for the novel.[21] One is exemplified by Joseph O'Neill's *Netherland*, a realist novel that is perfect – but (in Smith's view) 'anxiously' so. Its perfect realism is punctuated by interjections revealing the author's nervousness about this perfection, its performative nature, its inauthenticity – a perfectly performed realism that, by now, can no longer be considered realist because it has hardened as a genre. As an example of the other path, Smith proposes Tom McCarthy's novel *Remainder*, which is at the limits of realism, suffering (again in Smith's view) a 'nervous breakdown' of realism. This comes close to the postmodernist fiction that Wolfe in his manifesto resists in part by tracing its close relation to modernism. In Smith's reading, which she develops through a discussion of McCarthy's affiliation with the philosopher Simon Critchley, the realist novel of the future – *Remainder* rather than *Netherland* – presents us with the materialist collapse of the 'realist' form, revealing that the life around us, and indeed we ourselves, are 'defined by matter – though most of us most of the time pretend not to be'. It is this material remainder of the continuous elevation to form that realism *à la* McCarthy seeks to write. *Remainder* thus seeks to write something like the real contradiction that, as per Lévi-Strauss's reading, symbolic narrative always tries to resolve. It is narrative against narrative, in that sense: a narrative against symbolic resolution. A *material* story-*form*.

The result of such an attempt is a realism at the limits of realism – a realism that, within the limits of form, can only be achieved with difficulty.

The Realist Novel and 'the Great Outdoors'

It is obviously not a question here of moving to matter entirely, otherwise there would be no form left.[22] Instead, it seems that what is being pursued is a material crumbling of form – a form within which the materialization to which McCarthy aspires can be realized. One thus always still remains within the limits of realism, however minimally so, and a realist account of matter – one that would be able to capture the reality of matter *without* removing itself from it – is assumed impossible. Such a reality can only be captured negatively, as that which is either radically outside or (at best) present as a crumbling within (as in McCarthy's novel). While the RBH framework of the realist novel is evidently being challenged here, realism also never truly moves beyond it, leaving the realist novel ultimately always in a fix when it comes to actualizing its programme.

Now, I want to suggest that there is another, third path for realism that would be different from the two proposed above, one that would set it free from the RBH programme with which it struggles. I will readily admit that this third path is an *extreme*, if not *extremist*, path, one that realists like Wood might not hesitate to call *terroristic*. Indeed, it involves pushing the realist novel towards the experimental fiction from which it is traditionally separated, moving from a narrative realism towards a realism of juxtaposition, that is, from a realism associated with novels and films towards the realism of poetry and painting (as Houellebecq suggests in *The Map and the Territory*). To give an example of such a realism, let me return to Wood's characterization of Smith's *White Teeth* to show how that novel might already contain the possibility of such a third path. I want to propose that in its inhuman, quasimachinic generation of stories (to take up Wood's characterization), in its 'glamorous congestion' of dead narrative, and in its covering up of vitality by artificiality (all, of course, heavily criticized by Wood), *White Teeth* can be understood as a deathly, linguistic storytelling machine, generating tales outside of the RBH framework that has dominated the realist novel. The novel does not offer an account of the world or a living representation of the living; instead, the challenge would be to read Smith's novel as merely stories, just stories, as a kind of bare story-generation – by no one and for no one in particular.

This is an extreme, quasiterroristic position, as I have already indicated, one at the limits of writability and readability. For who can write like that, and who can read like that? However, I want to propose that, as such, *White Teeth* would still be a form of realism, specifically a realism that would write the reality that Wood cannot consider *within* the realist novel, and that is the very reality that realism, in its wildest dreams, wants to write: the great outdoors, the world as independent from the human beings who perceive it. It is in this way that realism would be able to write the real, material contradiction that remains at a distance from all narrative resolutions (as per modernism and postmodernism's criticisms of realism).

Indeed, there is no room for the great outdoors in the RBH novel – how could there be, given that its absolute outside is not relative to human beings, given as indifferent to its own givenness to be what it is, and exists in itself regardless of whether we are thinking of it or not? The great outdoors *breaks with all three credos of the realist novel.* It cannot be represented. It is not necessarily living. It is certainly not human. Clearly, a realist novel of the great outdoors can only be possible if realism leaves behind those values that it holds most dearly. Doing so, I propose, propels the realist novel towards the experimental fiction that is traditionally considered separate from it. It pushes the realist novel towards the speculative – towards the realm where it begins to exist independently from its human producer and receiver, while it can nevertheless still be written. It is here that literary realism, representation and language begin to approach something like the mathematical formula. Such an approach was perhaps most memorably staged in Herman Melville's famous story 'Bartleby, the Scrivener', which explicitly states that it fails in its representationalist and biopolitical attempt to write Bartleby's life and can effectively be condensed to the 'inhuman' scrivener's quasimathematical 'formula' (as Gilles Deleuze already put it): 'I would prefer not to'.[23] Meaning nothing, the formula's linguistic materiality becomes a writing of that 'foreign territory' or 'entirely elsewhere' that Meillassoux associates with the great outdoors. As such, it remains a realism – but a speculative one beyond the representationalism, biopolitics and humanism that constitute the trinity of traditional literary realism.

Second path: Meillassoux on narrative fiction

Let me now consider an aspect of Meillassoux's oeuvre that has largely been overlooked – namely, the role it attributes to literature, and specifically to narrative fiction – to see what literary solutions Meilassoux arrives at for the philosophical questions he raises. In an essay titled 'Metaphysics and Extro-Science Fiction' Meillassoux rehearses the philosophical argument for speculative realism that can also be found in *After Finitude*.[24] However, he also expands it to include a literary-theoretical argument about science fiction (SF) and specifically the genre that Meillassoux seeks to distinguish

The Realist Novel and 'the Great Outdoors'

from it, extro-science fiction (XSF). I want to consider both genres here against the background of the debates on literary realism rehearsed above in order to see, specifically, how Meillassoux's account of speculative realism can be brought into conversation with them.

Distinguishing between two regimes of narrative fiction, SF and XSF, Meillassoux points out that as far as its relation to science goes, SF preserves the existence of science. In SF, science 'may be profoundly transformed', he writes, 'but there will always be science'.[25] In XSF, this is not the case: this genre thinks a 'world outside science', '*where experimental science is in principle impossible*, rather than unknown'.[26] It is the latter that Meillassoux will be interested in – not because he is particularly interested in fiction, but because the distinction between SF and XSF will enable him to lay out a conceptual distinction that he deems to be of philosophical interest. Meillassoux's discussion revolves around 'Hume's problem', familiar to readers of *After Finitude*. How can we know, Hume asks, 'what truly guarantees – but also what persuades us – that physical laws will continue to hold in a moment's time, given that neither experience nor logic can assure us of this'?[27] Meillassoux goes on to discuss Karl Popper's answer to this question: Popper argues that 'nothing could guarantee it, but moreover that this was a good thing, since there is nothing fantastic about these possibilities – they must be taken entirely seriously'.[28] This is, Meillassoux points out, the SF answer: '[Popper] tells us that new experiences could refute our theories, but he never doubts that existing, well-established experiments will always produce the same results in the future.'[29] He thus confuses Hume's problem, which is ontological (a problem of being), with an epistemological problem (a problem of knowledge). Meillassoux argues, however, that Hume was interested in something else: 'Hume's problem mobilizes another imaginary, an imaginary of extro-science fiction, the fiction of a world that has become too chaotic to permit any scientific theory whatsoever to be applied to reality anymore.'[30] Here, Hume's problem becomes that of a billiards match 'during the course of which the laws of dynamics cease to hold'.[31] This is a problem of being (ontology) that cannot simply be recuperated by knowledge (epistemology). To illustrate, but also to further his thought on the problem, Meillassoux turns to an Asimov story that he considers to do both: it captures the XSF imaginary, since 'a totally unforeseen event occurs' in it, but it is ultimately an SF story, since this totally unforeseen event appears to *still* be explainable by the laws of science.[32] That is why, Meillassoux argues, the story works: narrative needs this SF resolution, since a world of 'pure chaos, a pure diversity ordered by nothing' would render narrative fiction impossible. With the XSF imaginary, fiction is able to go where science cannot; but it seems that narrative fiction can no longer happen there, unless (one imagines) it would be entirely transformed.

I will skip the crystal-clear albeit idiosyncratic pages that follow in Meillassoux's essay on Immanuel Kant's *Critique of Judgment*, in which the possibility of this 'some kind of thought' – this consciousness – is discussed. In view of my focus on literary realism, I want to jump instead to Meillassoux's list of extro-science fiction worlds with which the essay concludes: *Type One worlds* would be 'irregular, but too little to affect science or consciousness' – as he notes, these worlds are not extro-science fiction 'in the strict sense since they still allow the exercise of science';[33] the irregularity of *Type Two worlds*, by contrast, 'is sufficient to abolish science but not consciousness' – these worlds, he notes, 'are the real extro-science worlds';[34] finally, and most extremely, *Type Three worlds* are 'lawless universes in which disordered modifications are so frequent, that ... the conditions of science and those of consciousness alike, are abolished'.[35] This tripartite distinction brings Meillassoux to his final and – for my purposes here – most important question: how to *write* XSF? Which is another way of asking: what is narrative fiction's relation to the speculative realist worlds that Meillassoux sketches out, ranging from 'not strictly XSF' to the abolition of science and consciousness (and presumably also of narrative fiction as we know it)? Can there be a narrative fiction of XSF?

Meillassoux lists three literary solutions: first, introduce 'just one rupture without cause or reason' (he summarizes this as 'catastrophe'); two, 'nonsense'; or three, write 'stories of uncertain reality, those in which the real crumbles gradually and ceases to be familiar to us from one day to the next'.[36] It is this third solution that he considers to '[express] most faithfully the XSF genre'. Meillassoux summarizes this as 'the dreaded uncertainty of an atmospheric novel', and notes that there probably aren't enough of these novels around 'to constitute a genre'.[37] Apart from the reading of the Asimov story, there is no literary criticism in Meillassoux's essay to back up the list of worlds and solutions. Meillassoux gives an example of solutions One (René Barjavel's *Ravage*), Two (Douglas Adams's *Hitchhiker's Guide to the Galaxy*), and Three (Philip K. Dick's *Ubik*), but he seems to find none of them entirely satisfactory. Also puzzling in the essay is how the three solutions that Meillassoux lists at the end of the essay match the three types of worlds he describes earlier on. It seems that while the first solution would match Type One, and the second solution matches Type Three, the third

The Realist Novel and 'the Great Outdoors'

solution – 'the one that most faithfully expresses the XSF genre' – would match Type Two – 'the real extro-science world'.

What is clear, however – and this justifies the approach I develop in this chapter – is that the issue Meillassoux confronts is not only philosophical. Laying out three different worlds, all related to speculative realism *in philosophy*, Meillassoux then moves to *literature*, even if it doesn't come with an equally robust literary-theoretical framework, to ask what kind of narrative fiction would be capable of writing the XSF worlds he has theorized. Of course, the game is in a way already rigged, because he can only ask this question within the context of a discussion of science fiction. This indicates the limitations of literary realism, which cannot even be considered in this context as a viable candidate for investigation. However, given that realism is the correlationist aesthetic par excellence, it could be interesting to see where realism would need to be pushed in order to arrive at the philosophical mindset, and the literary solution, that Meillassoux proposes. In fact, I would argue that pursuing such a project and exposing realism's specific RBH limitations reveals some limitations of Meillassoux's approach to fiction, and the literary solutions to the philosophical problem of the great outdoors that he lays out. In short, I contend that the fact that Meillassoux limits himself to science fiction to ask about possible literary solutions to the philosophical problems he raises prevents him from fully leaving the RBH framework behind.

What are the relations between Meillassoux's speculative realism and the questions for literary realism to which it leads, and the contemporary debates in literary realism I engaged above? I will not attempt to 'map' here the three paths for the novel that I outlined above – the anxious perfection realism of O'Neill's *Netherland*, the nervous breakdown realism of McCarthy's *Remainder*, and (at least in my idiosyncratic reading) the literary-speculative realism of Smith's *White Teeth* – onto the three types of worlds and three types of storytelling solutions that Meillassoux proposes. As I have already pointed out, Meillassoux is a philosopher, and I consider him to be making analytical distinctions in his essay that, when considering works of narrative fiction, cannot hold in quite the same way. It is in this respect telling that Meillassoux's essay is, with the exception of the reading of the Asimov story, an entirely theoretical piece that includes no close-readings of actual literary texts; and even in the case of the Asimov story, where the story (in particular, the story's plot) is engaged, the story does not fully realize the XSF genre that Meillassoux theorizes. So we may be dealing with a philosophical horizon here that narrative fiction will always only be approaching. For my money, Tom McCarthy's novel comes closest to Meillassoux's Type Two world, and his third literary solution – but therein lies precisely the rub: for as I indicated above, McCarthy ultimately remains within the limits of a correlationist realism, something that – philosophically – Meillassoux wants to avoid.[38]

Remaining at the theoretical level, what I am interested in is to reconsider Meillassoux's types of worlds and solutions for narrative fiction, involving various configurations of science and consciousness, through the lens of theory of literary realism, which is arguably – with naturalism – the most scientific form of narrative fiction: one can think here, for example, of Emile Zola's scientific method in writing naturalist fiction. In Tom Wolfe's journalistic, nonfiction novel, we find one contemporary instantiation of such scientific realism. But it is worth noting again the challenge that Wolfe considers contemporary fiction writers to be up against: 'American society today is no more or less chaotic, random, discontinuous, or absurd than Russian society or French society or British society a hundred years ago,' he writes, 'no matter how convenient it might be for a writer to think so. It is merely more varied and complicated and harder to define.' At first sight, the two sentences in the previous quote may seem difficult to combine. On the one hand, Wolfe insists that contemporary society is no more chaotic than it was a hundred years ago (it is important to note an overlooked implication of this, namely that Wolfe thus seems to insist that society is and has always been irregular); on the other, he insists that it has become more varied, complicated and harder to define. It thus seems, upon further consideration, that variation, complication and interpretative difficulty cannot be equated to an increase in chaos, randomness, discontinuity or absurdism. The latter is still the same as one hundred years ago; its variations and complications have just made society harder to define. And thus, the novelist should apply himself more diligently to his 'science'.

This is, one could argue, a kind of science fiction imaginary, in which reality – by definition chaotic, random, etc. and ever more varied, complicated, etc. – is matched by science (I have called this realism's 'biopolitics'); reality's intensifications are to be matched by the intensifications of literary realism. However, I consider Meillassoux's three types of worlds to challenge Wolfe's belief in this biopolitical matching, which is itself a form of what Meillassoux calls correlationism. Instead, Meillassoux invites us to imagine worlds that would be irregular (though not quite in Wolfe's sense, as I will momentarily explain), but (i) not irregular enough to affect science or consciousness; (ii) irregular enough to abolish science, but not

The Realist Novel and 'the Great Outdoors'

consciousness; and (iii) so irregular that both science and consciousness are abolished. Now, while the first option may seem to match Wolfe's mode of science fiction – society is chaotic, random, etc. but literary realism can match that, as it did one hundred years ago – when Meillassoux gives an example of a literary work that matches this world, the difference between what he has in mind and Wolfe's chaotic, random, etc. society becomes clear: Meillassoux mentions René Barjavel's book *Ravage*, 'in which electricity suddenly no longer exists'.[39] In order for Wolfe's realism to begin to approach even the weakest of these XSF worlds, it would need to include an element that properly suspends the realist science, if only for a moment. Wolfe's point is, of course, that any degree of variation, complication or interpretative difficulty can be recuperated as part of the realist project – the novelist should simply try harder. But Meillassoux is asking for something else: in the case of a Type One world, a suspension that ultimately leaves realism and consciousness intact; in Type Two, one that abolishes realism but not consciousness; and, with Type Three, one that abolishes both realism and consciousness. In literary realism, Wolfe is like Popper to Meillassoux's Hume, confusing an ontological issue with an epistemological one.

To imagine narrative fictions that write each of those worlds is to go beyond the realism that Wolfe advocates. That would mean to practise a literary-speculative realism of varying degrees: first, second, or third solution, as per Meillassoux's suggestion. But when Meillassoux deems the 'stories of uncertain reality, those in which the real crumbles gradually, from one day to the next ceasing to be familiar to us' of the third solution to be the most XSF – that is, to match most closely the Type Two world in which science is abolished but not consciousness – one cannot help but notice that there isn't a single developed example in his essay that illustrates this solution and the speculative reality writes. The only example Meillassoux gives of it – Douglas Adams's *Hitchhiker's Guide to the Galaxy* – receives no further discussion. The example he does develop – the Asimov story that is reproduced in the essay's book version – includes the XSF mindset, but Meillassoux's argument is that this mindset is ultimately recuperated by the mindset of SF. Thus, even his only developed example is not really an example of a proper literary-speculative realism.

Needless to say, this is rather unsatisfying, since the RBH framework thus ultimately continues to hold sway in Meillassoux's text – at least in the literary examples he discusses. Part of the problem here, in my view, is the limitation of the SF and XSF framework, the fact that Meillassoux is *only* approaching the possibility of XSF fiction within the context of science fiction writing. If the (occluded) target of his discussion is literary realism as it is traditionally understood – if that is the most paradigmatic correlationist genre – then wouldn't it be more powerful to imagine Meillassoux's challenge to the genre from within that genre itself rather than from outside of it?

The Territory

I want to argue that one can find such a moment in Michel Houellebecq's novel *The Map and the Territory*. While Houellebecq's proximity to the science fiction genre deserves to be underlined in this context, I also want to emphasize that *The Map and the Territory* is an emphatically realist novel – emphatically so, because realism is one of its central themes.[40] Indeed, realism has been a recurrent concern in Houellebecq's oeuvre, starting with his first novel *Whatever* in which it takes up a central place. *The Map and the Territory* spans the arc of Jed Martin's artistic career, from his early photographs of industrial objects to his very last video works. I want to focus on the novel's closing pages, which discuss an interview that Martin gives at the very end of his life and in which he speaks about the artwork in which, in the late stage of his practice, he has been quietly engaged. As the novel explains, Martin speaks about the work while 'refus[ing] all comment'. 'I want to give an account of the world ... I want simply to *give an account of the world (Je veux rendre compte du monde ... Je veux simplement* rendre compte du monde)', Martin 'repeats for more than a page [of a 40-page interview]' to the journalist who has come to see him.[41]

It would be a mistake to only read this as a statement in the realm of visual art, especially after the novel has worked hard to set up an identification between Martin, the artist, and Michel Houellebecq, the novelist, who features prominently as a character in Houellebecq's book. The artist and the novelist share not just a mentality but also an aesthetic. When Martin states that he simply wanted 'to give an account of the world', and starts repeating this sentence for more than a page, the novel notes that the journalist 'turns out to be incapable of stopping this senile chatter', going on to say that 'this is perhaps for the best: the chatter of Jed Martin unfolds, senile and free, essentially concentrating on questions of diaphragm, amplitude of focusing, and compatibility between softwares'.[42] One can read this moment negatively, as a breakdown of visual and literary realism

The Realist Novel and 'the Great Outdoors'

and its RBH project. But it is also a performative moment that, positively, realizes another realism: one that does not seek to write the world, and be a living representation of the living by and for human beings. Going back to my earlier discussion of *White Teeth*, in Martin's chatter – the repetition of realism's programme 'I want to give an account of the world' – language takes on the form of a mathematical formula whose linguistic materiality ruptures the triple credo of traditional realism: it does not represent the world; it is not a living representation of the living; and while it is language it is no longer human related. Like Bartleby's formula, it continues a certain kind of realism but one that breaks with everything that traditional realism holds dear. Small surprise that one of the critics who were offended by Houellebecq's novel was James Wood,[43] who several years earlier had already attacked what I have tried to rethink in this chapter as the literary-speculative realism of Smith's *White Teeth*.

If a page-long repetition of 'I want to give an account of the world', a repetition that is not actually included in the novel, is the culmination of Houellebecq's literary realism, then the realization of this deathly, linguistic realism in Martin's visual art also needs to be considered. The novel tells us that Martin's last works were all made on his property, a house surrounded by seven hundred hectares of land that Martin was able to buy thanks to the immensely lucrative sale of his previous artworks. It seems Martin would drive his car out along the road traversing his property, stop it 'simply following the spur of the moment', and then leave a camera there – sometimes for a few hours, sometimes for an entire day or even several days – to film 'nature'. The novel notes that his frames would occasionally concentrate 'on a branch of a beech tree waving in the wind, sometimes on a tuft of grass, the top of a bush of nettles, or an area of loose and saturated earth between two puddles'[44] – but since such concentration happens only occasionally, one is left to assume that most of the time, he is simply filming 'nature' in general. At a later stage, he would superimpose edited versions of these films – 'those moving plant tissues, with their carnivorous supplements, peaceful and pitiless at the same time', representations of 'how plants see the world' – with his portrayals 'of industrial objects, first a cell phone, then a computer keyboard, a desk lamp, and many other objects', specifically 'those containing electric components'. Such a process (realized digitally) produces 'those long, hypnotic shots where the industrial objects seem to drown, progressively submerged by the proliferation of layers of vegetation. Occasionally they give the impression of struggling, of trying to return to the surface; then they are swept away by a wave of grass and leaves and plunge back into plant magma, at the same time as their surfaces fall apart, revealing microprocessors, batteries, and memory cards.'

Around the same time, and as part of the same project, Martin started filming 'photographs of all the people he had known': 'he fixed them to a neutral gray waterproof canvas, and shot them just in front of his home, this time letting natural decay take its course.' 'More curiously,' the novel continues, 'he acquired toy figurines, schematic representations of human beings, and subjected them to the same process.' It is unclear whether these films are then also superimposed with the plant films, but the novel suggests this is the case when it speaks of 'those pathetic Playmobil-type little figurines, lost in the middle of an abstract and immense futurist city, a city which itself crumbles and falls apart, then seems gradually to be scattered across the immense vegetation extending to infinity'.

How is one to interpret these artworks? One option would be, as the novel suggests, to focus on 'the human' and its disappearance. Martin's last works are, the novel suggests, 'a meditation on the end of the Industrial Age in Europe, and, more generally, on the perishable and transitory nature of any human industry'. The films of the decaying portraits 'make themselves the symbols of the generalized annihilation of the human species'. Like Houellebecq's novel, Martin's works obviously break with the humanist project. However, the closing lines of Houellebecq's novel focus not so much on what thus disappears – the human – but more on what such a disappearance reveals: 'Then everything becomes calm. There remains only grass swaying in the wind. The triumph of vegetation is total.' Here, a problem appears: vegetation – compared to the materialism of the formula 'I want to give an account of the world' – is still living. Is Martin's realism then still a living representation of the living? Does the novel then return to what I have called a biopolitical realism? I think that would be a misreading, one that would overlook the emphasis Martin gives, in the interview I discussed earlier on, to the technical, representationalist conditions of how this triumph was accomplished. Instead of leaving the reader with the triumph of actual, living vegetation, Martin (and Houllebecq's novel) leaves us with the *representation* of the total triumph of vegetation: a triumph that can only be achieved through the digital superimposition of layer of representation upon layer of representation. What we encounter here is not so much the absence of representation, but representation's materialization into a reality of itself – one that is not representationalist, living, or human. Ontologically, Martin's final artwork thus comes very close to his formulaic repetition of the realist credo 'I want to give an account of the world'. They are, within the visual and the literary realism, one and the same: they mark the moment where poetry encounters painting in the aesthetic of juxtaposition that the character of Michel Houellebecq in the book opposes to the narration of novels and films.

Houellebecq, then, presents a literary-speculative realism from within traditional realisms rather than from the more comfortable regions of its recognized outside: modernism, postmodernism, science fiction. Within literary approaches to speculative realism some of this project is realized by Graham Harman, a scholar of Meillassoux's work and a philosopher in his own right. Harman provocatively titled his book on H. P. Lovecraft *Weird Realism*.[45] The framework established here for the conversation is not that of science fiction; instead, *realism* becomes estranged from itself, turns weird – into a different (speculative) form of realism. And yet, the very fact that this conversation happens in a book about Lovecraft, not usually considered a realist writer, takes away some of the satisfaction. Harman's move is useful in that it invites us to read Lovecraft's SF as realist. But it is still not the same as rendering realism itself 'weird', which has been my project here. In his book *Alien Phenomenology*, in which Meillassoux's great outdoors is a recurring concern, Ian Bogost brings us closer to the project I am proposing. Bogost has noted there that literature's 'preference for traditional narrative acts as a correlationist amplifier'.[46] Surely, this is most paradigmatically the case with realism: 'Whether empathy or defamiliarization is its goal', he adds, 'literature aspires for identification, to create resonance between readers and the human characters in a work.' The 'whether' clause is important: for it thus seems that even literature that would defamiliarize by messing with traditional narrative can still be caught up in the correlationist bind, as long as it aims to create resonance between readers and characters. It is in this sense that I have argued modernism and postmodernism to continue the realist project. It may be, then, as Bogost recognizes, that it is nearly impossible for literature to break out of this bind. He does however offer a counterexample: Ben Marcus's *The Age of Wire and String*, which he characterizes as 'incomprehensible'.[47] It is 'within that incomprehensibility',[48] he argues, that something like a literature of the great outdoors becomes possible. I agree, even if I don't necessarily think literary-speculative writing needs to actually be incomprehensible – Marcus's certainly isn't. While Bartleby's formula may be incomprehensible and Martin's 'I want to give an account of the world' may become so after it's been repeated a number of times, Smith's *White Teeth* certainly isn't. The challenge, however, would be to read it as incomprehensible, so that the reality that traditional realism obviously continues to write in that novel becomes weird, throwing our reading back onto the writing that is trying to capture that reality, making that writing appear – in all of its proclaimed transparency – incomprehensible. Not representation, not living, not human. It exists, as writing, but independently from us. It is, I have argued, at this point that realist writing can take on a speculative reality of its own, one that (at long last) introduces us through its own deathly, linguistic reality; that is, to an absolute outside, the entirely foreign territory that Meillassoux has called the great outdoors. A language at the limits of language.[49]

Notes

1. Quentin Meillassoux, *After Finitude: An Essay on the Necessity of Contingency*, trans. Ray Brassier (New York: Continuum, 2008), p. 7. The present chapter is a companion to another essay in which I investigate Jacques Rancière's theory of literary realism through a reading of Michel Houellebecq's novels *Whatever* and *The Map and the Territory*; see my 'The Politics of Realism in Rancière and Houellebecq', in Grace Hellyer and Julian Murphet (eds), *Rancière and Literature* (Edinburgh: Edinburgh University Press, forthcoming). As such, it continues my investigation into the politics of the contemporary novel in view of selected arguments in speculative realism, which are to be integrated in a book tentatively titled *Finance Fictions* that examines literary-speculative realism in the context of the contemporary finance novel. Readers interested in tracing the development of this line of thought are referred to: '"All of us go a little crazy at times": Capital and Fiction in a State of Psychosis', in Arne De Boever and Warren Neidich (eds), *The Psychopathologies of Cognitive Capitalism: Part One* (Berlin: Archive Press, 2012), pp. 89–115; 'A Fiction of the Great Outdoors: The Psychopathology of Panic in Robert Harris' *The Fear Index*', in Warren Neidich (ed.), *The Psychopathologies of Cognitive Capitalism: Part Two* (Berlin: Archive Press, 2014), pp. 163–94; 'Creatures of Panic: Financial Realism in Robert Harris' *The Fear Index*', *European Journal of English Studies* 19(1) (2015): 24–38; 'Tom McCarthy's *Remainder* and "The Great Outdoors"', in a collection of essays on McCarthy edited by Dennis Duncan for Gylphi's *Contemporary Writers: Critical Essays* series (forthcoming). While the argument here differs considerably from what I have written elsewhere, it could not have come about without the preceding intermediary stages.
2. Meillassoux, *After Finitude*, p. 28.
3. Michel Houellebecq, *The Map and the Territory*, trans. Gavin Bowd (New York: Knopf, 2012), p. 161.
4. Quentin Meillassoux, *The Number and the Siren: A Decipherment of Mallarmé's Coup de dés*, trans. Robin Mackay (Falmouth: Urbanomic, 2012).

5. Tom Wolfe, 'Stalking the Billion-Footed Beast: A Literary Manifesto for the New Social Novel', *Harper's Magazine*, November 1989, pp. 45–56.
6. Wolfe, 'Stalking', p. 45.
7. Ibid., pp. 48, 50.
8. Ibid., p. 51.
9. Ibid., p. 55.
10. Arne De Boever, *Narrative Care: Biopolitics and the Novel* (New York: Bloomsbury, 2013).
11. Ian Watt, *The Rise of the Novel: Studies in Defoe, Richardson and Fielding* (Harmondsworth: Penguin, 1970), p. 25.
12. Daniel Defoe, *Robinson Crusoe* (New York: Random House, 2001 [original publication: 1719]).
13. Yann Martel, *Life of Pi* (Orlando: Harcourt, 2001), p. viii.
14. Michel Foucault, *The History of Sexuality Vol. 1: An Introduction*, trans. Robert Hurley (New York: Vintage, 1990), pp. 135–59.
15. Peter Sloterdijk, 'Rules for the Human Zoo: A Response to the *Letter on Humanism*', trans. Mary Varney Rorty, in *Environment and Planning D: Society and Space* 27 (2009): 23.
16. Claude Lévi-Strauss, *Structural Anthropology*, trans. Claire Jacobson and Brooke Grundfest Schoepf (New York: Basic Books, 1974), pp. 206–31.
17. Fredric Jameson, *The Political Unconscious: Narrative as a Socially Symbolic Act.* (Ithaca: Cornell University Press, 1982), p. 77.
18. Roland Barthes, *S/Z*, trans. Richard Miller (New York: Hill and Wang, 1974), p. 217.
19. James Wood, 'Human, All Too Inhuman', *The New Republic*, 24 August 2000, http://www.newrepublic.com/article/books-and-arts/human-all-too-inhuman [accessed 23 January 2015].
20. Zadie Smith, 'This is how it appears to me', *The Guardian*, 13 October 2001, http://www.theguardian.com/books/2001/oct/13/fiction.afghanistan [accessed 22 January 2015].
21. Zadie Smith, 'Two Paths for the Novel', *The New York Review of Books*, 20 November 2008, http://www.nybooks.com/articles/archives/2008/nov/20/two-paths-for-the-novel/ [accessed 22 January 2015]. I propose that this article is Smith's developed response to Wood's criticism in De Boever, *Narrative Care*, pp. 125–49.
22. The other option, trying to come up with perfect form, is not relevant given McCarthy's philosophical project. That option is represented in Smith's argument by O'Neill. There too, she finds a material crumbling of *Netherland*'s perfect form.
23. Herman Melville, 'Bartleby, the Scrivener; A Story of Wall Street', in *Billy Budd, Sailor and Other Stories* (New York: Penguin, 1986), pp. 3–46. For

Deleuze's commentary, see his 'Bartleby; or, The Formula', in *Essays Critical and Clinical*, trans. Daniel W. Smith and Michael A. Greco (London: Verso, 1998), pp. 68–90. The linguistic materialism of the quasimathematical formula is central to Tom Cohen's readings of Bartleby in his *Anti-Mimesis from Plato to Hitchcock* (Cambridge: Cambridge University Press, 1994), pp. 152–78.

24. Quentin Meillassoux, 'Metaphysics and Extro-Science Fiction', trans. Robin MacKay, in Christoph Cox, Jenny Jaskey and Suhail Malik (eds), *Realism Materialism Art* (Annandale-on-Hudson/Berlin: Center for Curatorial Studies, Bard/Sternberg, 2015), pp. 371–85. Meillassoux has also published the essay in book form: see his *Science Fiction and Extro-Science Fiction*, trans. Alyosha Edlebi (Minneapolis: Univocal, 2015). References to the essay here are to the version published in *Realism Materialism Art*.

25. Meillassoux, 'Metaphysics', p. 372.

26. Ibid.

27. Ibid., p. 373.

28. Ibid.

29. Ibid., p. 375.

30. Ibid.

31. Ibid., p. 373.

32. Ibid., p. 377.

33. Ibid., p. 381.

34. Ibid., p. 382.

35. Ibid., p. 384.

36. Ibid., p. 385.

37. Ibid.

38. See De Boever 'Tom McCarthy's *Remainder*'.

39. Meillassoux, 'Metaphysics', p. 58.

40. *The Map and the Territory* ends several years into the future. There are science fiction elements in several of Houellebecq's other novels, most notably in *Atomized* and in the science fiction novel *The Possibility of an Island*.

41. Houellebecq, *Map*, p. 264. For the French original, see Michel Houellebecq, *La carte et le territoire* (Paris: Flammarion, 2010), p. 406.

42. Ibid.

43. James Wood, 'Off the Map', *The New Yorker* 87(45), January 2012, p. 78. For another negative review that focuses on realism in Houellebecq's novel, see Laura Kipnis, 'Death by Self-Parody', *Bookforum*, December 2011–January 2012: 22.

44. Quotes from Houellebecq in this and the following paragraphs are from *Map*, pp. 265–9.

45. Graham Harman, *Weird Realism: Lovecraft and Philosophy* (Winchester: Zero Books, 2012).
46. This quote and the next one are from Ian Bogost, *Alien Phenomenology or What It's Like to Be a Thing* (Minneapolis: University of Minnesota Press, 2012), pp. 40–1.
47. Bogost, *Alien*, p. 82.
48. Ibid.
49. In this regard, Brian Kim Stefans's article on 'a speculative turn in recent poetry and fiction' has proven very instructive; see Brian Kim Stefans, 'Terrible Engines: A Speculative Turn in Recent Poetry and Fiction', *Comparative Literature Studies* 51(1) (2014): 159–83.

CHAPTER 8
MATERIALIST REASON AND ITS LANGUAGES. PART ONE: ABSOLUTE REASON, ABSOLUTE DECONSTRUCTION
Suhail Malik

The language of reason cannot be one of the ordinary languages because these are historically and culturally specific: formed in the contingencies of their histories they cannot not be sufficient to the universality that reason obtains by its deduction of invariants. Equally, however, the language of reason is not that of the notational scripts of mathematics or formal logic: these languages (if that is what they are) are formulated with wholly arbitrary and meaningless signs that, in their arbitrariness, negate the semantic necessities deduced by rational inference. As cursory as these propositions are, they directly state the predicament of the languages of reason; and, even in this highly abbreviated formulation, they immediately suggest two solutions: in the Derridean style, for these two reasons reason has no reason. Or, in the Meillassouxian style, reason is contingent, and absolutely so. These conclusions are at this point equivocal, and that presents another predicament: that the received opposition between speculative reason (SR), represented here primarily by Quentin Meillassoux, and poststructuralism (for which Jacques Derrida's deconstruction serves as a particularly staunch metonym) is at best partial, if not misconstrued or entirely unwarranted.

This last-mentioned opposition will be detailed shortly but even the reference to it imposes a caveat in arriving at these precocious conclusions: if the doctrinal opposition between SR and poststructuralism *is* well-founded, as will soon be seen to be the case, these rhetorically organized claims lead to a mistaken identity between the respective theories, or a metaphorizing of one for the other for the sake of some putative but misplaced consilience. The mistake here would be in countermanding each doctrine's distinctive and opposing determinations of language and reason. Yet, as will be substantiated later in this chapter, the rhetorical claim is in fact a preliminary indication that the predicament of the languages of reason itself proposes a theoretical axis that cuts across the opposition of SR and poststructuralism. This predicament must therefore be addressed from outside of the schema of that opposition, *both* sides of which are restricted determinations of a more comprehensive general theory of reason. This last result is obtained in Part Two of this essay, which will have to be taken up elsewhere: the comprehensively materialist determination of reason it requires is outside of the remit and space limitations of this volume. What can be only indicated here is that the general theory of materialist reason depends upon a reconfiguration of the quasiopposition between SR and poststructuralism, and this is the self-contained primary task of Part One presented here. The following introductory section outlines the received terms of this opposition before pivoting past it by recourse to structuralism – in particular, structuralism's premise of the scientificity of its endeavour qua method and object. These terms and the basic schema need to be in place before the further trajectory of the argument can be sensibly outlined. But, in brief, the reconfiguration of the theoretically organized opposition between SR and poststructuralism provides in turn the schema and conditions to resolve the predicament of the languages of reason by detailing (i) the materialist determination for language in general qua structure and sign, and (ii) a materialist account of the scientificity of reason. As will be seen, however, the latter determination is importantly constrained by the Meillassouxian determination of materialism that codes the argument to that point. Addressing that limitation provides the partial but for-now terminal conclusion to this chapter.

Subjectalism, structuralism, poststructuralism

Despite his objection to the term (for reasons presented shortly), SR is nonetheless represented here primarily by Meillassoux's philosophy. It is his term 'correlationism' that provides the minimal identifying trait of the paradigms to be repudiated and overcome by SR (a term extended here well beyond the four positions advanced at the 2007 symposium that gave initial traction to it).[1] Correlationism posits the *relation* between thinking and the real outside of thought as primary and ineliminable, stipulating that thought in its finitude can never get 'escape from itself' to think the real as such.[2] Correlationism is such an effectively comprehensive philosopheme because it is a highly reductive and generalizing determination of the primary praxical assumption of what are otherwise clearly distinct philosophies on both of the principal sides that it demarcates. Some SR doctrines are, for example, incoherent with one another, if not in direct opposition;[3] similarly for correlationist doctrines such as idealism, critique (contra idealism), vitalism (contra critique's representationalism), phenomenology, existentialism, and poststructuralism. But the paradigmatic rather than internecine difference at issue here is whether these and other philosophical doctrines are correlationist or not. Furthermore, and in direct response to the identifications SR suggests with philosophies that Meillassoux contests, his contribution to this volume generalizes the argument of correlationism beyond the limited condition of human cognition: while vitalism and other nonrepresentational or primarily intuitionist variants of thought's identification with the real (such as Bergsonian-Deleuzian immananetism, Nietzschean cosmopower, or object-oriented approaches) may look to get past rational cognition or discard anthropic thought or conceptualization as the premise for the correlation, Meillassoux recognizes that they no less 'hypostasize' their primary term as the absolute basis for the relation-to-the-world prior to all knowledge and so reproduce a correlationism in other terms. Meillassoux calls this generalized positing of a relational premise 'subjectalism'. Subjectalism 'identifies all reality with a sensible mode of subjectivity' that is not then to be restricted to the received anthropological determinations of subjecthood.[4]

The leading case of subjectalism in this chapter is Derridean deconstruction, which is a particularly cogent and incisive articulation of the basic claims of poststructuralism. In broad genealogical terms, and by way of brief introduction, poststructuralism may be characterized as the theoretical programme consequent to the identification of the dehiscences and limitations of structuralism, which itself dominated French rationalist thought in the humanities and social sciences for about two decades from the mid-1950s. Structuralism took Saussurean linguistics as the methodological paradigm across a range of disciplines because its account of the *structural* conditions and operations of language – rather than its individual, intentional, historical or other motivated dimension – sought to secure a desubjectivized (that is objective) and nonethnocentric (that is universal) validity for the phenomena it gives an account of, as well as for the account itself and for the results it obtained. The rationalist endeavour postulated by structuralism in general transposed this method to a variety of disciplines, identifying the impersonal and invariant structures of kinship, myth, psychosymbolic formation and so on, thus securing social *science* as such.[5] The fundamental premise of the scientificity of the structuralist paradigm is the identification of an immanent logic of the structures in question independent of its particular elements, the latter elements being differentially organized in it according to that logic. In his 1966 commentary on Claude Lévi-Strauss's structural ethnography, 'Structure, Sign and Play', Derrida accordingly identifies structuralism's primary task to be the identification of what he calls the 'structurality of the structure':[6] that is, the identifiable logic that constitutes an empirical system or phenomenon as a structure. The structurality of the structure is for structuralism an absolute for the examined system; but it is also and moreover the presumed condition for the paradigmatic method of structuralism's own scientificity.

Even if structuralism removes the subject as the assumed condition of the social and its praxes, and also locates itself outside of the subjective requirement of thought, its stipulation and reduction of what is to the terms of structure is, in Meillassoux's terms, nonetheless a subjectalism. In terms of the broader constellation of Meillassoux's terminology, which will govern this chapter, structuralism claims to establish knowledge of the real outside of thought and is therefore *speculative*.[7] Specifically, taking up Meillassoux's disambiguation of the general ambit of speculative thought into a realist variant, which claims to 'accede to absolute reality' even if it does not renounce subjectalism, and materialism, which 'affirms that one can think that which is, independently of all thought, of all subjectivity', it follows that structuralism is a speculative realism qua scientificity.[8] For Meillassoux, speculative thought is however only *fully* attained by a variant that is wholly nonsubjectalist, as a speculative materialism.[9] Any such materialism thus requires the surpassing of structuralism.

Poststructuralism meets this demand definitionally: it demonstrates that structuralism is intrinsically not cogent because the structurality of the structure cannot be apprehended in the terms of the distribution and affordances determined by the structure itself. As will be shown via Derrida's deconstruction of Levi-Strauss's structuralist ethnography, structures are shown to be always susceptible to an exogenous or extraneous supervention that the structure cannot apprehend in its own terms (variously called the event, singularity, irreducible heterogeneity, irreproducibility, and so on). But, to return to the terms of opposition between poststructuralism and SR, endorsing such an irrecuperable astructurality does *not* vitiate structuralism's subjectality. Exactly the contrary: what it maintains is the differential *relationality* of terms, which is the apprehending account of the structure, while refuting structuralism's speculative claim to determine the absolute of the structure itself. In other words, poststructuralism and deconstruction in particular *de*absolutize the real of structures and thereby rejects structuralism's scientificity and its realism, never mind its materialism. Poststructuralism is an absolute subjectalism, the deconstruction of the structurality of structure disarming any determination of even its own absoluity. It is a comprehensively irrealist correlationism for which asystemic and apparently exogenous terms are at once necessary and inexplicable.

Such, at least, is the basic scheme of the prevailing SR argument against poststructuralism. Beyond the intraphilosophical doctrinal positioning involved in that scheme, what is at issue in it is what modern rationality is and its viability. In particular: what is the status of the rational determination of the real and the scientificity of that knowledge (extended by structuralism to social and cognitive-subjective formations), of what is independent of all thought as well as the objective, universal and invariant real of thought itself? There are two dimensions to this subjectalist refutation of rational realism. First, as regards speculative theory, the absolutization of subjectalism, realist or not, vitiates materialism in principle and in practice. Which is to say that knowledge of the real outside of the terms of apprehension is *de*absolutized. All rational determinations of knowledge are then effects of a subject (or its proxy) that constitutes the absolute term of knowledge, as German Idealism concluded shortly after Kant's critical delimitations of rational finitude.[10] As such, and terminally, however realist or rationalist they may otherwise be, subjectalist (knowledge of) absolutisms are but fideisms.[11] In its concomitant sociopolitical dimension, and second, subjectalist knowledge of the absolute is wholly regressive with regard to the rational materialist determinations of the real and its consequent reorganization that, according to Enlightenment precepts, ought to characterize modernity.[12] Subjectalism in particular is not only the obstacle to materialism, as Meillassoux asserts; it is also the obstacle to rational determinations of the noncorrelational absolute. If philosophy is to regain its historical claim to rationally conceive the real and the absolute, to establish the basis for the rational *and materialist* task of modern science, correlationism must then be defeated and rationally so.

This is however only to reiterate that poststructuralism must be overcome, among other such subjectalisms. But a less evident counterargument can be made on the basis of the absoluity of the structurality of the structure that poststructuralism in particular identifies. That structurality is, recall, the absolute of any structure beyond its particular terms and, given the

Materialist Reason and its Languages

generality of structuralism's application, it can in principle be ascertained for conceptual thought itself. The received name for the structurality of conceptual thought and cognition, for the organizing matrix of its logic, relational structures, and regulating condition is, precisely, reason. It is on this basis that structuralism claimed a thematic and methodological scientificity for its task, incorporating the method and aim of its own project within that undertaking. As such, Derrida's deconstruction of how well the structurality of the structure can be identified and maintained *in principle* by structuralism itself does not then so much rescind the latter's speculative claim, as the standard SR criticism has it. Rather, it is the rigorous examination of the stability and validity of the scientificity of structuralism – of rationality as the necessary and absolute condition of its scientific endeavour – as much as its necessary fallibility. Specifically, and to preview the coming discussion, in surpassing the limited *ratio* of structuralism and the realist constraints thereby imposed on the speculative task, poststructuralism and deconstruction in particular are speculative theories of reason itself. It is then a *question* rather than a given as to whether the exorbitant determination of structuralism's speculative realism advanced by poststructuralism consolidates its subjectalist premise in the direction of an irrealist correlationism, as per SR's dominant account of poststructuralism, or rather – as the following argument contends – whether deconstruction ramifies structuralism's speculative claims in the contrary direction of a thinking of reason independent of the thought that rationally thinks it, of reason in its absoluity. In the direction, that is, of the materialism of reason itself.

The present chapter substantiates this hypothetical materialist counterdetermination of deconstruction. This in turn requires a double reconsideration of Meillassoux's endorsement of speculative materialism: first, materialism may not be quite as distinct from poststructuralism as Meillassoux contends; second, the knowledge of the noncorrelational absolute established by the speculative materialism as Meillassoux proposes it is itself rational, and so itself requires rational materialist determination. To be clear: because this latter consideration of the rationalism of Meillassoux's materialism concerns the absolute condition of the conceptual thinking that it is and *not* what it is outside of thought, it is, per Meillassoux's scheme, not *itself* a materialism but a speculative *realism*. This is to return to structuralism's primary cause of identifying the *ratio* determining a particular structure; but it also at once explicitly determines the precondition for speculative materialism to be a rational realism. Third, then, and to complete the circuit: given that the specific speculative determination of rational realism concerns precisely the structure, operation and manifestation of reason in its absoluity, the predicament of the languages of reason returns here as a direct problem of the determination of materialist reason. In other words, what is required to establish speculative materialism is not so much *what* it determines the nonsubjectal real to be – the 'absolute contingency' for which Meillassoux's philosophy has gained attention – but rather how and why the absolute real can be *rationally* known. And for that, the basics of Meillassoux's own philosophical system require elaboration.

Absolute materialism: Factial speculation

Meillassoux's principal historical achievement in *After Finitude* is his demonstration that correlationism is untenable even on its own terms. A 'weak' correlationism such as Kant's permits the possibility of a thing-in-itself outside of thought which, however, cannot be known as such precisely because it is outside of thought. 'Strong' correlationism, more typical of emphatically deabsolutizing doctrines, proscribes even the positing of the thing-in-itself precisely because any such proposition is presumed to identify any externality in terms of its apprehension.[13] Meillassoux demonstrates that the conclusion of correlationism, that thought in its finitude can never get 'outside of itself' because the *relation* between thought and being is primary and ineliminable for thought, is but a partial result foreclosing or repudiating thought's determination of its own *terminal* materialist constitution. This latter speculative materialism, as Meillassoux calls it, is established in four steps:

1. Facticity: For the weak correlationist the a priori categories of knowledge are invariant facts, distinct to the contingencies of what is empirical known. These categories are the conditions for the finite knowledge of empirical facts; and though empirical facts may be otherwise than they are, the *structure* of thought (qua logic and reason) does not change according to these empirical contingencies. Furthermore, with Kant, the a priori categories of thought are a given and can only be described, not deduced. Any such a deduction, Hegel's most notably, would mean that the categories of the understanding are unconditionally necessary and therefore adequate to determining the thing-in-itself (which is for Hegel finally just the concept).[14] The invariance of the facts that are the categories shaping correlationist thinking in its absolute finitude is what Meillassoux calls facticity.[15]

2. Unreason: Empirical facts are minimally contentful in that they are determined to be thus-and-so even while they can be otherwise, and so at least the fact of their contingency can be known. On the other hand, there can be no positive knowledge of the a priori categories of thought: they are not objects of experience and have no reason or foundation for being what they are. For correlationism, then, the facticity of thought is without reason and cannot be known to thought. But the *rationalist* inference that Meillassoux innovatively draws against that subjectalist conclusion is that what is known of the thing-in-itself, its truth, is precisely the absence of reasons for it: 'every hypothesis about the in-itself remains equally valid. [...] Facticity fringes knowledge and the world with an absence of foundation whose converse is that nothing can be said to be absolutely impossible, not even the unthinkable'.[16] Facticity is the 'unreason (*irrasion*) ... of the given as of the invariants'.[17]

Furthermore: (i) because it is the absolute prerequisite for rational cognition itself according to correlationism, facticity is not itself an empirical fact that could be otherwise than it is; rather, it is necessary – a necessary unreason; (ii) the unreason is that of the categories of knowledge and so ramifies in the knowledge of the empirical world constituted by those categories. It follows as a rational consequence that for weak correlationism the thing in-itself outside of thought – here called the exocognitive real – is without reason; it *can be* anything at all.

3. Nonnecessity: The unreason of the facticity of thought and *therefore* of the real outside of thought reverses correlationism's constitutively negative determination: that the thing-in-itself is necessarily unknowable, which result is premised on the inviolability of the finitude of thought. The speculative rationalist solution to the problem presented by facticity is the positive determination of the real as without reason, which is to say: as contingent. What is absolute – necessary and unconditional – of thought itself and now also of the exocognitive real is their contingency. The principal result here is that an absolute of thought *and* of the unthought thing-in-itself *can* be thought. This is the achievement of a speculative materialism, whose first result is that the *variability* of facticity is 'the absolute whose reality (*effectivité*) is thinkable as that of the in-itself as such in its indifference to thought'.[18]

This materialist determination of the absolute must be conceded even within strong correlationism, as demonstrated by the example of death: assuming the finitude of thought, death for the strong correlationist is at least conceivably the absence of her or his thought; for the atheist, death does not wait for its being thought in order to be actualized. The absence of thought that is death is conceivably independent of its thinking – meeting the criterion of a speculative materialism.¹⁹ The general lesson to be drawn from the example is that even granting the *de*absolutizing finitude of thought in its strongest formulation – to the point that the notion of the thing-in-itself is rescinded – requires positing *another* absolute: that of the variation without reason of what is, including that of its own nonexistence. Correlationism is therefore but an abjured speculative materialism – if, that is, it is not the repudiation of speculative materialism that is necessary insofar as thinking the absence of thought is the intrinsic vitiation of correlationism. Stated obversely, even when thought presumes its own deabsolutizing finitude it is nonetheless 'after finitude'; or, to introduce a term that is not Meillassoux's own, thought is *ex*finite.

4. Factiality: The positive determination of the thing-in-itself as absolutely contingent is *not* a knowledge of it in its particularities (what it is) but of its condition (how it is). Even so, this result is deduced by rational thought in *its* exfinitude, thereby performatively demonstrating (i) the thesis of speculative materialism and (ii) that speculative materialism is itself a rationalism. On this basis, the constraints and redeterminations speculative materialism imposes on reason can be elucidated. While Kant could only posit the exocognitive absolute without reason, it can now be understood that exfinite speculative materialism gives a positive determination of what is outside of thought and absolutely indifferent to it: that there *is* no reason, no necessity for the positing of the object. This is the condition proposed by Meillassoux's radicalization of doubt beyond Cartesian method: it is not the existence of the thinking subject that is absolute for thought, as Kant also maintains after Descartes, but the rationalist method of doubt to the cost of finitude and subjectivity. Furthermore, though the deduction of the necessity of what 'can be' seems to reiterate the Principle of Sufficient Reason in explaining why there is something rather than nothing, it is rather the revocation of that principle.²⁰ What is absolute for being is instead the necessity of contingency – a principle of unreason.

The principle of unreason – or the Principle of Insufficient Reason, as Meillassoux also calls it – restates the absolute contingency of what can be as it is deduced on the basis of the facticity of the categories of the understanding. In that the unreason that is the absolute condition of what can be is itself known as a necessity – precisely as a *Principle* of Insufficient Reason (PIR) – it secures the distinction between empirical facts and the given fact of rational thought. It is a necessity for thought and, no less, the necessity of thought itself. Facticity according to Meillassoux is then exempt from the contingency of facts; it cannot be applied to itself. Or: the principle of contingency is not itself contingent but necessary. That the principle of facticity is nonrecursive is why *it* is not subject to absolute contingency and, as such, is the condition for anything like a viable category of necessity or of principles. This is why contingency is absolute and only nonnecessity is 'eternal'.

Accordingly, a distinction must be made between the principle of facticity, by which what can be is subject to the principle of unreason, and what Meillassoux calls the principle of factiality, which speaks to 'the genesis of the only absolute necessity', namely 'the necessity for everything that is to be a fact'.[21] The rational deduction of the absolute outside of thought is, accordingly, 'factial speculation'.[22] The paradigmatic consequence of the principle of factiality is that there can then never be a metaphysics qua the assumption, stipulation or even hypothesis of a *necessary* being or becoming.[23] While the 'end of metaphysics' is a common enough theme in mid- to late-twentieth-century philosophy, Meillassoux's variant of it is distinguished from those proposed by strong correlationisms, including poststructuralism, by establishing that there *is* a knowable and necessary absolute: that of the nonnecessity of any- and everything – the necessity of contingency stipulating that 'there is nothing beneath or beyond the manifest gratuitousness of the given – nothing but the limitless and lawless power (*puissance*) of its destruction, its emergence, or persistence'.[24]

Null materialism

To summarize: PIR alone attests to the absolute of what can be: that there is *no* necessary reason for what is. However, as a *knowledge* of the absoluity of the exognitive real that is rationally deduced, PIR is not itself a materialist insight but one of the rational determination of the 'absolute reality' of what can be – ontology – which is why even the deabsolutizing finitude of strong correlationism must concede to it. Furthermore, because the necessity of contingency is premised on the facticity of the categories of knowledge – within the conditions of rational thought according to Kant – the rational determination of the absolute is formally contingent with regard to what the absolute real in fact is. Factial speculation determines the *conditions* of what can be, not of what in fact is. Meillassoux rearticulates this distinction in terms of primo- and deuteroabsolutory thought, as will be discussed later in this chapter; but, along with two further observations, this point marks a departure from the terms of Meillassoux's argument.

First, PIR is itself obtained not by a speculative materialism but by a *rational realism* of exfinite thought. Second, speculative materialism as such can not present any reasons for what is or can be other than PIR, and furthermore vitiates determining anything in the real other than its formal and otherwise empty contingency. And third, as noted, if Meillassoux's speculative materialism is to be comprehensively materialist, what is required is not just the rational realist determination of the *formal* contingency of what can be (which is the ontological argument) but also, necessarily, its own materialist determination of that formalism (which is a methodological and theoretical-rational argument). What is important in this provisional result is not the putative paradox it expresses in the conjunction of formalism and materialism but rather how rational realism's determination of speculative materialism qua factial speculation is terminally null: the only knowledge it provides of the real in its absoluity is the formalism of its contingency. Meillassoux's degree-zero determination of the exocognitive real can then be more explicitly announced by designating factial speculation as a *null materialism*.

The consequences of Meillassoux's null materialism, and that rational realism is not necessarily coherent – or even unique – to itself, are made apparent by comparing it to Ray Brassier's advocacy of nihilist rationalism. For Brassier, reason is a nihilism because rationalism – exemplified best by the natural sciences – is premised precisely on *nothing* other than its own revision under the twofold insistence of rational coherence on the one hand and an evidentiary basis on the other.[25] Brassier's account converges with Meillassoux's insofar as both endorse that it is rational, conceptually constituted thought that is alone the condition for a materialism, and that no positive contentful term underpins reason and the knowledge thereby acquired. Yet they diverge in that nihilist rationalism qua science endeavours to provide explanations and knowledge of what the real is in (empirical) fact as its positive content*s*, as well as the causal or other relational configuration of that real outside of thought. Such is the conventional task of rationalist modernity forged in the Enlightenment which Brassier seeks to vindicate with the caveat that nihilist rationalism affirms that there can be no positive determination of the absolute as such but only of the rational process itself (it is revisable).[26] For Brassier, it is by virtue of the latter realism that the knowledge of the real outside of thought – materialism – can be attained. Null materialism, on the other hand, indexes the formal condition of the

Materialist Reason and its Languages

rationally deduced positive knowledge of the absolute as such: it is necessarily contingent, meaning that no reason *can* be established and secured for what is and why. This is, to reiterate, not because of the limited knowledge that reason obtains thanks to the finitude of the knower (which is the correlationist's claim as much as, differently, that of the nihilist rationalist) but because of PIR. What can be is *necessarily* inexplicable in its ontology. The divergence in rational realism of these doctrines is not then just one of their incongruence but rather of their incompatibility: null materialism vitiates not just the materialist determination of knowledge garnered by nihilist materialism, it moreover vitiates the latter as a rational undertaking – if not *the* rational undertaking of modernity – in principle.

The only knowledge the null materialism of factual speculation can have of the real in its absoluity is that of its formal contingency. Any other determination of the absolute either veers into what Meillassoux calls metaphysics, by providing positive content to the absolute, thereby positing an absolute necessity where there is only nonnecessity, or, as with nihilist rationalism, cannot attain the minimally positive knowledge of the absolute as contingent, thereby maintaining the Principle of Sufficient Reason as a condition of rationality and its determinations. In either case, a rational realism that does not conform to Meillassouxian null materialism makes the error of giving reasons for the real (content, causes, a metaphysical basis, and so on).

Absolute reason

The comparison with nihilist rationalism, which is itself unexceptionally aligned with and subscribes to the operative assumptions of modern science, serves to expose one of three obstructions Meillassoux's philosophy presents to establishing rational realism as a comprehensively explanatory speculative materialism. The problem is internal to Meillassoux's own system in that, for him, the task of 'a factual derivation' is to 'legitimate the absolutory capacity of modern science – that is to say, Galilean science, which proceeds via the mathematization of nature'.[27] In programmatic terms that are not Meillassoux's own, an *explanatory* rather than legitimizing materialism must not only secure the conditions of knowledge of the exocognitive real, it must moreover ensure that such knowledge is not limited to the subjectalism of finite cognition but is exfinite. For Meillassoux, such an explanatory programme is not the task of speculative philosophy, which is rather to speak to eternities and inexplicable irruptions that can be occasioned by the absolute contingency of what can be.[28] But if it is to legitimize the mathematization of nature without recourse to idealism, the rational knowledge of the absolute-real to which speculative materialism is committed must *itself* be nonsubjectally absolute. However, the rational realism of factial speculation as Meillassoux presents it *proscribes* both sides of the double requirement – of being itself exfinite *and* absolute – from being simultaneously effected. Three analytically distinct limitations of rational realism can be identified for what factial speculation must be:

Formal contingency: as noted, the null materialism of factial speculation vitiates not just the materialist determination of knowledge of what is, itself endorsed by nihilist materialism, it moreover vitiates the latter as a rational undertaking – if not *the* rational undertaking of modernity – qua effectuation of the Principle of Sufficient Reason.

Ontology: null materialism establishes PIR as a formal determination of the ontology of what can be, not of particular facts. It is definitively not philosophy but the mathematical sciences that establish the comprehensive knowledge of the world in its particulars.[29] Philosophical materialism *must* then proscribe knowledge of what is in order to secure the formal contingency of what can be. This latter is what Meillassoux calls thought's primoabsolutory capacity.[30] Yet, in a near exact obverse of Kant's critical delimitation of cognitive thought to a weak correlationism proscribing rational speculation, exfinite factial speculation delimits the knowledge rational realism can attain to a descriptive rather than explanatory account of what is: mathematics as 'deuteroabsolutory thought' establishes knowledge of what the world is but cannot provide legitimate explanations for why qua its necessity – that is precisely what is ruled out by PIR. The capacity for the determination of the ontological absolute is therefore also an *in*capacity and stipulated limitation on knowledge, not as a consequence of thought's finitude but for reasons intrinsic and necessary to speculative materialism qua an exfinite rational realism.

Reason: The exfinite autolimitation of rational thought is not of a kind with that proposed by Kant because the latter's assumed and unsurpassable finitude and correlation is undone by factial speculation. It is rather an autolimitation of reason – and modification of its modern materialist determination – because of the formalism imposed by PIR: in its null materialism, factial speculation does not determine anything of the absolute-real other than its contingency. The factial-factual distinction effectively reiterates a form-content demarcation at the level of the rational determination of what

Materialist Reason and its Languages

can be. And the contention here is that this distinction is violated even as it is observed, with negative consequences for maintaining null materialism as a rational realism: recall that *realism* is only conceptual thought's 'acced[ing] to absolute reality', which makes no prescription as to what and how that access is to happen (general or particular) or to what the real is (endo- or exocognitive). It is then more precisely the *rationality* of a rational realism that commits it to its only formal, null determination of what can be. Factial speculation is then a formal rationalism. Hence, even taking into account that factial speculation is primarily a determination of ontology qua absolute contingency (or, from here, *ontocontingency*) and the PIR, and also the distinction between the principle of factiality against the contingency of facticity, the formalism of the rationality of null materialism is not just that of the determinations made by it but also of how that rationality is itself to be determined.

To be clear: this result is not in the dimension of the ontocontingency of thought – with regard to the *fact* of thought and reason, its anthropological or nonanthropological material basis, the universe in which it takes place, and so on – which Meillassoux affirms as one fact among others subject to PIR. Rather, and irrespective of its ontological determination or its material basis, because the determinations of factial speculation are *only* formal, its *rational* realism is itself subject to the PIR that it deduces. Or, without contradiction, in the formal determination of the absolute to which Meillassoux restricts factial speculation, reason is itself an absolute unreason.

Though this part-result seems to revoke rationalism per se, especially with regard to modern science, it is nonetheless a consequence of Meillassoux's vindication of reason as the route exfinite thought must take out of both the deabsolutizing finitude of correlationism and the inabsolute finitude of nihilist rationalism – if, that is, they are to establish the knowledge of what can be in its absoluity. Speculative materialism qua factial speculation is, in other words, committed to an irrational realism. If, then, speculative materialism is not to reverse to a fideism or even the relativism that assumes reason itself is only one discourse among others, what is imperative is to establish a speculative materialism that secures the rational realism by which the determination of absoluity can have validity (to itself, minimally). The difficulty is not insurmountable: as will now be seen, recourse to the Derridean deconstruction of structuralism's scientficity as a heterodox speculative theory of reason provides the basis for the vindication of the rational materialism that is now required. And not only that: given that the complaint of rational formalism put to Meillassoux's determination of speculative thought is made in view of establishing a comprehensive materialism, it also provides the schema by which the materialist determination of reason can itself be determined. However, in order to do so, the predicament of the language of reason first needs to be elaborated.

The languages of reason

The autolimitation and incapacity of factial speculation's rational formalism is redressed for Meillassoux by the 'mathematization of nature' of Galilean science, which formalizes the rational knowledge of the real.[31] As such, for Meillassoux mathematics 'founds the exploratory power' to obtain exact knowledge of the real qua facts without subjectalist premises. And this returns to the question of the languages of reason because the formalism of mathematics as itself a rational realism is for Meillassoux not that of its concepts or logics, but of its *signs*. Specifically, mathematical symbols for variables, constants, functions and so on are only proper names and *not* definitions for what they designate. Mathematical signs are therefore nonsemantic and referentless, and mathematics as a rational system of signs is irreducible to semantically dense ordinary language formulations and the consequent hermeneutical tasks, all of which prevent ordinary language discourses gaining knowledge of what the exocognitive in fact is – a limitation that, as seen, Meillassoux positivizes as philosophy's prerogative on the ontological absolute.

Asemantic and referentless, 'the initial object of mathematics' is 'the pure and simple sign that refers only to itself' – it is a 'sign devoid of meaning'. Mathematical formalism accedes to the speculative absolute because, unlike the semantic sign of ordinary language, the mathematical sign in its formalism does not refer to an idea or a signified. It is a sign without an ideal dimension. Mathematical signification is occasioned, Meillassoux proposes, because the sign is not governed by meaning; rather, for the pure sign, 'meaning is contingent in the constitution of the sign'. This does not prevent mathematics from making new statements with signification. To the contrary, mathematics generates statements which are 'rich in signification' – maybe even 'richer' than ordinary language can signify – *because* its syntactical operations 'remain empty of meaning'. Mathematics, then, is a semiotics that 'comes before' semantics.

The asemantic and anideal mathematical sign therefore instantiates the nonsubjectalist notion of 'dead matter'. Furthermore, because it is posited

Materialist Reason and its Languages

without motivation or semantic determination, the mathematical sign can be otherwise than it is without altering the mathematical operation or signification: replacing a q for a p makes no difference to the mathematical formalism if q is not already a term in the formalism. This 'eternal contingency' and variability without reason is the second trait of facticity as it is determined by factial speculation. What Meillassoux therefore establishes is that the formalism of the mathematical sign per a semiotic system with signification is comprised of what, for primoabsolutory thought, is the null materialism of ontocontingent facticity. While ordinary language is not 'dead' enough to be nonsubjectalist, on the basis of this semiotic and ontological formalism, speculative materialism can rationally apprehend the exocognitive real in a way that semantic language cannot. Equally, because they are factically constituted, mathematical truths are then not Parmenidean eternal and absolute necessities – which would contravene the stipulation that the only necessity is nonnecessity – but, precisely, the 'eternal' consequences of PIR.

For Meillassoux, then, the formalism of the mathematical sign provides the language of reason for the speculative apprehension of what is absolutely necessary qua nonnecessity – which is all that can be. Here, the highly abbreviated and rhetorically organized formulations that inaugurated this chapter – regarding how the predicament of the languages of reason crosses with the reorganization of the putative opposition between speculative realism and poststructuralism – come to the fore. The integrating theoretical point synthesizing these various and otherwise distinct issues, and around which the rest of this chapter turns, is the commonality of Meillassoux's and Derrida's accounts of the nonmetaphysical sign. Meillassoux's deduction of mathematical formalism is that it is constituted by the asemantic 'pure' sign that is itself a null materialist facticity, which 'neither signifies nor denotes anything'.[32] In this determination of the aneideitic sign, Meillassoux reiterates from another angle Derrida's remark in 'Structure, Sign and Play', that 'if one erases the radical difference between signifier and signified, it is the word "signifier" itself which must be abandoned as a metaphysical concept' – an 'abandonment' that for Meillassoux requires the redetermination of the mathematical sign as an empty token.[33] 'Metaphysical' for Derrida here means that the differential structure and operation constituting *both* the sign system in semiotics as an integrated whole as well as the 'radical difference' between signifier and signified is maintained and stabilized by a centre which acts as the final referent for that structure (historically: Man, ousia, meaning, Idea, etc.).[34] As a positive term that 'completes' the structurality of the structure, metaphysics is minimally consistent with Meillassoux's characterization of it as the mistaken attribution of ontological necessity to any term (including nothing and becoming) other than contingency. The homology is reinforced by Derrida's rejection, from the two 'heterogeneous ways' that the metaphysical concept of the signifier qua signifier-signified is abandoned, of the conventional 'metaphysical reduction' of the sign in which the sensible and historically contingent signifier is subordinated qua accident to the intelligible content of the signified; 'that is to say, ultimately in submitting the sign to thought', which conceptualization provides the contentful truth of the sign.[35] Derrida thus endorses, as Meillassoux does, the asemantic and aneideitic – and therefore nonmetaphysical – sign.

However, the apparent convergence between Derrida's and Meillassoux's common rejections of the metaphysical sign does not amount to an identity between their respective doctrines. To the contrary, with regard to whether a language of reason can be established at all, they propose obverse variants of the nonmetaphysical determination of the sign. As has been seen, for Meillassoux it permits a language of reason: the formal *sign* of mathematics is (adequate to) the factical contingency of what is and so establishes the language of speculative absolutization formulating rational knowledge, the truth, of what is. This language is for Meillassoux not just a rational realism but itself rational-speculative material*ist*. Derrida's argument, on the other hand, corrodes the metaphysical constitution of the sign not on the basis of the exceptionality of the pure sign to ordinary language but of the *structurality* of language that constitutes any and every sign (except the pure one). The centre of a semiotic structure, Derrida notes, must at once belong to and be part of the structure – otherwise, it is not immanent to the structural system and not its centre.[36] Yet it must nonetheless be simultaneously exempt from the substitutability, displacement and the infradifferential organization that characterize the semiotic structure, otherwise it has no prerogative as the unique and grounding referent for the structure it centres. The totality of the structure therefore has its centre elsewhere than the presumed centre. As Derrida puts it, 'the centre is then not the centre'. Or, in the terms of the maintained structure, the putatively plenitudinous centre is empty.

The major consequence of this paradigmatically poststructuralist deduction is that *any* metaphysical determination of structures and signs, each of which claims to fill or stabilize the centre of the structure and give its structurality a definition, is untenable. *This* 'abandonment' of the metaphysical concept of the signifier therefore makes the 'metaphysical

Materialist Reason and its Languages

reduction' of the signifier impossible. What is instead inaugurated with the *non*metaphysical determination of the sign is what Derrida calls the 'play' of signification. Play is in the first instance the structure's affordances to the sign's differential operations of substitutability and displacement; however, the structural elimination of the metaphysical concept of the signified as the basis of the sign together with the acentricity of the structure mean that the play of the signifier is in fact interminable and aneidetic – but *not* asemantic. Rather, the signifier liberated from metaphysics is supersemantic: in Derrida's own terminology it is 'overabundant' with regard to any capturing or stabilizing determination, necessarily overdetermined in a quasistructural 'play without security', the 'absolute chance (*hasard absolu*)' of the signifier's 'genetic indetermination'.[37]

Derrida's mention of the 'absolute chance' of the nonmetaphysical sign would seem to consolidate the homology of his deconstruction of the signifier with that of Meillassoux's speculative materialist pure sign. But such a consilience is unavailable because of their contrary conclusions with regard to the semanticity of the sign: contrasted to the supersemanticity and absolute chance of the sign that is for Derrida its deregulated and overabundant play, for Meillassoux the pure sign is asemantic because its facticity – its absolute ontological contingency – vitiates its capacity to signify in any way other than as a name without a referent. The pure sign makes for only syntactic significations – mathematics – because it is asemantic. The incompatibility between asemantic (factical) and supersemantic (structurally acentric) signs prohibits their identification or integration; yet, as will now be seen, it is precisely the synthetic combination of these two determinations of the aneidetic sign that overcomes the three obstacles preventing Meillassoux's rational realism from attaining the comprehensive speculative materialism he endorses. Moreover, the incompatibility of nonmetaphysical signs according to their doctrinal determination – deconstruction or speculative materialist – directly restates the predicament of the languages of reason at the level of the sign as theoretical object. Resolving the apparent contradiction as to the semanticity of the nonmetaphysical aneidetic sign thus at once engages with the predicament of the languages of reason, and vice versa. The following sections of this chapter are dedicated to integrating these otherwise disparate theoretical demands as a unified problem of materialist reason, the basis for which is surpassing the dichotomy of the aneidetic signification as finite or not. Their common resolution in a general theory of reason is the task of Part Two.

Subtractive finitude

For Derrida, the nonmetaphysical sign is not an effect or consequence of cognitive or historical finitude, because 'the infiniteness of a field cannot be covered by a finite glance or a finite discourse'; rather, the finite field of signs 'excludes totalization' by necessity because its acentric *structurality* can not 'arrest and ground the play of substitutions'.[38] The 'absolute chance' of the aneidetic yet supersemantic sign is that of the play of 'a field of infinite substitutions' of signifier for signifier occasioned *because* that field 'is finite'. Or, to paraphrase several similar Derridean formulations, infinite signification is finite.[39] This result is the now-standard deconstruction of the sign – and it is also the precise rearticulation on Derrida's part of the finite deabsolutization of signification that is characteristic of strong correlationism: the condition of the specific finitude of the structure is that 'there is something missing' from it, and that 'something' is the absolute. It is because the acentric structure is *subtractive* of the absolute that it constitutes the infinite movement of signification.

The contrast to Meillassoux's thesis of exfinite thought, which not only affirms that there is an exocognitive absolute but also that it can be known, is manifest here: the deconstruction of the structural absolute prohibits identifying the absolute chance of the supersemantic sign with the asemantic pure sign in its absolute contingency. But it also permits the homology between deconstruction's finite deabsolutization and exfinite speculative materialism to be precisely determined beyond the received terms of their opposition. That contiguity is methodologically demonstrated by Meillassoux's own deduction of factial speculation from within the stance of the strong correlationist. The explicit thematic determination of that contiguity however relies on noting that, on the one side, the deconstruction of the absolute qua structurality of the structure determines that structure to be an unsurpassable finitude: absoluity as such is subtracted – vindicating if not inaugurating the deabsolutization of the ontology and structure of finitude. On the other side, that of exfinite thought, the absolute is ontocontingent – which is the minimally positive determination granted by the null materialism of speculative thought. Each determines the absolute: as subtracted, from the side of finitude; as ontocontingent, from the side of exfinite materialism. Put in abbreviated form: deabsolutized finitude is the subtracted obverse of exfinite absoluity.

This proposition not only requires the finite-exfinite scheme to be comprehensively redetermined and the consequences to be drawn up. It also substantiates the counterintuitive homology between deconstruction and speculative materialism that was presented in the introductory comments to this chapter and, with that, provides the basis for the resolution of the predicament of the languages of reason. The predicament, recall, is that the sociohistorical contingencies of ordinary languages are inadequate to the universalities and invariances that rational thought is to establish; equally, and on the other hand, the formal languages of mathematics and formal logic that claim to establish such invariances are wholly contingent and so also themselves inadequate to the horizon of reason they posit. Formulated in terms more proximate to the current argument, in its contingency the sociohistorical dimension of language is that of the supersemantic sign, the conditions of which are identified by Derrida; *equally*, the contingent formalism of the mathematical sign is precisely what Meillassoux calls the pure sign in its asemantic null materialism. The obverse contiguity between absolutizing and deabsolutized thought just proposed means that the predicament of the languages of reason is premised on and integrated by the aneideticity of the signs comprising *both* ordinary and formal languages (which also means that the Saussurean account of language, premised as it is on the signifer-signified relation, is in no case valid).

The angle between the two vectors of language's inadequacy to reason is then determined by whether the aneidetic sign is constituted according to the subtractive finitude of language (which is ordinary language) or exfinite null materialism of the absolute (formal language). This angle makes for a discrepancy: the supersemantic sign concomitant to subtractive signification is the finite obverse of the asemantic sign of exfinite speculative absolutization. In order to advance to the concluding section on what the obverted continguity of the languages of reason – meaning now also that of deconstruction and speculative materialism – entails for reason as such, the ramifications of the comprehensive account of the aneidetic sign for the systemic account of language must first be elaborated.

Absolute supplementarity

If the *obverse* discrepancy between the deconstruction and speculative metaphysics is made evident via their respective determinations of the aneideitic languages of reason, their *contiguity* is on the other hand demonstrated by their respective establishments of that sign as nonmetaphysical. For Meillassoux, any positive determination of the absolute-real other than that of its formal contingency or mathematical description is the mistake of metaphysics. For structuralism, recall, the absolute of the structure is the scientificity of the rational undertaking that is the structuralist paradigm itself; and it is precisely any such absoluity that deconstruction discovers to be subtracted, with the concomitant result that finitude is deabsolutized. To a minimal yet critical degree of difference which will be taken up in a moment, the *variety* of hypostasizing determinations of the absolute-real that are for Meillassoux the common mistake of metaphysics (in the plural) are for Derrida precisely and also the mistaken positive determinations of the absent structuralities of the structure, a 'series of substitutions of centre for centre', by which the centre 'receives different forms or names', that he calls the history of metaphysics.[40] The united repudiation of metaphysics by speculative materialism and deconstruction proposes a quasicoherence between them that neither side alone can establish: that the rescinding of metaphysics by deconstruction is an immanently constituted proxy within deabsolutized finitude of the null materialism of the absolute-real that exfinite absolutizing thought comprehends as such. Elaborating the terms for this quasicoherence provides the specific determination of reason that not only conditions speculative materialism but is moreover itself materialist.

On the side of deabsolutized finitude, the history of substitutions filling the necessarily subtracted centre of the structure – constituting its scientificity, according to structuralism – is precisely what Derrida identifies via Lévi-Strauss (and via Rousseau, in *Of Grammatology*) as the 'movement of supplementarity'.[41] The supplement gives a stabilizing centre to the structure, *halting* the indefinite play of deabsolutized signification. The nonmetaphysical determination, however, is that though it is but an instance of the play of the acentric structure, the movement of supplementarity is the *condition* for the metaphysical determination of structure and the signifier. Which is to say that metaphysics is an effect of supplementation and no such determination *can* be stabilized. From within deabsolutized finitude, this is why and how metaphysics has a history. Despite the metaphysical designation of the nonterminal elements of a structure as accidents and play – for example, the arbitrary signifier that comprises the fact of language – in its determination of its own positive term as unique centre within generalized play, it is metaphysics that is the accident, a mistake. The supplement is how a metaphysics proposes its own nonmetaphysical condition without having the capacity to know it as such.

In a stylized Derridean formulation, metaphysics is possible (in fact) because it is impossible (in principle). The cliché has traction here because

Materialist Reason and its Languages

the nonmetaphysical determination of the movement of the supplement it formulates *within* deabsolutized finite language and thought is what exfinite materialism apprehends as the minimal positive determination of the formal contingency of the absolute-real. On this basis the discrepancy in what the aneidetic sign is, which arises from maintaining *both* salient nonmetaphysical determinations of language, can be eliminated: the supersemantic aneidetic sign is the finite rendition of the pure aneidetic sign identified by exfinite primoabsolutory thought. A first specification for the resolution of the predicament of the languages of reason follows directly: ordinary language as it is constituted by the supersemantic sign is the finite deabsolutization of formal mathematical absolutization; or, stated the other way, formal mathematical absoluity is the exfinitization of ordinary language.

This result is however only available unilaterally to exfinite thought. It cannot be comprehended from within deabsolutized finitude: *any* determination of the absolute is for it mistakenly metaphysical and must be rescinded. Accordingly, play 'must be conceived of before the alternatives of presence or absence', which is to say before metaphysics or the missing origin – which is to say, in any case, without the absolute, including that of the ontocontingency deduced by exfinite thought.[42] Apprehended in its exfinite determination, however, the deconstructive operation of aneidetic language that is supplementarity is *itself* the absolute-real of the structure, its formal ontocontingency. In its full account: with regard to the language of reason, the play of the supersemantic sign is the manifestation of the null materiality of the absolute-real of the formal asemantic sign within a finitude that abjures its own exfinite apprehension. And with regard to doctrinal terms: deconstruction is the finite variant of the absolute-real qua formal contingency. Deabsolutized finitude cannot apprehend this absolute-real as such but in fact effectuates it while renouncing it. Hence, though the interminable movement of the supplement is the Derridean quasidetermination of the subtracted absolute of the structure, and so is in some sense a realism by default, it is more precisely yet a *subtractive* realism – an unspeculative realism – that, as such, and as Meillassoux diagnoses via the putative doctrine of strong correlationism, can never be a materialism.

Ratiocontingency

If the formal ontocontingency of the absolute deduced by factial speculation is subtractively transcribed as the 'movement of supplementarity' of the sign and structure, it is manifest as both the play of that sign-system *and* the history of metaphysics. Derrida remarks in passing that the 'supplementary allowance (*ration supplémentaire*) of signification', the affordance of play permitted under the metaphysical constraint, 'could no doubt be demonstrated ... [to be] the origin of the *ratio* itself'.[43] As noted, *ratio* here means two things: first, that the metaphysically determined *ratio* is constituted by and in the movement of supplementarity that mistakenly gives a (contingent but) positive content to the subtracted centre; second, that the play of signification is limited to a more or less complementary relation of the signifier to the signified qua the sign's intelligibility. Two distinct positive determinations of that structural absolute have been endorsed here:

From structuralism: the metaphysical determination that the structurality of the structure is the determinant of the scientificity of the structure and also of the structuralist endeavour.

From exfinite materialism: that the absolute, which is the structurality of the structure qua *supplementary* metaphysical constraint, is absolutely contingent.

This latter determination returns to the result established earlier: that the structurality of the structure qua *ratio* is absolutely contingent. The PIR, recall, is premised on a formalist determination of the absolute-real leading to the determination of reason as itself absolutely contingent not only with regard to its ontology (the fact of reason) but also as regards what and how reason is as such. That exfinite hypothesis is here vindicated from within deabaolutized finitude: starting from the thesis of exfinite materialism, the *supplemental* 'origin of the *ratio*', of the arbitrarily organizing absolute of the structure as such (including that of thought), is the transcription within deabsolutized finitude of absolute ontocontingency, the contingency of which is rendered within the structure as its acentricity. For Derrida, this *is* deabsolutized finitude but mistakenly and only contingently determined via supplementarity as the 'origin of the *ratio*'. In its absoluity and null materialism, however, this origin, the structurality of the structure, *can* be positively identified without metaphysical determination, minimally so, as the formalism of the absolute contingency of the *ratio*. That is, the origin of reason is not the play of supplementarity but *absolute* unreason – and this is what Derrida theorizes as the supersemantic sign in play.

This *ratiocontingency* of the structurality of structure stipulates that any and every *ratio* is absolutely contingent in its constitution of a structured and systemically coherent organization – of reason and, per structuralism, of scientificity. Ratiocontingency must be severally demarcated: on one side, it is distinct to *onto*contingency as Meillassoux establishes it with PIR, as is methodologically apparent in its effective but curtailed identification by Derrida via the unspeculative realism that is deconstruction. On another side, absolute ratiocontingency does not mean that rational thought is itself a fideism. Though each faith also holds that its *ratio* or system of belief is absolute – a result that deconstruction permits and also denounces as metaphysical – ratiocontingency is, to the contrary, rationally known and deduced by exfinite thought, and is therefore irreducible to fideism. On yet another side, which returns to the predicament of the languages of reason for the last time, ratiocontingency in its absoluity must also be demarcated from the geohistorical contingency of the language in which rational thought is articulated. Here, Derrida's argument for the supersemantic sign together with his countermanding of Lévi-Strauss's critique of scientific ethnocentrism elaborates the predicament of the languages of reason not with regard to the discrepancies between those languages, which was taken up earlier via the aneidetic sign, but along the axis from *any* language (qua finite contingent, or inadequately universal sign-system) to reason as such. At the point, this predicament is directly apprehended as the problem of how the scientificity of any rational realism is warranted and, on that basis, how a comprehensive explanatory speculative materialism is established.

Contingent absoluity

Deconstruction shows that the *ration supplémentaire* constitutes the necessary destabilization *and* accidental relative stabilization of the 'complementary' relation between the signifer and signified, which means that: (i) the signified is, as noted, aneidetically constituted; (ii) the signified is only ever partially constructed *on the basis of* the contingencies of the signifier; and (iii) the sign and signification therefore have a relative freedom with respect to any organizing *ratio*. This triumvirate conditioning of signification is that of the supersemanticity of the sign, and it is the operation of writing that Derrida primarily identifies as literature. In view of the ratio-contingency of the structure of signification – that is, respecting writing as literature – it is then necessary to

> avoid the violence that consists in centering a language which describes an acentric structure ... [and therefore] to forego scientific

or philosophical discourse, to renounce the *epistéme* which has the absolute exigency, which is the absolute exigency to go back to the source, to the centre, to the founding basis, to the principle, and so on.[44]

Derrida's direct argument here is against Lévi-Strauss's reclamation of myth as an ersatz basis for the structuralist ethnological discourse, but it can be extended to Lévi-Strauss's broader claim that structuralism is a true science of social systems thanks to its objective, impersonal and universalist account (paradigmatically including language). Such a rationally constituted scientificity even takes into account the ethnologist's own position in systemic terms – hence, *structural*ism – thereby establishing the critique of ethnocentrism. For Derrida, such a scientistic claim perpetrates two violences simultaneously: one is the structural and theoretical 'violence' mentioned in the passage just quoted; the second is the historical and geopolitical violence concomitant with Eurocentrism, perpetrated because if 'ethnology – like any science – comes about within the element of discourse' then the ratiocontingency of signification means that 'it is primarily a European science employing traditional concepts, however much it may struggle against them'.[45] That is, signification's ratiocontingency qua movement of supplementarity – subtracting absoluity as a condition for scientificity – requires that the putative universality of ethnography (and of science more generally) is constrained to the contingency of sociohistorical terms and concepts even in the attempt to leave them. In Derrida's words, 'this necessity' – to relativize the scientific claim once the assumed scientificity of the structure and its discourse are deabsolutized – 'is irreducible; it is not [itself] a historical contingency'. This is the necessity that is explicit and manifest qua literature, which is then a simultaneously ethical, political and epistemological task.

The 'necessity' Derrida identifies here is however only irreducible, and literature the truth of science, if the absolute structurality of the structure *is* subtracted and correctly unthinkable as a positive term. These are the constitutive requirements of the deabsolutized finitude Derrida endorses and substantiates. Apprehended as the obverse of exfinite ontocontingency, however, the necessity of a sociohistorical determination of the *ratio* is *not* irreducible. Exfinite speculation determines that onto- and ratiocontingency are absolute, not historical, and this in turn warrants precisely the universalisms that according to Derrida – and for the deabsolutized finitude that he rigorously theorizes – are impossible, including, most immediately, the scientificity on which structuralism is premised.

Rational absoluity qua ratiocontingency however entails an obvious recursive consequence that seems to vitiate the basic claims to universality, invariance or anonymity that are indispensable for establishing modern scientificity and returns its basic operation to literature in the Derridean sense: if every and any rational realism is itself ratiocontingent in its reason, this includes the speculative materialism that rationally identifies the absolute or, on the other hand, deconstruction's unspeculative realism. In particular, ratiocontingency presents a fundamental obstacle to positing absolute contingency itself: any deduction or demonstration of absoluity requires the establishment of invariances, universals and necessities, and this is precisely what ratiocontingency *in its absoluity* vitiates. Ratiocontingency in its absoluity is immediately self-contradictory. Meillassoux resolves this quandary with respect to the ontology of the absolute-real with the factial-factical difference, but that resolution itself presumes the rational realism that is undermined by the contradiction of ratiocontingency.

Here, the contiguity of deabsolutized finitude and exfinite speculation extricates rational absoluity – including the thought of absoluity – from its autonegating recursion. Deconstruction establishes that because discourse and the supersemantic sign are both ratiocontingent and ontocontingent, *no* element of discourse can be absolute or necessary – a reformulation of the recursive negation of absoluity just noted. If there were any such necessary sign, then the absolute contingency of both the real and the *ratio* would be abrogated by a term or discursive element that would be absolute and so in fact constitute a metaphysics (in both Derrida's and Meillassoux's terms). In addition to the nonnecessity of any element of any language, Meillassoux establishes the null materialism of mathematical formalism via the pure sign of mathematics as the manifestation of the ontocontingency of the sign; mathematical signification develops only thanks to the formal sign being aneidetic and asemantic. Consequently, (i) the sign is in the *pure* movement of supplementarity within a given ratiocontingent *mathematical* formalism (one sign is replaceable by another up to a syntactic limit without transformation of the significance of the mathematical expression); and (ii) mathematical formalism as a rational construction makes explicit the contingency of the *ratio* – the contingency and variability of its axioms and its formalism *as a formalism* – *without* assuming or stipulating any necessary conditions for the constraint of play that it constructs (not even self-consistency in the case of paraconsistent logics). Without, that is, any metaphysical supplementation for the operational or structural *ratio* of signification or necessity to the complementation of signifier to signified.

The mathematical sign is not then in or of the supplemental 'play' of the signifier before presence (metaphysics) or absence (subtractive finitude), surpassing-subtracting the metaphysical determination of the sign as Derrida identifies and endorses it. On the other hand, that metaphysical elimination is, recall, the subordination of the signifier by the signified qua the sign's intelligible content, contrasted to which the pure sign of mathematical formalism is aneidetic and asemantic, intelligible only by way of its syntactical operations – by its structural signification – rather than its intelligible content. Yet, though the aneideitic-asemantic sign is not metaphysical in the full sense that Derrida proposes, it is nonetheless constituted according to the formal onto- and ratiocontingency of all languages of reason. However minimal and null-formal this exfinite positive determination of the absolute of the sign-system may be, as such it is a metaphysical sign per Derrida: the metaphysics (or formalism) of a necessary contingency. In Derrida's terms, formal contingency is the transcendental signified of the pure sign. This transcendental signified is the ultimate intelligible content of the signifier, and it is the null materiality that for Meillassoux *precludes* any metaphysical determination of the absolute.

The pure aneidetic sign is, in sum, *both* metaphysical (for deabsolutized finitude) *and* nonmetaphysical (for exfinite thought). While this dual determination only reiterates that one doctrine of the aneidetic sign obverts the other – now with regard to the metaphysicality or not of the pure sign rather than its semanticity – it also proposes an unheralded third option for eliminating the necessary and 'radical difference between signifier and signified' in addition to those that Derrida presents. Specifically, that the pure sign of mathematics is metaphysical with regard to subtractive finitude in that the signifier *is* wholly subordinate to the intelligible content, but that content is itself the null materiality of absolute contingency and not at all eideitic. And insofar as the materialist aneidetic 'pure' sign of mathematics mitigates against any positive determination of its intelligible content other than/because of this degree-zero condition, the structurality of the sign-system remains absolutely contingent and formal with regard to being or reason. Which is to say, in fact empty. The movement of supplementarity and the subtractability of positive determination of the absolute for finite thought – deconstruction – is then a consequence of the null materiality of the absolute which that deabsolutized finitude cannot itself apprehend (and for deabsolutory finite language this is precisely the necessary and supposed – but here deduced – transcendentality of the degree-zero signified that is onto- and ratiocontingency).

Materialist Reason and its Languages

Countermanding Derrida's predilection for literature as the demonstration of the nonmetaphysical construction of supersemantic signification, it is therefore, and rather, asemantic mathematical formalism that is the overt manifestation of the 'pure' play of structurality. What in Derrida's terms would be the metaphysical erasure of the signifier in mathematical (or, more broadly, scientific) formalism, because of its subordination to the intelligible content of the *ratio*, is shown by the exfinite absolutory thought that Meillassoux instigates to be in fact the complete and explicit affirmation of the onto- and ratiocontingency of the sign-structure of *all* languages of reason. Mathematical formalism and the pure aneidetic-asemantic sign by which the explicit affordances of the structure constructs signification (which Derrida calls 'play') is, in sum, the rational elimination of metaphysics *whether or not* finitude is assumed. That elimination does not leave the absolute of the structure and the knowledges constructed from it empty – that would be to return to the deconstructive determination. Rather, it establishes that the rational realism that secures speculative materialism as a nonfideistic knowledge of the absolute must itself be a ratiocontingent mathematical formalism.

Such a language of reason is materialist reason. It is premised on the contingency of its signs and structurality as condition for its construction of the determination of the absolute outside of thought – which may or may not be exocognitive facts. The consequent constructions of invariances, universalities and absoluities – which are necessarily at least as multiple as the formalisms of contingent rational languages – is how materialist reason establishes knowledge of the absolute-real qua fact. But, surpassing the constraints Meillassoux proposes for reason and speculative materialism, materialist reason so-constituted does not just obtain knowledge of what is outside of thought, moreover it is *itself* a rationalism that is outside of thought *and* which constructs absolutes outside of thought and subjectalism. Materialist reason is therefore a speculative materialist reason; and because these constructions establish knowledge of the absolute that is more than minimal, the scientificity of the aneidetic language of reason is not just thereby vindicated but also invented again and again – as then are the languages of reason and that of which they provide knowledge.

Notes

1. For a transcription of the Speculative Realism conference see Robin Mackay and Dustin McWherter, *Collapse III: Unknown Deleuze [+ Speculative Realism]* (Falmouth: Urbanomic, 2007), pp. 307–449. A concise summary of the principal arguments of the four presenters at the conference – Ray Brassier, Iain Hamilton Grant, Graham Harman and Quentin Meillassoux – is presented in Christoph Cox, Jenny Jaskey and Suhail Malik, 'Editors' Introduction', in Christoph Cox, Jenny Jaskey and Suhail Malik (eds), *Realism Materialism Art* (Center for Curatorial Studies, Bard/Sternberg: Annandale-on-Hudson/Berlin, 2015), pp. 16–25. However, speculative realism is taken here as the cover term for a series of philosophies, theories and praxes defined by a primary commitment to anticorrelationism – which is itself taken here to be clearly theorized by Meillassoux – and so the applicability of the name extends beyond the four presenters at the 2007 conference.

2. Quentin Meillassoux, *After Finitude: An Essay on the Necessity of Contingency*, trans. Ray Brassier (London: Continuum, 2008), p. 5; see also the elaboration of the term in Quentin Meillassoux, 'Iteration, Reiteration, Repetition: A Speculative Analysis of the Sign Devoid of Meaning', trans. Robin Mackay and Moritz Gansen, this volume, p. 118.

3. Between the four presenters at the 2007 Speculative Realism conference, for example, the arguments and commitments of Harman and Brassier almost entirely countermand one another. See Ray Brassier, 'Postscript: Speculative Autopsy', in Peter Wolfendale, *Object Oriented Philosophy: The Noumenon's New Clothes* (Falmouth: Urbanomic, 2014), pp. 407–21, as well as Wolfendale's own substantial argument comprising that book; and Graham Harman, 'Realism without Materialism', *SubStance* 40(2) (2011): 52–72.

4. Meillassoux, 'Iteration', p. 124

5. For a historico-theoretical overview of 'peak' structuralism see François Dosse, *History of Structuralism Volume One: The Rising Sign 1945–1966*, trans. Deborah Glassman (Minneapolis: University of Minnesota Press, 1998).

6. Jacques Derrida, 'Structure, Sign and Play', in *Writing and Difference*, trans. Alan Bass (London: Routledge, 2001 [original French publication 1967]), p. 352 and passim.

7. Meillassoux, 'Iteration', p. 119.

8. The distinction permits Meillassoux to demarcate his own philosophy from that of other positions in SR (Harman and Grant in particular affirm a subjectalist variant of SR) but also draws attention to the broad affirmation of realism in rational thought: as limit examples, Hegelian idealism establishes the absolute reality of the concept and so is a variant of realism, as is the noetic intentionality of Husserlian phenomenology, or the immanentism of concept

formation to ordinary language in post-Wittgensteinian analytic philosophy. See Meillassoux, 'Iteration', pp. 133ff. and 191n. 19.

9. Meillassoux, *After Finitude*, p. 38, and 'Iteration', p. 134.
10. Notable here in a complex and densely articulated set of philosophies are Johann Gottlieb Fichte, *Foundations of Transcendental Philosophy (Wissenschaftslehre) nova methodo (1796/99)*, ed. and trans. Daniel Breazeale (Ithaca: Cornell University Press, 1992); and G. W. F. Hegel, *Phenomenology of Spirit*, trans. A. V. Miller (Oxford: Oxford University Press, 1977 [original German publication: 1807]).
11. Meillassoux, *After Finitude*, chapter two.
12. Jonathan Israel provides a detailed and comprehensive vindication of the Enlightenment as a philosophically-constituted rationalist materialism. See for example *Radical Enlightenment: Philosophy and the Making of Modernity 1650–1750* (Oxford: Oxford University Press, 2002)
13. The stances of strong and weak correlationisms are spelt out in Meillassoux, *After Finitude*, pp. 35–36.
14. Meillassoux, *After Finitude*, pp. 38.
15. Ibid., p. 39.
16. Ibid., p. 40.
17. Ibid., p. 41.
18. Ibid., p. 57.
19. Ibid.
20. Ibid., p. 71ff. for quotes in this and the next paragraph.
21. Ibid., p. 79. 'Factiality' is Ray Brassier's translation of Meillassoux's neologism (see *After Finitude*, pp. 132–33, note 6). It is sometimes rendered in English as 'factuality' (for example, 'Presentation by Quentin Meillassoux', in Mackay and McWherter (eds), *Collapse III*.
22. Meillassoux, *After Finitude*, p. 101; Meillassoux, 'Presentation', p. 434.
23. Meillassoux clearly differentiates absolute contingency from the doctrines that propose becoming and flux as the ontological condition. These philosophies propose a reason for what is – becoming – and as such violate PIR. See Meillassoux, *After Finitude*, pp. 64–66.
24. Meillassoux, *After Finitude*, p. 63.
25. See Ray Brassier, *Nihil Unbound: Enlightenment and Extinction* (Basingstoke: Palgrave Macmillan, 2007), p. 17.
26. Ray Brassier and Suhail Malik, 'Reason is Inconsolable and Non-Conciliatory: Ray Brassier in Conversation with Suhail Malik', in Cox et al. (eds), *Realism Materialism Art*, pp. 214–15.
27. Meillassoux, 'Iteration', p. 155
28. Ibid., p. 143

29. Quentin Meillassoux, Florian Hecker and Robin Mackay, *Documents UF13-1*, 22.7.10, p.4 (Falmouth: Urbanomic, 2010), http://www.urbanomic.com/Documents/Documents-1.pdf [accessed 10 January 2015].

30. Meillassoux, 'Iteration', pp. 156–7.

31. Ibid., pp. 155–6. The exposition in this and the next two paragraphs paraphrases Meillassoux, 'Iteration', pp. 155–62.

32. Derrida, 'Structure', p. 164.

33. See Derrida, 'Structure', p. 355; Meillassoux, 'Iteration', pp. 167–8.

34. Ibid., pp. 352–3.

35. Ibid., p. 355.

36. See Derrida, 'Structure', p. 352 for the argument on the unviability of the 'classical' determination of the centredness of the structure. This 'classical' determination is that of a logic of sovereignty, in which the sovereign is at once the primary figure of the state and therefore wholly exemplifies it while also being distinct to every other figure that constitutes it. The nonmetaphysical deconstruction of this condition configures a regicidal wake that is nonetheless constrained by the premises of its initial configuration: for example, that *any* absolute determination is metaphysically compatible. Such determinations are, in a word, intrinsically postsovereign rather than ex- or a-sovereign. This logic permeates Derrida's arguments through to his final seminars. See Jacques Derrida, *The Beast and the Sovereign, Vol. 1 (2001–2002)*, trans. Geoffrey Bennington, eds. Michel Lisse et al. (Chicago: University of Chicago Press, 2009).

37. Derrida, 'Structure', pp. 367 and 369 for the 'overabundance' of the signifier.

38. Ibid., p. 365.

39. See Jacques Derrida, *Speech and Phenomena and Other Essays on Husserl's Theory of Signs*, trans. David B. Allison (Evanston: Northwestern University Press, 1973 [original French Publication 1967]), p. 102.

40. Derrida, 'Structure', p. 353.

41. Ibid., p. 365. See also Jacques Derrida, *Of Grammatology*, trans. Gayatri Chakravorty Spivak (Baltimore: Johns Hopkins University Press, 1997 [original French publication: 1967]), Part II.2.

42. Derrida, 'Structure', p. 396.

43. Ibid., p. 366.

44. Ibid., p. 362.

45. Ibid., p. 356.

PART III
SCIENCE

CHAPTER 9
UNDERLABOURING FOR SCIENCE: ALTHUSSER, BRASSIER, BHASKAR
Nathan Coombs

How philosophy should respond to modern science is a great unresolved question. The Galilean mathematicization of nature and the Baconian controlled experiment undermined the aprioristic method of classical philosophy and medieval scholasticism. Since then, cognisance of nature's contingency has provoked conflicting responses. In proposing the transcendental aesthetic of space and time, Immanuel Kant's critical revolution would be the first to respond systematically to the challenge.[1] G. W. F. Hegel's dialectic would then seek to supersede Kant's insights: assimilating finite understanding in the Absolute Idea and speculatively reconciling Reason with natural scientific knowledge.[2] Edmund Husserl's phenomenology would circumvent the dualism of appearances and reality altogether in an imperative to go back to the 'things themselves' from the first-person perspective of conscious intentionality.[3] That these responses have come to be identified with certain antiscientific implications – Kantianism with agnosticism about the objective world;[4] Hegelianism with contempt for determinate objects;[5] phenomenology with a reversion to prescientific common sense – indicates that the question of how philosophy should relate to natural science remains open. Still, an epistemological orientation has proved attractive for philosophers wishing to defend the cognitive autonomy of science from philosophical encroachments upon its terrain.[6] On the side of analytic philosophy, Rudolf Carnap's logical positivism, Karl Popper's falsifiability criterion and Wilfrid Sellars's naturalism have all promised a role for philosophers in clarifying the rational basis of scientific knowledge. Among Continental philosophers, a postwar period encompassing the work of Alexandre Koyré, Georges Canguilhem and Gaston Bachelard theorized the epistemic discontinuity of the prescientific and the scientific.

The factions forming after the 2007 Goldsmiths speculative realism workshop thus redraw a well-scoured line of demarcation within philosophy. The clash between Graham Harman's phenomenological object-oriented philosophy and Ray Brassier's nihilism provides the case in point: the former's commitment to philosophy serving as an equal partner to science is opposed by the latter's claim to defend science by insisting that philosophy justify itself in light of modern science's sundering of reality and ideality. Or in the words of one of Brassier's disciples, the astringent theorizing of object-oriented philosophy, unconcerned with the dualism of concepts and world opened up by post-Galilean science, enjoins us to 'reactivate the methodological primacy of epistemology'.[7] Central to Brassier's critique are two main concerns. The first is the relation between what Sellars termed the 'manifest image' and the 'scientific image' – these images respectively corresponding to the world of midsized objects we inhabit phenomenologically and the world of imperceptibles posited by natural science.[8] Brassier calls into question philosophies which attempt to tether the scientific image to manifest foundations, and which refuse to cede cognitive priority to science. Brassier's second move involves a rejection of empiricist epistemology and pragmatist instrumentalism when theorizing changes in scientific theory. This allows him to assert the necessity of philosophy working through new scientific discoveries without 'engaging in an ontological hypostasis of entities and processes postulated by current science'.[9] The pursuit of both desiderata animates Brassier's advocacy of a Sellarsian 'critical epistemology-rationalist metaphysics' nexus, which he believes is well suited for satisfying the demands of scientific realism.

This essay frames Brassier's interventions with respect to Louis Althusser's epistemological programme of the 1960s. What justifies the comparison? Importantly, it helps to illuminate the genealogical thread linking Brassier's realist project to Althusser's via the influence of Alain Badiou and Quentin Meillassoux (whom Brassier translated). For those unacquainted with this lineage, the reasons why realism and a defence of the autonomy of science are such pressing concerns for Brassier may be opaque. Hence, linking Brassier's project to Althusser's helps us to understand better the former's polemical interventions against antirealist tendencies in Continental thought. Another motivation for comparing Brassier's project to Althusser's is that setting it within a broader context sheds light on the possible limits of Brassier's Sellarsian realism. In particular, following Althusser's project through its key moments of elaboration, culminating in a self-critique of his speculative-rationalist deviation in the 1970s, allows us to reflect on the problems with mobilizing epistemology in the defence of science. Delineating the Althusserian link will then pay further dividends in thinking possible alternatives to Sellarsian epistemology. I

Underlabouring for Science

introduce Roy Bhaskar's account of scientific ontology, inspired in part by Althusser's self critique, to point to what is missing from such critical epistemologies: their lack of an account of scientific experimentation and their reduction of science to the singular (positioning scientific method under the umbrella of a more general theory of knowledge). Given that Brassier's main target, Bruno Latour's Actor Network Theory,[10] is much more than a mere antirealist provocation with respect to the natural sciences and is instead a fully fledged social metaphysics, Bhaskar's work is, I argue, important for sensitizing us to the specificity of social science within realist philosophy and alerts us to the current incompleteness of Brassier's critique. More than just aiming to provide genealogical depth to Brassier's project, then, the greater ambition of this chapter is to inspire a future encounter between Sellarsian critical epistemology and Bhaskar's scientific ontology capable of advancing realism in the social sciences.

The discussion that follows is divided into four sections. The first section addresses how Althusser drew inspiration from Bachelard's notion of the 'epistemological obstacle' and enriched it with antisubjectivist, antiempiricist and antiteleological arguments. The second section examines Althusser's attempt to identify breaks from ideology to science and how this led him to criticize his speculative-rationalist deviation. The third section presents the Sellarsian 'critical epistemology-rationalist metaphysics' nexus identified by Brassier, comparing and contrasting it with the Bachelard-Althusser programme. The fourth section offers reflections on the lasting significance of Althusser's self-critique and argues that Bhaskar's scientific ontology provides a compelling, though not mutually exclusive, alternative to Sellars's critical epistemology.

Althusser's epistemological programme of the 1960s

Given that Althusser was no ordinary scholarly epistemologist and is best known for his innovations in Marxist theory, this section provides the necessary historical background to make sense of why he would turn to epistemology to defend the autonomy of science.[11] In so doing, it shows that although Althusser's motivations were highly idiosyncratic and shaped by the French theoretical conjuncture of the 1960s, his epistemological programme nonetheless prefigures some of the moves taken by Brassier's realist project. As we will see in subsequent sections, Althusser's rejection of empiricism and pragmatism, his turn to epistemology to defend scientific realism and his affirmation of a muscular rationalism will be echoed in Brassier's employment of Sellars's naturalist epistemology against Harman's object oriented philosophy and Latour's Actor Network Theory. Beginning this essay with Althusser's epistemological programme thus allows us to appreciate the genealogical lineage of which Brassier is a part and to understand better the sometimes cryptic political motivations of Brassier's appeals to realism and rationality against his theoretical adversaries.

Transforming French historical epistemology

To begin with just a sketch of a complex political and intellectual career, Althusser was a theorist operating on the philosophical fringe of the French Communist Party (PCF), which dominated Marxist politics in postwar France.[12] The decisive events animating Althusser's philosophical work were Nikita Khrushchev's de-Stalinization programme, announced in 1956, and its culmination in the Sino-Soviet split of the early 1960s. Althusser's response to these events was to mount a scathing criticism of the humanist critique of Stalinism promoted by existentialist and phenomenological currents. Lenin's motto 'Without Revolutionary theory, there can be no Revolutionary Movement' provided the source of Althusser's disquiet with this trend. Only by refusing the reduction of Marxist theory to humanist invocations of praxis could the PCF's opportunist slide towards pragmatism and reformism be resisted theoretically.

On another, closely related front, Althusser's project was lent urgency by the need to uphold the autonomy of science in the wake of the Lysenko affair.[13] The disastrous application of political criteria to Soviet agricultural projects, justified by Engelsian dialectical materialism under the pretext of Stalinist-Zhadanovian proletarian science, far from compelling the abandonment of the project of Marxist science in Althusser's estimation entailed the need for its thoroughgoing renewal. The ironical result of Althusser's hard-line position, resisting both humanism and Stalinism, would be a remarkably heterodox synthesis of intellectual traditions. Althusser would partition Marx's early works from the scientific analysis of his mature political economy by emphasizing the structural determinations of Marx's scientific breakthrough (hence the temporary alliance with the anthropological structuralism of Claude Lévi-Strauss), as well as thinking the rupture between ideology and science as an epistemological break. His main influences belonged to an historical epistemological school represented by the work of Alexandre Koyré, Georges Canguilhem and Gaston

Bachelard.[14] Although Althusser's debts would be owed to all these thinkers in seemingly equal measure, the similarities between Bachelard's notion of the 'epistemological obstacle' and Althusser's 'epistemological break' make it the easiest concept through which to trace a line of continuity.

An important text for understanding Bachelard's influence on Althusser is *The Formation of the Scientific Mind*, which employs psychoanalysis in order to diagnose the impedimenta to scientific progress. For Bachelard, inferring the 'epistemological obstacles' in scientific pedagogy and persisting in the minds of scientists is a matter of grasping the invariant errors of prescientific thought, a claim he illustrates by drawing on examples from a wealth of eighteenth-century scientific texts which revel in spectacle and awe at the expense of the sober elaboration of the abstract laws underpinning phenomena. The lesson Bachelard draws from this is that standing between prescientific thought and scientific thought is an 'experience that is ostensibly concrete and real, natural and immediate present[ing] us with an *obstacle*'.[15] In search of the science of reality as 'the mathematical *why*' entails resistance against '*obvious and deep-seated empiricism*' because 'nothing is given. Everything is constructed'.[16] The process of science, where an initial generality about an object can be flawed in the extreme, implies 'a very real break between sensory knowledge and scientific knowledge'.[17]

The conclusion Bachelard reaches flies in the face of the empiricist image of science as a method concerned with uncovering the secrets of the object, believed to be there just waiting to be discovered. In Bachelard's words, 'the twentieth century has seen the beginning of scientific thought against sensations ... we need to construct a theory of the objective *against* the object'.[18] Science, as befits the ideal type Bachelard finds in physics, is an enterprise concerned with the efficaciousness of conceptual innovation, taking us away from the blooming, buzzing confusion of the subjective phenomenological world. Despite the presence of psychological elements in Bachelard's epistemology, the points below summarize it in the schematic terms in which it would be taken up in Althusser's appropriation.

1. Discontinuity in scientific practice.
2. A strong divide between the prescientific (errors) and scientific approach (correction).
3. Science as the realm of mathematical abstraction, set against the diverse, sensuous concrete.

4. Development in science as proceeding from initial overgeneralization and proceeding with caution in the increasing particularization of analysis.

5. The objective of science distinguished from the object of scientific investigation.

In his attempt to firm up the line of demarcation with Hegelian humanism, Althusser would enrich Bachelard's account of the discontinuity of the prescientific and the scientific with antisubjectivist, antiempiricist and antiteleological arguments. While this attempted transformation of French historical epistemology into a new Marxist dialectical materialism would be directed towards thinking Marx's epistemological break with his youthful humanism, Althusser's arguments would also comprise genuine interventions in the philosophy of science supporting an implicitly anticorrelationist realism.

Antisubjectivism

Althusser's critique of the subject is generally associated with political debates concerning structure and agency in Marxist theory. But it is also of great importance for his interpretation of epistemological breaks. With Althusser's antihumanist insistence on history as a 'process without a subject' there can be no recourse to the category of genius, or to the world-historical individual gifted by nature with a capacity to see what others could not.[19] The problem thus posed is of 'the relation between the *events* of … thought and the one but double history which was its true *subject*'.[20] Where the famous American philosopher of science, Thomas Kuhn posited moments of revelation giving rise to a new scientific paradigm, Althusser decries the vacuity of such psychological explanations.[21] The passage below from *Reading Capital* captures well the reasons for Althusser's resistance to subjective accounts of the origins of knowledge.

> To see the invisible … we need an *informed* gaze, a new gaze, itself produced by a reflection of the 'change of terrain' on the exercise of vision … The fact that this change in terrain, which produces as its effect this metamorphosis in the gaze, was itself only produced in very specific, complex and often very dramatic conditions; that it is absolutely irreducible to the idealist myth of a mental decision to change 'view-points'; that it brings into play a whole process that

Underlabouring for Science

the subject's sighting, far from producing, merely reflects in its own place; that in this process of real transformation of the means of production of knowledge, the claims of a 'constitutive subject' are as vain as are the claims of the subject of vision in the production of the visible.[22]

Althusser's rejection of subjective experience as an account of epistemological breaks also lies behind his rejection of 'subjective empiricism'.[23] Althusser sees a Humean empiricism, in which knowledge derives from impressions tied together solely by subjective ideas, as opening the door to agnosticism about the independence of the objective world (the same concern emerges in Quentin Meillassoux's critique of 'correlationism').

Antiempiricism

Althusser prosecutes empiricist epistemology through a critique of the Hegelian notion of contradiction within the real. In this conception, Althusser argues, the object is considered the source of all knowledge, and science succeeds only insofar as it extracts the essence of the object. On the empiricist account there are thus essential and inessential qualities to objects: the former falling under the purview of science, extracting it from the barriers imposed by the latter.[24] This is because in order for empiricism to maintain its realist credentials knowledge has to be posited as preexisting within the internal relations between the object's essential and inessential traits. Scientific cognition merely takes hold of the essential by way of a relation already lying within the object itself. Science does not construct its scientific object by way of *creative* mathematical abstractions; according to empiricist epistemology, it grasps the abstraction within the real object itself. To surmise the above using Althusser's words: 'for the empiricist conception of knowledge, the whole of knowledge is invested in the real, and knowledge never arises except as a relation inside its real object between the really distinct parts of that real object'.[25] Consequently, 'empiricist abstraction, which abstracts from the given *real* object its essence, is a *real abstraction*, leaving the subject in possession of the *real* essence'.[26]

Empiricism thereby falls foul of Althusser's antisubjectivism by enjoining the metaphor of the invisible (essential) being covered up by the visible (inessential), consecrating the conception of the uniquely brilliant scientific subject who can peer through the inessential fog into the essential heart of the object. Vice versa, 'an empiricism of the subject always corresponds to an idealism of the essence (or an empiricism of the essence to an idealism of the subject)'.[27] The empiricist conception of knowledge, Althusser writes, is 'the twin brother of the problematic of the religious vision of the essence in the transparency of existence'.[28] Empiricism is represented as a philosophical (ideological) incursion in the realm of science, embroidering the mobile scientific process into a philosophical tapestry of stable objects. Althusser here repeats Bachelard. For cutting across Bachelard's writings lies a critique of the way philosophy lags behind science: an observation undermining philosophy's claims to provide a discourse assuring or dissuading its readers of science's truth claims. Bachelard's point is that seemingly innocent words like 'object' shared by science and philosophy compel philosophy to criticise its inhibiting drag on science.[29] It follows that Althusser could be quoting Bachelard when he declares: 'I am interested in the *play on words* itself'.[30] For Althusser, the word 'object' is the rug under which empiricism's ideological manoeuvres are swept; the word 'real' provides the decoy. Attributing his counter-insight to Marx and Spinoza, Althusser sets up his epistemology in opposition to empiricism when he claims that 'the production of knowledge which is peculiar to theoretical practice constitutes a process that takes place *entirely in thought*'.[31]

Antiteleology

If it is possible to isolate the point at which Althusser transcends Bachelard unequivocally, it is his attempt to subsume these insights into a new Marxist science of history. In Resch's incisive words, 'Althusser forces French historical epistemology beyond the limits of its own self-understanding'.[32] The problem, Althusser argues, rests with 'the traditional concept of the history of the sciences, which today is still profoundly steeped in the ideology of the philosophy of the Enlightenment, i.e. in a teleological and therefore idealist rationalism'.[33] And since for Althusser science is associated with discontinuous breaks, then Hegel's teleological philosophy assumes the role of absolute ideology. Rescuing epistemological breaks from teleology demands their extrication from ideologies of history carried over into empiricism. Althusser recognizes in empiricism an originary *mythos*, whereby knowledge is excavated from the relation of real objects' essential and inessential features. It is a 'myth of the origin; from an original unity undivided between subject and object, between the real and its knowledge'.[34] What Althusser calls an 'idealism of the ante predicative' throws into suspicion philosophical terminology for the production of the new. Origin, genesis and mediation – all these terms are infected by teleological ideology; and empiricist epistemology is on this basis isomorphic with humanist political ideology.

Althusser's unsparing criticisms of subjectivism, empiricism and teleology therefore sit at the foundations of his new Marxist epistemology. They comprise the key arguments which Althusser employs to enrich Bachelard's philosophy of scientific discontinuity and to translate it into a Marxist idiom which can map onto the critique of ideology (a critique of the prescientific). Brassier will pursue his realist project in a way only connected tangentially to Marxism, but he shares with Althusser the conviction that a philosophical defence of science is necessary to maintain a place for reason in politics. Equally so, Brassier repeats Althusser's adoption of an epistemological orientation for distinguishing the prescientific from the scientific; hence the salience of the question of whether Althusser's epistemology can actually distinguish the break from ideology from science. But can it support the heavy expectations placed on it? The seeds of the problem, we will see, lie in the absence of an account of knowledge of the real object in Althusser's epistemology – a problem opening up the path to the critique of his speculative-rationalist deviation.

Epistemology without the real object?

Althusser's work has been criticized from almost every conceivable angle. Its flirtation with structuralism has been accused of denying the creative capacities of human agency, and its defence of science has been seen as shoring up the French Communist Party and the staid hierarchies of the University system. Perhaps the most damning charge of all is that Althusser's epistemology fails to deliver on its own terms: that it has no account of how science gains traction on the real object and only formalizes processes of ideational transformation. Below we see that this charge carries weight and that Althusser came to recognize the failings of his epistemology. At the same time, I also argue that Althusser's excoriating self-critique of the 1970s, involving a sweeping Feyerabendian dismissal of epistemology, overgeneralizes from the specific failings of his own epistemological programme.

For want of the empirical

What ailed Althusser's epistemological programme, leading to its disavowal by its author in such a short space of time? The rub of the matter comes down to whether Althusser's claim that he 'take[s] this transformation [i.e. the epistemological break] for a fact, without any claim to analyse the mechanism that unleashed it' is a defensible proposition. Given that for Althusser the transformation from ideology to science takes place entirely in thought, the question that he would ultimately be forced to confront is how his epistemology accounts for correspondence between scientific concepts and reality. Aware of the problem of how science is supposed to refine its grasp on the real object, Althusser famously leaves the question unanswered when he writes that the 'reader will understand that I can only claim, with the most explicit reservations, to give the arguments towards a sharpening of the question we have posed, and not an answer to it'.[35] Alex Callinicos takes the consequences of this evasion to their logical conclusion: 'if theoretical practice [for Althusser] can cognitively appropriate its real object despite the fact that it takes place completely in thought it is because thought and the real are homologous', to which he continues, 'to employ an asserted homology between thought and the real as the foundation for an epistemological positions, is to fall into the empiricist problematic'. The damning conclusion in Callinicos's eyes is that 'above all, it becomes impossible to avoid idealism'.[36]

In the 1966 text, 'The Philosophical Conjuncture and Marxist Theoretical Research', Althusser conceded how his desire to combat empiricism led to him to bend the stick too far against the empirical and to foment a phoney war with sociology.[37] The problem is dramatically highlighted by how Althusser earlier appraised the significance of Marx's scientific contributions, which subtract them entirely from empirical verification. 'No mathematician in the world', Althusser says, 'waits until physics has verified a theorem to declare it proved ... the truth of his theorem is a hundred percent provided by criteria purely internal to the practice of mathematical proof.' What goes for mathematics goes for Marx: 'It has been possible to apply Marx's theory with success because it is "true"; it is not true because it has been applied with success.'[38] But if Marx's discovery of the continent of history is a merely rational transformation of ideological philosophies of history regardless of potential empirical verification, then Marxism retreats into a hermetically self-referential rationalism (or even irrationalism).

Here analogous pitfalls in Alain Badiou's and Quentin Meillassoux's neo-Althusserian philosophies become apparent.[39] While both thinkers operate in the realm of ontology, in theorizing order and change they repeat Althusser's identification of science with radical discontinuity, resulting in ambiguous views on real scientific practice. In Badiou's case, this takes the form of an axiomatic commitment to Marx's critique of political economy which obviates the need to engage with contemporary political economy.[40] At no point does Badiou deem it necessary to recommence Marx's scientific dissection of the mechanisms of capitalist exploitation; for him, it is enough to affirm the persistent form of capitalism from Marx's day to the present. In Meillassoux's case, his rationalist commitments take his defence of science in an even more dubious direction. For if we were to take seriously Meillassoux's claim to deduce the emergence of matter, life and thought as reasonless *ex-nihilo* events, then real scientific practice would come to a standstill.[41] As Gabriel Cartren has argued perspicaciously, Meillassoux's ontology of absolute contingency sits in stark contrast to the project of theoretical physics, concerned with uncovering the necessity of the laws governing the Universe.[42] And one can equally – in fact, more damningly – extend this point to the more empirically oriented fields of chemistry, biology and neuroscience too. For all the respect for science announced by Badiou's and Meillassoux's ontologies, their Platonic belief in the purchase of the logico-deductive method is of a piece with Althusser's rationalist epistemology.

Althusser's Feyerabendian self-critique

In his 1974 'Elements of Self-Criticism' Althusser expands upon his earlier critical reflections about his evasion of the empirical, which he now defines as a 'speculative-rationalist' deviation within Marxist theory. He presents the deviation as resulting from the identification of science with truth and ideology with error, permitting a representation of Marx's epistemological break in entirely rationalist terms.[43] Although readings of Althusser's self-critique have tended to focus on his remarks that he left class struggle out of his earlier work, more interesting for our purposes are his intraphilosophical criticisms of his epistemology, and indeed of epistemology *tout court*. In this text, Althusser defines the speculative-rationalist deviation according to three features:

1. A (speculative) sketch of the theory of the difference between science (in the singular) and ideology (in the singular) in general.

2. The category of 'theoretical practice' (*insofar as*, in the existing context, it tended to reduce philosophical practice to scientific practice).

3. The (speculative) thesis of philosophy as 'Theory of theoretical practice' – which represented the highest point of this theoreticist tendency. [44]

Divesting philosophy of its pretensions thus entails a revaluation of his earlier identification of philosophy with epistemology. A lengthy footnote to the text recounts how his 'speculative-rationalist' deviation was organized, as if often the case, around the manifest form of a word, whose credentials seemed beyond doubt:

> *Epistemology* ... [is] the theory of the conditions and forms of scientific practice and of its history in the different concrete sciences ... [which can lead to] a *speculative way*, according to which Epistemology could lead us to form and develop the theory of scientific practice (in the singular) in distinction to other practices: but how did it now differ from philosophy, also defined as 'Theory of theoretical practice'? ... If epistemology is philosophy itself, their speculative unity can only reinforce theoreticism ... one must give up this project, and criticize the idealism or idealist connotations of all Epistemology.[45]

The most significant point here is that in reifying a single category of science, inattentive to the diversity of the practices subsumed under the word, Althusser recognized that his epistemology flattened the distinctions between philosophy, theoretical practice, social science and natural science. Also important to note is how Althusser then generalizes the result of his self-critique by claiming that all epistemology inevitably transits towards idealism in seeking to provide a philosophical guarantee to scientific process (a sweeping dismissal of epistemology in keeping with Paul Feyerabend's in *Against Method*).[46] This scepticism explains why, after the 1968 texts *Lenin and Philosophy* and *Philosophy and the Spontaneous Philosophy of the Scientists*, Althusser demoted philosophy from any role in determining truth/error and ideology/science distinctions.[47] From this point onwards, all that is left for Althusser to do is to wage an arbitrary philosophical battle of ideas in defence of spontaneous scientific realism – a position just presumed to be favourable to working-class struggle.[48]

Althusser's lesson?

It is my belief that Althusser went too far in his self-critique, generalizing from legitimate criticisms of his epistemology to a broader, illegitimate critique of epistemology. As well as being insufficiently argued – a knee-jerk reaction to disillusionment with his own project – Althusser's newfound scepticism also undermined the basis for some of his most innovative social ontological concepts such as overdetermination and structural causality (ideas that would be elaborated only cryptically in Roy Bhaskar's scientific realism).[49] Still, for all the unnecessary *Sturm und Drang*, Althusser was correct in diagnosing his insufficient theorization of how scientific method gains empirical traction on the real object and his critique of how he reduced science to the singular. With Althusser's story in mind we will judiciously employ elements of his self-critique when reflecting on the limits of Brassier's Sellarsian critical epistemology over the following sections.

Brassier's Sellarsian epistemology

Bringing the discussion forward to the present, what might Althusser's story tell us about the recent speculative turn? Despite the lesser role of class struggle and political intrigue today, it is possible to see the debates since the Goldsmiths speculative realism workshop of 2007 as reviving elements of the theoretical conjuncture of the 1960s and 1970s. In particular, the rift between Graham Harman's and Brassier's realisms, the latter aiming for coherence with the findings of cognitive neuroscience, resuscitates old lines of demarcation concerning the legitimacy of philosophical conceptualization in the wake of developments in natural science. Here I want to focus solely on one side of this debate by providing a sympathetic yet critical assessment of Brassier's contribution.[50] My proposition is that while Brassier's Sellarsian 'critical epistemology-rationalist metaphysics' nexus might be adequate to call into question the legitimacy of Harman's object-oriented philosophy, in light of Althusser's self-critique it may however *not* be adequate to defend the cognitive autonomy of science. The question, then, is whether Brassier's adoption of Sellars's *naturalist* epistemology exempts him from the problems diagnosed in Althusser's self-critique or if it just runs into them from a different direction. In order to find answers it is first necessary to present core components of Brassier's Sellarsian critical epistemology and to flag up continuities and discontinuities with Althusser's epistemological programme.

Sellars's two images

To trace genealogically Brassier's project back to its Althussersian roots would be to undertake the arduous task of following its branches threading through Meillassoux's and Badiou's philosophies (whom Brassier has translated and played a part in promoting in the Anglophone academy). For our purposes, it is sufficient to note that Brassier shares with Althusser an opposition to phenomenology, empiricism and pragmatist-instrumentalist conceptions of science. Most importantly, both Althusser and Brassier oppose these conceptions when theorizing the epistemic discontinuity of the prescientific with the scientific. That Brassier does not adopt the framework of French historical epistemology, but rather endorses Sellars's account of the relationship between the scientific and manifest image, signals a commitment to naturalism that distinguishes his philosophy from Althusser's while still remaining genealogically explicable in terms of that tradition.

Sellars's distinction between the 'manifest' and 'scientific' image distinguishes between our phenomenal submersion in a world of midsize objects and the scientific world of imperceptibles creating science's novel categorical framework. However, unlike the stark discontinuity between prescientific and scientific cognition proposed by Bachelard's philosophy of science – a discontinuity presented as a simple break between falsehood and truth – Sellars's naturalism will demand a more subtle account of their differences. Sellars insists that the opposition of these images is not 'that between a prescientific, uncritical, naive conception of man-in-the-world, and a reflected, disciplined, critical – in short a scientific – conception'.[51] The manifest and scientific images should not be construed simplistically as a neat break between a naive, mythical understanding of the world opening up to rigorous science. Rather, in permitting valid statistical inferences within its own domain, the manifest image is in many ways 'itself a scientific image'.[52] Sellars expressly refuses to endorse a stereoscopic view of both images in which the manifest is 'overwhelmed in the synthesis'.[53] Sellars therefore leaves his discussion on an equivocal note: on the one hand, while the scientific image emerges from the manifest image it has the potential to break free of its tethers and displace it entirely; on the other, as a matter of practical necessity we will continue to rely upon the manifest image for understanding our place in the world.

Initially, Brassier's project in *Nihil Unbound* was to affirm the metaphysical consequences of the scientific image against philosophy's recalcitrant attachment to the manifest image.[54] While this compels him to lend a sympathetic ear to philosophers willing to engage cutting-edge science in revising their categorical frameworks, it does not, *mutatis mutandis*, entail an unbridled endorsement of the eliminative materialism of the right-Sellarsian neurophilosopher Paul Churchland. Brassier finds wholly unsatisfactory Churchland's attempt to eliminate both folk psychology and metaphysics in favour of a neurocomputational notion of vector space, supported by the pragmatic virtue of maximal explanation purchased with the greatest conceptual parsimony. That this account can be found self-contradictory and harbouring impoverished metaphysical presuppositions leads Brassier to instead suggest that the 'goal is surely to devise a metaphysics worthy of the sciences, and here neither empiricism nor pragmatism are likely to prove adequate to the task'.[55] Brassier's speculative realism will be a 'metaphysical radicalization of eliminativism' defending scientific realism without supposing that scientifically informed philosophizing obviates the need for a rational metaphysics.[56]

If the next stage of Brassier's project from his essay 'Concepts and Objects' onwards marks something of a retreat from the desire to liquidate metaphysically the manifest image (the obverse of his warming to Robert Brandom's account of inferential rationality), Brassier's continuing attack on antirationalism is no less fanged.[57] The critical force of this work has been directed principally at Bruno Latour's Actor Network Theory for its debilitation of truth-falsity distinctions and for promoting an 'irreductionism' rendering scientific knowledge a mere instrumentalism.[58] For Brassier, this has the result of forcing Latour to lean on rhetoric and metaphor in the place of reasoned arguments addressing the 'epistemological obligation to explain what meaning is and how it relates to things which are not meanings'.[59] Placing his reflections in a lineage running from Plato to Hegel to Sellars, Brassier's two-fronted war against object-oriented philosophy and Actor Network Theory will stress the need for tying a knot between critical epistemology and a rationalist theory of conceptual change.[60]

The 'myth of the given' and conceptual change

Sellars's critique of the 'myth of the given' is an important starting point for understanding this thematic intersection. As most famously presented in *Empiricism and the Philosophy of Mind*, Sellars shows, contra empiricist epistemology, that the desire to locate foundations for knowledge in sense-datum or in an intuitive-rationalist access to objects will always run up against inconsistencies.⁶¹ Sellars insists that even objects that are putatively immediately sensed, such as triangles and colours, are conceptually mediated; there is no preconceptual knowledge or facts about things. And once empiricist and rationalist foundational safe harbours are flooded by doubt, the epistemological scrutiny of all knowledge claims becomes imperative. Relatedly, if critical epistemology is not just to involve invoking caution about access and the necessity of deferring truth claims to the normative adjudication of the epistemic community, Sellars needs to show how the scientific image emerges from the manifest without falling into Kuhnian/Feyerabendian relativism or proposing a stark Bachelardian truth/error distinction. Sellars's theory of conceptual change navigates between these undesirable poles by providing a naturalist evolutionary account of conceptual succession covering both the development of the scientific image from the manifest image as well as developments internal to the scientific image.⁶²

A complete exegesis of Sellars's theory of conceptual change is impossible within the space afforded by this chapter.⁶³ Let it suffice to note how Sellars's theory aims to satisfy two desiderata: first, explaining how language can be acquired under the condition of conceptual holism; second, how the addition of new objects to a conceptual system does not render a system incommensurable with that which it supersedes. Sellars's answer to this problem can be grasped intuitively as a conceptual topography where a concept can be retained even in its transportation into a new conceptual system.⁶⁴ To use Sellars's own example, he aims to show how a Euclidean triangle and a triangle in Riemannian geometry can both be said to share the same concept of triangle, even though the categorical space of the latter opens up new, previously unexplored dimensions. Proposing a solution similar to Hegel's idea of *Aufheben*, Sellars writes that we must 'distinguish between the conceptual structure to which a proposition *belongs* and the conceptual structure *with respect to which its truth is defined*'.⁶⁵ That this is possible without defaulting to an instrumentalism wherein it is only our beliefs about concepts that change in a scientific revolution, or without tending towards a Platonism defending the existence of mind-independent abstracta, rests for Sellars on *epistemologically* interrogating the basis of concepts.

Sellars's epistemology thus enjoins an account of how a conceptual structure can be more or less adequate to the world it maps when employing first-order, matter-of-factual statements – a process Sellars terms 'picturing'.⁶⁶ Sellars's notion of picturing is intended to resolve the problem of how even though truth-assertability is normatively governed within a conceptual-linguistic system, a conceptual system can nonetheless refer to nonlinguistic reality as a measure of its adequacy. As a derivative of the causal relations between events and physical objects, picturing supplies nonpropositional, atomic statements comprising maps of the world, opening up the nonlinguistic world to a form of linguistic representation.[67] This nonconceptual account of correspondence allows for the 'fact that we can define a sense in which expressions in a different but related conceptual structure can be said to refer to or denote that which is denoted by expressions in our conceptual structure'.[68] For Brassier, Sellars's insight is of the utmost significance and 'is at once dialectical and materialist'.[69] It follows that Sellars's account of theory-change and picturing furnishes the linchpin for Brassier to resolve the problem of 'granting maximal (but not, please note, incorrigible) authority to the scientific representation of the world while acknowledging that science changes its mind about *what* it says there is'.[70] Or, to put this in Sellars's own words:

> the importance of this analysis lies in the fact that it permits the extension of epistemic notions to conceptual items in the framework which is other than, but related to, the conceptual structure which is embedded in our language as it now stands. In other words, the connection of these epistemic notions with our current conceptual structure (which is necessarily the point of view from which we view the universe) is loosened in a way which makes meaningful the statement that our current conceptual structure is both more adequate than its predecessors and less adequate than certain of its potential successors.[71]

The upshot is that Sellars's account of how we acquire representations of real causal relations allows the scientific image to escape the manifest image even though it evolves out of it. Sellars provides the means by which Brassier can square the need for a line of demarcation between the manifest and scientific images without engaging in the kind of reification of contemporary scientific knowledge that he sees in Churchland's eliminativism. Significant in terms of Brassier's broader genealogical context, Sellars's notion of picturing also provides an interface between a theory of conceptual change and a theory of our access to the real object – the latter being exactly what is sorely lacking in Althusser's epistemology.

Axiomatic or naturalist epistemology?

As we have seen, although Althusser's epistemological programme and Brassier's Sellarsian critical epistemology share similar aims, Brassier's commitment to naturalism entails notable philosophical differences. In particular, Sellars's account of conceptual change is squared with a naturalistic epistemological account of how languages are learned and translated. Sellars's idea of theory-change maintains a nonempiricist theory of representation in the notion of picturing; and these representations can be judged more or less adequate to real objects as measured against prevailing scientific norms. Where Althusser's demarcation of the break from ideology to science foundered on its lack of a theory of how science gains empirical traction on the real object, Sellars's evolutionary notion of theory change is, on the contrary, connected intimately with the question of how we gain ingress on the nonlinguistic real. In this sense, Brassier's turn to Sellars represents an improvement upon Althusser's epistemology. For though Sellars's naturalism addresses a number of issues that Althusser was never concerned with, it is still consistent with the core aims of Althusser's project: namely, a refutation of empiricism, pragmatism and instrumentalist conceptions of science, all of which open up a space for phenomenology (and the likes of Latour's Actor Network Theory) to claim cognitive equality with science. While there is much to be commended about Sellars's naturalism, a question remains however as to what extent it matches up to the real practice of science. The scientific ontology proposed by philosopher of science, Roy Bhaskar, will show why there are reasons to doubt if this is the case.

Bhaskar's scientific ontology

Given their affinities, it is odd that Bhaskar's transcendental realism has rarely been compared to Sellars's. Perplexing too is the fact that Brassier has not seen fit to engage Bhaskar's realist oeuvre when considering their many shared commitments. Bhaskar is perhaps the leading realist figure occupying the space between the decline of Althusser's project in the 1970s and the rise of speculative realism in the late 2000s; and he is responsible for founding the school of critical realism counting among its number famous theorists such as Tony Lawson, Margaret Archer and Andrew Collier.[72] Taking inspiration from both Althusser's epistemological programme of the mid-1960s and his post-'68 rejection of epistemology, Bhaskar's philosophy is animated by the desire to defend scientific realism against empiricist epistemology and pragmatist instrumentalism.[73] Thus, Bhaskar's philosophy marks a point of intersection between Althusser's and Brassier's projects – and this essay will conclude with some brief remarks aiming to encourage their future encounter. In seeing how Bhaskar's scientific ontology addresses two problems identified by Althusser's self-critique – his lack of an account of how science gains traction on the real object and the reduction of science to the singular – the aim is to raise questions about the adequacy of Brassier's Sellarsianism for defending the cognitive autonomy of science. Of course, it might be rightly said that Sellars and Bhaskar count more as allies within the realist camp than they do as rivals. The point of concluding this essay by contrasting Bhaskar's ontology with Brassier's Sellarsian critical epistemology therefore lies in a spirit of provocation, hoping to open up new lines of dialogue between these approaches.

Bhaskar's critique of epistemology

In his most famous texts, *A Realist Theory of Science* and *The Possibility of Naturalism*, Bhaskar presents philosophy's underlabouring role as that of defending an ontology adequate to real scientific practice.[74] Pivotal to this endeavour is Bhaskar's argument against what he calls the 'epistemic fallacy': that is, the severing of questions about knowledge from questions about being, resulting in an anthropocentric philosophy of science out of step with its real practice. Throughout his work Bhaskar's main targets are positivism and empiricist epistemology, neither of which accusations can be levelled against Sellars. But Bhaskar also offers a more general argument against epistemology's tendency to render the philosophy of science a mere subset of the theory of knowledge. Bhaskar provides a programmatic statement of why philosophy should not neglect scientific ontology:

> Philosophers, including philosophers of science, have for too long regarded the philosophy of science as a simple substitution instance of some more general theory of knowledge ... If, however, we reverse the customary procedure and substitute the more specific 'science' (or even better 'sciences') for 'knowledge' considerable illumination of many traditional epistemological problems can, I think, be achieved.[75]

The resonances between Bhaskar's position and Althusser's self-critique are plain to see. Not only does Bhaskar see philosophy's vocation as supporting the practice of science – a position in keeping with Althusser's *Philosophy and the Spontaneous Philosophy of the Scientists* – but he also sees this move as being necessary for the demarcation of the specific sciences. In so doing, Bhaskar provides a compelling response to two of the greatest flaws Althusser identified with his epistemology in his self-critique: the lack of an account of how we gain knowledge of the 'real object', and the presentation of science in the singular.

The centre of Bhaskar's case for the necessity of a scientific ontology of invariant generative mechanisms and striated structures lies in his contention that without it the scientific experimental method would be unintelligible. In Bhaskar's words, the transcendental deduction is that 'given that science does or could occur, the world *must* be a certain way'.[76] Since experiments involve creating a closed system where findings are repeatable, for Bhaskar scientific practice has to assume that it is hunting generative mechanisms impeded by countervailing tendencies in the open systems of the nonexperimental domain. The upshot for Bhaskar is that we must reject the notion of causal laws grounded in Humean event regularities. In isolating generative mechanisms in a closed experimental setting, scientists evidence their conviction that generative mechanisms must continue to be operative in the open, nonexperimental domain where they only rarely contribute to event regularities. Otherwise, it would be unclear as to why science would need the experimental method in the first place. Bhaskar concludes that when causal laws are conceived as event regularities, à la Hume, this misses the actual purpose of, and methodological approaches taken by, real scientific practice. The idea of a causal law as tracking event regularities is for Bhaskar a philosophical illusion promoted by positivism and empiricist epistemology.

The limits of Sellarsian realism

In that Sellars is one of the great critics of empiricism, he obviously escapes the full brunt of Bhaskar's critique. Indeed, Bhaskar admits that in maintaining scientific realism, 'Sellars [is] nearer the position characterized here as transcendental realist'.[77] Nevertheless, it should be noted that Sellars's notion of picturing seems to remain beholden to a notion of science as the generalization of Humean event regularities. So, Sellars's attempt to understand scientific realism within the remit of a more general theory of knowledge falls squarely in the line of sight of Bhaskar's critique. In Sellars's notion of picturing, providing an account of how we represent the nonlinguistic real through mapping causal relations nonpropositionally, we seem to be back to something incommensurate with the experimental method. Bhaskar's scientific ontology therefore represents a serious problem with employing critical epistemology in the defending science – a problem which to my knowledge has not been addressed by its advocates, Brassier included.

The second major problem identified by Althusser's self-critique and insufficiently addressed by Brassier's critical epistemology is the reduction of science to the singular. One of the great virtues of Bhaskar's scientific ontology is that though monist, traversing both the natural and social scientific domains, it allows for the transcendental deduction of the specificity of the social science and, consequently, informs the application of social scientific research methods.[78] For Bhaskar, conceiving the social as an open system allows for a social ontology with emergent properties and causally determinant structures. It opens up a gateway to rich theoretical debates about the causal powers of social structure interlacing with classical sociological debates on structure and agency, and synchronic and diachronic causation.[79] What is more, the critical realist school Bhaskar founded has taken these ontological insights and used them as a guide for conducting productive social scientific studies underwritten by a conviction in the efficaciousness of knowledge in transformative social practice.[80]

Lack of attention to the specificity of social science (or to the social practices of scientists) is a significant weakness of any self-proclaimed realism. Yet, like Sellars, Brassier has little to say about social science. Indeed, Brassier tends to assume that Meillassoux's critique of correlationism can be transferred to the human sciences relatively unproblematically. For instance, as noted, Brassier laments 'correlationism's status as the regnant intellectual orthodoxy throughout the humanities and the social sciences'.[81] Or consider the moments when Brassier announces an Althusserian calling for philosophy: 'philosophy intersects with politics at the point where critical epistemology transects ideology critique'.[82] Despite repeated intimations that his project interfaces with social theory, nowhere however does Brassier actually attempt to grapple with the unique properties of the social from a realist perspective: its reflexivity and emergent structures. Nor does Brassier attempt to explain how critical epistemology constitutes ideology critique in light of sophisticated debates on the nature of political ideology.[83]

Brassier's curiously insubstantial interaction with social theory is all the more strange when one considers that his principal target, Bruno Latour's Actor Network Theory, has never really claimed to be a philosophy of science as such. From the 1990s onwards, Latour's main contribution has been to elaborate a new social ontology in which the question of how scientific facts are constructed is subsumed into a theoretical endeavour exploring how the social in its broadest sense is assembled. To continue to focus solely on the status of natural scientific realism in Latour's work is therefore just to repeat the dismissal of Latour's contributions by professional philosophers of science since the 1980s. If Brassier's aim to is to mount a defence of realism capable of engaging Latour on the multiple fronts on which Actor Network Theory operates, then he will need to do more than just continue to pick at Latour's antirealism about natural scientific objects; Brassier will also have to make explicit his own position on how and in what sense one can also be a realist about social scientific objects. Of course, it may be objected that it is churlish to accuse Brassier of neglecting to also elaborate a social scientific realism when his core concerns lie in exploring naturalism and rationalism at the most universal level (that is, with respect to natural science). Yet from the perspective of Bhaskar's transcendental realism, Brassier's insensitivity to the specificity of social ontology follows with necessity from his adherence to critical epistemology, taking us back to reasons why Althusser's project ran aground in the 1970s. In light of Bhaskar's scientific ontology, then, Althusser's critique of his speculative-rationalist deviation continues to pose a series of salient problems which epistemological realisms would be well advised to confront.

Conclusion

The point of this chapter's entwining of realisms across the twentieth century – from Bachelard to Althusser, from Sellars to Brassier, from Althusser to Bhaskar – is to highlight their shared support for science's cognitive autonomy against phenomenology and empiricism (today represented by the duumvirate of Harman's object-oriented philosophy and Latour's actor-network theory). Although the motivations for Althusser's epistemological programme of the 1960s were Marxist in orientation, defending the need for theory in political practice, this chapter showed that echoes of this spirit live on in Brassier's realist project. Insofar as Brassier has embarked upon a full-frontal assault on Latour's Actor Network Theory, and has associated himself with the accelerationist current's promotion of rationalism and Prometheanism, it is not hard to see his assault on the French neoliberal's sophism as a continuation of politics by other means.[84] The elucidation of the genealogical thread which ties together Althusser, Brassier and Bhaskar was therefore written with further partnership in mind. It pointed to ways in which these thinkers can inform new theorization about how philosophy can support science against philosophical transgressions running counter to its spirit.

To make the case for a genealogical thread running through the work of Althusser, Brassier and Bhaskar, three arguments were introduced corresponding to the thinkers in question. First, Althusser's self-critique highlighted the need for epistemology to provide an account of how science gains traction on the real-object and why we should avoid speaking of science in the singular. Second, Brassier's Sellarsian critical epistemology was shown to provide a more subtle take on how the scientific image can break free of the manifest image. I argued that Sellars's naturalist commitment to ensuring a theory of conceptual change is commensurate with an account for how we acquire language, marking an improvement on Althusser's arbitrary demarcation of the break from ideology to science. Third, Bhaskar's scientific ontology was shown to respond effectively to the problems articulated by Althusser's self-critique. Not only does Bhaskar provide a convincing account of why scientific method gains traction on the real object; his ontology also supports the heterogeneity of the sciences. Thus, we concluded, Bhaskar's ontology suggests limits to Sellars's critical epistemology. From a Bhaskarian perspective, Sellars's notion of picturing, which is a concomitant of Sellars's reduction of scientific method to a more general theory of knowledge, seems out of step with science's experimental method.

However, the aim of this chapter was expressly not to put forward an argument against Brassier's Sellarsian critical epistemology so as to simply lay the groundwork for endorsing Bhaskar's scientific ontology. Instead, it was to invite a dialogue between these approaches which has so far remained silent. I agree with the epistemological pitfalls identified by Althusser's self-critique, but see merits in both Sellars's naturalism and Bhaskar's transcendental realism. The aim here, then, is to make the suggestion that it would be highly constructive if Brassier were to engage Bhaskar's work in the future. After all, Bhaskar's school of critical realism has done the most to maintain realism within the philosophy of natural and human sciences over the past forty years. The speculative turn need not reinvent the realist wheel. Therein, I hope, lies the value of this genealogy.

Notes

1. Immanuel Kant, *Critique of Pure Reason*, trans. Werner S. Pluhar (Indianapolis: Hackett, 1996).
2. G. W. F. Hegel, *The Science of Logic*, trans. A. V. Miller (Atlantic Highlands, NJ: Humanities Press, 1969).
3. Edmund Husserl, *Logical Investigations – Second Edition*, trans. J. N. Findlay, ed. Dermot Moran (London: Routledge, 2001), p. 168.
4. V. I. Lenin, 'Materialism and Empirio-Criticism. Critical Comments on a Reactionary Philosophy', in Clemens Dutt (ed.), *V. I. Lenin Collected Works, Vol. 14*, trans. Abraham Fineberg (London: Lawrence & Wishart, 1962), pp. 13–358; Quentin Meillassoux, *After Finitude: An Essay on the Necessity of Contingency*, trans. Ray Brassier (London: Continuum, 2008).
5. For a sophisticated and underappreciated critique of Hegel, see Galvano della Volpe, *Logic as a Positive Science*, trans. John Rothschild (London: NLB, 1980).
6. By the 'cognitive autonomy' of science I do not mean autonomy from the social conditions of knowledge production, about which the field of science and technology studies has left us with no illusions. Rather, the word 'autonomy' here signals the intellectual autonomy of scientific practice from philosophy in the Bachelardian sense – science does not need philosophy and philosophy's engagement with science acts as a fetter on science's development when it is taken too seriously.
7. Daniel Sacliotto, 'Realism and Representation: On the Ontological Turn', *Speculations* IV (2013): 59.
8. Wilfrid Sellars, 'Philosophy and the Scientific Image of Man', in *Science, Perception and Reality* (Atascadero, CA: Ridgeview Publishing Company, 1963), pp. 1–40.
9. Ray Brassier, 'Concepts and Objects', in Levi R. Bryant, Nick Srnicek and Graham Harman (eds), *The Speculative Turn: Continental Materialism and Realism* (Melbourne: re.press, 2011), p. 49.
10. Bruno Latour, *Reassembling the Social: An Introduction to Actor-Network-Theory* (Oxford: Oxford University Press, 2005).
11. As a reformulation of dialectical materialism, Althusser's epistemological theories are situated in a discourse alien to most philosophers of science. Add to this Althusser's engagement with French historical epistemology – circling theoretical loci foreign to a field dominated by the names of Popper, Kuhn, Feyerabend and Lakatos – and his seemingly traceless contribution is not surprising. Unusual indeed is a book like A. F. Chalmers's *What Is This Thing Called Science?* (St. Lucia: University of Queensland Press, 1976) which discusses Althusser's theories – and even here Althusser is consigned to the end of the book as just a 'radical critic'. Regarding the broader split in schools of historical epistemology, Dominique Lecourt observes that '*The New Scientific Mind*, Gaston Bachelard's first great work, was published in 1934, the

same year in which Karl Popper's famous book *The Logic of Scientific Discovery* appeared in Vienna. During the subsequent thirty years the works of the one and the other have been developed, enriched, corrected and broadcast without it ever being possible to register either the beginnings of a confrontation or a sign of any emulation between them.' See Lecourt, *Marxism and Epistemology: Bachelard, Canguilhem and Foucault*, trans. Ben Brewster (London: NLB, 1975), p. 9.

12. For the best account of Althusser's intellectual and political trajectory, see Gregory Elliott, *Althusser: The Detour of Theory* (London: Verso, 1987).

13. For a full account of the Lysenko affair, see Ethan Pollock, *Stalin and the Soviet Science Wars* (Princeton and Oxford: Princeton University Press, 2006), chapter three.

14. See Alexandre Koyré, *From the Closed World to the Infinite Universe* (Baltimore: The Johns Hopkins Press, 1957); Georges Canguilhem, *The Normal and the Pathological*, trans. Carolyn R. Fawcett and Robert S. Cohen (New York: Zone Books, 1991 [original French publication: 1966]); Gaston Bachelard, *The Formation of the Scientific Mind*, trans. Mary MacAllester (Manchester: Clinamen Press, 2002 [original French publication: 1938]).

15. Bachelard, *Scientific Mind*, p. 18.

16. Ibid., pp. 17, 39, 25.

17. Ibid., p. 237.

18. Ibid., p. 248.

19. Louis Althusser, *Lenin and Philosophy and Other Essays*, trans. Ben Brewster (New York: Monthly Review Press, 2001), p. 81.

20. Louis Althusser, *For Marx*, trans. Ben Brewster (London: Verso, 2006 [original French publication: 1965]). p. 71.

21. Thomas Kuhn, *The Structure of Scientific Revolutions, Third Edition* (Chicago: The University of Chicago Press, 1996 [original publication: 1962]), pp. 122–3.

22. Louis Althusser and Étienne Balibar, *Reading Capital*, trans. Ben Brewster (London: Verso, 2009), p. 28.

23. Joel Reed, 'Althusser and Hume', in Stephen H. Daniel (ed.), *Current Continental Theory and Modern Philosophy* (Evanston: Northwestern University Press, 2005), p. 213.

24. Althusser and Balibar, *Reading Capital*, pp. 36–40.

25. Althusser, *For Marx*, p. 41.

26. Ibid., p. 38.

27. Ibid., p. 228.

28. Ibid., p. 40.

29. See Lecourt, *Marxism and Epistemology*, p. 53.

30. Althusser and Balibar, *Reading Capital*, p. 42.

31. Ibid., p. 45.
32. Robert Paul Resch, *Althusser and the Renewal of Marxist Social Theory* (Berkeley: University of California Press, 1992), p. 181.
33. Althusser and Balibar, *Reading Capital*, p. 47.
34. Ibid., p. 68.
35. Ibid., p. 56.
36. Alex Callinicos, *Althusser's Marxism* (London: Pluto Press, 1996), pp. 76–7.
37. Louis Althusser, *The Humanist Controversy and Other Writings*, ed. François Matheron, trans. G. M. Goshgarian (London: Verso, 2003), pp. 1–18. The text referred to here was written in 1966.
38. Althusser and Balibar, *Reading Capital*, p. 64.
39. The genealogical continuities between Althusser, Badiou and Meillassoux are elaborated in Nathan Coombs, *History and Event: From Marxism to Contemporary French Theory* (Edinburgh: Edinburgh University Press, 2015), Part II.
40. See Alain Badiou, *Being and Event*, trans. Oliver Feltham (London and New York: Bloomsbury, 2007).
41. Quentin Meillassoux, 'Excerpts from *L'inexistence Divine*', trans. Graham Harman, in Graham Harman, *Quentin Meillassoux: Philosophy in the Making* (Edinburgh: Edinburgh University Press, 2011), pp. 175–238.
42. Gabriel Catren, 'A Throw of the Dice Will Never Abolish the Copernican Revolution', in Damian Veal (ed.), *Collapse V: The Copernican Imperative* (Falmouth: Urbanomic, 2012), pp. 455–502.
43. Louis Althusser, *Essays in Self-Criticism*, trans. Grahame Locke (London: NLB, 1976), p. 106.
44. Ibid., pp. 123–4.
45. Ibid., p. 124.
46. Paul Feyerabend, *Against Method, Third Edition* (London: Verso, 1993).
47. Althusser, *Lenin and Philosophy*; and Louis Althusser, *Philosophy and the Spontaneous Philosophy of the Scientists and Other Essays*, trans. Gregory Elliott (London: Verso Books, 2011).
48. Jacques Rancière objects pointedly to this assumption. He alleges that Althusserian philosophy was used as a discourse to reassert order in the universities after the 1968 student revolts. For Rancière, Althusser accords science neutrality only because for him 'class struggle is not already there, for example, in the social function of the scientific institution and its concomitant modes of selection ... in the double relationship scientific activity entertains with power and with the masses. All of this is replaced by a class struggle conceived through the opposition between a materialist element originating in science and an idealist element intrinsic to it' (*Althusser's Lesson*, trans. Emiliano Battista [London: Continuum, 2011], p. 63). Gregory Elliott also

demurs: 'The imputation of a spontaneous materialism to the proletariat integral to the "representative" function of Marxist philosophy is at best implausible' (*Althusser*, p. 188).

49. See Roy Bhaskar, *A Realist Theory of Science* (Hassocks: The Harvester Press, 1975).

50. The foundational text of Harman's philosophy is *Tool-Being: Heidegger and the Metaphysics of Objects* (Chicago: Open Court, 2002). In this essay I focus on Brassier's work in recognition of Peter Wolfendale's penetrating critique of Harman's object-oriented philosophy and because of my own concerns about the repercussions of Harman's philosophy throughout the humanities. See Peter Wolfendale, *Object-Oriented Philosophy: The Noumenon's New Clothes* (Falmouth: Urbanomic, 2014). Although Harman has been careful to distinguish his realism from materialism, interpreting the latter as reducing objects to their smallest atomic components and denying reality to composites, his philosophy has emboldened some political thinkers to stake a claim to the term by way of phenomenology. Foremost among this tendency are the 'new materialists': see Diana Coole and Samantha Frost (eds), *New Materialisms: Ontology, Agency, and Politics* (Durham, NC: Duke University Press, 2010). As catalogued by Nathan Brown in his review of Timothy Morton's *Realist Magic*, the result of such thinkers' abandonment of prudence in their engagement with science is a litany of nonsensical statements browbeating the reader unfamiliar with the primary scientific material: see Nathan Brown, 'The Nadir of OOO: From Graham Harman to Timothy Morton's Realist Magic: Objects, Ontology, Causality (Open Humanities Press, 2013)', *Parrhesia* 17 (2013): 62–71.

51. Sellars, 'Scientific Image', p. 6.

52. Ibid., p. 7.

53. Ibid., p. 9.

54. Ray Brassier, *Nihil Unbound: Enlightenment and Extinction* (Basingstoke: Palgrave Macmillan, 2007).

55. Ibid., p. 25.

56. Ibid., p. 31.

57. The key work is Robert Brandom, *Making It Explicit: Reasoning, Representing, and Discursive Commitment* (Cambridge, MA: Harvard University Press, 1994).

58. Brassier, 'Concepts and Objects'.

59. Ray Brassier, 'That Which Is Not: Philosophy as Entwinement of Truth and Negativity', *Stasis Journal* 1 (2013): 182.

60. I must caution that Brassier is not entirely clear about what he takes from Sellars. Consequently, my reading of Brassier's Sellarsianism is a somewhat speculative reconstruction. I also do not take account of Brassier's arguments drawing on the work of Robert Brandom. These are the inevitable drawbacks

of attempting to capture a philosopher's ideas in motion before they have been systematized, as is promised by Brassier's forthcoming book(s).

61. Wilfrid Sellars, *Empiricism and the Philosophy of Mind* (Cambridge, MA: Harvard University Press, 1997).

62. Wilfrid Sellars, 'Conceptual Change', in *Essays in Philosophy and Its History* (Dordrecht: D. Reidel, 1974), pp. 172–88. See also Harold I. Brown, 'Sellars, Concepts and Conceptual Change', *Synthese* 68 (1986): 275–307.

63. For a systematic presentation of Sellars's philosophy of science that puts it into dialogue with Kuhn and Feyerabend, see Joseph C. Pitt, *Pictures, Images, and Conceptual Change: An Analysis of Wilfrid Sellars' Philosophy of Science* (Dordrecht: D. Reidel, 1981).

64. Wilfrid Sellars, *Science and Metaphysics: Variations on Kantian Themes* (London: Routledge & Kegan Paul, 1963), pp. 133–9.

65. Ibid., p. 134.

66. Steven M. Levine, 'The Place of Picturing in Sellars' Synoptic Vision', *The Philosophical Forum* (2007): 247–69.

67. Sellars, *Science and Metaphysics*, p. 137.

68. Ibid., p. 138.

69. Ray Brassier, 'Nominalism, Naturalism, and Materialism: Sellars's Critical Ontology', in Bana Bashour and Hans D. Muller (eds), *Contemporary Philosophical Naturalism and Its Implications* (New York: Routledge, 2014), p. 102.

70. Brassier, 'Concepts and Objects', p. 64.

71. Sellars, *Science and Metaphysics*, p. 138.

72. For a welcome encounter between speculative and critical realism, see the following exchange: Fabio Gironi, 'A New Realist Landscape', *Journal of Critical Realism* 11(3) (October 2012): 361–87; Alison Assiter, 'Speculative and Critical Realism', *Journal of Critical Realism* 12(3) (July 2013): 283–300.

73. Roy Bhaskar, 'Feyerabend and Bachelard: Two Philosophies of Science', *New Left Review* I(94) (December 1975): 55; Michael Sprinker, 'The Royal Road: Marxism and the Philosophy of Science', *New Left Review* I(191) (February 1992): 122–44.

74. Roy Bhaskar, *The Possibility of Naturalism: A Philosophical Critique of the Contemporary Human Sciences, Third Edition* (London: Routledge, 1998).

75. Bhaskar, *A Realist Theory of Science*, p. 10.

76. Ibid., p. 29.

77. Ibid., p. 26.

78. Bhaskar, *The Possibility of Naturalism*, chapter two.

79. See Dave Elder-Vass, *The Causal Power of Social Structures: Emergence, Structure and Agency* (Cambridge: Cambridge University Press, 2010).

80. For examples of how complexity theory and critical realism have contributed to empirical studies, see David Byrne and Gillian Callaghan, *Complexity Theory and the Social Sciences: The State of the Art* (London: Routledge, 2013).
81. Brassier, 'Concepts and Objects', p. 59.
82. Ibid., p. 54.
83. See Michael Freeden, *Ideologies and Political Theory: A Conceptual Approach* (Oxford: Clarendon, 1996).
84. See Ray Brassier, 'On Prometheanism and its Critics', in Robin Mackay and Armen Avanessian (eds), *#accelerate: The Accelerationist Reader* (Falmouth: Urbanomic, 2014), pp. 467–88.

CHAPTER 10
FORMALISM, MATERIALISM AND CONSCIOUSNESS
Dorothea Olkowski

Introduction: Formalization and scientific systems

In *Postmodern Philosophy and the Scientific Turn,* I used the phrase 'the scientific turn' to characterize a philosophical paradigm widely utilized in twentieth-century Continental philosophy but which, I argue, originated primarily in analytic philosophy as a turn toward the language of *logic,* and toward discrete and formal computation in the philosophy of language and philosophy of mind.[1] I made the claim that a number of significant postmodern philosophers and theorists embraced this turn, but that among these theorists it is referred to as the *linguistic* turn, and that the linguistic turn, like its correlate in analytic philosophy, finds its theoretical roots in a methodology broadly construed as mathematical or logical formalism. What I would like to do in this essay is to briefly discuss the nature of formalism, and then to focus on its relationship to materialism in order to ask if it is the case, as some newly emerging neomaterialist claims coming from Continental philosophy imply, that formal brain mechanisms and the matter of the brain will ultimately suffice to explain all psychologically described phenomena.[2] I pursue this route in order to ask to how it is that postmodern philosophy seems to have given rise to materialism in contemporary Continental philosophy and because it appears to me that it is important to address the sudden rise of materialism in Continental thought, especially its negative relation to consciousness. Although poststructuralist and postmodern philosophies have been willing to set aside consciousness along with the idea of the subject, phenomenology in general has not. The impact of materialist critiques on phenomenology must then be taken into account.

The move toward formalist thinking had numerous originators, among them Bernhard Bolzano (1741–1848), who argued that science is a demonstrated theory that dispenses with verification. According to Jean Cavaillès, this means that science is independent of both the human mind and being in itself, and it becomes an 'object *sui generis*'.³ This is not a trivial conclusion, for it indicates that science is not one object among others in a cultural milieu but that it is autonomous, capable of generating its own intelligible elements. Different sciences are unified by their common inclusion in this one system, 'a self-enclosed dynamism' without beginning or end that is therefore outside of time; in particular, it is outside of the 'lived experience of a consciousness'.⁴ What this establishes is that science is seen to be an unending and unstoppable conceptual becoming, independent of what the scientist herself understands.

As Cavaillès states, for all the natural sciences, including the biological sciences, 'growth occurs without external borrowing … [thus] there is a break between sensation or right opinion, and science'.⁵ This is why the structure of science is and only can be demonstration defined as logic, 'the internal rule which directs it posits each of its steps', as well as its essential traits: unity, necessary indefinite progression and closure upon itself.⁶ However, unlike the logical positivists, Cavaillès does not accept the idea that the theory of science is logic alone, for that position ends up abandoning even truth as correspondence and leaves only a coherence theory, which stipulates that so called 'atomic' statements or judgements of perception – the reported sensations of a particular observer at a specific moment in time, formerly said to be irrefutable and therefore foundational – are really only the result of syntactical commitments, that is, the arrangement of signs.⁷ The general problem with this approach is that syntactical formalization cannot complete itself by itself; it cannot help but refer to objects, so the system is not in fact self-enclosed.⁸ For philosophers like Cavaillès, the logic of a formal system requires an ontology to complete it; that is, in addition to the formal system it requires that there is a reference to an exteriority, to objects, and not just to other signs in the system.⁹ But for hardened formalists 'all external questions are "metaphysical" and therefore nonsensical', the 'external' referring only to systems of signs or, at most, to marks on paper and foregoing the necessity that signs are not objects and imply a reference to an external actuality.¹⁰

This is a problem to which postmodern philosophers sought to find a solution. Here, a bit of historical information may be revelatory. Cavaillès, a leader of the French Resistance, was captured and after several escapes recaptured, then murdered in 1944 by the Nazis.¹¹ Georges Canguilhem, who was both a friend and colleague, was recruited into the Resistance by Cavaillès, where he served as a medical doctor. After Cavaillès's death, Canguilhem wrote a book on the work and life of Cavaillès.

In 1948, Canguilhem became the director of the *Institut d'histoire des sciences* at the Sorbonne. 'Canguilhem also served from 1964 to 1968 as the President of the *Jury d'Agrégation* in philosophy, which provided him an institutional influence over the teaching of philosophy and which helped consolidate the future influence of students.'[12] Among these students were Gilles Deleuze, Michel Foucault, Louis Althusser and Jacques Derrida. With this in mind, we might want to look more closely at ideas developed by Cavaillès that seem to have made their way into the work of postmodern philosophers.

Although Cavaillès stood in opposition to logical positivism, he is thought to have been influenced by the mathematician David Hilbert's formalism.[13] Both argue that the truth of mathematics is in the demonstration, in the *method* of mathematics, so that science cannot be the product of the intentions of scientists. It is rather science itself that demonstrates what is true or not, so 'the credit should and does go to *science itself*.'[14] Thus, mathematical objects – such as the square root of -1 – are merely the product of the mathematical system that produces them and outside of this formal-linguistic context they are meaningless. They represent no idea until and unless such formulations become objects of study.[15]

If mathematical language extends itself, introducing its own formal idealizations, then the universe of mathematical objects is always in the process of formation, a conceptual becoming that cannot be stopped, that will always be beyond the reach of individuals.[16] As the mathematician Vladimir Tasić points out, the same thing can be said about 'truth', especially the claim that 'all truth changes all the time', a statement that cannot itself be proven to be true since no formal language can formulate its own theory of truth, and even higher concepts of truth are needed to do this.[17] The implication is that if mathematics is always and endlessly formulating its own object, mathematical truth cannot possibly be formulated by finite human understanding. Gödel's famous incompleteness theorem expresses this by claiming that higher concepts will have to be continued into the transfinite, part of a conceptual continuum that never ends.[18] Yet even Gödel notes that such concepts are put to the test, judged in human practice, in the lifeworld, in the cultural, social and intellectual milieu. Let us now turn to an examination of how this is done in mathematical formalism, and how this might have led to neomaterialist philosophical positions.

The structure of science

Cavaillès's chosen task seems to have been to reconcile formal logic with worldly applications. 'Through the detour of abstract axiomatics, the formalist elevates himself to the general theory of formal systems and succeeds in constituting systems in which the structure has completely eliminated the content.'[19] For this reason Cavaillès rejected at least some aspects of Edmund Husserl's account of the relation between mathematics and the physical world which, for Cavaillès, remained too much embedded in such a logical empiricism. Essentially, if it is the case that 'physical theory is simply an empty mathematical form applied to the invariant intuitive contents of the lifeworld', then mathematics does not truly augment our knowledge of the lifeworld, but rather merely idealizes our power to predict.[20] In other words, this is the old problem of the Kantian schematism that is supposed to bring together an empirical intuition and a radically heterogeneous concept.

Cavaillès thought he could do better. Thus, he proposed that matter or content is unintelligible without its concept, so the condition and the conditioned must be within one system, and the connection between them is realized anew in a 'conceptual becoming that cannot be halted'.[21] As Cavaillès argues, science cannot be the intermediary between the human mind and the empirical world. Science is not a cultural object. 'Now science is regarded as an object *sui generis*, original in its essence, autonomous in its movement.'[22] Furthermore, science is unified and its unity is the 'self-enclosed dynamism' that is outside of the lived experience of consciousness, a conceptual becoming that cannot be stopped. Experience is thereby the incorporation of the world into the scientific universe.[23] This means that the assertions of science appear as the 'self-illumination of the scientific movement', and that the structure of science simply 'speaks about itself'. It is demonstration; a unified, necessary and indefinite progression.[24]

Although at this point I can see significant resonances between the position of Husserl, that of Gilles Deleuze, Cavaillès, and that of Michel Foucault, it is more productive for my purposes here to turn directly to the neomaterialist position of Quentin Meillassoux who, without mentioning Cavaillès in his texts or placing his work in the bibliography of his primary book, *After Finitude,* nevertheless seems to have followed Cavaillès to a rather high degree. Like Cavaillès, Meillassoux formulates his thesis in opposition to Kant. He proclaims the existence of worldly manifestations that arose prior to human existence, and that may continue after human extinction, so as to reveal a temporal discrepancy between thinking and being, between what is known and what exists.[25]

This is a discrepancy that arises with modern science because it is only insofar as the formalist mathematization of nature has come to define modern science that this question has even been raised.[26] This discrepancy rests originally on the fact that science is not based on simple observations but on data that has been produced, processed and quantified by increasingly elaborate measuring instruments.[27] Meillassoux renders this statement in the context of another distinction, the distinction between inorganic matter and life, and this distinction reinstates an older one, the distinction between primary and secondary qualities. Primary qualities are inseparable from the object and belong to things. The modern modification is that primary qualities can be formulated in mathematical terms.[28] Secondary qualities are affective or perceptual, and so exist only as a relation between things and living beings.[29]

The division between life and matter, the organic and inorganic is hard and fast for Meillassoux, and does not take into account either the physics of energy and matter or evolutionary biology. Matter or the inorganic appears to be anything that is not life, such as the luminous emission of a star or an isotope undergoing radioactive decay.[30] Scientific statements about matter can be formulated as mathematical data, for example, that the earth began occupying a certain volume that varied through time, starting 4.56 billion years ago. The claim is that it is safe to assume that statements backed by mathematical data are true unless and until the theory that produced this data is replaced by more elegant or accurate theories.[31] This 'realist attitude' is set forth as normal and natural for the scientist, as well as the ultimate regime of meaning for understanding matter.[32] Like Cavaillès, who opposes the Kantian a priori, Meillassoux objects to what he calls the correlationalist position in Kant and Husserl. The correlationist is a philosopher who maintains that it is impossible to hold the realms of subjectivity and objectivity as independent of one another.[33] In other words, correlationalism is when events take place for thought, *for a thinker*.

The first objection Meillassoux anticipates from the correlationalist, whom he characterizes as an idealist, is that if there had been a witness to the origin and emergence of the planet earth, this occurrence would have been perceived in the manner the data tells us it did occur. The origin of the earth is no different, in fact, from a vase that falls off a shelf and breaks in a room where *no one sees or hears it*.[34] What is different, however, for

Meillassoux is that the origin of the earth is an event anterior to human terrestrial life, and hence, anterior to givenness, to perception or thought. It is a nongiven, an unwitnessed occurrence, that is not of the time of consciousness but another time, the time of 'science' which engenders – that is gives rise to or makes possible – the time of consciousness and of life.[35]

Meillassoux's position leads him to ask how is it that 'mathematical discourse [is] able to describe a world where humanity is absent, a world crammed with the things and events that are not the correlates of any manifestation ... not the correlate of a relation to the world'?[36] Mathematical discourse is described as a *temporal discrepancy* between thinking and being with respect to *statements* about events prior to and after the existence of human beings.[37] It is a question, then, about *scientific discourse*, about which statements can be verified or falsified, and how throughout his discussion Meillassoux, like Cavaillès, refers to what 'science' has discovered or said: 'Science could have discovered a synchronicity between humanity and the world'; or, 'if science had discovered this synchronicity it would still have been a *discovery*'; or, that it is 'the capacity of scientific discourse which concerns us'.[38]

Modern science arose when its statements became part of a cognitive process and when these statements became hypotheses able to be corroborated by experiments as instances of knowledge. All of this is part of the *discourse* of empirical science and its rational debate is what 'science made it meaningful to debate' and 'to disagree about'.[39] This argument continues until there is eventually an acknowledgement that even though science gives the means to rationally favour one hypothesis over another to humans it is, in the end, human beings who do the rational favouring.[40] In other words, this argument inevitably collapses because something is, in the end, being thought, some choice is made, and so speculative materialism is not the inevitable remainder. Except possibly along some narrow cultural extremes, it seems largely indisputable that whatever is mathematically conceivable is certainly possible, but declaring it absolutely possible has the effect, in this case, of using this claim to an absolute status to rule out theories of consciousness without positing an alternative to how something can be thought without consciousness. Moreover, the claim that whatever is mathematizable can be posited *hypothetically* as existing independently of humans seems to be uncontroversial and is generally acknowledged.

Given this, what we might wish to pay attention to here is that, in spite of Meillassoux's admission that Kant radically promoted science over metaphysics, too many *philosophers* have veered away from speculative materialism toward transcendental idealism.[41] It seems that speculative materialism presents us with a dichotomy: either speculative materialism or correlationalism. That is, *either* thought now thinks the events that occurred prior to all thought (because science gives it) *or* the events occurred prior to the existence of thought but *for thought* through the necessary a priori *forms* by which a thinking being thinks. The question is: what would be necessary with respect to human thinking for Meillassoux's thesis to hold? The apparent claim that something occurred for thought before there was any thought just seems to be exaggerated, and surely no Kantian or Husserlian would make this sort of claim. So, we can ask, is Meillassoux asserting a false dichotomy by exaggerating the claims of philosophers whose position he opposes?

We might also ask if these positions leave Meillassoux subject to the same unanswered questions as the analytic philosophers of mind. Like those materialists Meillassoux has no coherent account of psychological processes of the mind including thoughts, beliefs, desires and sensory experience, as he refers only to cognitive processes and, like the philosophers of mind, he offers no convenient explanation for how psychological phenomena are related to physical systems, either causally or functionally. Nor does Meillassoux tell us how it is possible for material phenomena to give rise to conscious states understood as subjective qualities. In fact, these considerations are precisely the ones that Meillassoux is eager to eliminate by claiming that aspects of objects formulable in mathematical terms – such as length, width, movement, depth, figure and size – are purely properties of the object in itself and have nothing to do with any subject's relation to the world.[42] Similarly, as he states, the truth or falsity of a physical law is not established with regard to human existence – a conclusion that is indicative of why philosophy is defined by him primarily, if not exclusively, as the invention by philosophy of strange forms of argumentation, making use of internal mechanisms for regulating its own inferences and eliminating the inadequacies of reasoning.[43] This is particularly evidenced in his extensive argument against the Christian dogmatist and the agnostic, which leads him to the conclusion that there are no necessary entities, only necessary contingency; and – perhaps more telling – that following the example of paraconsistent logic, at least some contradictory statements are necessary.[44]

In choosing this route, Meillassoux has accomplished at least one thing in particular: he has released philosophy from dependence on any and all versions of subjectivity insofar as they all treat something abstract, something conceptual, as if it were concrete reality. Included in this list are

Formalism, Materialism and Consciousness

Leibniz's monad, Schelling's Nature, Hegel's Mind, Schopenhauer's Will, Nietzsche's Will to Power, Bergson's ontological memory and Deleuze's conception of Life. For each of these concepts, the contention is that there is no separation between the act of thinking and its content, a position contrary to the speculative realist position, that absolute reality is an entity without thought. Thus, thought is not necessary insofar as we can think a given reality by abstracting from the fact that we are thinking it but because thought, on this account, is random and immanent to 'contingent atomic compounds'.[45] In propositional logic, an atomic statement such as 'A' is said to affirm its own truth, and all atomic sentences are purely contingent. Compound atomic sentences are built from atomic sentences using sentence connectives.[46] As Ken C. Klement put it,

> propositional logic does not study those logical properties and relations that depend upon parts of statements that are not themselves statements on their own. This would include parts such as the subject and predicate of a statement, because simple statements are considered to be indivisible wholes, thus are not divisible into subject and predicate.[47]

With this, we enter the realm of axiomatic systems, a set of properties that are consistent, thus contain no contradiction, from which other properties may be derived.[48] Nevertheless, given Cantor's theorem, that the cardinal number of any set is lower than the cardinal number of the set of all its subsets, these systems or sets are never complete, never able to be totalized.[49] Cardinality refers to the size of a set, not the order of its members, and if two sets each have an infinite number of elements, one may have a greater cardinality, which is to say that one may have a 'more infinite' number of elements and is therefore called the *transfinite* or an aleph, without reaching an absolute infinity.[50] One may construct an unlimited series of infinite sets, each of which is some quantity superior to that of the set whose parts it collects together, but the series can never be totalized, never brought to an end as this or that ultimate quantity. Using Cantor's concept of the transfinite, the quantifiable totality of what *is* thinkable cannot be thought without falling into contradiction and therefore cannot be said to even exist.[51]

Meillassoux admits that other systems are entirely possible, that standard set-theory is only one among many, but we have no way of knowing if any of them would guarantee necessity. Nevertheless, set-theory thinks the transfinite, the possible as untotalizable. Meillassoux thinks or assumes the truth of this system, which allows him to cease believing in the existence of necessary physical laws as opposed to mere stability. Thus Kant is scolded for claiming that, absent the transcendental ground of unity or, in other words, the claim that conceivable possibilities constitute a totality, there would be no knowledge. Kant bases this on a pre-Cantorian application of the calculus of probability to the world as a whole. If it is the case that the possible either does or does not constitute a totality, there is nothing to prevent one from choosing the latter and concluding that physical laws carry no necessity but are merely stable.[52]

Mind-brain interaction

Meillassoux states repeatedly that *science gives the discourse of empirical science* to cognition. Science relies on self-evident axioms that are consistent but seem not to originate with the human mind since they are given to cognition to think. How is it possible for science to be the structure that gives cognition its thoughts? If it is possible, what are the implications and what does this imply? Contemporary neuropsychological research frequently puts forth the thesis that the brain consists of material particles and fields that ultimately explain all mental phenomena. Thus terms like *feeling*, *knowing* and *effort* play no role; they are not 'primary causal factors'.[53] This view has been amplified by brain-imaging technology, which has correlated areas of the brain with a large number of mental activities including learning, memory and symbol manipulation. This has led many scientists to conclude that such measurable properties of physical brain mechanisms are all that is needed to explain mental or psychological events.[54] In part, this is due to the classical physical models that have been used to understand the functional activity of the brain.

According to these models, all causal connections between observables are explainable in terms of mechanical interactions between material realities, an effect of experimental paradigms that focus primarily on changes in brain activation as primary variables used to explain observable behavioural changes in subjects who are primarily passive in the experimental situation.[55] These situations reinforce the supposition set out above, that *science gives the discourse of empirical science* to cognition, and subsequently the material activation of the limbic system, the hypothalamus, the thalamus and subthalamus structures generates emotion and memory, while activation of the cerebral cortex generates thought, language and consciousness.

Although Meillassoux argues that nature's laws are merely stable, and not absolute, this does not mean that they are not deterministic, meaning that the state of the physical world of matter at one time determines the state of the physical world at a future time although not necessarily absolutely. Of course physics must make use of mathematical models for the sake of intelligibility. Thus, a physical system defined by *deterministic chaos* is relatively indeterminate because even though the laws governing the field do not alter, there is an indeterminacy regarding which elements in the field will interact with one another, making predictability more difficult. It is true that cosmologists such as Lee Smolin have posited that when working on 'the theory of spacetime and quantum space ... we draw pictures which are networks of relations and how they change in time and our pictures look just like pictures of ecological networks that these people study'.[56] Smolin hypothesizes that there is a deep relation between Einstein's notion that everything is just a network of relations and Darwin's notion of an ecological community as a network of individuals and species in relationships which evolve. But the question remains: is such a model necessarily materialist?

Perhaps of greater importance in Meillassoux's model is that brains seem to be mechanical, the effect of material interactions governed by physical laws or forces. Emotion and cognition are redundant, and intentions are misleading illusions. They are either epiphenomenal by-products of matter or they are identical with the patterns taking place in the brain; they are so-called emergent properties.[57] However, if it is possible within the conceptual framework of classical physics to take away consciousness while leaving intact the properties that enter into the materialist construct, namely the locations and motions of the tiny physical parts of the brain and its physical environment, then it is possible that materialism is either incomplete or simply incorrect.[58] As we can see, the problem remains that of the connection between the mathematical system, consciousness and the world; and, for us, that is a question of the relation between physics and philosophy.

It has been pointed out by neuroscientists that understanding the connections between phenomena in terms of the mechanical interactions of material entities conforms to the conception of the world developed by *classical* physics. However, 'terms such as "feeling", "knowing" and "effort", because they are intrinsically mentalistic and experiential, cannot be described exclusively in terms of material structure'.[59] The claim has been made, however, that human choices and intentions can be described more accurately by means of quantum-based theories. This, I would argue, is an approach that was signalled in Maurice Merleau-Ponty's early work, *The Structure of Behavior*.[60] There, Merleau-Ponty raises the question we have been asking here: how to understand the relation between behaviour and physical events? He takes up the question by introducing the concept of form: form for Merleau-Ponty is not a material, physical reality but an object of perception, a perceived whole, the 'empty x'. 'This unity is the unity of perceived objects .... It is encountered in physics only to the extent that physics refers us back to perceived things as to that which it is the function of science to express and determine.'[61]

In other words, for phenomenology physical form is not the foundation or cause of the structure of behaviour. It is rather an object of perception, which in this case is expressed as an idea. The physical form is an object of knowledge (the empty x) of the fields of force and the dynamic unities of perception: just as perceived objects change properties when they change place, so in the physical structure of, for example, system wave mechanics the wave associated with the entire system propagates itself in an abstract configurational space.[62]

A wave function is the mathematics that accounts for how a wave varies in space and time. It describes the probable values of the attributes of quantum objects, but the equation for calculating the quantum wave function 'has defied all attempts to give it an interpretation in terms of physically observable entities'.[63] Once an actual physical observation/measurement is made, the wave collapses into a single determinate value, yet no one seems to know why. Unlike system wave mechanics, classical science appears to have constructed the image of an absolute physical reality and then proposed that perceptual structures are simply manifestations or projections of this fundamental ontological foundation. But the phenomenological concept of form indicates that this is not so: although the laws of physical reality conceptualize the perceived world, reference to the perceived world is nevertheless essential to knowledge of the physical world.[64]

Werner Heisenberg discovered the first successful mathematical quantum theory in 1925. He postulated that quantum behaviour, which represents the unobserved world, must consist of 'possibility waves' – that is, when not observed, the world might exist as waves of possibility.[65] Atoms and elementary particles might form a world of potentialities or possibilities with numerous tendencies and not a world of determinate things. 'As long as they remain unobserved, events in the atomic world are strictly in the realm of possibility ... [but] because certain facts have become actual in our world, not everything is equally possible in the quantum world.'[66] It is only in the act of measurement, an act chosen and carried out by human beings with consciousness, that quantum possibility becomes an actual event.

But in addressing quantum physics, Merleau-Ponty wisely asks: 'what can one say, in a serious way, when one lacks technical competence?'[67] The philosopher, he concludes, can best address that moment where science connects with prescientific being, at the point where science requires an image of reality and a language that gives meaning to its formalist structures.[68] Merleau-Ponty therefore turns his attention to the question of probability in the standard model of quantum physical behaviour, stating that existing things such as particles or waves might best be taken not as individual but as generic or species behaviour.[69] More specifically, in the prequantum theory classical model, apparatuses utilized to measure the movement of atoms can still be understood to be 'prolongations of our senses ... a more precise sensoriality'.[70] That this is no longer the case for phenomena is nontrivial. The quantum measuring apparatus collapses the quantum wave into a particle provoking the appearance of a subatomic particle, fixing or sampling it in relation to the wave and leaving in question the gap between what is 'perceived' and what can be known, so that it appears to be the case that 'known nature is artificial nature' – that it is an effect of the measuring apparatus.[71]

But we must also be aware of the fact that the quantum measuring process involves the object to be measured, the measuring apparatus – both of which belong to the external world – and the observer herself who does not, who has a relationship with herself and whose observation and thought makes possible the emergence of an individual existence.[72] Merleau-Ponty recognizes that formalist accounts of physics allow a lot of freedom but signify no reality because as formalist systems they are in actuality a radical nominalism. Likewise, against what would amount to a materialist position like Meillassoux's, he argues that relations between reality and measurement must be conceptualized outside of the in-itself/representation dichotomy, thus outside of so-called correlationalism that Meillassoux attributes to phenomenology.[73]

What Merleau-Ponty calls for from a philosophy that corresponds to quantum physics is something both more realist – specifically, a philosophy *not* definable in transcendental terms – and more subjectivist, in the sense of a situated incarnate physicist who does not claim to be a universal and transcendental 'I think'.[74] Thus we may distinguish a plane of reality in which physical systems from a second plane of reality exist, that of the process of taking the measurement, and also a third plane, that of the structure independent of the measurement process and relative to the species being studied. Because the structural relations refer to the mathematical forms needed to describe the relations of the subject to the object and also to the theory in which they intervene as the schematism of the relation between observers and objects, this structure is for Merleau-Ponty 'comparable to the Platonic objectivity of the idea vis-à-vis its sensible realizations'.[75]

Once again, this conception of structure takes us back to the perceived thing, not as a finished product but in its full ambiguity, which would affirm that there are ambiguous beings that are neither waves nor particles. If we accept, for example, that the perceived wind is 'a continuation of movement without mobiles, of behaviors without subjects' then what is perceived are beings that are probable, indeterminate, negative (defined by their absence) and neither infinite nor finite.[76] Why is this the case? Because nothing about the scale of particles or waves can be understood without the existence of an incarnate subject whose perceptual experience includes the experience of space as ambiguous and thus not as an immediate given.[77]

Although Merleau-Ponty does not express his conceptualization of quantum theory in terms of what I will clarify as Intuitionist logic, his position nevertheless appears to me to able to be commensurate with that of physicist Fotini Markopolou, whose work I utilized in both *The Universal (In the Realm of the Sensible)* and in *Postmodern Philosophy and the Scientific Turn*. Markopolou characterizes her work as the effort to describe what the universe looks like from *inside,* eschewing formalist mathematical logic in favour of Intuitionism. She proposes a causal structure of space-time, the view from inside, meaning, what an observer inside the universe can observe.[78] Arguing against classical models precisely because they lead to uncertainty, Markopoulou suggests utilizing causal sets, that is, large collections of events in discrete space-time partially ordered by temporal causal relations. Moreover, Markopoulou proposes to work with evolving sets that bring the causal past of each event as well as the causal structure of each event into a causal set. She further suggests that evolving sets satisfy a particular algebra called Heyting algebra, which utilizes a nonstandard logic whose historical development has been related to understanding the passage of time. Intuitionistic logic does not adhere to the Law of Excluded Middle. Whereas the classical Boolean mathematician believes that a statement x is true or false whether or not she has proof for it, Intuitionism does not allow proof by contradiction. From the onset, it does not consider x to be true or false unless there is a proof for it. In other words, without a proof the option is open as to whether x may be true tomorrow or false tomorrow. Intuitionistic logic is thus suited to time evolution, where certain physical statements become true at a certain time.[79]

This logic appears to correspond to Merleau-Ponty's critique of the logic of classical physics. Quantum physics is probabilistic – that is, for objects with tiny masses and sizes such as atoms and molecules the statistical distribution of energy microstates in a system can be predicted but not that of individual particles. Thus quantum can be said to be ambiguous or indeterminate where this means *uncertain*, revealing not realities, but two phantoms, the particle and the wave.[80] The problem lies in thinking that classical Boolean logic is the only valid logic and that the physical incompossibility of particle and wave is equivalent to and determined by logical incompossibility in a logical discourse in which the law is that of existence and nonexistence, and the passage from one to the other, the movement of time and change, the open future, the nonexcluded middle, is forgotten. It is the limitation of classical logic to consider only positive determinations and to be blind to the temporal movement that is change.[81] The latter is a logic of ambiguity; it is still a logic but temporal and probabilistic, as we have defined this above.

What becomes crucial here for the reconceptualization of quantum physics as prescribed by Merleau-Ponty is that 'a theory with internal observables is fundamentally different than a theory describing a system external to the observers' insofar as this theory refers to observations made from 'inside'.[82] For physicists, this means inside the universe, a point of view from which such observations can only be partial. That is, they contain information that is in the causal past of an observer in a particular region of spacetime but, significantly, they do not contain predictions, meaning information about the future, information that should be obtainable from a classical dynamical perspective. When this partiality is represented in terms of light cones – light rays that form the outer boundary of the past in roughly the shape of a cone – information that constitutes a particular point of view is shown to be the effect of mutually influencing and overlapping light cones. If the causal past of an event consists of all the events that could have influenced it, these influences travel from some state in the past at the speed of light or less. The light rays arriving at an event form the outer boundary of the past of an event and make up the past light cone of an event. Under these conditions, the causal structure of states evolves and the motion of matter is a consequence of that evolution. Here we have the Intuitionist conception according to which intuition is a process of building or constructing, a time-bound process beginning in the past, existing in the present and evolving into an open future.

Because the information from the past evolving as the present into an open future occurs on the quantum scale, the scale of photons, the world can be said to be composed of discrete states that may be on a very small scale but are nevertheless discrete in space and time. Under such conditions, what might be observed? Called spin network graphs, representations of mutually influencing and overlapping light cones have been used to model spatial geometry in quantum physics as well as evolving events in a causal set, yielding a quantum causal history.[83] Unlike other models, one significant implication of these graphs is that the manifold of space-time is not pregiven. Rather than a dynamically changing form of content and form of expression taking place in a preestablished space-time manifold yet produced or assembled from outside by the elements of that manifold, the model of quantum causal histories specifies that space-time and the states that evolve – the stage and the actors – evolve together.[84] This is particularly useful for the exploration of states that occur at the Planck scale of quantum states where classical physics fails; in addition, it allows for the construction of a point of view that is not that of an atomistic individual but of a network. *It is a point of view according to which different observers 'see' or 'live' partly different, partial views of the universe – partial views that nonetheless overlap.*

What I have been pursuing throughout my work is the possibility that this structure and these processes might involve the participation of vulnerable and sensitive beings in an ontological spatiotemporalization, an ever-changing perspective made up of a crowd of perspectives in the heterogeneity of space and time. Such a perspective, if it is thinkable, if it is real, could manifest itself as a sort of history; but is more like a complex causality – layers and layers of states always susceptible to realignment, its patterns and particles resolving in a point of view that is the effect of a crowd of influences and itself contributing to a crowd of influences. These light rays, conical flows of information that are often imperceptible, influence one another and in this they influence the sensibility of all things.

As models of quantum consciousness proliferate, it is my hope that they will supplant the rough materialism favoured today in philosophy as well as in some quarters of natural science. If it is the case, as John von Neumann posited in the 1930s, that the quantum physical world consists of nothing but possibility waves, then the collapse of the wave function requires something outside of the physical realm. If that something truly is, as von Neumann concluded, consciousness, then the world remains in a state of possibilities except wherever a conscious mind takes the measure of that world and actualizes it.

Notes

1. Vladimir Tasić, *Mathematics and the Roots of Postmodern Thought* (Oxford: Oxford University Press, 2001), pp. 27, 31.
2. Jeffrey M Schwartz, Henry P. Stapp and Mario Beauregard, 'Quantum Physics in Neuroscience and Psychology: A Neurophysical Model of Mind–Brain Interaction', *Philosophical Transactions of the Royal Society B* 360 (2005): 1309.
3. Jean Cavaillès, 'On Logic and the Theory of Science', trans. Theodore J. Kisiel, in Theodore J. Kisiel and Joseph J. Kockelmans (eds), *Phenomenology and the Natural Sciences: Essays and Translations* (Evanston: Northwestern University Press, 1970), pp. 370–1.
4. Ibid., pp. 371–2.
5. Ibid., p. 372.
6. Ibid., p. 373.
7. Ibid., p. 350. As Kirk Ludwig remarks, such statements are called 'protocol sentences':

    If we want to know whether a given sentence is meaningful or not, we must decide whether or not we associate with it a method of verification, for the meaning of a sentence lies in the method that we would employ to verify or falsify it. This means that we must specify the conditions under which it would be possible to verify the sentence. In stating what those conditions are, of course, we must use sentences. Unless we want to be involved in an infinite regress (or a circle), there must be some sentences that we can verify directly, which will then form the foundation for verifying other sentences. Those sentences are the protocol sentences. Protocol sentences were taken (initially at least) to express conditions whose obtaining or not is directly verifiable. ('Carnap, Neurath, and Schlick on protocol sentences'. Available from http://www.clas.ufl.edu/users/ludwig/PHP5785/set8%202009.pdf [accessed 7 January 2013].)

8. Cavaillès, 'On Logic', p. 350.
9. Ibid., p. 350.
10. Ibid., p. 350.
11. Peter Hallward, *Concept and Form: The* Cahiers pour l'Analyse *and Contemporary French Thought*. Available from http://cahiers.kingston.ac.uk/names/cavailles.html [accessed 28 January 2015].
12. Ibid.

13. Tasić, *Mathematics*, p. 85.
14. Ibid., pp. 87–8. Emphasis added.
15. Ibid., pp. 86, 87
16. Ibid., pp. 88, 89.
17. Ibid., p. 88.
18. Ibid., p. 89, citing Kurt Gödel.
19. Jean Ladrière, 'Mathematics in a Philosophy of the Sciences', trans. Theodore J. Kisiel, in Kisiel and Kockelmans (eds), *Phenomenology*, p. 472.
20. Cavaillès, 'On Logic', p. 351.
21. Ibid., p. 360. See also Tasić, *Mathematics*, p. 86.
22. Cavaillès, 'On Logic', p. 371.
23. Ibid., p. 372.
24. Ibid., p. 373.
25. Quentin Meillassoux, *After Finitude: An Essay on the Necessity of Contingency*, trans. Ray Brassier (London: Continuum Books, 2008), p. 112.
26. Ibid., p. 113.
27. Ibid., p. 114.
28. Ibid., pp. 2–3. The distinction is explicitly that of John Locke's but Meillassoux traces it back to René Descartes as well.
29. Ibid., p. 2.
30. Ibid., p. 9.
31. Ibid., p. 12.
32. Ibid., p. 14.
33. Ibid., p. 5.
34. Ibid., p.19; I have simplified the argument for the sake of clarity.
35. Ibid., pp. 20–1.
36. Ibid., p. 26.
37. Ibid., p. 112.
38. Ibid., p. 113.
39. Ibid., p. 114.
40. Ibid., p. 114.
41. Ibid., pp. 120–1.
42. Ibid., p. 3.
43. Ibid., pp. 76–7.
44. Ibid., pp. 55–7, 64, 76–9. Full analysis of these arguments requires an essay in itself. We will therefore restrict our analysis to the more familiar arguments against causal necessity.

45. Ibid., pp. 36–7. What is here called 'Life' on Deleuze's behalf is presumably more usually referred to in Deleuze's own work as 'desire'.

46. Nancy A. Stanlick, 'Logic: Clarification of Terms and Concepts in Sentence Logic'. Available from http://pegasus.cc.ucf.edu/~stanlick/slterms.htm [accessed 28 January 2015].

47. Kevin C. Klement, 'Propositional Logic', *Internet Encyclopedia of Philosophy*. Available from http://www.iep.utm.edu/prop-log/ [accessed 28 January 2015].

48. Carl Lee, 'Axiomatic Systems', *Topics in Geometry*. Available from http://www.ms.uky.edu/~lee/ma341/chap1.pdf [accessed 10 January 2013].

49. Eric W. Weisstein, 'Cantor's Theorem', *MathWorld – A Wolfram Web Resource*. Available from http://mathworld.wolfram.com/CantorsTheorem.html [accessed 28 January 2015].

50. Aaron Krowne, 'Cardinality' (version 21), *PlanetMath.org*. Available from http://planetmath.org/ [accessed 10 January 2013].

51. Meillassoux, *After Finitude*, p. 104.

52. Ibid., p. 107.

53. Schwartz, Stapp and Beauregard, 'Neuroscience', p. 1.

54. Ibid., p. 2.

55. Ibid., pp. 3–4.

56. Lee Smolin, 'Cosmological Evolution', *Edge*. Available from http://edge.org/conversation/-cosmological-evolution [accessed 28 January 2015].

57. Schwartz, Stapp and Beauregard, 'Neuroscience', pp. 7–8.

58. Ibid., 'Neuroscience', p. 9.

59. Ibid., 'Neuroscience', p. 2.

60. Maurice Merleau-Ponty, *The Structure of Behavior*, trans. Alden L. Fisher (Boston: Beacon Press, 1967). Originally published in French as *La Structure du Comportment* (Paris: Presses Universitaires de France, 1942). Page references are given first to the English translation then the French original.

61. Ibid., p. 144/156; emphasis added.

62. Ibid., p. 144/156. This appears to be a reference to what mathematicians call 'state space'.

63. John Casti, *Complexification: Explaining a Paradoxical World Through the Science of Surprise* (New York: HarperCollins, 1994), pp. 205–6.

64. Merleau-Ponty, *The Structure of Behavior*, p. 145/157. This concept of form reverses the view of the natural sciences that perceptual reality is only a projection of an absolute physical reality.

65. Nick Herbert, *Elemental Mind, Human Consciousness, and the New Physics* (New York: Penguin Books, 1993), p. 157.

66. Herbert, *Elemental Mind*, pp. 158–9.

67. Maurice Merleau-Ponty, *Nature. Course Notes from the College de France,* trans. Robert Vallier, compiled by Dominique Séglard (Evanston: Northwestern University Press), p. 89. Originally published in French as *La Nature, Notes, Cours du Collège de France,* établi et annoté par Dominique Séglard (Paris: Éditions du Seuil, 1995), p. 125. Page references are given first to the English translation then the French original.

68. Ibid., p. 90/125.

69. Ibid., p. 92/128.

70. Ibid., p. 93/129–30.

71. Ibid., p. 93/130.

72. Ibid., p. 94/130–1.

73. Ibid., p. 96/133.

74. Ibid., p. 97/134.

75. Ibid., p. 98/136.

76. Ibid., p. 99/137.

77. Ibid., pp. 99–100/137.

78. Fotini Markopoulou, 'The internal description of a causal set: What the universe looks like from inside', *Communications in Mathematical Physics,* 211, (2000): 559–83. Available from http://arxiv.org/pdf/gr-qc/9811053.pdf [accessed 28 January 2015].

79. Ibid.

80. Merleau-Ponty, *Nature,* p. 91/127.

81. Ibid., p. 92/128.

82. Fotini Markopoulou, 'An insider's guide to quantum causal histories', *Nuclear Physics – Proceedings Supplements,* 88 (2000): 308–13. Available from http://arxiv.org/abs/hep-th/9912137 [accessed 28 January 2015].

83. Ibid.

84. Fotini Markopoulou, 'Planck scale models of the universe', in John D. Barrow, Paul C. W. Davies and Charles L. Harper, Jr (eds), *Science and Ultimate Reality: Quantum Theory, Cosmology, and Complexity* (Cambridge: Cambridge University Press, 2002), pp. 550–63. Available from http://arxiv.org/abs/gr-qc/0210086 [accessed 28 January 2015].

CHAPTER 11
SUBTENDING RELATIONS: BACTERIA, GEOLOGY AND THE POSSIBLE
Myra J. Hird and Kathryn Yusoff

Wasting (in) the Anthropocene

If the Subcommission on Quaternary Stratigraphy Working Group recommends to the International Commission on Stratigraphy in 2016 that the 'Anthropocene' be designated as an epoch, stratigraphers will then be tasked with determining how to mark this unit of geological time.

Will the Anthropocene be designated with a Global Stratigraphic Section and Point (GSSP) – a golden spike; or will it be signposted by a Global Standard Stratigraphic Age – a designated time boundary? If stratigraphers opt for the latter, where would this time boundary begin?

Some say it was the late seventeenth century's Industrial Revolution when the accelerated extraction and burning of fossil fuels began to take place. Others place it some 8,000 years earlier in the Neolithic, with the clearing of forests for agriculture. An even longer, deeper, Anthropocene stakes a claim for the Promethean moment of the harnessing of fire, and widespread use of landscape burning.

Until recently, Paul Crutzen had been of the opinion that the Anthropocene began with the large-scale extraction of fossil fuels, but recently changed his mind. He now places 'the real start of the Anthropocene' on July 16, 1945 – the Trinity detonation – and its fallout, radioactive waste.

Perhaps stratigraphers will opt to place a golden spike in a specific physical place. The Pleistocene-Holocene boundary, for instance, is in Greenland at 75.1000°N 42.3200°W.[1] In which case, any number of candidates are viable: there's the Clarke Belt, approximately 35,786 km above sea level, where orbiting satellite debris will outlast most if not all life on Earth, or anywhere within the 124,000 sq km range that the Soviet satellite Cosmos 954 exploded over Canada's Northwest Territories in 1978, spreading some 65 kilograms of fissionable uranium 235.

The spatial-temporal claims of these wastes, among a host of possible others, lay geologic markers in the strata with cosmic signatures.

Whether it is the large-scale industrial use of fossil fuels (a form of necro-waste formed from the mainly anaerobic decomposition of buried dead organisms),[2] or the Trinity detonation that deposited radioactive waste into the stratosphere, or any one of the subsequent nuclear accidents that added further radioactive debris into this stratospheric soup, or the ubiquitous dumps and landfills that proliferate the globe archiving a timeline of extraction, consumption and disposal, a strong case can be made for waste as *the* signature of the Anthropocene. While some, including Crutzen, see the Anthropocene as a thesis of critical reflection on humanity's material impact on the earth and its threatened futurity, the Anthropocene is by no means an epoch in which all organisms are deprived of their future. Anthropocene futures read through waste may have a lot less to do with humanity's awesome capabilities of destratification and a lot more to do with the creative and autonomous activity of bacteria. The question then becomes: how has waste inaugurated an epoch, and the only epoch to mark the point at which human activity has intersected, in its significance and magnitude, with planetary geophysical forces? And, furthermore, what does this epochal wasting do to accounts of a human agential claim on geologic force in Anthropocenic thought?

Geologists study the Earth as a vast 'strata machine' whereby the earth 'phoenix-like, has kept renewing itself' through a relentless process of vertical and horizontal sediment flows that move material – over millions of years – up through the biosphere and down through the lithosphere.[3] The temporal and material calibration of this machinic earth is recorded by geologists as epochs marked by distinct material features and events. And for the past four billion years or so – almost the entire history of the earth – bacterial metabolic processes working in tandem with geologic forces have indelibly influenced (and often enacted) this restratification. The earth, as Tyler Volk puts it, is 'one big waste world' fuelling the world's organic and inorganic metabolism.[4] We breathe tree and bacteria waste products (that is, oxygen). And we feed off the mineralogical byproducts of the folding, erupting and implosions of the Earth's crust. The Earth's soil and water consist in large degrees of the built-up waste products of living and nonliving matter (the mass of once-living organisms that have returned to base matter is estimated at somewhere between 1,000 and 10,000 times the mass of the Earth itself).[5] As such, waste is materially world-making, connecting geosphere, biosphere and stratosphere (beyond the various gases and solid particles expelled as waste from organic and inorganic matter, myriad space junk orbits the earth).

Human waste contributes to, and is ineradicably caught up in, the flux of earthly waste restratifications.

To wit: the Giant mine, located on the Ingraham Trail, close to Yellowknife in Canada's Northwest Territories, produced over seven million ounces of gold in its heyday, as well as some 237,000 tonnes of arsenic trioxide dust – a highly toxic form of arsenic – as a byproduct.[6] The plan, so far, is to restratify this waste in the mine itself, using the Frozen Block Method to freeze this highly toxic waste in perpetuity for a future generation of engineers, scientists, politicians and publics to resolve.[7] Or we might consider the mundane dump or landfill that is civilization's preferred method of disgorging its past. The intention is that these unfathomable tonnes of waste be kept in place: not leaking, not exploding, not combusting, not flowing beyond the boundaries we have imposed. Or we might consider the Waste Isolation Pilot Plant about 26 miles from Carlsbad, New Mexico, which is storing transuranic nuclear waste for at least the next one million years. This site is already cut through with stratifications: the nuclear waste from hospitals and plutonium from some 30,000 US nuclear weapons is stored in the hole created by the extraction of salt produced during the flooding and evaporation of the Permian Sea some 250 million years ago. And then there's the potash, oil and gas mining that plunges excavation below the salt table. Warning future generations about this nuclear waste means 'saying something about a future twice as far from us as human written culture lies in the past – or roughly the entire span of time since the ice age … [which] seems utterly impossible'.[8]

The Earth, we might say, is filling up with waste. We are refilling it with materials we have already extracted, often in combinations that are highly toxic to humans and other animals. In this way, the environmental crisis of the Anthropocene is a succinct nomination for the empirical crises of waste: the wastes of modernity, of fossil fuels, of biodiversity, of the toxicity and porosity of contaminated materials, of pollution's leakage into bodies of water, air, skin, shell, land, plant and microbe. The Anthropocene also names an ontological crisis in the perceived separation of hitherto distinct categories of matter: organic and nonorganic, human and inhuman, object and subject. In understanding the Anthropocene as primarily an epoch of waste practices, attention must shift to the shadow economy that haunts relational approaches to materiality: the exuberant, unforeseen and often indeterminate consequences of material relations. This shadow economy, like waste, subtends relational approaches to materiality and has a determining and differentiating force in constituting the very possibilities of those relations. As waste is sorted, categorized and determined through waste practices, in the subterranean *ur*landscape of bacteria, waste is incorporated and excreted through the labour of microbial digestion to generate new strata of waste-like entities that are in large part determined through the activities of those bacterial communities.[9]

This bacterial waste work is not without consequence. For reasons to be outlined later, bacterial mutation can be seen as a form of material speculation that generates new forms of life, which throw off the category of 'waste' as it is designated within a subject/object relation (that is, human waste becomes the basis of new, autonomous forms of materialization that are unperturbed by human categorizations). Bacteria engage in their own forms of objectification to reveal hidden dimensions of the mutable objects that are socially deemed as 'waste'. These forms of bacterial object orientation have very little to do with how these objects function (materially or relationally) in human social worlds. Thus, bacteria reveal an insurgency at the level of the object that is inadequately captured in understandings of the relationality between humans and objects. While focus remains on human waste as a stratification of the Anthropocene, retaining the anthropocentric focus of human-environment relations, bacteria are restratifying this waste stream with largely unknown results. As bacteria digest waste, they do not remain unchanged by this process of indigestion.[10] Thus, empirical questions about microbiological life forces raise ontological questions about what counts as waste matter, and how we should begin to apprehend the capacities of such matter to speculate in evolutionary and materially inventive ways. In this chapter we argue that waste is transformative, not only of material conditions and spatiotemporal responsibilities, but also of the ontologies of matter and their theorization. To materialize this claim, we look at the often obscured and indeterminate materialism that subtend biological and geological relations in the Anthropocene, to ask whether relationality is sufficient enough to encompass these speculative material futures *and* whether speculative thought is sufficiently engaged with matter's own speculative capacities.

Waste's proclivities

Far from the debris that lies forgotten in what we hope are stagnant and immobilized global dumps and landfills, waste *flows*.[11] That is, waste does not stay stratified within the social designations accorded it. Waste itself

– assuming for the moment that we may define it simply as such[12] – is a compendium of already extracted, assembled, reassembled and transformed materials that, when dumped in a hole in the ground or modern landfill, is taken up – engaged – with leachate. So, all of those diapers, food scraps, metals, plastics, holiday wrapping paper, Styrofoam, wood, liquids, refrigerators, pets, their shit and litter, batteries, chairs, fabrics and so on are restratified and compacted with rather less expected materials such as products of common industrial processes like coal fly ash (of which over 50 per cent ends up landfilled),[13] plastics (more than 308 million tons of plastics are consumed worldwide each year, most of which still ends up landfilled),[14] and food waste and its some 14,000 different kinds of additives and contaminants (over 97 per cent of which is landfilled in the United States).[15] Landfills also mix hazardous and nonhazardous waste, including over seven million known chemicals, 80,000 of which are in commercial circulation (and with a further 1,000 new chemicals entering into commercial use each year).[16] The engineering and science of waste disposal, in other words, must contend with a vast heterogeneous mix of known, unknown and unknowable material. Indeed, this is not a stable heterogeneity; it is dynamically reconstituting the terms of that heterogeneity.

Landfills assemble billions of heterogeneous bacteria whose 'variations may be cyclical, directional, stochastic, or chaotic'.[17] Aerobic bacteria metabolize a landfill's early life, which produces material that is highly acidic and toxic to surface water. Anaerobic bacteria do the bulk of the metabolizing work deeper in the landfill's strata, producing leachate. Leachate is a heterogeneous amalgamation of heavy metals, endocrine-disrupting chemicals, phthalates, herbicides, pesticides and various gases including methane, carbon dioxide, carbon monoxide, hydrogen, oxygen, nitrogen and hydrogen sulphide. Factors affecting leachate production rate and composition include the

> characteristics of the waste (initial composition, particle size, density and so on), the interaction between the percolating landfill moisture and the waste, the hydrology and climate of the site, the landfill design and the operational variables, microbial processes taking place during the stabilization of the waste, and the stage of the landfill stabilization. Most of these factors change during the operational period of the landfill as the landfill is developed causing significant changes in leachate quality and quantity.[18]

Genealogies of Speculation

Leachate travels vertically and horizontally within landfills, and continues to travel when it leaks beyond landfill cells, and sometimes through geological strata. That is, leachate may percolate into soil and groundwater where it moves into and through plants, trees, animals, fungi, insects and the atmosphere. Via leachate, bacteria create well-known, little-known and new biological forms. Waste flows are always contingent, uncertain and temporal. 'Trash may dissemble the truth of its being by presenting itself as [an] immaterial, innocuous substance divorced from the relations to physicality', but in actuality, biogeological processes are always already actively *involved*.[19] The millions of people who live in and on dumpsites, survive by directly handling waste, or live downstream from waste's fallout are acutely aware of waste's proclivity to materially flow.[20]

The point here is that when it comes to what bacteria ultimately make of this 'good soup', and what in the process they make of themselves, we simply have very little idea.[21] Yet the unfathomably rich and complex feedstock that we are pumping underground has a special significance in the magnification of the insensible and the unknown, and its unintended consequences comprises one of the deepest and darkest ecologies of the current material-historical juncture. And it is at least as important to consider the future of this dark ecology as it is to speculate on the nascent ends of humanity, not least because bacteria have been geologizing a great deal longer. A quite feasible but utterly unconfirmable consequence of human subterranean waste disposal is a stimulation of bacterial proliferation that is likely to involve adaptation and diversification.

Waste's relationality

A compelling case may be made to analyse landfilling and waste generally from a relational materiality perspective, with human and nonhuman actants in shifting assemblages.[22] Within this formulation, waste emerges as a force that queers 'thinghood', traversing bio and geo worlds and complicating what counts as living matter. Distinct, overlapping, contradictory and variously concurrent conceptualizations suggest that waste isn't a 'thing' or even a distributed set of things: waste requires material-discursive constructions that create, bring to the fore, and sustain particular relations as well as deaden, obfuscate and otherwise limit other relations. As such, waste has a genealogical trajectory that subtends and exceeds objectification.

Karen Barad's agential realism offers a rich theory concerned with phenomena's relationality and is inspiring new ways of engaging in philosophical discussions about long-standing concerns with ontology and epistemology, naturalism, realism, constructivism and more recent calls for interdisciplinary modes of theoretical and empirical engagement. Located within a trajectory of materialist science studies, Barad's work both extends materialist feminist concerns with how matter comes to matter into a realist mode (while keeping with the demand to instantiate power relations there within), and pushes poststructuralist accounts of the performativity of matter beyond discursive registers. From an agential realist theoretical perspective, the world is not composed of entities that we may or may not come to know; it is composed of 'phenomena' produced through measuring. Agential realism's focus on phenomena rather than things requires careful attention to the myriad 'material-discursive practices' through which these phenomena are (re)constituted, (re)arranged and abandoned.[23]

Within this theoretical formulation, then, waste is not a pregiven thing that awaits analysis and critique (as well as sorting, reclaiming and disposing). Waste only becomes a phenomenon through various agential cuts, or 'cutting together-apart'.[24] These cuts require various apparatuses and practices such as mass production and consumption, anaerobic digestion, global transportation and communication, statistical modelling, organismal differentiation, cheap mechanized labour, heavy water, cultural analysis, nonrenewable fossil fuels, regulations and so on. Agential realism, then, provides us with a theoretical framework within which to analyse the various material-discursive 'apparatuses' that '(re)configure' and literally make and remake the world's waste.[25] Measuring, or knowing, is 'world-making'. Measuring 'entangles'; as Barad puts it, measuring 'cuts together-apart'.[26] From this ontoepistemological perspective, matter and meaning are measuring 'effects'.[27] They do not preexist as individual entities, nor are they inherently static in time or space (to make them so is itself to exact an agential determination or 'cut', as Barad puts it).[28]

Barad refers to our 'thingification' of relations, which requires that things have at least partial autonomy that precedes their relating to each other.[29] This attention to 'things' obscures, for Barad, the primacy of phenomena as 'dynamic topological reconfigurings/entanglements/relationalities/ (re)articulations'.[30] When waste is considered a thing it may risk appearing as rather static, like the garbage dumped in landfills or the plutonium buried in nuclear repositories, as though materiality is just waiting there, passively, not doing much. But waste is anything but static and submissive: waste flows and mobilizes relations; waste enacts new material phenomena; and waste *forces* new social and geological formations into being.[31] The unfathomably diverse and multitudinous bacteria that metabolize landfills, and the half-lives of iodine, strontium-90, plutonium and other nuclear materials suggest just the kind of (re)configurings, entanglements, and relationalities that agential realism forefronts.

This is not to say that agential realism denies the existence of objects outside of or prior to relations. As Barad writes:

> properties that we measure are not attributable to independent objects. Independent objects are abstract notions. This is the wrong objective referent. The actual objective referent is the phenomenon – the intra-action of what we call the electron and the apparatus.[32]

Although we do not have access to objects in themselves, we may gain some insight into what agential realism refers to as phenomena or what speculative realism details as the types of relations objects may have (containment, contiguity, sincerity, connection, none), and how these relations affect objects.[33]

What makes agential realism particularly stimulating is that it forefronts the inhuman in measuring/knowing. Barad's work reminds us that world-making is not effected through human measuring/knowing alone; myriad unfathomable inhuman phenomena including quarks, photons and those not/there virtualities within the quantum field, measure. Inhuman measurements render the world determinate as much as, if not more than, human measurements. 'The world', Barad reminds us, 'theorizes as well as experiments with itself.'[34] Turning human exceptionalism on its head, Barad argues that:

> if we thought the serious challenge, the really hard work, was taking account of *constitutive exclusions*, perhaps this awakening to the infinity of *constitutive inclusions*, the in/determinacy that manifests as virtuality calls us to a new sensibility.[35]

A plate tectonics of ontology

This attention to the inhuman is taken up within the expanding swathe of speculative realism, object-oriented philosophy, object-oriented ontology, and their variations. A central concern uniting these metaphysical approaches – whether Ray Brassier's 'eliminative nihilism', Iain Hamilton Grant's 'cyber-vitalism', Quentin Meillassoux's 'speculative materialism' or Graham Harman's 'speculative realism' – is an objection to Kant's settlement or what Quentin Meillassoux defines as *correlationism*: 'the idea according to which we only ever have access to the correlation between thinking and being, and never to either term considered apart from the other'.[36] 'Every philosophy', writes Meillassoux, 'which disavows naïve realism has become a variant of correlationism.' This includes, then, all variants of phenomenology, structuralism and poststructuralism, and certainly postmodernism. Speculative realism takes issue with phenomenology's insistence that we cannot know reality itself but only objects as they appear to us (through experience, scientific experimentation, modelling, traditional ecological knowledge and so on). It also takes issue with those formulations of Science and Technology Studies (STS) such as Actor Network Theory and the Strong Program for their tendency to reiterate the salience of human consciousness within analyses whose ostensible focus is objects themselves. As Harman observes:

> [Latour's] examples are drawn from the human realm, not from general cosmology. And in this way, the more difficult cases are left in shadow. With a bit of work, it is not difficult to see why all objects that enter human awareness must be hybrids, why the ozone hole or dolphins or rivers cannot be viewed as pure pieces of nature aloof from any hybridizing networks. The harder cases involve those distant objects in which human awareness is currently not a factor at all. Where are the hybrids in distant galaxies? If they are not present, then the purifying discourse of nature wins the war, and the rule of hybrids can be viewed to some extent as a local effect of human perception.[37]

Speculative realism, within Harman's metaphysics, attempts to prioritize objects themselves rather than their relations with humans or, indeed, other objects. Objects, in this formulation, are somewhere between the tendencies to either 'undermine' or 'overmine' within philosophy. When objects are undermined a form of recursive monism occurs, as what appear to be autonomous objects turn out to be aggregates of smaller objects. If these objects are not distinct from one another, then we have monism; if they are distinct, then their relation to each other is merely an assertion that objects are 'both connected and unconnected at the same time'.[38]

This assertion may come in the form of popular tropes of 'becoming' or 'difference' but leaves unaddressed the issue of the object itself – if each becoming or difference is merely an instance of one underlying becoming or difference, then we are back to monism, and if each is distinct, then we have objects whose becoming or difference from other objects remains to be explained. When objects are 'overmined', argues Harman, their only existence consists of their relation with other things. Here the object itself recedes as relationality takes precedence. This may not need to be relations between humans and objects, to be sure, but we are left with the same issue we have with undermining: relationality is abstracted such that objects only count as such when they effect other objects (objects are entirely exhausted by this relationality – nothing is kept in reserve), which forecloses the possibility of change.

Working from the rich philosophical lineage of Martin Heidegger, Alfred North Whitehead, Alphonso Lingis, Edmund Husserl and others, Harman's object-oriented philosophy (OOP) is at pains to separate object from subject. Indeed, Harman defines an object as 'anything that has a unified reality that is autonomous from its wider context and also from its own pieces'.[39] Or as Ian Shaw puts it, 'objects reduce each other to caricatures – they literally "objectify" each other'.[40] Instead, relations 'do not exhaust' the things that relate; objects are more than the sum of the relations and networks within which they (at times) participate.[41] Thus, whereas in some STS formulations black-boxing is something for social scientists to work on, for Harman it is something objects themselves do.

Objects, within Harman's metaphysics, do not have to be physical things; they may equally be deities, dreams, faeries or fantasies. Thus all objects have hidden qualities, and may also be dormant for short or eternally long periods of time. In an oft-cited illustration, Harman writes:

> When fire burns cotton, it makes contact only with the flammability of this material. Presumably fire does not interact at all with the cotton's odour or colour, which is relevant only to creatures equipped with sense ... The being of cotton withdraws from the flames, even if it is consumed and destroyed.[42]

Unable to fully touch or otherwise experience other objects, objects affect each other through what Harman terms 'vicarious causation'.[43] Two or more objects can only influence each other by forming, as it were, a third object, which becomes 'the molten inner core of objects – a sort of plate tectonics of ontology'.[44] Given that neither of these objects need to be – or indeed within the scale of the universe are likely to be – human, vicarious causation holds that *relationality* itself (and not human consciousness) necessarily and always distorts the reality of objects. Being in relation within Harman's speculative realism does not refer to the essence of any object in itself but only with a part of that object (which Harman refers to as its 'sensual' element). This determination of relationality as distortion fits well within agential realism's proposal that phenomena are produced through intraactive cutting together-apart.

Waste's agential speculative possibilities – the inhuman and indeterminacy

STS analyses bring into sharp relief the processes through which things become objects, objects become black-boxed, and humans enact classificatory and other practices such that objects appear to be stable or unstable, fixed or transitory, hidden or exposed. What brings agential and speculative realisms together is, as we have outlined, a concern with the inhuman, and more specifically with figuring out ways to explore a universe that does not require human consciousness to either exist or be understood. Both agential and speculative forms of realism ask us to contemplate a world of objects unmediated by human consciousness, one emphasizing the cutting together-apart that all objects (human or otherwise) *are*, and the other emphasizing the withdrawn unavailable aspects that maintain object autonomy. Within both approaches, we get a keen appreciation of the unending becoming of objects and their relations; that there is no relation or object that is so durable that it cannot be worn out, overthrown, bribed, caressed or otherwise moved by its own 'will' towards something else. At the same time, an object is not simply the sum of its relations, and can withhold, suspend or reserve forms of relation. For Shaw a 'geo-event' occurs when these transcendental objects – objects that affect all of the objects in a world – 'are overthrown by inexistent objects' thereby bringing forth a new constellation of objects, a new world; worlds brought forth by bacterial oriented objectification in the Anthropocene, for example. This is made possible because no object is exhausted by its relations to other objects. There is always a surplus. And 'object by object, the geoevent deanchors the integrity of the world'.[45] If, indeed, the Anthropocene is a geoevent of epochal magnitude, there is much need to address not just this exhaustion and survival of objects (species, biodiversity, minerals, fuels, humanity) but the inexistent objects that form both the shadow economy of these social relations and exceed them.

What also unites these metaphysics is a strong recognition of indeterminacy. Within speculative realism, vicarious causation maintains that all relations must, in the relating objects' refusal to reveal all of their qualities, be indeterminate. When objects form relations with other objects, the withdrawn aspect(s) of each object means that each relation can only be partial and never entirely known or certain. For agential realism, indeterminacy is the condition of measuring: 'how strange', writes Barad, 'that indeterminacy, in its infinite openness, is the *condition for the possibility* of all structures in their dynamically reconfiguring in/stabilities'.[46] Astrid Schrader describes the articulation of the trace, when indeterminacies are rendered determinate phenomena through measuring:

> There is no measurement without memory, no intraaction that wouldn't leave a trace. But the trace by itself is not. Memories have to be read in order to 'be'. That is, they require work that involves material determinations.[47]

The work Schrader refers to is determining phenomena – the work that comprises knowing. The trace, then, is a provocation and knowledge is a form of cutting. Moreover, we cannot, writes Schrader, both be part of nature and examine nature from an external position. It is not that we are part of a system of which particular parts are currently inaccessible but accessible in some future (Heisenberg's uncertainty), but rather 'because the scientist's work helps to enact the system boundaries she will have become part of'.[48] Knowing, then, is about determining the indeterminate. We *make* determinations of the indeterminate. This is a limitless process; so long as there are phenomena, there is indeterminacy rendered determinate:

> Matter is never a settled matter. It is always already radically open. Closure can't be secured when the conditions of im/possibilities and lived indeterminacies are integral, not supplementary, to what matter is.[49]

Thinking with indeterminacy as an integral condition of matter provides a much more expansive mode of recognition of the speculative possibilities of objects than is admitted within an anthropocentric view of the Anthropocene and its waste-worlding. Recalling Barad's provocation that the world experiments with itself, we have little idea what the multitudes of bacteria that metabolize landfills will make of its ingredients, of themselves as they proliferate and differentiate into new forms, or of the geosphere and biosphere given enough time.[50] The issue is that the radical openness of matter does not cease being 'open' to various forms of experimentation when it is designated as waste or put in a hole. Bacteria continue to metabolize the various assortments of left-over materials that are aggregated together in a landfill in ways that defy their given stratification as waste, enacting new flows that exceed this physical containment. More than the Anthropocene's discontents, its undergrounds or waste sites cannot simply be understood as a collective unconscious of industrialization that will return, like the repressed, to offer a critique of the psychic life of wasting. The point of landfills was – at least until recently – not to dig them up: to keep the indeterminate as such. But spatially and temporally such a practice of internment is insufficient to contain waste's exuberant materiality. The generative life of waste suggests a need to liberate an understanding of geologic forces from the fetters of surface chauvinism, whose determinations obscure the comprehension of other organisms to territorialize the strata on their own terms.

Unsurprisingly, engineers and scientists respond to this interdeterminacy with efforts to *manage* waste. Waste management is all about determination and containment. Within engineering and science, determining waste is a highly complex process, and the constitutive inclusions are extensive. Certainly, landfills, nuclear repositories, incinerators and other management techniques have become more technically sophisticated as engineers and scientists develop better liners, gradient specifications, barriers and so on (which doesn't mean these techniques are always or most often adopted). This 'so on' is wide-ranging: for instance, modern landfills are lined with a complex layering of rocks, clay, sand, geotextile membranes and/or liners, and are physically structured in waste cell layers, which are placed on top of each other to form a number of waste columns.[51] Estimating landfill settlement depends upon, among other things, the 'type of waste, moisture content, compaction density, porosity, compressibility, biodegradation rate (level of nutrients available for biological activities, presence of enzymes, sludge addition, pH, temperature) and mode of landfill operation'.[52]

Engineers and scientists are fully cognizant that they are building conceptual and statistical models of the movement of moisture, bacterial metabolism, soil integrity and so on, and then testing these models empirically in controlled experiments. To take just one example, conceptual models constructed to test landfill quality assume each layer is a completely mixed reactor with uniformly distributed waste, moisture, gases and bacteria – but this is not actually the case, with cells containing decomposed material of varying degrees.[53] Engineers and scientists, in other words, know they are creating conceptual models (rather than reality) in order to derive determinate matters of fact. Describing the principle of *renormalization* in physics, Barad writes:

> if it turns out to be possible to get finite results by subtracting infinities via a process that cuts out the domain of unknown physics, then the theory is said to be renormalizable. The cut-off method of renormalization is a mathematical way of bracketing out what you don't know.[54]

This is what the engineering and science of waste management does: it makes certain facts about landfills, bioreactors and the like known through a process of bracketing out or minimizing indeterminacy; not just what is as-yet unknown, but what is unknowable. This is necessary to the acquisition of knowledge. And as Barad argues, it explicitly builds ignorance into theory.[55]

Engineers and scientists are well aware of indeterminacy in, for example, their attention to issues such as 'contaminants of emerging concern', which include chemicals such as BisPhenol-A (BPA) that have been used in many plastic products and are believed to mimic human oestrogen at low concentrations, PolyBrominated Diphenyl Ether (PBDE) which is an additive flame retardant in plastics, foams and fabrics that may cause liver, thyroid and neurodevelopmental toxicity, as well as new materials such as nanoparticles which were not part of the waste stream at the time many landfill regulations (for example, US Subtitle D) were developed.[56] Issues such as contaminants of emerging concern are not only 'known knowns' (the things we know we know), 'known unknowns' (the things we know we don't know), or 'unknown unknowns' (the things we don't know we don't know):[57] the words 'contaminants', 'emerging' and 'concern' are themselves agential cuts. Suspending the connotative powers of language in bracketing off indeterminacy is but the first step towards the kind of disruption that might allow another economy of relations to be disclosed that keeps with waste's own indeterminations as a concurrent concern, so that for every cut of knowledge there is a corresponding remembrance of what is withdrawn in the process of determination and in that account of matter. In a somewhat strange philosophical coupling, Barad's theorization of indeterminacy together with Harman's understanding of the objects withdrawal provide a way to articulate a form of material speculation – that may or may not be called the Anthropocene – that is neither wholly determined by human relations, nor immune to the political accounts of matter that seek to determine it.

If a concern with the Anthropocene is that it characterizes humans' destratification of billion-years-old fossil fuel and other material layerings from the earth's strata, then landfills and nuclear waste repositories articulate a concern in the opposite direction, with a kind of earthly restratification or relayering.[58] A landfill's contaminating lifespan is estimated at hundreds to thousands of years, and nuclear contamination endures for upwards of 100,000 years, or 3,000 generations, making the consequences of this restratification indeterminable. Yet, such sudden de- and re-stratifications of the earth's geologic layers have consequences as new formations of matter are brought together with little or no knowledge of how these cuts continue to germinate (or evolve) into new historic strata. While waste may be often categorized as the end-life of 'thinghood' and material utility, it is the starting point of a new form of material ontological speculation.

Not only are these wastes materially indeterminable, but their temporal duration promises much more of a future than humanity might lay claim to. The geologic-like cut in time that waste practices present establishes something akin to what Meillassoux has called 'ancestral statements' (albeit from the future anterior rather than the past).[59] Meillassoux makes the distinction between primary and secondary qualities in objects, primary qualities being nonrelational and secondary properties being relationality enacted. Primary qualities are not available to enter into relationals (because they either proceed or exceed human consciousness) and can only be inferred through the fossils that exist in the present. He defines ancestral statements as events that are anterior to the emergence of all conscious apprehension and therefore have no body of affects or perceptions to register their event. This matter is not a fossil in the traditional sense that is a trace of life, but an archefossil that indicates the existence of realities anterior to all life, such as a radioactive isotope. Meillassoux's point is that we can have knowledge of nonrelational properties that are not *for us*, in so much as they preexist or, as in the case of waste, will certainly outlive us. If we view waste as a 'ruin in reverse', producing its own futurity or deep time, independent, but not unconnected to human futures, this makes room for thinking the ontological junctures of determining indetermination beyond what determination means for us.

Genealogies of Speculation

From a waste studies perspective, attending to the ways in which humans create waste from objects, and then attempt divestiture through various forms of disposal (whether in underground nuclear lairs, landfills, dumps, energy-from-waste facilities and so on) and by empowering engineers and scientists with the task of dealing with this dispossession's remainder – fly and bottom ash, leachate, contamination and so on – is an important contribution to contemporary studies of the Anthropocene, especially when this divestiture is considered within the context of the already dispossessed, human or otherwise. Waste in this sense *is* the cutting together-apart of a complex array of objects, measuring practices and humans.

At the same time, we might also be drawn to the reminder that real objects are withdrawn from apprehension. In their awkward and stubborn refusal to be easily characterized as species as well as their sheer numbers and diversity, bacteria, for instance, certainly defy – and indeed are largely indifferent to – the claiming and naming practices of humans.[60] But, it is the very relations that bacteria form with each other, with moisture, soil, sunlight, various chemicals and so on within landfills, that makes the phenomenon of landfill waste what it is. And what makes radioactive uranium is its relation with time and organic bodies. In other words, leachate, as an object, is already a network. It is difficult, by definition, to separate it from the masses of objects, moisture, and teeming bacteria that make it up. As Mattias Kärrholm points out, we are left with a relational typologization.[61]

Moreover, one of the things that characterizes scientific and applied scientific approaches to forms of waste (radioactive material, leachate, fly ash and so on) is precisely to disaggregate – to 'undermine', as Harman would have it – these objects into their constituent parts. It is difficult to examine any one constituent of leachate, let alone one constituent's synthesis with one or more others. As waste becomes gathered up into the term leachate, a further mode of differentiation between matter that stays stratified and matter that flows, is made. We can see waste as this double articulation (in Deleuze's terms) of the unstable forms between strata – waste as an interstratum between social and geophysical processes that regulates relations between strata. Gilles Deleuze and Félix Guattari refer to a 'double articulation' that is meant to take account of the constitution of entities[62] – not, as Aristotle articulated it, through 'essence', but rather through a process of, first, the selection or 'sedimentation' of materials that will make up the object and, second, through the 'cementation' of these materials into an entity with its own properties. For leachate to be such an object, there must be an ongoing process of extraction, sedimentation, resedimentation and so on. What marks these Anthropocenic stratifications of waste is the mixing of wildly different strata with no single plane of consistency, such that it is not enough to merely confirm the exclusion of the indeterminate without a corresponding acknowledgement that the indeterminate determines future possibilities, even as these remain anterior to human life. Landfills and other forms of waste may have the appearance of sedimentation, but this is in human time, and sometimes not even then. But landfills are relationality all the way down: sometimes fast, and sometimes slow. Such strata mixing is a new form of geologizing with the planet in so much as it risks on the one hand a wild and furious destratification of the earth (of the carbon, nitrogen, atmospheric and ocean cycles) and on the other it introduces unknown stratifications of indeterminate parts that materially refute staying stratified.

If waste phenomena (humans, strontium 91, landfills, recycling, nonrenewable fossil fuels, anaerobic bacteria) are always already relational and marked as distinct through ongoing processes of cutting together-apart, what might this add, challenge, or otherwise provoke in discussions about the politics and ethics of waste? And, how might this working-through of the cuts of relationality begin to prompt a need to understand matters' own modes of differentiation apart from, but also together with, our own waste-making practices? Examining waste as a speculative material practice involved in processes of stratification requires an understanding of the interpolation of epistemological and ontological terms in acts of cutting by both human and nonhuman agents. While managing waste lends a spatial and temporal specificity to these practices in the short term, their indeterminate futurity suggests that waste practices need to include a consideration of waste beyond the human in their knowledge practices. If, as Michel Foucault reflected, 'knowledge is not made for understanding; it is made for cutting', then an acknowledgement of the speculative dimensions of waste's mattering beyond human determinations actualizes different sets of ontological relations to that waste that are nonrelational, in the sense of being anterior to the present and independent of human attempts to designate waste as such.[63] Through the transformative capacities of waste, then, there is the identification of relationality to an inaccessible deep time in which the human subject is necessarily discarded as an object of primary concern, but nonetheless such an identification may be without agency but it is not without decision. Thinking with the speculative possibilities of bacterial waste-life inadvertently lays open political and material possibilities in processes of in/determination that might transform what it becomes.

Ultimately, Barad's agential realism is a theory about ethics: it seeks to address the difficult ground of social obligation through phenomenal (re)articulations, which, to use Isabelle Stengers's words, 'allow us to inherit our history otherwise'.[64] It also requires, even *demands* (in a Derridean poststructuralist sense), that we pay attention to the indeterminate inheritances that compose and foreshadow our extraordinary responsibility for the future to come.[65] While the concerns of these all-too-human ethical relations may seem at odds with some of the claims made in this chapter with regards to inhuman agency, it is precisely the mode in which matter is politicized through ontological inquiry that informs processes of in/determination. Barad's contribution is to take these ethical concerns through a formal engagement with matter across the field of human and inhuman cuts, while retaining a hold on the agential specificity of those cuts. In dual concern for responsibility to both matter and its determinations, there is a sympathetic taking up of the obligations to the future that motivated some poststructuralist thought, alongside an understanding of inhuman agency within and on the outer reaches of that thought.

The indeterminacy of waste draws our attention to the *imprescriptibility* of our ethical responsibility to future generations and environmental sustainability.[66] In law, prescription infers a statute of limitations for the identification and assignation of guilt: after a certain time, crimes must be forgiven. Imprescriptibility refracts a global futurity of indeterminate entanglements, of cuttings together-apart, and of collective (in)human vulnerability and responsibility:

> ethics is not simply about responsible actions in relation to human experiences of the world; rather, it is a question of material entanglements and how each intraaction matters in the reconfiguring of these entanglements, that is, it is a matter of the ethical call that is embodied in the very worlding of the world.[67]

Waste, then, draws our attention to the complex destratifications and restratifications, the limitless potential intraactions corralled into composing waste as human, inhuman, disposable, reusable, risky, determinate, containable, profitable, inert, anthropogenic and ethical.

Conclusion

So where does the indeterminacy of waste lead us? Is viewing waste as a semiautonomous object that generates its own futures, as Nils Johansson and Jonathan Metzger fear, to treat it as somehow preordained or given?[68] If an acknowledgement of the futurity of waste, independent of human concerns, provides too much of an ethical alibi by disowning the inheritances that are clearly part of industrial relations, then there is at least a need to retain a dual aspect of objectification (as inheritance and material speculation). The role of speculation then forms an important 'lure' into the existences of those dual aspects, not to resolve that indeterminacy, but to partake of its inaccessibility.[69] Attention to that which is insensible or anterior is part of noticing how determination cuts out that which 'troubles of sensibility/sense-of-ability as well as limiting our comprehension and compassion for that which is outside of our sphere of experience'.[70] How matter is made to appear, and the ontological and epistemological technologies of recognition that certify its appearance, are clearly part of the aesthetic-ontic politics of waste, but it is only one part of the story. What becomes crucial in these aesthetic-ontic politics is how we both speculate about the agency of indeterminate matter and account for the speculative capacities of that matter to become otherwise along radically different spatial and temporal axes. This is perhaps the 'lure' of the conceptualization of the withdrawn in Harman's OOP in the context of waste. What objects appear – their aesthetic and sensible allure – is a matter of politics, not all of which is human (*pace* DeLanda).[71] We want to be mindful of the constant worlding taking place that is insensible to us, rather than assume that all that matters is what affects us and provokes us to notice. Furthermore the topology of affects that waste might generate is simultaneously happening on a much different temporal and spatial configuration than is often given through the determining cuts of policy legislation and waste-practice management.

If the surface of the earth commands most of our attention, it is worth registering the limitations of our surface exclusions. The dark biosphere refers to the ecosystem at least one metre below the continental surface or seafloor. Up to 95 per cent of bacteria and archaea live in this deep subsurface and exist independent of light as a source of energy.[72] These lithotrophic microbes rely on various gases (such as CO_2 and H_2) for energy to do their metabolic work. That we know so little about this dark biosphere, literally beneath our feet, may well be one of the biggest blind spots in Anthropocenic practices. Grappling with the indeterminacies of this dark substratum requires searching out modes of recognition that do not depend upon our usual human sensorium both ontologically and through our various epistemic cutting tools. If 'existence is coexistence, as it were, through mutual abandonment and exposure rather than enclosure', then the containment of waste as a category of disappearance in Anthropocenic thought needs to be thrown off.[73] As Kevin Hetherington argues, 'disposal is about placing absences and this has consequences for how we think about "social relations"'.[74] On one level, the formulation of waste *as waste* obscures the very fact that it is the disappearance of these objects from social view that renders the ontology of these objects indeterminate (as well as rendering the work of determination doubly problematic because it is proceeded by human indeterminations and exceeded by bacterial determinations). Both actions (human and nonhuman) collude to generate indeterminate objects. A politics of recognition, then, is not the point: a careful reading of the speculative possibilities of what that waste might become through its own inventive capacities, with and without a human subject, possibly is.

Notes

1. Mike Walker et al., 'Formal Definition and Dating of the GSSP (Global Stratotype Section and Point) for the Base of the Holocene Using the Greenland NGRIP Ice Core, and Selected Auxiliary Records', *Journal of Quaternary Science* 24(1) (2009): 3–17.

2. Phillip Olson, 'Knowing "Necro-Waste": A Reply to Hird', *Social Epistemology* 2(7) (2013): 59–63.

3. Jan Zalasiewicz, *The Earth After Us: What Legacy Will Humans Leave in the Rocks?* (Oxford: Oxford University Press, 2009).

4. Tyler Volk, 'Gaia Is Life in a Wasteland of By-Products', in Stephen H. Schneider, James R. Miller, Eileen Crist and Penelope J. Boston (eds), *Scientists Debate Gaia: The Next Century* (Cambridge MA: MIT Press, 2008).

5. See Mike Davis, 'Cosmic Dancers on History's Stage? The Permanent Revolution in the Earth Sciences', *New Left Review* (1996): 73.

6. The effects of arsenic depend on the dose. Arsenic is lethal to humans at a range of 70–180 milligrams. Doses below this threshold produce various effects including vomiting, diarrhoea, muscle pain, skin rashes, parenthesia and keratosis. Lower doses over longer periods of time (years) produce black spots on the skin, and very low doses indicate arsenic is a carcinogen, producing lung, liver and bladder cancers. Arsenic trioxide resembles dust and is soluble in water, and is therefore a health threat to any organisms drinking from or potentially from living near streams, lakes, puddles or snow contaminated by arsenic dust. There has been a long series of complaints, an

unconfirmed number of human (child) deaths, livestock and wildlife death and illness, investigations, commissioned and uncommissioned reports, denials of responsibility, further reports, media exposés, and now a lengthy assessment process to determine what to do with the Giant mine's mammoth waste.

7. The Frozen Block Method is a remediation technique that involves drilling holes into the rock around an arsenic trioxide chamber and pumping super-cooled liquid through pipes which freezes the rock and nearby water to 'trap' the arsenic trioxide dust in a frozen storage block. The method takes ten years, costs approximately $200 million, and requires indefinite monitoring and maintenance.

8. Peter Galison and Jamie Kruse, 'Waste-Wilderness: A Conversation between Peter Galison and Smudge Studio', *Discard Studies*, 2014, http://discardstudies.com/2014/03/26/waste-wilderness-a-conversation-between-peter-galison-and-smudge-studio/ [accessed 10 March 2015].

9. Jennifer Gabrys, 'Plastic and the Work of the Biodegradable', in Jennifer Gabrys, Gay Hawkins and Mike Michael (eds), *Accumulation: The Material Politics of Plastic*, (Abingdon: Routledge, 2013), p. 208.

10. See Nigel Clark and Myra J. Hird, 'Deep Shit', *O-Zone: A Journal of Object-Oriented Studies* 1 (2014): 44–52.

11. Industrialism, capitalist economies and neoliberal governance means that this expurgation is now global in scale and topography: see Gert Spaargaren, Arthur P. Mol and Frederick Buttel (eds), *Governing Environmental Flows* (Cambridge, MA: MIT Press, 2006); Peter Dauvergne, *The Shadows of Consumption: Consequences for the Global Environment* (Cambridge, MA: MIT Press, 2010).

12. See Myra J. Hird, 'Knowing Waste: Towards an Inhuman Epistemology', *Social Epistemology* 26(3–4) (2012): 453–69.

13. Marian Chertow, 'The Ecology of Recycling', *UN Chronicle* 46(3) (2009), http://unchronicle.un.org/article/ecology-recycling/ [accessed 10 January 2015].

14. Plastics Europe, 'Plastics Europe', *Plastics Europe*, 2012, http://www.plasticseurope.org/ [accessed 14 March 2015].

15. J. W. Levis et al., 'Assessment of the State of Food Waste Treatment in the United States and Canada', *Waste Management* 30(8) (2010): 1486–94.

16. See Brian Wynne, *Risk Management and Hazardous Waste: Implementation and the Dialectics of Credibility* (Berlin: Springer, 1987).

17. Scott L. Collins, Fiorenza Micheli and Laura Hartt, 'A Method to Determine Rates and Patterns of Variability in Ecological Communities', *Oikos* 91(2) (2000): 285–93.

18. Ebru Demirekler Yildiz, Kahraman Ünlü and R. Kerry Rowe, 'Modelling Leachate Quality and Quantity in Municipal Solid Waste Landfills', *Waste Management & Research* 22(2) (2004): 78.

19. See Greg Kennedy, *An Ontology of Trash: The Disposable and Its Problematic*

Nature (New York: SUNY Press, 2007), p. 162; Myra J. Hird, *The Origins of Sociable Life: Evolution after Science Studies* (New York: Palgrave Macmillan, 2009); Myra J. Hird, 'Waste, Landfills, and an Environmental Ethic of Vulnerability', *Ethics & the Environment* 18(1) (2013): 105–24; Clark and Hird, 'Deep Shit', pp. 44–52; and Hird, 'Knowing Waste'.

20. See Josh Lepawsky and Charles Mather, 'From Beginnings and Endings to Boundaries and Edges: Rethinking Circulation and Exchange through Electronic Waste', *Area* 43(3) (2011): 242–49; Dan McGovern, *The Campo Indian Landfill War* (Oklahoma: University of Oklahoma Press, 1995).

21. Clark and Hird, 'Deep Shit'.

22. Bruno Latour, 'Where Are the Missing Masses? The Sociology of a Few Mundane Artifacts', in Wieber Bijke and John Law (eds), *Shaping Technology/ Building Society: Studies in Sociotechnical Change* (Cambridge, MA: MIT Press, 1992), pp. 225–58.

23. Karen Barad, 'Posthumanist Performativity: Toward an Understanding of How Matter Comes to Matter', *Signs* 28(3) (2003): 818.

24. Karen Barad, 'On Touching – The Inhuman That Therefore I Am', *Differences* 23(3) (2012): 14.

25. Barad, 'Posthumanist Performativity', p. 816.

26. Barad, 'Touching', p. 14.

27. Ibid.

28. Ibid.

29. Barad, 'Posthumanist Performativity', p. 812.

30. Ibid., p. 818.

31. See Zsuzsa Gille, 'Actor Networks, Modes of Production, and Waste Regimes: Reassembling the Macro-Social', *Environment and Planning A* 42(5) (2010): 1049–64; Hird, 'Knowing Waste'; Hird, 'Landfills'.

32. Karen Barad, 'Interview with Karen Barad' in Rick Dolphijn and Iris van der Tuin (eds), *New Materialism: Interviews & Cartographies* (Ann Arbor: MPublishing, 2012), p. 61.

33. Graham Harman, *The Quadruple Object* (Winchester: Zero Books, 2011).

34. Barad, 'Touching', p. 207.

35. Ibid., p. 216.

36. Quentin Meillassoux, *After Finitude: An Essay on the Necessity of Contingency*, trans. Ray Brassier (London: Continuum, 2008), p. 5.

37. Graham Harman, 'The Metaphysics of Objects: Latour and His Aftermath', *Draft Manuscript*, 2008, p. 8. Available from https://pervegalit.files.wordpress.com/2008/06/harmangraham-latour.pdf [accessed 18 March 2015].

38. Harman, *Quadruple Object*, p. 9.

39. Ibid., p. 116.

40. Ian G. R. Shaw, 'Towards an Evental Geography', *Progress in Human Geography* 36(5) (2012): 620.
41. Harman, *Quadruple Object*.
42. Ibid., p. 44.
43. Graham Harman, 'On Vicarious Causation', in Robin Mackay and Damian Veal (eds), *Collapse Volume II: Speculative Realism* (Falmouth: Urbanomic, 2007), pp. 187–221.
44. Ibid., p. 174.
45. Shaw, 'Evental', p. 622.
46. Barad, 'Touching', (2012b) p. 16.
47. Astrid Schrader, 'Haunted Measurements: Demonic Work and Time in Experimentation', *Differences* 23(3) (2012): 43 (emphasis added).
48. Ibid., p. 44.
49. Karen Barad, *What Is the Measure of Nothingness: Infinity, Virtuality, Justice* (Ostfildern: Hatje Cantz, 2012), p. 16.
50. Likewise, our knowledge of the effects of nuclear fallout and low-level radiation exceed current spatial and temporal fallout demarcations. For example, consider the Russian thistle that absorbs strontium-90 and cesium and metabolizes it from nuclear contaminated areas, its head eventually severing from its stem, thus becoming a source of windblown distributed radiation. See John Stang, 'Tainted Tumbleweeds Concern Hanford', *Tri-City Herald*, 27 December 1998, https://www.mail-archive.com/nativenews@mlists.net/msg01073.html [accessed 15 March 2015]; Clark and Hird, 'Deep Shit'.
51. Yildiz, Ünlü and Rowe, 'Leachate'.
52. Sherien A. Elagroudy et al., 'Waste Settlement in Bioreactor Landfill Models', *Waste Management* 28(11) (2008): 2366–74.
53. Yildiz, Ünlü and Rowe, 'Leachate'.
54. Barad, 'Touching'.
55. Barad, *Nothingness*.
56. On BPA see Elizabeth W. LaPensee et al., 'Bisphenol A at Low Nanomolar Doses Confers Chemoresistance in Estrogen Receptor-α–Positive and –Negative Breast Cancer Cells', *Environmental Health Perspectives* 117(2) (2009): 175–80; Y. Takai et al., 'Estrogen Receptor-Mediated Effects of a Xenoestrogen, Bisphenol A, on Preimplantation Mouse Embryos', *Biochemical and Biophysical Research Communications* 270(3) (2000): 918–21.

    On PBDE see US EPA, 'Polybrominated Diphenyl Ethers (PBDEs) Action Plan Summary', 2015, http://www.epa.gov/oppt/existingchemicals/pubs/actionplans/pbde.html [accessed 13 March 2015].

    On nanoparticles see M. Z. Islam and R. Kerry Rowe, 'Permeation of BTEX through Unaged and Aged HDPE Geomembranes', *Journal of Geotechnical and Geoenvironmental Engineering* 135(8) (2009): 1130–40; R. K. Rowe, 'Design and Construction of Barrier Systems to Minimize Environmental Impacts due to Municipal Solid Waste Leachate and Gas', *Indian Geotechnical Journal* 42(4) (2012): 223–56; LaPensee et al., 'Bisphenol A'; Takai et al., 'Estrogen'.

57. Donald Rumsfeld, *US Department Defense Briefing*, 2002, http://www.youtube.com/watch?v=GiPe1OiKQuk [accessed 10 February 2015].

58. Clark and Hird, 'Deep Shit'.

59. Meillassoux, *After Finitude*, p. 10.

60. Hird, *Origins*.

61. Mattias Kärrholm, 'Building Type Production and Everyday Life: Rethinking Building Types through Actor-Network Theory and Object-Oriented Philosophy', *Environment and Planning D: Society and Space* 31(6) (2013): 1109–24.

62. Gilles Deleuze and Félix Guattari, *A Thousand Plateaus: Capitalism and Schizophrenia*, trans. Brian Massumi (Minneapolis: University of Minnesota Press, 1987), p. 39.

63. Michel Foucault, 'Nietzsche, Genealogy, History', in Paul Rabinow (ed.), *The Foucault Reader* (New York: Pantheon, 1984), pp. 76–100.

64. Quoted in Erik Bordeleau, 'The Care of the Possible: Isabelle Stengers Interviewed by Erik Bordeleau', *Scapegoat* 1 (2011): 17.

65. Rosalyn Diprose, 'Derrida and the Extraordinary Responsibility of Inheriting the Future-to-Come', *Social Semiotics* 16(3) (2006): 435–47.

66. See Hannah Arendt, 'Irreversibility and the Power to Forgive', in *The Human Condition* (Chicago: University of Chicago Press, 1958), pp. 233–47; Gregory Benford, *Deep Time: How Humanity Communicates Across Millennia* (New York: Harper Perennial, 2000); Peter C. Van Wyck, *Signs Of Danger: Waste, Trauma, and Nuclear Threat* (Minneapolis: University of Minnesota Press, 2004).

67. Karen Barad, *Meeting the Universe Halfway* (Durham, NC: Duke University Press, 2007), p. 160.

68. Nils Johansson and Jonathan Metzger, 'Experimentalizing the Organization of Objects: Some Why's and How's Discussed in Relation to Mineral Resource Becomings', Unpublished Paper, 2014, p. 4.

69. Kathryn Yusoff, 'Insensible Worlds: Postrelational Ethics, Indeterminacy and the (k)nots of Relating', *Environment and Planning D: Society and Space* 31(2) (2013): 211.

70. Ibid.

71. On bacterial politics, see Hird, *Origins*.

72. Katrina J. Edwards, Keir Becker and Frederick Colwell, 'The Deep, Dark Energy Biosphere: Intraterrestrial Life on Earth', *Annual Review of Earth and Planetary Sciences* 40(1) (2012): 551–68.

73. Yusoff, 'Insensible Worlds', p. 220.

74. Kevin Hetherington, 'Secondhandedness: Consumption, Disposal, and Absent Presence', *Environment and Planning D* 22(1) (2004): 159.

INDEX

absolute, the
   absolute contingency 15–16, 128, 244, 263 see also ontocontingency
   absolute realism 249–52
   absolute supplementarity 257–9
   absolutism 120–1
   absolutist metaphysics 120
   absolutization 176, 242, 254, 257, 259
   absolutory speculation 120
   deabsolutization of thought 117, 119 see also correlationism
   deabsolutized finitude 256, 258–9
   deuteroabsolutory properties/thought 157–8, 162, 178, 183, 186, 247, 250
   primoabsolutory properties/thought 156–8, 177–8, 247, 250, 253, 259
   properties of 156–7
Accidental Mind: How Brain Evolution Has Given Us Love, Memory, Dreams, and God, The (Linden, David) 60
Actor Network Theory 285
affective dynamism 48
After Finitude (Meillassoux, Quentin) 37, 122, 139, 142, 147, 153, 244
Agamben, Giorgio 43–4, 212, 216 n.25
agential realism 324–6, 329–30, 335–6
'Aggressiveness in Psychoanalysis' (Lacan, Jacques) 47, 48–9, 50
Alice in Wonderland (Carroll, Lewis) 101
Alien Phenomenology (Bogost, Ian) 233
allure 35
Althusser, Louis 19, 272–4
   antiempiricism and 277–8
   antisubjectivism and 276–7
   antiteleology and 278–9
   Bachelard, Gaston and 275–6, 278
   'Elements of Self-Criticism' 281 279–83
   empiricism and 277–8, 280–1
   epistemological programme 273–83, 288
   'Philosophical Conjuncture and Marxist Theoretical research, The' 280

   self-criticism and 281–3, 293
   speculative-rationalist deviation 281–2
analytic philosophy 1, 3, 200, 202, 203, 205–7, 271
anatomopolitics 220
ancestral, the 30
ancestral statements 333
aneidetic sign, the 253, 255, 257, 259, 263–5
anorganicism 46–7, 50, 52–4, 57–64
Anthropocene, the 319–22, 329, 333
anthropocentrism 1, 4–5, 125–6
anthropomorphism 126
antiempiricism 277–8
antifoundationalism 6, 11, 12
antiidealism 124
antirealism *see* correlationism
antisubjectivism 276–7
antiteleology 278–9
arbitrariness of the sign, the 168–9, 180–2
arche-fact, the 136–7
architecture 85, 174–5
Aristotle 76
Artaud, Antonin 101–2
atomic statements 301, 307
atomism 95
axiomatic systems 307

Bachelard, Gaston 278
   Formation of the Scientific Mind, The 275–6
bacteria 322, 323–4, 326, 330, 334
Badiou, Alain 43–4, 280–1
Barad, Karen 324–6
Barthes, Roland:
   S/Z 221
'Bartleby the Scrivener' (Melville, Herman) 224
base signs 160–1
Baudrillard, Jean: *System of Objects* 84
behaviour 310
Bergson, Henri 173–4, 179, 192 n.24

Index

Time and Free Will 173, 179
Berkeley, George and 187 n.3, 132
　subjectalism and 132
Bhaskar, Roy 272–3, 288–93
　Possibility of Naturalism, The 289
　Realist Theory of Science, A 289
Bibliothèque François Mitterand 174–5
bifurcation of nature 15, 35–9
biopolitics 218–20, 228
body, the 106–8
body-in-pieces 51–2, 53–4, 56–8, 61
body without organs 102, 103, 106–7
Bogost, Ian: *Alien Phenomenology* 233
Bonfire of the Vanities, The (Wolfe, Tom) 219
brain, the 308–9
Brassier, Ray 10, 30
　bifurcation of nature and 38–9
　Nihil Unbound 284
　nihilistic rationalism and 248
　science and 33, 271–2, 279, 283–8, 291–3
　scientific representation and 33
　Sellarsian epistemology and 283–8, 293
　social science and 291–2
Buren, Daniel: 'Peinture acrylique blanche sur tissu rayéet rouge (White Acrylic Painting on White and Red Striped Fabric)' 175
Butler, Judith 77, 82

Callinicos, Alex 280
Canguilhem, Georges 301–2
Cantor's theorem 307
Capital (Marx, Karl) 75
cardinality 307
Carroll, Lewis: *Alice in Wonderland* 101
causal sets 312
Cavaillès, Jean 300–3
central nervous system 60–1
Chance and Necessity (Monod, Jacques) 63
chaos 191 n.17
chemisms 53
Chomsky, Noam 209
Churchland, Paul 285
climate change 83
cognition 308–9
colonialism 6
commodity fetishism 75

communication technology 88–9
conceptual change, theory of 286–8, 293
consciousness 314–15
Continental philosophy 42, 44, 73–4, 90 n.10, 95, 121, 201, 271, 300
contingency 97–8, 104, 128
　Meillassoux, Quentin and 135, 138, 142, 147, 179–81
contingent, the 135, 138
contingent absoluity 261–5
Copernican revolution 108
correlation 123, 134–7
correlational circle 32–3, 36
　Meillassoux, Quentin and 118–20, 134
correlational facticity 134–5, 137
correlationism 5, 70–3, 239–40, 327 *see also* correlational circle; correlational facticity
　commodities and 75
　Hegel, Georg and 31–2
　language and 211
　Meillassoux, Quentin and 5, 10, 71–2, 74, 117–23, 136, 240, 244, 304–5
　observers and 74, 77–82
　pluralist 73, 75
　politics and 75–7
　poststructuralism and 73–4, 80–3
　poststructuralist correlationism's critique (PSC) 83–6
　second-order observation and 80–3
　universal 73
counteractualization 102–3
counternature 49
critical theory 75–7
critique 4–5
critique of the subject 124–5, 130, 133
cryptophysics 153–4

dark biosphere, the 337
Darwin, Charles 44–5
Davidson, Donald 207
dead, the 126–8, 131, 133, 157–8
deconstruction 18, 82, 203, 221, 240–3, 256–9, 263–5 *see also* structuralism
Defoe, Daniel: *Life and Strange Surprising Adventures of Robinson Crusoe, Mariner, The* 119
Deleuze, Gilles 93
　body without organs and 103, 106–7
　Difference and Repetition 103

344

Index

fold, and the 105
immanence and 98, 100
language and 100–1, 102, 103
Logic of Sensation, The 100
Logic of Sense, The 100, 102, 103
materialism and 103, 106
naturalism and 95, 98–9
Nietzsche, Friedrich and 96–7
observers and 82
philosophical principles and 97–8
principle of sufficient reason (PSR) and 94, 97–8, 108
sense/nonsense and 100–2
univocity and 97, 102
What is Philosophy? 104
denaturalization 46
deontologization 72, 81
Derrida, Jacques
  metaphysics and 258
  movement of supplementarity and 258
  semiotics and 253–6, 261, 264
  structuralism and 241, 243, 258, 262
  subtractive finitude and 256–9
determinations 330–7
Difference and Repetition (Deleuze, Gilles) 103
'Direction of the Treatment and the Principles of Its Power, The' (Lacan, Jacques) 49
discourse 83–4
distinction 78–82

Eddington, Arthur Stanley 37
elasticity 108
'Elements of Self-Criticism' (Althusser, Louis) 281 279–83
ellipse, the 109
emancipatory political thought 3–4, 7, 24 n.11, 75–6
empiricism 144, 277–8, 280–1
Empiricism and the Philosophy of Mind (Sellars, Wilfrid) 285
environment, the 83 *see also* waste
  Luhmann, Niklas and 87–9
  systems and 87–8
epicureanism 120
Era of Correlation 122–3, 133, 135
eternal return 97
ethics 3, 21, 95–7, 151, 335–7
  imprescriptibility of 336

Ethics, The (Spinoza, Benedict de) 95–6
ethnology 262
Euclid 159–60
evolutionary theory 44–5, 59–61, 192 n.24
  Monod, Jacques and 63
exfinite materialism 259, 260
exfinite thought 246, 250, 256, 259, 265
extro-science fiction (XSF) 224–30

Fabre, Jan: *Vleekskomp* (*Meat*) 127
fact, the 136
factial speculation 247–8, 250–1 *see also* null materialism
factiality 104, 137–8, 141, 153, 246–7 *see also* factuality
facticity 138, 151–2, 194 n.31, 207, 244–7
(f)actual investigations 149–54
factuality 207 *see also* factiality
'Family Complexes in the Formation of the Individual, The' (Lacan, Jacques) 47–8
Figures 138
finitude 102–3, 121
  deabsolutized finitude 256, 258–9
fissures 145, 146–7, 149
flatus vocis 164
fold, the 105, 107
form 310
formal language 161–2, 208–9
formal meaning 162
formalism 158–9, 162, 300–2
Formation of the Scientific Mind, The (Bachelard, Gaston) 275–6
formulatory contradictions 118–19
Foucault, Michel 77, 82
  History of Sexuality, The 220
  Order of Things, The 82
Francis Bacon: The Logic of Sensation (Deleuze, Gilles) 100
Frankfurt School, the 6
Freud, Sigmund 44, 52
'Freudian Thing, The' (Lacan, Jacques) 50
function of lack 56

Galileanism 139
gender 77, 82
geology
  geoevents 329
  geological markers 319–20

Index

geological restratification 333–5 *see also* waste
Giant mine, the 321
Gödel, Kurt 302
Grant, Iain Hamilton 30, 34, 37
great outdoors, the 29, 217, 223–4, 227, 233–4
ground, the 99, 103–7
Guattari, Félix 82
   What is Philosophy? 104
'Guiding Remarks for a Convention on Female Sexuality' (Lacan, Jacques) 53

Harman, Graham 30, 297 n.50, 327–9
   allure and 35
   bifurcation of nature and 37
   science and 271–2
   Weird Realism 233
Hegel, Georg 31–2, 63, 271
   anorganic, the 46
   Phenomenology of Spirit 58–9
   Philosophy of Nature 46
Heidegger, Martin 103–4
Heyting algebra 312
Hilflosigkeit 45–51, 54–5
History of Sexuality, The (Foucault, Michel) 220
holistic semiotics 202
home, the 85
Houellebecq, Michel 218
   Map and the Territory, The 218, 230–3
human, the
   affective dynamism 48
   body-in-pieces 51–2, 53–4, 56–8, 61
   central nervous system 60–1
   dissemination of 130
   function of lack and 56
   Hilflosigkeit and 45–51, 54–5
   libidinal dynamism 47–8
   mirror stage, the 46–51, 55–8
   need and 45–6, 47 *see also Hilflosigkeit*
   negativity and 42–4
   prematurity of 47–50
   qualities of 128
   science and 305
'Hume's problem' 35, 136, 191 n.18, 194 n.33, 225, 229, 277, 290
hylozoism 123–4
Hyperchaos 142, 152

idealism 123–4
immanence 98, 103–7
   Deleuze, Gilles and 93–5, 98
   Lacan, Jacques and 55–7, 59
   language and 100, 204, 212
   logic and 78
   organicity and 46, 50, 55–7, 63
   structuralism and 240, 254, 258
   thought and 307
inconsistency 138, 286
indeterminacy 330–7
indication 78, 80
infinite, the 95, 100, 102, 155, 196 n.42, 197 n.51, 312
   cardinality and 307
   fold, and the 105
   indeterminancy and 330
   infinitesimal limits 99–100, 131, 210
   renormalization and 332
   signification and 256
   signs *dm* (devoid of meaning) and 155, 170–7
   speculation and 100
infraconscious subjectalism 138–9, 148
instrumental rationality 2
intelligent design 60–1
intentional act 119, 266 n.8, 271
intentional object
interstices 107–8
intrinsic essence 70
Intuitionism 312–14
irruptive fulgurites 150–1
iteration 176–9

Jameson, Fredric: *Political Unconscious, The* 220
joy 95–6

Kant, Immanuel 271, 308
   correlationism and 72–3
   Sublime, the 31–2
kenotypes 166–7, 179
Kepler, Johannes 109
Keplerian revolution 108–9
Kripke, Saul 206–7

Lacan, Jacques 13, 82
   'Aggressiveness in Psychoanalysis' 47, 48–9, 50

Index

anorganicism and 46–7, 50, 52–4, 57–62
atheism and 41, 45
body-in-pieces 51–2, 53–4, 56–8
'Direction of the Treatment and the Principles of Its Power, The' 49
ego and 45, 47–50
'Family Complexes in the Formation of the Individual, The' 47–8
Freud, Sigmund and 52
'Freudian Thing, The' 50
function of lack 56
'Guiding Remarks for a Convention on Female Sexuality' 53
Hegel, Georg and 58–9
mirror stage, the 46–51, 55–8
myth of the nongiven and 43–5
narcissism and 54
nature and 45–6, 58–9
'On a Question Prior to Any Possible Treatment of Psychosis' 49
'On My Antecedents' 52, 54
ontogenesis and 45, 38–9
organic, the 46–7, 50, 52–3
phylogenesis and 41
religion and 41, 45
'Remarks on Daniel Lagache's Presentation: "Psychoanalysis and Personality Structure"' 52
science and 55–6
landfills 323, 331–2, 335 see also waste
language 11–12, 17–18, 200 see also semiotics and signs
abitrariness of 200–2, 203, 209
aesthetic philosophy of 212–13
analytic philosophy and 205–7
correlationism and 211
Deleuze, Gilles and 100–1, 102, 103
formal language 161–2, 208–9
iconoclasm and 204
Meillassoux, Quentin and 156, 158, 161–2, 208–9
natural language 161–2, 208–10, 213–14
ontology of 199–201
realism and 17–18, 199, 210
recursion and 201, 202, 210–12
reference and 206–7, 213
reflection and 212–13
speculative philosophy and 200–1, 204
speech and 209–10
languages of reason 18–19, 238–9, 244, 252–5, 257, 261
Latour, Bruno 285, 291–2
leachate 323–4, 334–5
Left, the
Left Accelerationism 4
leftism 3, 7
Leibniz, Gottfried 104–5
Leiss, Elizabeth 209–10
Lévi-Strauss, Claude 220, 262
speculative realism and 262
libidinal dynamism 47–8
life 30, 63, 103, 125–8, 146, 155, 190 n.14
see also dead, the
bacteria and 322, 323, 335
biopolitics 218–20, 228
Deleuze, Gilles and 100, 113 n.54, 189 n.10
evolutionary theory 44–5, 59–61, 63, 192 n.24
homes and 85
irruptive fulgurites and 150–1
life sciences 45, 46, 49, 51–2, 55
lifelessness 38
mathematics and 303–5
realist novels and 219, 221, 223, 224, 231, 232
vitalism 123–4, 134, 139, 194 n.28, 240
waste and 320, 331, 333
Life and Strange Surprising Adventures of Robinson Crusoe, Mariner, The (Defoe, Daniel) 119
light cones 313–14
Linden, David 59–61
Accidental Mind: How Brain Evolution Has Given Us Love, Memory, Dreams, and God, The 60
linguistics 163, 165, 199–205, 209–13, 240, 287–8,
linguistic realism 218, 231
linguistic turn, the 213, 300
literary fiction 224–30 see also literary realism; literature
literary realism 218–24, 227–32
anatomopolitics and 220
big, ambitious novel and 221–2
biopolitics and 219–20, 228
literary-speculative realism (LSR) 17–18, 217–18, 233–4

347

Index

modernism and 220–1
narrative fiction and 224–30
postmodernism and 220–1
poststructuralism and 221
representational, biopolitical and humanist framework (RBH) and 218, 222, 223, 224
representationalism and 218–19, 221–2
Smith, Zadie and 222
structuralism and 220–1
literary-speculative realism (LSR) 17–18, 217–18, 233–4
   Bogost, Ian and 233
   great outdoors, and the 223–4, 233–4
   Harman, Graham and 233
   Houellebecq, Michel and 233
   literary realism and 218–24
   Meillassoux, Quentin and 224–30
   narrative fiction and 224–30
literature 17–18, 200 *see also* literary fiction
   extro-science fiction (XSF) 224–30
   science fiction (SF) 224–30
logic 100, 301
Logic of Sense, The (Deleuze, Gilles) 100, 102, 103
Lucretius 75–6
Luhmann, Niklas 86
   environment and 87–8
   poststructuralist correlationism's critique (PSC) and 89
   Social Systems 86
   theory of distinction 78–82
   theory of observation 77, 80–3, 86–9
   theory of systems 86–9

McCarthy, Tom: *Remainder* 222–3, 228
manifest image 38, 272, 284–7
Map and the Territory, The (Houellebecq, Michel) 218, 230–3
Markopoulou, Fotini 312
Marx, Karl 44
   Capital 75
   commodity fetishism and 75
materialism 9–12, 103, 118–19, 297 n.50, 309
   Berkeley, George and 187 n.3
   Boolean logic 312–13
   Deleuze, Gilles and 106
   dialectical 274, 276
   eliminative 285
   materialist realism 134
   materialist reason 45, 50, 56, 62–3, 239, 241–52, 255, 257–9, 265
   materialist subject 131, 151
   materiality 84–6
   Meillassoux, Quentin and 11–12, 105, 120, 130, 133, 139, 144, 157–8
   principle of sufficient reason (PSR) and 105–7
   relationship to consciousness 300
   relationship with formalism 300
   waste and 322, 333 *see also* waste
mathematical discourse 305
mathematics
   formalism and 302–3
   Kepler, Johannes and 109
   mathematical formalism 33–4, 37, 109, 263, 300, 302–6, 312
   Meillassoux, Quentin and 14–15, 33–4, 139, 141, 145–6, 154, 156–63, 252
   quantum theory 310–11
   set theory 159–61
   signs and 160–4, 184–5, 252–3, 263–4
   wave functions 310
matter 10, 38, 106, 128, 131, 133, 145–6
   agential realism and 325, 336
   geology and 320–1, 333
   indeterminancy and 330
   life and 304
   physical world of 309
   realism and 223,
   waste and 320–2, 333, 337
meaning 7
Meillassoux, Quentin 154–5
   absolute, properties of 156–7
   absolutism and 120–1
   absolutist metaphysics and 120
   absolutory speculation and 120
   After Finitude 37, 122, 139, 142, 147, 153, 244
   ancestral statements and 333
   ancestral, the 30
   arbitrariness of the sign, and the 168–9, 180–2
   arche-fact, and the 136–7
   base signs and 160–1
   bifurcation of nature and 37–8
   contingency and 135, 138, 142, 147, 179–81

Index

correlation and 123, 134–7
correlational circle and 118–20, 134
correlational facticity and 134–5, 137
correlationism and 5, 10, 71–2, 74, 117–23, 136, 240, 244, 304–5
cryptophysics and 153–4
deabsolutization of thought and 117, 119
death and 157–8
deuteroabsolutory properties 157
empiricism and 144
Era of Correlation and 122–3, 133, 135
exfinite thought and 256, 265
extro-science fiction (XSF) and 224–30
Fable of the Overjoyed Palaeographer, The 172–3
fact, and the 136
factiality and 137–8, 141, 153, 247 *see also* factuality
facticity and 138, 151–2, 194 n.31, 207, 246–7
(f)actual investigations 149–54
Figures and 138
fissures 145, 146–7, 149
formal meaning and 162
formalism 158–9, 162
formulatory contradictions and 118–19
Galileanism and 139
great outdoors, and the 217, 227, 234
Hume's problem and 225–6
Hyperchaos and 142, 152
inconsistency and 138
irruptive fulgurites 150–1
iteration 176–9
kenotypes and 166–7, 179
language and 156, 158, 161–2, 167–70, 208–9
literary-speculative realism (LSR) and 224–30
materialism and 11–12, 105, 120, 139, 157–8
materialist subject and 151
mathematical signs and 160–4
mathematics and 14–15, 33–4, 139, 141, 145–6, 154, 156–64, 252
metaphysical materialism and 120
metaphysics and 119–22, 139, 144, 153, 257–8
'Metaphysics and Extro-Science Fiction' 224–5
monotonous-chant effect and 173–4

narrative fiction and 224–30
numbers and 184–6
operator signs and 160–1
ordinary meaning and 162
organigrammes and 144–5
philosophical principles and 97
philosophy and 306–7
positivism and 193 n.25
primoabsolutory properties 156
principle of factuality and 104
principle of sufficient reason (PSR) and 143, 147
pure sign, and the 252, 255 *see also* signs *dm* (devoid of meaning)
realism and 133
reason and 93–4, 98
reiteration and 177–9
repetition and 172–7, 179
resemblance and 171
sceptico-fideism and 93
science and 33, 139–41, 155–7, 281, 304–5
science fiction (SF) and 224–30
scientism and 193 n.25
set theory and 159–61, 307–8
signs and 160–84
signs *dm* (devoid of meaning) and 156, 161, 162, 163–83, 186–7, 207–8, 211
space and 174–6, 178–9
speculative materialism and 14–15, 134, 138, 141–2, 144–8, 243
speculative philosophy and 119, 143–4
subjectalism and 10, 14, 121–3, 129–30, 133–4, 138–9, 148–52, 240
subjectivity of reality and 148, 151–3
thought and 117
type/tokens 165–8, 170–3, 176
melody 173–4
Melville, Herman: 'Bartleby the Scrivener' 224
Merleau-Ponty, Maurice 20–1, 310–13
Structure of Behavior, The 310
metaphysics 119–22, 139, 144, 153, 188 n.5, 192 n.23, 257–9
Brassier, Ray and 273, 285
Deleuze, Gilles 97
Derrida, Jacques and 253–4, 258
end of metaphysics 247
metaphysical materialism 120

Index

metaphysical sign, the 254–5
meta-physis and 141
movement of supplementarity 258–9
subjectalism and 134
'Metaphysics and Extro-Science Fiction' (Meillassoux, Quentin) 224–5
Miller, Jacques-Alain 41–2
mirror stage, the 46–51, 55–8
modernism 220–1
monism 327–8
Monod, Jacques: *Chance and Necessity* 63
multiplicity 173
Musée des Beaux-Arts de Pau 126–7
myth 220, 262
myth of the given 285–6
myth of the nongiven 42–5, 61

narcissism 54
narrative fiction 224–30 *see also* literary realism
natural language 161–2, 208–10, 213–14
naturalism 95–8
nature 13
    bifurcation of 13, 35–9
    Lacan, Jacques and 45–6, 58–9
    Meillassoux, Quentin 131
    power of 31, 34
    weaknesses in 63–4
    Whitehead, Alfred North and 13, 35–6
negativity 42–4
Netherland (O'Neill, Joseph) 222
new materialism 71
Nietzsche, Friedrich 44
    Deleuze, Gilles and 96–7
    eternal return and 97
    will to power 124–5
Nihil Unbound (Brassier, Ray) 284
nihilistic rationalism 248
nonnecessity 245–6
nonsense 101–2
nothingness 41–2
noumena 73
nuclear waste 321, 341 n.50
null materialism 248–51

object-oriented ontology 89 n.1
object oriented philosophy (OOP) 4–5, 10–11, 271–2, 328–9
objects 33, 74, 84, 327–30, 334
    signification of 84

waste and 334
observation 74, 77–83
'On a Question Prior to Any Possible Treatment of Psychosis' (Lacan, Jacques) 49
'On My Antecedents' (Lacan, Jacques) 52, 54
'On the Dignity of Man' (Pico della Mirandola, Giovanni) 42
O'Neill, Joseph:
    Netherland 222
ontocontingency 251, 256, 259, 261 *see also* absolute contingency
ontogenesis 43
    Lacan, Jacques and 45, 48–9
ontology 76, 127–8, 247–8, 250, 255–6, 333
    deontologization 72, 81
    of language 17, 199–201, 209
    logic and 100
    mathematics and 163, 166, 310
    object-oriented ontology 89 n.1
    ontological crisis 321
    scientific ontology 273, 288–93
    semiotic ontology 214
OOP (object oriented philosophy) 4–5, 10–11, 328–9
operator signs 160–1
oppression 76
Order of Things, The (Foucault, Michel) 82
ordinary meaning 162
organic, the 46–7, 50, 52–3
organigrammes 144–5
organism, the 53

'Peinture acrylique blanche sur tissu rayé et rouge (White Acrylic Painting on White and Red Striped Fabric)' (Buren, Daniel) 175
Peirce, Charles Sanders 163, 165–6, 203–4
performative contradiction 32–3
Perrault, Dominique 174
perspectives 314
phenomena 72, 325–6, 330
phenomenology 56–7, 271
Phenomenology of Spirit (Hegel, Georg) 58–9
'Philosophical Conjuncture and Marxist Theoretical Research, The' (Althusser, Louis) 280
philosophy 16, 24 n.11, 94, 102, 122, 146, 242

Index

analytic 1, 3, 200, 202, 203, 205–7, 271
Continental 42, 44, 73–4, 90 n.10, 95, 121, 201, 271, 300
Deleuze, Gilles and 97–8
epistemology and 282, 289
language and 20, 200–1, 204, 205–7, 212–13
Meillassoux, Quentin and 10, 97, 119, 143–4, 306–7
naturalism and 95
object oriented philosophy (OOP) 4–5, 10–11, 271–2, 328–9
philosophical materialism 250
realist 71, 72, 86, 133, 204, 221, 232, 273, 288–92, 311
science and 271–2, 278, 282, 289
speculative 10, 93, 106, 119, 143–4, 152, 188n.5, 200–1, 204, 249–50, 282
split in 200–3
tests 36
Philosophy of Nature (Hegel, Georg) 46
phylogenesis 41, 45
physics 309–14, 332
Pico della Mirandola, Giovanni: 'On the Dignity of Man' 42
picturing 286–7, 290–1
Plague of Fantasies, The (Žižek, Slavoj) 84
plasticity 107–8
Platonism 99
PNC (principle of noncontradiction) 97, 104
poetics 199–200, 210–13
poiesis 17, 190 n.14, 204, 212, 216 n.25
Political Unconscious, The (Jameson, Fredric) 220
politics 2–4, 75–7
  literature and 219–20
  poststructuralist correlationism's critique (PSC and) 85–6
polydualism 132
Popper, Karl 225
positivism 193 n.25
Possibility of Naturalism, The (Bhaskar, Roy) 289
postmodernism 220–1
poststructuralism 1–3, 221, 240, 241–2
  compatibilities with SR 7
  correlationism and 5, 73–4, 80–3
  criticism 6
  incompatibilities with SR 7–9
  language of reason and 238–9

politics and 2–3, 76–7
poststructuralist correlationism's critique (PSC) 83–6
power systems and 76–7
reason and 7
poststructuralist correlationism's critique (PSC) 83–6, 89
power 85
  systems of 76–7
principle of factiality 104, 137–8
principle of insufficient reason (PIR) 246–8, 250, 260
principle of noncontradiction (PNC) 97, 104
principle of sufficient reason (PSR) 94, 108–9, 119–20, 246
  counteractualization 102–3
  Deleuze, Gilles and 94, 97–8, 108
  immanence and 103–5
  materialism and 105–7
  Meillassoux, Quentin and 143, 147
  naturalism and 95–8
  structuralism and 98–101
  univocity and 101–3
principle of unreason 246
PSC (poststructuralist correlationism's critique) 83–6, 89
psychoanalysis 57
pure sign, the 252, 255 *see also* signs *dm* (devoid of meaning)

qualitative multiplicity 173–4
quantitative multiplicity 173
quantum physics 310–11, 313–14
Quine, Willard Van Orman 206

Rancière, Jacques 296 n.48
rational realism 242, 243–4, 248–51, 263, 265
realism 10–12, 14, 70, 83, 272, 288–92 *see also* literary realism
  agential realism 324–6, 329–30, 335–6
  biopolitics and 219–20
  language and 17–18, 199, 210
  Luhmann, Niklas and 88
  Meillassoux, Quentin and 133
  philosophy and 71, 72, 86, 133, 204, 221, 232, 273, 288–92, 311
  rational realism 242, 243–4, 248–51, 263, 265

Index

representational, biopolitical and humanist framework (RBH) and 218, 222
subtractive realism 259
theories of 85
Realist Theory of Science, A (Bhaskar, Roy) 289
reality 72–3, 74–5
  deontologization of 72
  Lacan, Jacques and 83
  Luhmann, Niklas and 80, 81
reason 6–7, 243 *see also* principle of sufficient reason (PSR)
  languages of 18–19, 238–9, 244, 252–5, 257, 261
  Meillassoux, Quentin and 93–4
  PIR (principle of insufficient reason) 246–8, 250, 260
  ratiocontingency 259–63
  rational materialism 242, 243
  rational realism 249–51
  rationalism 6–7, 11
reiteration 177–9
relationality 329
relations 199–200
Remainder (McCarthy, Tom) 222–3
'Remarks on Daniel Lagache's Presentation: "Psychoanalysis and Personality Structure"' (Lacan, Jacques) 52
renormalization 332
repetition 172–7, 179
resemblance 171

Saussure, Ferdinand de 169
sceptico-fideism 93
Schrader, Astrid 330
science 3–4, 19–21, 271, 301, 305
  Althusser, Louis and *see* Althusser, Louis
  Bachelard, Gaston and 275–6
  Bhaskar, Roy and 288–93
  Brassier, Ray and 33, 271–2, 279, 283–8, 291–3
  Cavaillès, Jean and 300–3
  cognition and 308–9
  data and 304
  determinism and 309
  evolution of 139–41, 143, 156–7
  Intuitionism 312–14
  Lacan, Jacques 55–6
  logic and 301
  Markopoulou, Fotini and 312
  Meillassoux, Quentin and 33, 139–43, 155–7, 281, 304–5
  Merleau-Ponty, Maurice and 310–13
  philosophy and 271–2, 278, 282, 289
  physics 309–14
  Sellars, Wilfred and 283–8, 290–1, 293
science fiction (SF) 224–30
scientific discourse 305
scientific image 38, 272, 284–7
scientific representation 33
'scientific turn, the' 300
scientism and 193 n.25
second-order observation 80–3
Sellars, Wilfrid 283–8, 290–1, 293
  Empiricism and the Philosophy of Mind 285
  theory of conceptual change and 286–8
semiotics 201–4 *see also* semiotic triangle *and* signs
  analytic philosophy and 205–7
  Derrida, Jacques and 253–6, 261, 264
  holistic semiotics 202, 204
  reference 206–7
  semiotic triangle 201, 203, 204, 210
set theory 159–61, 307–8
signification 84–5
signs 160–87 *see also* languages of reason; semiotics
  aneidetic sign 253, 255, 257, 259, 263–5
  arbitrariness of the sign, the 168–9, 180–2
  asemantic sign 252–7, 259, 263–5
  contingency and 179–81
  Fable of the Overjoyed Palaeographer, The 172–3
  iteration 176–9
  kenotypes and 166–7, 179
  language and 161–2, 167–78
  mathematical 160–4, 184–5, 252–3, 263–4
  metaphysical sign 254–5
  numbers and 184–6
  pure sign, the 252, 255 *see also* signs *dm* (devoid of meaning)
  reiteration 177–9
  repetition and 172–7, 179
  resemblance and 171–2
  supersemantic sign 257, 259, 260, 261

Index

type/tokens 165–8, 170–3, 176
signs *dm* (devoid of meaning) 210, 211, 214, 252–3 *see also* pure sign, the aneidetic sign, the 253, 255, 257, 259, 263–5
  kenotypes 166–7, 179
  Meillassoux, Quentin and 156, 161, 162, 163–83, 186–7, 207–8, 253
Smith, Zadie 221, 222
  White Teeth 221, 223
social hierarchy 76
social science 291–2
Social Systems (Luhmann, Niklas) 86
solipsism 121
space 174–6, 178–9
space-time manifold 314
speculation 12, 100, 108
  absolutory speculation 120
speculative materialism 14–15, 134, 138, 141–2, 144–8, 243–6
  null materialism and 248–9
  rational realism and 251
  science and 305–6
  waste and 322, 333, 335
speculative philosophy 10, 93, 106, 119, 249–50, 282
  language and 200–1, 204
  Meillassoux, Quentin and 143–4, 188 n.5
speculative realism (SR) 1–2, 71, 133–4, 327–30
  2007 Goldsmiths workshop 1, 13, 71, 271, 283
  anthropocentrism and 4
  compatibilities with poststructuralism 7
  criticisms of 5–6
  drama and 2
  incompatibilities with poststructuralism 7–9
  languages of reason and 238–9, 243–4
  Lévi-Strauss, Claude and 262
  object-oriented approaches to 5–6
  object-oriented variants of 10–11
  politics and 4
  poststructuralism and 241–2
  structuralism and 241
  theories of 62–3
speculative rhetoric 203
speech 209–10
Spencer-Brown, George 77–9

spin network graphs 314
Spinoza, Benedict de: *Ethics, The* 95–6
SR (speculative realism) *see* speculative realism
'Stalking the Billion-Footed Beast: A Literary Manifesto for the New Social Novel' (Wolfe, Tom) 218–19
structuralism 98–101, 220–1, 240–3, 258, 260
  Derrida, Jacques and 241, 243, 258, 262
  Lévi-Strauss, Claude and 262
Structure of Behavior, The (Merleau-Ponty, Maurice) 310
subjectalism 10, 15, 242
  Berkeley, George and 132
  Meillassoux, Quentin and 10, 14, 121–3, 129–30, 133–4, 138–9, 148–52, 240
subjectalist absolutism 134, 136
subjectivist metaphysics 122
subjectivity 42, 121–6 *see also* critique of the subject
  negativity and 42–3
  Pico della Mirandola, Giovanni and 42
  solipsism 121
subjectivity of reality 148, 151–3
Sublime, the 31–2
subtractive finitude 256–9
subtractive realism 259
supersemantic sign, the 257, 259, 260, 261
supplementarity 258–9
System of Objects (Baudrillard, Jean) 84
systems 86–9
S/Z (Barthes, Roland) 221

technology 88–9
technoscience 21
Thacker, Eugene 29
theories, evolution of 139–41
'Thirdness' 204
thought 30–1, 304–7
  being and 105
  correlationism and 32, 304
  exfinite thought 246, 250, 256, 259, 265
  madness and 101–2, 103
  Meillassoux, Quentin and 117, 191 n.20
  perversion and 103
  relationship with being 105
Time and Free Will (Bergson, Henri) 173, 179

353

Index

transfinite theory 307–8
type/tokens 165–8, 170–3, 176

universal correlationism 73
universe
    distinction and 91 n.21
    end of the 30
univocity 97, 101–3
unreason 18, 98, 135, 183, 245–7, 251, 260

vicarious causation 328–30
vitalism 123–4, 134, 139, 194 n.28, 240
Vleekskomp (*Meat*) (Fabre, Jan) 127
von Neumann 314–15

waste 21, 320–6, 329–38
    agential realism and 324–6
    ancestral statements and 333
    bacteria and 322, 323–4, 326, 330, 334
    contaminants of emerging concern 332
    double articulation of 334–5
    ethics and 336–7
    indeterminancy of 330–7
    leachate 323–4, 334–5
    managing 331–5
    materialism and 322
    restratification and 333–5
Waste Isolation Pilot Plant, the 321
wave functions 310–11, 314–15
Weird Realism (Harman, Graham) 233
What is Philosophy? (Deleuze, Gilles/
    Guattari, Félix) 104
White Teeth (Smith, Zadie) 221, 223
Whitehead, Alfred North 13, 35
    bifurcation of nature 13, 35–6
Wolfe, Tom 218, 220, 228–9
    Bonfire of the Vanities, The 219
    'Stalking the Billion-Footed Beast: A Literary Manifesto for the New Social Novel' 218–19
Wolfendale, Peter 297 n.50
Wood, James 221–2
World, distinction and 91 n.21
world-without-us 29–30
    Hegel, Georg and 32

Zermelo–Fraenkel set theory 159–60
Žižek, Slavoj: *Plague of Fantasies, The* 84

www.ingramcontent.com/pod-product-compliance
Lightning Source LLC
Chambersburg PA
CBHW050134240426
43673CB00043B/1666